D0190365

The Puritan Ordeal

The Puritan Ordeal

Andrew Delbanco

Harvard University Press
Cambridge, Massachusetts, and London, England

Copyright © 1989 by the President and Fellows
    of Harvard College
All rights reserved
Printed in the United States of America
10 9 8 7 6 5 4 3 2

First Harvard University Press paperback edition, 1991

Library of Congress Cataloging-in-Publication Data

Delbanco, Andrew, 1952–
    The Puritan ordeal / Andrew Delbanco.
        p.   cm.
    Bibliography: p.
    Includes index.
    ISBN 0-674-74055-6 (alk. paper)
    ISBN 0-674-74056-4 (pbk.)
        1. Puritans.   2. Puritans—United States.   I. Title.
BX9322.D45 1989
285'.9'0973—dc19   88-11218
                                                    CIP

To Benjamin and Yvonne
who have shown me a new world

Acknowledgments

Over the years of work that such a book as this requires, most of the help one gets from family and friends—which has nothing immediately to do with the task of writing—cannot be reduced to a list of favors and so is belittled by any effort at enumeration. There are, nevertheless, a few particulars I would like to mention.

After showing me where the book was out of shape or out of tune, my wife, Dawn, tolerated my fits of resistance and indignation, and kept after me to make it right. To the extent that it has found its proper form, I owe her many thanks. To the extent that it has not, I should have asked her to read it again. Those who know her (and especially those among them who know me too) understand that this is only one small way in which she is my great good fortune.

Since all writing, no matter how responsive to the experience of others, is a form of autobiography, I should acknowledge here my most basic debt: to my mother (who I wish had lived to tell me if these pages approach her high requirements of sympathy and honesty) and to my father, who shared with her and continues to pass on to his children an openness and a resilience not unrelated to the experience of uprooting and emigration.

My friend John Klause has read the whole manuscript and helped me to eliminate some foolishness. Many long talks with Patricia Caldwell have been of great importance to me as well. Some of the concerns in the early sections were suggested to me by Wallace MacCaffrey's lucid and comprehensive lectures on Tudor and Stuart England. Others developed years ago in Herschel Baker's seminar on literature and religion in the same period—and from stimulating talks with a fellow student in that class, Ritchie D. Kendall. Frederick Wertheim assisted me with some of the research, and Albert J. von Frank made helpful suggestions on an early draft, as did my brother Nicholas.

I am grateful to Camille Smith for her expert editing, among other reasons because I have tried to use the English language as an instrument of affective as well as cognitive communication, and she has believed in that possibility. Aida Donald once again saw my work through the stages of acquisition, review, and revision.

Though the book mainly took shape in the solitude of libraries and at the writing desk, I have been able to try out some of its themes in my classes at both Harvard and Columbia. I am especially aware that Laura Henigman and Jeannie van Asselt, who will soon be making their own contributions to American studies, helped me think harder and in unanticipated directions. I have also had valuable responses to the work in progress from audiences at Princeton University, the University of Michigan, and the American Literature Section of the Modern Language Association, and from other scholars who kindly responded with criticism and encouragement—including Daniel Aaron, Stephen Fender, Paul Lucas, Michael McGiffert, William Spengemann, Robert Weisbuch, and especially Lewis P. Simpson.

Michael Kaufmann, another student of great devotion and promise, deserves special thanks for the excellent job he did for and with me in seeing the manuscript through its final stages. While graciously putting up with my muttering and looking over her shoulder, Linda Ainsworth produced an index that meets the high standard of all her work.

The bulk of my reading was done in the Houghton and Widener libraries at Harvard, and in the McAlpin Collection of the Union Theological Seminary, where I am particularly grateful to Mr. Seth Kasten. For many courtesies I thank as well the staffs at the American Antiquarian Society, the Andover-Newton Library at the Harvard Divinity School, the Boston Atheneum, the Boston Public Library, the British Library, the Butler Library at Columbia University, the

Connecticut State Library, the University of Illinois Library, and the New York Public Library.

Though the book was completed at Columbia, the writing was begun during a year of freedom from teaching duties at Harvard University, made possible by a grant from the National Endowment for the Humanities. An earlier version of Chapter 6 has been published in the *New England Quarterly,* portions of the Introduction in the *Journal of American Studies,* and parts of Chapter 5 in *Harvard English Studies,* No. 8. I am grateful to the editors for permission to use this material here.

Finally, I must acknowledge, as I have done before, the central importance to my work of Alan Heimert. Others who have been privileged to be among his students will recognize that a good deal of this book constitutes a series of responses to questions first raised by him and, indeed, refinements and expansions of ideas presented in his teaching. There are many other young Americanists who have said, or will be saying, much the same thing—which is one mark of his impact on a generation of students. As a teacher and a scholarly example he gave to us, without demanding discipleship, the chance to earn the knowledge that any truths we make or find will always be provisional. He has always required that we honor the presence of history by never regarding it as closed. For that lesson, and for much else, I thank him.

I have taken the opportunity to correct several typographical and factual errors for this paperback edition.

Contents

The Puritan Ordeal

Who and what is an alien, when it comes to that, in a country peopled from the first under the jealous eye of history?—peopled, that is, by migrations at once extremely recent, perfectly traceable and urgently required . . . Which is the American, by these scant measures?—which is *not* the alien, over a large part of the country at least, and where does one put a finger on the dividing line, or, for that matter, "spot" and identify any particular phase of the conversion, or any of its successive moments? The sense of the interest of so doing is doubtless half the interest of the general question—the possibility of our seeing lucidly presented some such phenomenon, in a given group of persons, or even in a felicitous individual, as the dawn of the American spirit while the declining rays of the Croatian, say, or of the Calabrian, or of the Lusitanian, still linger more or less pensively in the sky.   Henry James, 1907

What comes into being when two contradictory emotions are made to confront each other and are required to have a relationship with each other is . . . quite properly called an idea. Ideas may also be said to be generated in the opposition of ideals, and in the felt awareness of the impact of new circumstances upon old forms of feeling and estimation, in the response to the conflict between new exigencies and old pieties.

Lionel Trilling, 1949

Introduction

This book is about the experience of becoming American in the seventeenth century. It has in some respects the appearance of a study in intellectual history, but I prefer to think of it as a contribution to the history of what the Puritans called affections. My hope is to help advance our understanding not of ideas so much as of feeling—specifically of the affective life of some of the men and women who emigrated to New England more than three hundred fifty years ago, but also of the persistent sense of renewal and risk that has attended the project of becoming American ever since. As a result of the labors of several generations of remarkable historians, we now know a great deal about the beliefs these particular Englishmen and women brought with them, as well as about the material circumstances in which they lived, and the ecclesiastical and social forms they created (or recreated) in the New World. The historiography that has brought us to this point has been, with the possible exception of recent work on slavery in the nineteenth-century South, the most impressive collective achievement yet made by American scholarship. Still, it should be recognized that the ideas and events with which most of our historians have been concerned, though they are very complex in their origins, development, and consequence, and though they have required enormous learning and precision in the act of description, are yet relatively static entities from which the observing historian works at a stable distance.

With feeling it is different. The act of writing about even a small moment in the history of human feeling is rather like a game of catch carried on between players who are both in motion—a game with no clearly demarcated location. Feeling undergoes continual and unpredictable change, and the historian's own capacity to respond to it and to grasp it is equally in flux. I would invoke here Raymond Williams's salutary caution that "the strongest barrier to the recognition of human cultural activity is [the] conversion of experience into finished products." Despite the many advances we have made in understanding the conditions of life in seventeenth-century New England, it is still the case that most "analysis [remains] centered on relations between these produced institutions, formations, and experiences, so that . . . only the fixed explicit forms exist, and living presence is always, by definition, receding."[1]

One of the concerns of this book, for example, is with something called the doctrine of preparation. This was a model for the process of salvation—a regimen of self-examination by which the repentant sinner could estimate his readiness for receiving grace—that became current in late Elizabethan and Stuart Puritanism and was transferred to the New World, where it was in some respects augmented. To describe this doctrine is first of all to exhibit its intellectual content, to say what it prescribed, how many stages toward salvation it defined, how much it was modified over time—to treat it, in other words, as a material substance that can be charted and summarized. There are, to be sure, differences among the accounts of it by different historians. Perry Miller, in his magnificent works on *The New England Mind* (1939–1953), ascribed to the doctrine a kind of crypto-Arminian voluntarism—an enlargement of the role of man and a proportionate reduction of the role of God in determining the fate of the soul. More recently, the preparatory process has been seen not so much as setting the conditions for conversion, but as a spiritual discipline stretching forward throughout the sanctified life of the Puritan saint, who felt himself perpetually subject to the divine will as he grew in grace toward "an exact, total, and Adequate Union, of the understanding with the truth of the Gospel." Despite these differences in emphasis, the governing assumption behind most discussions of the doctrine has been the notion that preparation represented a divine gift, a mitigation of the harshness of an aloof and unpredictable God who had decreed all human destinies from before the beginning of time—a "decree [which] is that everlasting womb, wherein is conceived whatsoever hath been, is, or shall be." Modern commentators tend to understand the preparatory process as a form of reassurance (offered by ministers to a needy laity) that God had placed himself in intimate dialogue with every sinner—that he was concerned with individual men as well as with the aggregate, man.[2]

These assumptions derive, I think, a great deal more from our automatic resistance to the idea of arbitrary governance, and from our commitment (however chastened by historical awareness) to the ideal of individual autonomy, than from a consideration of how the doctrine *felt* to seventeenth-century New Englanders—for whom it often increased rather than allayed anxiety because it transferred authority over the self to the self. If we are to learn anything about religious experience in early New England—as opposed to bare doctrine—we must listen as best we can to the dialogue between congregants and preachers. The questions that arose between them can still be overheard: whether, for example, "a distinct Experience of the several Heads of Preparatory Work" is necessary to salvation; or "whether may it not come to pass [that one] . . . may yet be unable, distinctly to call to mind [the] former experiences of some principal part of preparatory work," and yet be saved. It is still possible to recover the urgency of such questions. For some who were "cast out of the Church," the pressure to answer them must have been unbearable, until relief was sought in "open blasphemous speeches of hatred against God" (out of terror at his relentless demands?), and in "sundry scandalous Attempts to drown [their] children" (out of despair at their prospects for salvation?). The chance—indeed the requirement—to perform meticulous self-examination at each stage of the soul's progress was by no means a universal comfort. One minister consoled the members of his church by assuring them that "we are no where commanded to know the time of our conversion." By watching New Englanders divide over the meanings and effects of such inquisitorial doctrines (pressed by some of the clergy; eased and softened by others) we are able to witness the division of early American culture into premodern and modern selves.[3]

Some of the most exciting work in American studies is coming to focus on this sort of issue, on, that is, the ideological origins of contemporary culture—a tendency with which I am in sympathy, since it is upon such a basis that humanistic scholarship may hope to sustain its traditional function of nurturing self-knowledge. If we understand ideology to mean "thought which is socially determined yet unconscious of its determination," then any effort to situate thought in history should require no defense. Yet at the same time it remains a matter of urgency to recognize that certain forms of ideological criticism tend to underestimate, even to mock as a figment of naive belief, those aspects of human experience which remain at least partly free from ideological coercion—aspects which fall under the rubric of what has been called "the unchanging human heart." "When ideology . . . acquires a human face," as I hope it will do in the ensuing pages, "it draws the reader's consciousness to sympathy with the attitudes and forms of thought being advanced."[4] To identify the constricting power of the unarticulated premises by which human beings think and act at different historical moments is a difficult and desirable achievement, and it is my hope that this book may make some contribution toward that end. Yet our responsibility to those who lived before us surely includes as well an obligation to defend what Williams calls their "living presence" in history, and to protect them from becoming merely stick-figure messengers of an ideology from which we may wish to free ourselves, or, for that matter, which we may wish to embrace.

A further problem with contemporary American ideological criticism is its liability to the same weaknesses that afflicted what used to be called "consensus" historiography. In a beautiful and prescient essay published not long before his death, Richard Hofstadter observed that although the chief proponents of the consensus theory of American history (such writers as Louis Hartz and Daniel Boorstin) were mindful of defeated fascism and prospective communism abroad, and were therefore writing about America in a celebratory mood, their particular political orientation did not convince him that "the idea of consensus is . . . intrinsically linked to ideological conservatism." On the contrary, Hofstadter remarked, "in its origins I believe it owed almost as much to Marx as to Tocqueville, and I find it hard to believe that any realistic Marxist historian could fail to be struck at many points by the pervasively liberal-bourgeois character of American society in the past. Many aspects of our history, indeed, seem to yield to a 'left' consensus interpretation, and some radical historians have in fact begun to see it that way." If Hofstadter's prophecy had any deficiency, it would seem to have been its understatedness. Much interesting work in American literary, social, and political history now oscillates between demonstrating (and lamenting) how limited an ideological range has been available within American culture, and displaying, with affection and hope, certain minor but inspiriting exceptions to the rule: proto-socialist political movements, working-class subcultures, minority writers in protest, and so on. What was even more telling in Hofstadter's assessment of the future of American self-reflection was his recognition that

> the important ground on which consensus as a general theory of American history should be quarreled with is not its supposed political implications but its intrinsic limitations *as history*. Having come into being as a corrective [to the Progressive emphasis on economic conflict as the chief feature of American development], the idea of consensus as an interpretative principle has the status of an essentially negative proposition. It demarcates some of the limits of conflict in American history, and underlines some other difficulties in the historical legacy of the Progressive, but as a positive principle it does not go very far . . . It has somewhat the same relation to historical writing as an appropriate frame has to a painting: it sets the boundaries of the scene and enables us to see where the picture breaks off and the alien environment begins; but it does not provide the foreground or the action, the interest or the pleasure, the consummation itself, whether analytical or esthetic.[5]

To an impressive degree, Hofstadter's warning has been heeded, and a vital series of monographs has begun to emerge from a new generation of social historians who are complicating and deepening our sense of the past by attending, above all, to its diversity.[6] But Hofstadter would have also recognized and, I think, regretted, that American literary studies (which will soon be dominated by critics who came of age since his death in 1970) are again showing signs of being charmed by the attractions of consensus theory. I regret this too, not out of any antagonism to the left-liberal view of the travesties and missed opportunities in American history, but rather because of the attenuated sense of our contentious past with which, as Hofstadter predicted, much of this current work leaves us. We are getting again— at least from scholars of literary training and leftist inclination—a thin and colorless version of our history, as if all who lived before us were running on a treadmill, charged with an occasional burst of sprinter's energy by which they may have briefly advanced into new terrain (as did the Populists, say, or certain black nationalists), but mostly making no progress, yet pathetic and exhausted from the effort. All American history becomes, through the lens of this new criticism, one and the same—a tedious sequence of bourgeois consciousness in version after indistinguishable version. "Significant issues divided various segments of society," concedes a leading proponent of this view, "and . . . the antagonists differed significantly from each other in purpose, approach, and quality of mind, [but] these were divisions, antagonism, *within the culture.*" Is there any culture, we must ask, about which this statement cannot be made? Is it really true that only in "Europe . . . [have] the creators of its culture . . . been able and prone to imagine a different social model altogether"; is it unusually characteristic of modern America that it has "spawned a normative ideal of culture which served as protection against other realities"?[7] These are, I think, the mechanisms by which any culture defines itself. The real force of these sorts of argument is always an adversarial one: that our particular culture has been peculiarly impoverished—that the range of its intellectual and political possibilities has been straitened, and that we are the poorer for it.

Following Tocqueville, Louis Hartz said nothing less than this more than thirty years ago in *The Liberal Tradition in America* (1955): "This then is the mood of America's absolutism: the sober faith that its [middle-class] norms are self-evident." The question was—and still is—whether this can become something more than a lament; whether closer study of our cultural genealogy by means of an essentially literary method might not disclose internal tensions and even cleavages along the way to the apparently consensual present; whether we might not achieve a better sense of the living virtue (in the classical sense of that word) of our past rather than of its deadening weight. Occasionally, transcendence has seemed possible: "Literature," Emerson declared, with similar fatigue at the constrictedness of his own American moment, "is a point outside of our hodiernal circle through which a new one may be described." The possibility of such transcendence is now being everywhere denied, even as literature is once again being situated where it belongs—in history. "Somewhat like Archimedes," writes one acute feminist critic, "who to lift the earth with his lever required someplace else on which to locate himself and his fulcrum, feminists questioning the presumptive order of both nature and history—and thus proposing to remove the ground from under their own feet—would appear to need an alternative base."[8] Contemporary feminist scholars have in fact gone a good deal further toward achieving such a base than have most others, who are less alert to the specific debilitations inflicted by middle-class American culture, and much less clear about preferred alternatives. And though polemics against tradition can conceal their own brands of intolerance, there has been a salutary impulse in the canon-revising of contemporary literary studies—a process through which new voices have been admitted to enrich the collective inheritance which we call American literature. By and large, however, the contemporary ideological critic consents to no shared history and proclaims no loyalties; he does not declare primitivist, or socialist, or welfare-capitalist, or fascist allegiances. He is usually content with a vaguely communitarian ideal that he finds nowhere realized in what he describes as the laissez-faire culture of American self-reliance. He tends to do criticism on the move—as if trying to push the heavy family furnishings out of the room while jumping off the floor.

There is apparently a compensatory pleasure in the adversarial critical attitude that is on the ascendant at the present time. With respect to Puritan studies in particular, it may be said that the historiographical revolution effected in the 1930s (by the Harvard scholars Samuel Eliot Morison, Kenneth Murdock, and Perry Miller), and variously reinforced by many others since, is proving to be insecure. We seem to be returning to an older, hostile view of the Puritans, as expressed in the 1920s by William Carlos Williams and recently summarized with sympathy by a sitting president of the Modern Language Association: the Puritans were the people, *tout court,* "who massacred the Indians and established the self-righteous religion and politics that determined American ideology."[9]

The present book is unabashedly devoted to a different possibility: the possibility of fervor rather than embarrassment in our membership in the American "hodiernal circle," in our inescapable linkage with the objects of our attention as we move with them in a perpetual dance. It is quite true that we are analytically disadvantaged by this proximity. We may mistake small, local conflicts for large, portentous ones. In forfeiting critical distance, we may fall prey to the spirit of boosterism. But it is surely also true that detail and conflict are the stuff of history. If we keep the materials of the past at a longer, safer range, we lose all sense of their associational meanings, of their texture and particularity; all sense of their beauty as creations of a human consciousness to which we may feel related—with the mixed indebtedness and recoil that are the emotions with which relation is always acknowledged.

2

To establish such a human relation with the Puritans, it is necessary to look deep into their religious experience—by which I do not primarily mean their doctrinal convictions, or their specific ecclesiological practices, but the fund of basic attitudes by which they confronted and transformed reality. This kind of inquiry is now beginning to be undertaken by other scholars, some of whom have already shown that the emigrant Puritans were far from convinced of their place in what Henry Vane (after he returned to England) called "the GENERAL ASSEMBLY of the FIRST-BORNE." They were, rather, like Willa Cather's pioneers, "huddled [with no] appearance of permanence" on the New England coast; their purpose in being there remained long in doubt to themselves. It was in doubt, for instance, to Anne Hutchinson, who shuddered at "the meanness of the place," and to Anne Bradstreet, whose "heart rose" in anger at being carried like baggage into a wasteland which her father forlornly hoped might someday become a new "Macedonia." "After I came hither," declared one candidate for communion in the newly gathered church at Cambridge, the town which the emigrants named after the ancient university that had nurtured many of them, "I saw my condition more miserable than ever." It is not fanciful to imagine this immigrant generation, like a later one described by the Jewish writer Abraham Cahan, collectively wishing "a curse upon Columbus."[10]

That the Puritans were first and foremost *immigrants* has been a fact too little reckoned with by historians whose primary interest is in the life of the mind. "It is with God," wrote one of their early leaders, "that knoweth the heart of exiles to comfort exiles." We cannot build a deeper understanding of the Puritan experience upon the premise that they installed themselves in the New World as a people essentially unchanged by their mental and physical journey. We cannot accept the proposition that "the finest creations of the founders . . . proceeded from a thoroughly European mentality upon which the American scene made no impression whatsoever." Nor, on the other hand, should we leap to the more recent view that they were a people of unique eschatological aspiration—enormously more bold than their English brethren in their sense of their place in history as settlers of a new promised land.[11] The fact is that it took a long time, at least a generation, for these people to become in any intelligible sense Americans. I have concentrated on those for whom this transformation was never quite completed—the first generation— about whom (to borrow a phrase from Henry James), "half the interest of the general question [is] to put a finger on the dividing line . . . [to] identify any particular phase of the conversion." Since it will not do simply to deny or assert the Americanness of this founding generation, I have tried to listen to them closely enough to make a better transcription of their thought and feeling than the either/or question permits. Such attentiveness includes the obligation to distinguish wherever possible between what they said and felt in Old England and what they said and felt in New England. Fortunately, certain of the major figures did a good deal of speaking in both, and it is sometimes possible to distinguish between the two.

In the course of exploring such distinctions I have been struck by how often the themes around which this book is composed are recapitulated by the experience of subsequent immigrants to the New World. Here, for instance, is one historian writing about the Methodist emigration from Yorkshire to Nova Scotia in the years just before the Revolution: "The distressed—tradesmen, craftsmen, farmers, and the laboring poor, seeking security, spiritual and psychological as well as economic—found relief in this religion of evangelical renewal. And the abuse they received for their deviance from the world at large—the condemnation, physical intimidation, and contempt they endured—confirmed them in their sense of isolation and made them even more susceptible than they otherwise would have been to blandishments from abroad."[12] These sentences, which appear in the first volume of Bernard Bailyn's massive ongoing work on the peopling of North America in the period before industrialization, rest on a great deal of research into the archival remains of a dispersed and complex population movement: on emigrant registers and ship-arrival notices, on customs lists and other civic records, but most of all, on surviving letters and the few diaries and other jottings that preserve something of the immediacy of dislocation and renewal (or despair) that every immigrant underwent. Despite such research, the largest and often insuperable difficulty for the historian of immigration has been the fact that this best of sources—the immigrants' words—is generally scarce. That is one reason why the experience of the Puritans, who were an exceptionally voluble and curatorial people, is more abundantly available than that of any immigrant group until the twentieth century. It is also the reason that the indispensable interpretative tool, if we are to recover something of the inner experience of these (as of any) past lives, must finally be a literary one: an ear for emotional inflection, for convention as opposed to confessional authenticity, in short for the nuances of rhetoric, and more basically, for language itself.

Here is another historian, Charlotte Erickson, who is sensitive in exactly these ways, writing about nineteenth-century British emigration to the United States: "In assessing motives for emigration from emigrant letters one must be careful not to infer reasons which were ex post justifications, made from the point of view of the migrant in America." We find W. I. Thomas, the pioneer Chicago sociologist, making similar discriminations fifty years earlier: "In examining the letters between immigrants in America and their home communities I have noticed that the great solicitude of the family and community is that the absent member shall not change . . . And the typical immigrant letter is an assurance and reminder that the writer, though absent, is still a member of the community." These are just the kinds of cautions that must inform any satisfying study of the Puritan experience. The historian must sort out the complex elements that add up to motive: in some cases Erickson finds "a discontent arising out of economic ambition," as opposed to the desperation of unbearable want, or the fear and self-disgust attendant upon the risk of "sinking to the status of day-labourers" in an industrializing England. "My flight allowed me to escape destruction," she quotes from one Robert Bowles, an English emigrant to the Ohio valley in the 1820s—a note strikingly close to the Puritans' conviction that Christian England under the Stuarts was in its death-throes.[13]

There is, then, a general agreement among diversely focused historians that what Bailyn succinctly calls an "absence of poverty" is more often to be found in the precedent conditions of emigration than the "poor, tired, huddled" existence of the mythic American pilgrim.[14] The sobering point for students of immigrant experience is that the most widely applicable generalization (which has, of course, its own exceptions) is a negative proposition—"the absence of poverty"—a concept not unlike Hofstadter's picture frame. It tells us nothing except that the range of motivation tends to begin somewhere above the literal level of self-preservation. To offer some better representation than this of one immigrant experience is the task of this book.

In pursuing that objective, I have relied mainly, though not exclusively, on published statements drawn from the Puritan leadership. Such a method need not and cannot be justified by appeal to the conviction (here expressed by one of Archbishop Laud's biographers) that "those who hold the Helm of the Pulpit alwayes steer the peoples hearts as they please." It is a much more complicated matter than that, as all intellectual historians have been forced to recognize under the pressure of such disclosures as the fact that only about half the adult males in Winthrop's Boston were church members at all. Nevertheless, our best sense of *mentalité* in seventeenth-century New England remains consistent with the conviction that "the ministers . . . used no other language than the one they shared with the people." This assumption has been buttressed in recent years by the publication of a variety of documents in which the outlines of something we may call "lay piety" can begin to be discerned. It should also be said in this connection that the study of early American writing has always perforce been concerned with the uses of rhetoric, with the political design of literary and religious texts, and has long been informed by the sense of an active audience. Although the congregational system was once defined by its New England leadership as "a speaking *Aristocracy* in the face of a silent *Democracy*," the ministers' texts do give voice to the "people" as well. The pressure of audience, of resistance and assent, can be felt.[15]

This audience has been studied in a very sensitive book by Patricia Caldwell, *The Puritan Conversion Narrative: The Beginnings of American Expression* (1984); Caldwell points out that "of forty-eight completed [conversion] narratives" recorded by Thomas Shepard (pastor at Cambridge) in his church-notebook, "only nine of the saints indicate that they have actually had the joyful experience that Shepard calls 'first conversion' *before* their voyage to the new world." One twenty-five-year-old woman in Shepard's congregation put it touch-

ingly: "Making way for New England, I thought I would find feelings."
That exquisitely simple explanation seems to me close to the heart
of the matter. It is consistent with the sense of incompletion that fills
the early New England sermons, and consistent with what we know
of the internal struggles precipitated by the prospect of migration. A
young Essex chaplain who ultimately declined to make the journey
(even after he was visited by a New England minister on a mission
of recruitment) wrote in his diary as he tried to work up the will to
go, "Oh, more Lord; more, more of Thy self of whose love I have
tasted . . . oh the vail, the vail to be removed." Such men and women
felt their spiritual yearnings deflected by life in England; they fled a
land where, according to Governor Winthrop, "children, servants,
and neighbors . . . are counted the greatest burthen, which if things
were right . . . would be the chiefest earthly blessing." Seven decades
later, Solomon Stoddard took Winthrop's lament seriously, and so
should we: "Our fathers . . . would not have left *England* meerly for
their own quietness; but they were afraid that their Children would
be corrupted there."[16]

By fear of corruption, the Puritans meant fear of the emergent
self. Behind Winthrop's remark and Stoddard's reconstruction lay the
fact that they were retreating from much more than hard times. They
were in flight from what they themselves were becoming in England—
a people fully involved in the pursuit of economic advantage, playing
by the new capitalist rules, engaged in casuistical compromise over
everything from church ceremonies to poor relief. Those who chose
to emigrate under these conditions were perhaps most poignant in
their effort to dissociate themselves from the demeaning contractual
idea that had invaded their religion and their lives. Gentry like Winthrop faced a constant pressure to enter the modern world of rational
computation, which meant, for instance, charging real instead of traditionally nominal "fines" when a tenant's son stood to inherit his
father's copyheld deed. To be squeamish about such balance-sheet
realities was to court serious economic decline, which, in turn, meant
not only the shrinkage of one's assets and the contempt of cannier
neighbors, but also the distress of one's own sons, whose inheritance
grew smaller with every qualm their father felt at pressing his tenants
for more. "We are grown to that height of Intemperance in all excess
of Riot," Winthrop wrote in the year before he left England, "as no
man's estate almost will suffice to keep sail with his equals: and he

that fails in it must live in scorn and contempt."[17] Yeoman farmers were similarly caught: as they found themselves producing more than a subsistence crop, it became necessary to deal with the growing numbers of "higglers, badgers, poulterers, fishmongers" who bought at the local market and dealt profitably from town to town. Objects of disgust at a time when the Christian proscription of usury still retained a certain force, such middlemen were considered meddlers who drove up prices for their own benefit. And yet nothing much beyond local barter could exist without them—and without such an extended market there could be no growth, or even stability, in one's household economy. There seemed no way to tend to the self without dirtying it. "The Harlot," wrote Thomas Fuller in an effort to make such a distinction, "is one that her self is both merchant and merchandise." Puritans in Stuart England felt that the difference between selling oneself and selling for oneself was breaking down.[17]

These were people, moreover, who did not want to accept performance for reward as the standard of virtue. They wanted to believe in the pure generosity of God, and that such selfless divinity was within reach of human emulation—that the true saint was an "assimilating" person, who when "he . . . changes his course, would have others to change with him." Such was the hope for a contagion of grace that Anne Hutchinson (a merchant's wife) expressed when she cried out, "tell not mee of . . . duties, but tell me of Christ." Her mentor, John Cotton, who had declared before he left England that "love is an affection, whereby we desire communion one with another, and communication of good one to another," continued in his great New England sermons on *The Covenant of Grace* (preached in 1636) to struggle against the idea of self-interested reciprocity—of material exchange—as the governing structure of experience.[18]

Another way of putting this is to say that the Puritans in America wished not to lose what has been called "their long nurture as an outgroup." Pressed into comradeship by their sense of difference in England, they were forged as a spiritual movement in a minority experience, and some knew that that spirit would inevitably be threatened by their coming to what Cotton thought of as "a country of universal profession." And sure enough, they scattered quickly. The "dispersion troubled some of us," wrote Thomas Dudley within a year of his arrival, "but helpe it wee could not." Soon thereafter Thomas Shepard offered his own analysis of the spiritual depression that preceded the economic breakdown of the forties: "Here are no enemies to hunt you to heaven . . . no sour herbs to make the lamb sweet." Feeling the absence of "pinching persecutions," they created new enemies. "Offend not the poor natives," Cotton had told the passengers of Winthrop's fleet in 1630; "make them partakers of your precious faith." Within the decade he was demanding that the savages be "blast[ed in] all their green groves, and arbours."[19]

"Resistance to something," as Henry Adams put it, "was the law of New England nature." It was these first New Englanders who established that law. Seeking opposition in America—in Indians, "Antinomians," eventually Quakers and "witches"—they risked losing their concept of sin itself. There is a remarkable structure of irony to their experience of evil: in England they had struggled to apprehend it as the absence of God—compared to whom "there's no other object so lovely"—but in the isolation of the New World, where unobstructed growth in grace had seemed a possibility, they came more and more to feel it as the presence of Satan. The most discerning among them knew that this was happening. "In truth," insisted Anne Bradstreet, in her private effort to slow the change, "it is the absence and presence of God that makes heaven or hell." But "after a persecuting Spirit arose amongst the Priests," wrote one of Anne Hutchinson's exiled allies—using that filthy Romish word, "priests," to defile the ministry—"all Persons that were against [us] were noted as the removing Party." This was what New Englanders' claim to Christian militancy had quickly come to—whether they had begun as the self-proclaimed vanguard of the millennium (as some scholars claim), or (according to others) as the model for English churches—their ambition was ineluctably reduced to being noted in the wilderness as "the removing Party." With the "wars of truth" under way in England, even the strident Edward Johnson had to admit that "it may seeme a mean thing to be a New England soldier."[20]

We can begin to apprehend the manifold complexity of this immigrant experience only if we bend close to the words with which the Puritans recorded it. Theirs was a language under terrible stress, threatened by the migration itself. How could one continue to speak convincingly of the "suburbs of salvation" (a common metaphor for the preparatory stages) in a land without cities? How could one press home the reality of evil through its old (now foreign) associations—mumbling Catholics, or prelates with golden goblets and scarlet robes?

How could the force be preserved of such rebukes as Katherine Chidley's (author of an apology for English Independency in the 1640s) who, recoiling from the idea that needlework could be devoted to comfort in the pews, charged that Presbyterians "sow pillowes of flatteries under [the] elbows" of their parishioners?" Once topical and even urgent, such images, in Emerson's phrase, "lose ... power to stimulate the understanding or the affections" as "old words are perverted to stand for things they are not." When John Norton wrote to his English readers from New England, it was in the imperative mood: "You are our companions in this Patmos."[21] He knew that this was more wishful than true. The Puritans in America needed to devise a new language even as they clung to the old; in the process—as in every immigration—there was loss as well as gain.

If we take seriously the proposition that the settlement of New England was a paradigmatic immigrant ordeal, then a number of ironies come immediately into view. In discovering a judgment in their backsliding children, the Puritans strikingly resemble, for example, the immigrant Jews who came to America nearly three centuries after them:

> These American children, what is to them a mother's feelings? ... A fire should burn out the whole new generation. They should sink into the earth, like Korah.   (Anzia Yezierska, 1920)

> There are divers Children who ... grow to that pride, and unnaturalness, and stubbornness, that they will not serve their Parents except they be hired to it ... Perhaps [they] are ready to say as the Prodigal, *Luke* 15:12, *Give me the portion of goods that falleth to me, &c.* ... I wish there might be seasonable redress thereof.   (Thomas Shepard, Jr., 1672)[22]

When the profligate children of the Puritan founders expropriated the rhetoric of Jeremiah to declare themselves still in covenant with God, they were eventually greeted with a sarcasm that mimicked their claims: "New England they are like the Jews / As like as like can be." Peter Folger's contempt for New England's self-importance foreshadows the sort of filial rebuke that later American-born children aimed at their immigrant parents; one may think of the comment Philip Roth offers to the pious manager of a deluded baseball team: "Surely it is going a little bit overboard to start comparing a sorry second division club like yours to the people of Israel."[23]

There is, of course, risk as well as profit in pressing the immigrant analogies. Coming in 1630 to a "voyd [and] vacant" place free of obstructive and competing cultures (native Americans were effectively invisible, at least as human beings, to most English settlers) was, after all, quite a different thing from threading one's way to Delancey Street through the New York of 1890. There lurks an ahistorical absurdity within every analogy that might be drawn between such vastly divergent experiences. Still, it is overly scrupulous to avoid remarking the connections. With suitable adjustments in the word "frontier," we may say with Frederick Jackson Turner that "at the Atlantic frontier one can study the germs of processes repeated at each successive frontier." In many cases land-distribution practices, for example, and those of local governance, survived the migration relatively intact for a time, but the story of seventeenth-century New World communities is overwhelmingly one of a falling away from the transplanted ideals with which they were founded. As in subsequent migrations (consider the romanticization of the shtetl in early American Jewish writing), those ideals were largely retrospective constructs. England in 1650, no less than Poland in 1900, looked better from afar. If we place the colonial experience beside later migrations we discover two versions—developing at different speeds—of the same process: the Puritans called it declension; later immigrants, with a beckoning human world before them, called it assimilation.[24]

The history of American immigration (which, as Oscar Handlin has famously remarked, is the history of America) is replete with available illustrations of this linked power and impotence of memory. Turn-of-the-twentieth-century Irish workers, for example, brought with them the boycott as a time-honored political strategy. In the Old World this had been an effective means of ostracizing exploitative and competitive enemies by public taunting and shunning. But in the much more dispersed market economy of urban America, it became quickly clear that such community-based techniques could no longer work. One may think with equal aptness of English middle-class emigrants in the 1830s to the Michigan frontier, of whom it was written by a contemporary observer: "After one has changed one's whole plan of life, and crossed the wide ocean to find a Utopia, the waking to reality is attended with feelings of no slight bitterness. In some instances . . . these feelings of disappointment have been so severe as to neutralize all that was good in American life, and to produce a degree of sour discontent which increased every real evil, and went far towards alienating the few who were kindly inclined toward the stranger." Or we may notice the fate of Polish wedding traditions in Upton Sinclair's Chicago:

A trouble was come upon them. The *veselija* is a compact, a compact not expressed, but therefore only the more binding upon all. Every one's share was different—and yet every one knew perfectly well what his share was, and strove to give a little more. Now, however, since they had come to the new country, all this was changing; it seemed as if there must be some subtle poison in the air that one breathed here— it was affecting all the young men at once. They would come in crowds and fill themselves with a fine dinner, and then sneak off. One would throw another's hat out of the window, and both would go out to get it, and neither would be seen again. Or now and then half a dozen of them would get together and march out openly, staring at you, and making fun of you to your face. Still others, worse yet, would crowd about the bar, and at the expense of the host drink themselves sodden, paying not the least attention to any one, and leaving it to be thought that either they had danced with the bride already, or meant to later on.

All these things were going on now, and the family was helpless with dismay. So long they had toiled, and such an outlay they had made![25]

Recent historians have made it clear that the seventeenth-century emigrants to New England—although insulated by choice from the corrosive influence of other peoples—were not as unitary as they once were thought to be. They were not transporting intact a shared Old World culture. At Plymouth, for example, they displayed a high rate of geographical mobility—into, out of, and within the villages; while Dedham and Andover showed a "glacial stability." Yet the members of the Dedham church came "from se'rall pts of England: few of them knowne to one an other before," and thereby tasted some of the bewilderment of starting anew among strangers in a strange place. It is striking, too, how soon an internal critique (led at first by Cotton, Hutchinson, and Henry Vane) arose within the central Puritan settlement at Boston, and how bitterly they indicted their new society for its legalism, for abandoning the spiritual coherence that had held together the groups of faithful covenanters in England. When Anne Hutchinson accused the New England ministry of preaching works, of defiling the faith for which they had come, or when Cotton (recalling the conventicle he had formed in old Boston) mused on "the sweet and gracious company / That at Boston once I had," and pronounced himself "afraid [that in New England] there is more reformation than resurrection," they were expressing the immigrant's shock that their besieged solidarity in Europe was turning into mutual assessment and suspicion in America. This is the specter to which Cotton addressed himself in his sermons on the new covenant (1636); it is, *mutatis mutandis,* the same transformation that Sinclair described in *The Jungle* (1906), or that Arthur Miller treated in *A View from the Bridge* (1956)—his drama of an Old World Italian family breaking apart under New World pressures. It is, finally, "the American peculiarity" with which the immigrant imagination has always had to come to terms—as here defined by New York–born Jerre Mangione, visiting for the first time the Sicilian relatives whom he has never known: "I was astonished how quickly they accepted me as one deserving of their affection and loyalty simply because we were closely related. As one whose habit it is to judge a person by his individual traits, I felt guilty for not being able to respond in kind. But if they were aware of this American peculiarity, there was no sign of it."[26] The American requirement of self-definition is at hand.

3

As I am concerned with the fate of feeling in this process of Americanization, I am obliged above all to confront in immigrant Puritanism what is perhaps the ultimate test of any ethical or metaphysical system—namely, its response (of which the doctrine of preparation was but one version) to the universal problem of coming to terms with the fact of evil. "In one form or another," as Max Weber puts it, "this problem belongs everywhere among the factors determining religious evolution and the need for salvation." "It is a problem," writes one of its closest theological students, "equally for the believer and for the non-believer. In the mind of the latter it stands as a major obstacle to religious commitment, whilst for the former it sets up an acute internal tension to disturb his faith and to lay upon it a perpetual burden of doubt." In the literature of Puritanism, as in any body of metaphysical speculation, there are many succinct statements of the centrality of this problem—of which one by a first-generation New England immigrant may serve here as representative: "There is never a childe of *Adam,* but so soone as hee is borne into the world, hee falls to crying, and so he continueth in Sorrowes all the dayes of his life . . ."[27]

Who, in the dwindling years of the twentieth century, stands ready to say different? Pain remains an elemental experience in human lives—the child's first attempt to come to terms with visceral hurt, then with the more abstract but less comprehensible fact of death; the parent's efforts to explain suffering; the manifold experience of betrayal. The growth of technology, we surely know, has done as much to inform us of the undiminished dominion of pain as it has done to limit it. Everyone endures assault upon the conviction of order, and yet, because everyone thinks about such experience differently, it is extremely difficult to render our repertoire of response (which varies, of course, with historical moment, with class, and with the particular portion of the human past upon which each individual draws) either as an act of contemporary criticism from within one's own culture, or as an act of historical recovery from the distance of time. Yet if one thinks of culture as the shared inventory upon which human beings depend in interpreting and responding to phenomena, and of experience as the cumulative impact of such responses upon the self, then the conceived nature of evil is among the most sensitive indices to any culture at any time.

I am persuaded that the history of mind in America reveals a traceable contour of feeling about this problem. In this sense I agree with a remark made nearly twenty years ago by a scholar of colonial American literature: "just as the intellectual side of man may be said to have a history, so may human feeling." It is, moreover, a dialectical history, into which we must look "for the coloration or discoloration of ideas received from the sometimes bruising contact of opposites." The most difficult historical questions—not just the problem of formulating the relationship between ideology and action, but also the problem of understanding cultural transmission—can be seen, at least for early America, centrally to involve certain basic differences over the apprehension of evil. Here is to be found a large part of the process by which our "culture [has achieved] identity not so much through the ascendancy of a particular set of convictions as through the emergence of its peculiar and distinctive dialogue."[28]

Our best historians have made scattered forays into this dialectic, but not in any systematic way. Tocqueville (and his many followers) made paramount the relative absence of class antagonism in early

republican America, and suggested thereby that the appetite for enmity within American culture fed on the presence (or perceived presence) of aliens—those who were racially or nationally distinct—rather
than on the next social rank that threatened from above or below.
This is one way, but only one, by which we may approach the nature
of evil as it has been culturally defined in America. Although I have
tried to be mindful of the inadequacy of any single method for re-
solving this problem, the final chapter of this book represents a preliminary sketch of what I hope may someday become a sustained
account of our culture as it has provided (or failed to provide) the
means by which human beings can make some sort of sense of their
experience of deficiency, danger, and pain. In the present work I
confine myself to arguing that by the end of the seventeenth century
one important group of new Americans had already become generally
committed to a conception of evil as positive entity rather than as
absence of the good—a commitment that has since been more renewed than repealed, and which, as a defended norm or as an ideological principle under assault, underlies our politics, our literature,
and our sense of ourselves.

Let me here be clear about some of my assumptions. The idea of
moral evil has been said to begin in Western culture with images of
defilement. "Dread of the impure and rites of purification are in the
background of all our feelings and all our behavior relating to fault."
According to this sort of argument, there is preserved somewhere in
human consciousness a determinative moment at which "evil and
misfortune have not been dissociated, in which the ethical order of
doing ill has not been distinguished from the cosmo-biological order
of faring ill . . ." We retain, in other words, a pre-ethical fear of stain
as symbol, or (in the terms of Puritan discourse) as type, of suffering.
This is why

> we are astonished . . . when we see involuntary or unconscious human
> actions, the actions of animals, and even simple material events called
> defilements—the frog that leaps into the fire, the hyena that leaves its
> excrements in the neighborhood of a tent. Why are we astonished?
> Because we do not find in these actions or events any point where we
> might insert a judgment of personal imputation, or even simply human
> imputation; we have to transport ourselves into a consciousness for
> which impurity is measured not by imputation to a responsible agent
> but by the objective violation of an interdict.[29]

There may have been, then, a time in the history of human consciousness at which the concept of defilement—as disease, deformity, the suffering of wounds, sexual transgression—coincided entirely with the concept of evil. The genealogy of morals may consequently be understood as the expansion of the concept of evil until it exceeds the more limited idea of defilement and begins to distinguish between the material and the volitional, between taboo and law. The widening of these distances can be seen to accelerate during certain periods in Western history—with the development of Judaism, for instance, or, much more recently, with the rise of what is known as the Enlightenment. Indeed we may say that the essence of what we call liberalism (the chief legacy of the Enlightenment) can be understood as a commitment to keep these distances large: murder is quite a different thing when regarded as an unconditioned act that leaves the perpetrator with "blood on his hands" than it is when regarded through the liberal consciousness as a complex coordination of volition with coercion, of intention with circumstance. This is why such notions as national guilt (an issue that is still current, for example, in discussions of the moral relation between Nazi Germany and the postwar Federal Republic, or, closer to home, between the historical fact of slavery and the reparative policy of affirmative action), may strike us as unenlightened holdovers from a premodern way of thinking about evil as an inheritable entity that exists independently of the individual will.

The English Puritans of the seventeenth century who came to America were a people in flight from manifold turbulence in their understanding of these issues. Theirs was a psychic upheaval that accompanied the material transformation of English society in which they themselves had been participating. This transformation, which is often denoted by such phrases as "the rise of capitalism" or of "bourgeois" society, has been described as the slipping away of a "time . . . when the whole of life went forward in the family"; the authority of the national church was waning, and the individual (including his or her identity as a member of new entities such as corporations or professions) was beginning to emerge in recognizably modern form. The present book is about a relatively small number of people who were part of a movement—religious, political, and geographical—that was committed, among other things, to preserving their endangered sense of family, and to withdrawing from the corporate Church of England and the English nation into churches of their own creating and under their own control. The word "brethren" became, for both the Puritans and their enemies, the seventeenth-century equivalent of "comrades"; while within the movement one faction (Independents) charged another (Presbyterians) with selling out to a "hireling ministry" instead of committing themselves to ministers who could truly act as "Fathers and Nurses." The language of family was sent into combat against the language of commerce.[30]

These come-outers were attempting an unachievable return to a mythic stage of communal innocence—an impulse that eventually found expression in the organizational structures of New England towns and churches. Fleeing from a society where "the strongest social controls" were less and less "exerted in the personal mode," they tried to restore an alternative world of fading memory where "the private individual sees his interests and . . . society . . . expects him to respond" in ways that "more or less coincide." In such a world of harmony, which required for its formation the withdrawal of its citizenry into an essentially separatist sect, individuals tended "to class themselves as members or strangers," and were increasingly "preoccupied with rituals of cleansing [and] expulsion." The outer world loomed as irrational menace, full of "foreign danger[s], introduced by perverted or defective" human beings.[31]

These are not a historian's descriptive phrases, but the terms employed by the anthropologist Mary Douglas in her apposite account of "the sociological matrix in which ideas about sin and the self are generated."[32] What makes the story of the Puritans generic in Douglas's sense, and yet more than an anthropological illustration, is the dynamic and complex process by which these chosen values ran both *with* and *against* their deepest beliefs. The emigrant Puritans fought against a sense of malignant evil that threatened their faith in redemption, even as they more and more encountered such a sense through their willed relation to the world.

In describing the origins and effects of the collective thought and action of these people it is necessary to consider motives of which they themselves may not have been fully conscious. I have tried, with this in mind, to show what I judge to be certain fundamental sources of tension within Puritan culture itself: their flight from individualism even as they consecrated the individual in his unmediated relation to God; and especially their intellectual and affective discord over the question of how evil could best be understood in such a contradictory world—a question that is always especially volatile at moments of fundamental social change. In large measure, then, this story concerns the Puritans' ill-fated defense of their conviction, in St. Augustine's terms, that

> that evil then which I sought, whence it is, is not any substance: for were it a substance, it should be good. For either it should be an incorruptible substance, and so a chief good: or a corruptible substance; which unless it were good, could not be corrupted. I perceived therefore, and it was manifested to me that Thou madest all things good, nor is there any substance at all, which Thou madest not; and for that Thou madest not all things equal, therefore are all things; because each is good, and altogether very good, because our God made all things very good.[33]

One sees in this passage from the *Confessions* that the concomitant ideas of all materiality as the creation of God and of all evil as the privation of good are, in the Augustinian view, one and the same idea. Conversion is the felt apprehension of this idea, and the Puritans who came to America came in hopes of securing (or in some cases of attaining) just such a conversion. They resisted all other conceptualizations of sin.

To make this point clear, it may be useful to turn to one of the most direct treatments of the issue, by John Norton, minister at Ipswich (later John Cotton's successor at Boston), who devoted a lengthy treatise, *A Discussion of that Great Point in Divinity, the Sufferings of Christ* (1653), to refuting certain heretical propositions that had been put forward by William Pyncheon in a book entitled *The Meritorious Price of Our Redemption* (1650). Pyncheon, founder and chief landowner of the western settlement at Springfield, was accused by the New England clerical leadership of Socinian tendencies—of diminishing the divinity of Christ with respect to that of God the Father. (Pyncheon's offense was particularly galling because he was writing as a layman, and thereby giving comfort to those in England who were decrying New England as a "nurserie of schismaticks.") He had argued that the atonement consisted not in God's imputation of sin to his begotten child, but in Christ's exemplary act of self-sacrificing obedience (as a kind of symmetrical cancellation of Adam's original disobedience in Eden). Orthodox Puritans considered that such views amounted to a dangerous portrayal of Christ as a teacher by example rather than as a divine being. In his rebuttal

Norton begins with a narrative of God's judicial relation to man:
"God in the first Covenant (the substance whereof is, *Do this and
thou shalt live,* Lev. 18.5. *But in the day thou eatest thereof thou shalt
surely dye,* Gen. 2.17.) proceeded with man in a way of justice." As
the scripture proclaims, "God by his *free Promise* hath made himself
a debtor according to order of Justice . . . [and] the demerit or desert
of man by reason of sin being death . . . justice now requireth that
man should dye." Norton's God has caught himself in a contradiction
of his own making; the just desert of death for sin must somehow
be accommodated to the free promise of eternal life to the elect:

> The elect then having sinned, the elect must die; if they die in their
> own persons, Election is frustrate, God is unfaithfull; if they die not at
> all, God is unjust, the Commination is untrue: If elect men die in their
> own persons, the Gospel is void, if man doth not die the Law is void;
> they die therefore in the man Christ Jesus, who satisfied Justice as their
> Surety, and so fulfilled both Law and Gospel.[34]

As much as Christ is God's gift to man, he is God's gift to God.

Norton now dwells with scholastic precision upon the etiology of
morals. "What is the supream and first cause why justice requireth
that sin should be rewarded with the punishment?" Why should there
be any moral economy at all in the universe, any consistent or proportionate relation between action, desert, and punishment or reward? Norton's answer is the Puritans' unanswerable credo: because
of "the free constitution of God." There is no appeal here to the rule
of utility, to the social value of discipline and punishment, as there
was, say, in Thomas Shepard's contemporary statement that God's
decrees are "commanded . . . because [they are] good . . . not . . . good
because [they are] commanded." Norton delights in the unconditioned nature of the divine axiom: "This great principle is all along
to be kept in minde . . . The good pleasure of God is the first rule
of Righteousness, the Cause of all Causes, the Reason of all Reasons,
and in one word *all Reason* in *one Reason."*[35]

This is Puritan piety at its purest. "The love of God to us," as
Norton's friend and mentor, John Cotton, put it, "was not procured
by our love to him, but from his own good pleasure." When Norton
turns to the consideration of punishment, we can see the implications
of such an uncompromising faith for the understanding of sin: "The
essential punishment of the curse, is the total temporal privation of

all the sense of the good of the promise, called by some, *The pain of losse . . .*"[36] For both the doomed and the saved there is no other than a privative language; to be damned is not to be burned or violated or pilloried; it is to be separated from the promises—a more devastating sentence than any penance. All the rhetorical power of this pure form of Puritanism is devoted to helping the penitent feel that his separation from God can be closed. There is not a word about Satan.

This vision—with its significant absence—did not endure in America for very long. The concept of evil as a thing with an ontological essence of its own eventually became dominant in New England culture, and the idea of privation was relegated to minor status. This I take to be a transformation with enduring consequences for the culture that defeated the Puritans' holding action against it—namely our own. From time to time the resurgence of the privative idea, with its corollary conviction that human beings are still capable of organic growth into a fulfilled harmony with the divine, has marked a disruption in American life, disruptions that we tend to refer to by the name "revival." But when we hear those Puritans, like Norton, who tried to conserve this conviction in the years immediately following the Great Migration, we are already listening to eulogy.

In recounting some early instances of this conflict as it took form and played itself out in the small and homogeneous society of Puritan New England, I have tried to write a work of history rather than of taxonomy. By this I do not mean that the present book is in any sense an exhaustive account of ecclesiastical or doctrinal developments, or, I trust, that I have written about what Freud called "the narcissism of minor differences." It has been remarked that "it is a vice of the biographical method and of histories of doctrine to make much of apparent distinctions among the ministers." Yet in casting this book in roughly narrative form, I have stressed the importance of some of those distinctions, and have aimed through them to express the rhythm of competition between opposing ideas and feelings that strike me as lying close to the heart of Puritan experience. If we accept the view, as I do, that "the real, central theme of History is not what happened, but what people felt about it when it was happening," then it should be clear how much work remains to be done until we will have met the challenge, issued thirty years ago by Alan Simpson, to confront the "stretched passion" that was working deep within the intellectual edifice of Puritan doctrine.[37] In this spirit I have tried to show that the essential distinction between positive and privative, whose oppositions are usually treated as fixed intellectual positions denoted by such terms as Manichean and Augustinian, represented much more than a scholastic debate for many men and women in early New England. It is my hope not merely to furnish an illustration of a contest between ideas but to show their interpenetration with experience.

The first decades of New England's existence were, as almost all historians have agreed, a generative time for much that came later in our culture—which is to claim a good deal more for the Puritans than mere chronological priority. As common as that claim has become, it still needs defending and explaining. To this end it is possible, I think, to see how the idea of sin as entity leads directly to a very high valuation of psychological and political control, and thereby puts a premium on socially approved behavior (what the Puritans called sanctification) as the best measure of virtue. The idea of sin as stain, in other words, guarantees a shudder in the perception of deviance— and is therefore at the heart of middle-class culture, even perhaps as a constitutive element. The idea of sin as privation, on the other hand, can only exist simultaneously with (indeed is the same thing as) a felt conviction that a transcendent realm of plenitude exists by which human beings can, if they are open to its influence, transcend their moral limitations, or even their mortality.

If it were possible to imagine a culture fully committed to the latter view—whether we call it Platonic or Augustinian or Antinomian— such a culture would yield an entirely different sort of social world from the one in which we live or the one we know from the record of history. It is the world imagined by our ecstatic writers—by Edwards in *The End for Which God Created the World,* by Emerson in *Nature,* by Melville in the "Squeeze of the Hand" chapter of *Moby-Dick,* by Whitman in *Democratic Vistas,* by Henry Adams in *Mont St. Michel and Chartres.* It is the transcendent vision that contemporary ideological critics of American culture have tended to devalue as escapist or apolitical. At certain times in American history it has even been announced as on the verge of incarnation. The Puritan moment remains, I believe, not only the first, but possibly the last time at which Americans were deeply—because almost evenly—divided between those who judged such notions to be visionary fantasies and those who felt them to be realizable. This, to my mind, is the paramount reason—and one that subsumes many other compelling reasons—that the Puritans should continue to exert a special, even an urgent claim on our attention.

What is all history but the work of ideas, a record of the incomputable energy which his infinite aspirations infuse into man? Has anything grand and lasting been done? Who did it? Plainly not any man, but all men: it was the prevalence and inundation of an idea. What brought the pilgrims here? One man says, civil liberty; another, the desire of founding a church; and a third discovers that the motive force was plantation and trade. But if the Puritans could rise from the dust they could not answer. It is to be seen in what they were, and not in what they designed . . .

Ralph Waldo Emerson, 1841

1 The Prophecies of Richard Hooker

When the first four books of Richard Hooker's *Treatise of the Laws of Ecclesiastical Polity* appeared in London in 1593, the forces against which they were directed were already in disarray. The Marprelate press had been shut down for nearly a decade, and its satiric tracts against the clerical establishment had been disavowed by much of the Puritan leadership. The homes of Puritan preachers were being ransacked for scurrilous pamphlets, while agents of the High Commission worked the booksellers' stalls in St. Paul's churchyard, goading or enticing clerical customers into revealing themselves as seditious dissidents. In 1590 a major figure in the movement, John Udall, had been sentenced to death, and though he was pardoned a year later through the personal intervention of the future King James, he died a broken man soon after his release. In the year following Udall's arrest, Thomas Cartwright himself, the Puritans' leading spokesman for a quarter-century, was brought before Star Chamber along with others accused of subscribing to the Book of Discipline. "Long imprisonment and trial had worn down and all but defeated" this core of the Puritan leadership, and what was worse, the setbacks of the eighties did not promise a new martyrology that might inspire those who were left to carry on. The times seemed, for the Puritan party, to be an endless series of discouragements.[1]

Yet anyone who reads through Hooker's *Laws* cannot miss its urgency. The impetus behind Hooker's book was to awaken the nation to what he still considered a clear and present danger. If his Episcopal predecessors and contemporaries—Bishop Jewel in the 1560s, Archbishop Whitgift in the 1580s—had written their defenses of the Anglican *via media* in order to allay the suspicions of Catholic Europe toward a heretic England, or to consolidate the support of a restless gentry, it is less easy to say for whom Hooker was writing. He did, to be sure, make certain gestures of conciliation that seem to have been aimed at the Puritan opposition itself—proposing a "conference or disputation . . . for the ending of contentions," and insisting that "it is no part of my secret meaning to draw you hereby into hatred, or to set upon the face of this cause any fairer glass than the naked truth doth afford; but my whole endeavour is to resolve the conscience . . . without either cloud of prejudice, or mist of passionate affection."[2]

Hooker's disclaimer notwithstanding, there was a "secret meaning" in the *Laws*. Hooker did not seriously expect that the "you" of his address would come to the conference table, or that the inflamed Puritan conscience could be cooled by reason. He was writing, on the contrary, in order to expose the surviving Puritan agenda, which had become, as its leading modern historian puts it, "only a blurred impression" to even its most strenuous observers.[3] The *Laws* was an effort to smoke out a clandestine enemy, to make him show himself so that queen and country would not be lulled into thinking him gone. It was an attempt to demonstrate the end to which this weakened but still living ideology would necessarily lead if it were not utterly stamped out. "The more harmlesse men be," protested one beleaguered Puritan leader a decade later, "the more they shall be molested."[4]

To see the Elizabethan Puritan movement in this way through Hooker's eyes is to complicate our vision not only with our own retrospect but also with his enmity. But there is a compensation in his sheer astuteness about the phenomenon before its translation to America. Although some recent scholars have begun to see Puritanism as "comprising a kind of moral majority of the late Elizabethan and Jacobean Church," we have been mainly schooled to think about it as an organized and self-conscious movement that was somehow of the left, of its Fifth Monarchist fringe as "preach[ing] anarchist revolt against the state," and even of its mainstream intellectual leadership as "the first of those self-disciplined agents of social and political reconstruction who have appeared so frequently in modern history . . . the destroyer[s] of an older order for which there is no need to feel nostalgic."[5] One therefore expects Hooker, severe Erastian that he was, to confirm this sense of Puritanism as an impulse deeply dangerous to the well-ordered society. And so he does. Yet if we listen to his articulation of what he deems to be the proper understanding of history (and therefore of one's responsibility as an actor within history), we are forced to modify our picture of the conservative Anglican as bound to the past and of the radical Puritan as committed to an open future:

> True it is that the ancienter, the better ceremonies of religion are; howebeit, not absolutely true only so far forth as those different ages do agree in the state of those things, for which at the first those rites, orders, and ceremonies, were instituted. In the Apostles' times that was harmless, which being now revived would be scandalous; as their *oscula sancta*.[6]

This is a full-fledged historical relativism that will permit "loose construction" of the Bible itself. It is the heart of Hooker's assault on what he regards as the mad absolutism of his opponents. He is alarmed by the extent to which the Puritan mind has been mastered by its subservience to scripture—or, to put it more accurately, by the extent to which it thinks itself capable of discerning the prescriptive intent of scripture, and thereby of recovering the original intent of God:

> [B]y fashioning the very notions and conceits of men's minds . . . when they read the Scripture, they may think that every thing soundeth towards the advancement of [their ecclesiastical] discipline, and to the utter disgrace of the contrary. Pythagoras, by bringing up his scholars in the speculative knowledge of numbers, made their conceits therein so strong, that when they came to the contemplation of things natural, they imagined that in every particular thing they even beheld as it were with their eyes, how the elements of number gave essence and being to the works of nature.[7]

Hooker's critique becomes much more than a rejection of particular scriptural interpretations with which he takes issue. It becomes almost an assertion of what is nowadays called the "undecidability" of texts. Hooker reduces the authority of scripture because he doubts that it has any recoverable pure meaning apart from the contingent meanings that its readers bring to it.

The Puritans who emerge from this total (and eerily modern) assault are naive believers—committed not only to the notion that they can read God's intention in scripture, but to the more basic proposition that history itself is an unremitting, if sometimes temporarily obstructed, revelation of preexisting truth. If we read the best modern historians on Puritanism, we come away with a healthy skepticism toward "any scheme of categorisation for which 'Anglican' and 'Puritan' are hard and fast entities." Yet if we read Hooker and his contemporaries, we must still be impressed by the evident division of their culture into what may be called two styles of knowing. For the Puritan, history is genuinely progressive, but only in the sense that it manifests the slow adjustment of continually changing human arrangements into congruence with God's eternal intentions. Here is a clear assertion of this view, as expressed decades later by one of the emigrants to America:

> Even Fundamental Truths which have been the same in all generations, have been, and shall be transmitted more clear from age to age in the times of Reformation: untill that which is perfect is come, and that which is imperfect be done away . . . Such addition, is no innovation, but an illustration, not new light, but new sight.

For the Anglican, in contrast, history requires that the search for order be adjusted on both sides—that is, by both God and man:

> Laws though both ordained of God himself, and the end for which they were ordained continuing, may notwithstanding cease if, by alteration of persons or times, they be found insufficient to attain to that end.[8]

Hooker's language here is significantly imprecise: he attaches no agency to the verb "cease," as if he is hesitant to specify who holds the power to introduce and terminate such laws—God or man. The elision did not go unnoticed; Puritans loudly objected to the main principle Hooker was determined to uphold—the principle of *adiaphora,* which declared that God required men to exercise their reason in order to find the best means for establishing Christian order according to the times in which they lived. In one age, according to the Anglican argument, this may have meant small gathered churches with no central or even synodical authority; but in another it meant a national church organized into parishes and dioceses. The apostles' kiss had given way to the bishops' decree—a change that Hooker did not regard as ordained by God from the beginning of time, but that he thought reasonable and just according to prevailing conditions.

The mind that has no room for such adjustments to the temper of the times is a mind obsessed, says Hooker, with submitting itself to a divine authority that is beyond interpretation. To such a mind the idea of alternative truths is more than nonsense; it is an obscenity. "The Scripture saith," as another Puritan emigrant to New England was to put it in the 1640s, "there is nothing makes free but Truth, and Truth saith, there is no Truth but one." About this sort of mind Hooker says what William James will say of the "absolutist" three hundred years later:

> The indeterminism I defend . . . gives us a pluralistic, restless universe, in which no single point of view can ever take in the whole scene; and to a mind possessed of the love of unity at any cost, it will, no doubt, remain forever inacceptable. A friend with such a mind once told me that the thought of my universe made him sick, like the sight of the horrible motion of a mass of maggots in their carrion bed.[9]

What James is describing here is the psychic risk to the monist when confronted by the possibility of an indeterminate universe in which God has not decreed the shape and content of every moment for every inhabiting consciousness. As Hooker defended such a possibility—specifically an ecclesiastical system for which he made no claim of transcendent truth—he was, in effect, inviting the same revulsion. His text is the best commentary on the size of the Puritan investment in divine authority, and on the cost the believer must pay when that investment appears to be lost. The recoil of the distressed believer in the seventeenth century was much less likely to be a repudiation of God's authority than a vilification of the wayward self. In the case of those Puritans who journeyed to the New World, this self-doubt was soon to be manifest.

2

Among the clues Hooker gives us to the size of the Puritans' wager on their own centrality in the divine consciousness is his recognition that they "impute all faults and corruptions, wherewith the world aboundeth, unto the kind of ecclesiastical government established." This imputation implied a belief in the limitless potentiality of the unregulated human soul. "I see it not necessary," preached John Preston in the 1620s, "that a finite facultie, should have an infinite object, if that which is proportionable be enough; but this I affirme withall, that unlesse *God* were infinite, he could not satisfie the soule of man, for this is the nature of the soule, if it finde a bottom in any particular, it passeth over that, and hasteth after more."[10]

Hooker sensed that Puritanism expressed a deep desire to believe in human moral capability. The ethical teachings of writers like Theophilus Golius (whose extracts from the *Nichomachean Ethics,* compiled in the late sixteenth century, became a standard text in the Cambridge and Harvard curricula) addressed in a Platonic spirit the question of how desire for the good can be ineffectual in the making of moral choice. A number of themes in classical ethical theory converged upon this question, not the least of which was the Aristotelian notion that virtue, like a muscle or a limb, requires continual strengthening through exercise. The response of writers such as Golius to the problem of moral education was to make a distinction between sensory and true knowledge. Both good and evil actions stem equally from desire; the question is always whether a man's perception is trained upon an elevated or a base object of desire. Satan, in other words, misleads by interjecting an immediately tempting object between the perceiver and the true good. Men have no active preference for evil, but they are subject to misperception, in which fleeting pleasures can be mistaken for the enduring good.[11]

From this sort of moral theory it can be readily seen that the challenge for the Christian teacher of ethics was to direct the mind to divine objects of desire ("It is the nature of sound love to covet nearer union with the thing beloved") and to free it from illusory ones ("What is it to enjoy the creature for a season, and be deprived of the creator for ever?"). One way to make these discriminations was to render God's truth sensually enticing; another was to darken the aspect of whatever carnal satisfactions masquerade as truth. All Puritan ministers did some of each. "We are dealing," as one scholar puts it, "not with separate theologies [within Puritanism], but with shades of emphasis that sometimes generate conflict."[12] The incipient conflicts within Puritanism that would emerge full-blown upon its transferral to the New World can be apprehended if we take seriously the changing proportions of Christ-preaching and devil-preaching from one historical moment to another. The possibility of a privative conception of evil always hung, as it were, in that balance.

To Hooker, however, no matter how much hellfire the Puritans stoked in the service of moral reform, they were fanatics who held out the fantastic promise of renovating human nature by effecting institutional change. This is why the real audience for the *Laws* was not the immovable enemy but those for whose allegiance he and the Puritans were contending: drowsy members of the English clerical class, whom Hooker thought unaware that their church was destined to come yet again under radical assault. Hooker grasped the Puritans' inveterate antagonism toward hierarchy (or at least toward the prevailing form of it that held them low), and so he devoted much of the *Laws* to defending the techniques that the maintenance of hierarchy seemed to require:

> The end which is aimed at in setting down the outward form of all religious actions is the edification of the Church. Now men are edified, when either their understanding is taught somewhat whereof in such actions it behoveth all men to consider, or when their hearts are moved with any affection suitable thereunto; when their minds are in any sort stirred up unto that reverence, devotion, attention, and due regard, which in those cases seemeth requisite. Because therefore unto this purpose not only speech but sundry sensible means besides have always been thought necessary, and especially those means which being object to the eye, the liveliest and the most apprehensive sense of all other, have in that respect seemed the fittest to make a deep and a strong impression: from hence have risen not only a number of prayers, readings, questionings, exhortings, but even of visible signs also; which being used in performance of holy actions, are undoubtedly most effectual to open such matter, as men when they know and remember carefully, must needs be a great deal the better informed to what effect such duties serve. We must not think but that there is some ground of reason even in nature, whereby it cometh to pass without some visible solemnity: the very strangeness whereof and difference from that which is common, doth cause popular eyes to observe and to mark the same.[13]

This is a manifesto of what may be called the party of the eye—a commitment to sensory manipulation of "popular eyes," to keep them gazing upward at fixed points of authority: Bishop, King, God. "For the Anglican . . . the church expresses the deep sense of the English nation on its knees . . . owing allegiance to their sovereign who is both king and supreme governor of the church."[14] In such a worshipping posture there can be little sense of the worshipper by one's side, except as a fellow supplicant suffused with awe.

That was Hooker's vision of the church. It was not, he knew, shared by the Puritans:

> whatsoever is spoken concerning the efficacy or necessity of God's Word, the same they tie and restrain only unto Sermons, howbeit not Sermons read neither (for such they also abhor in the church), but sermons without book, sermons which spend their life in their birth and may have public audience but once.[15]

Puritans were obsessed with the Pauline doctrine that "faith cometh by hearing" (Romans 10:17) and contemptuous of what they considered the residual "dumb-shows" that still dominated Anglican ritual— "altar-decking, cope-wearing, organ-playing, piping and singing, crossing of cushions and kissing of clouts, oft starting up and squatting down, nodding of heads, and whirling about till their noses stand eastward . . ."[16]

Even when the vernacular gradually entered the church and recitation from the Edwardian prayer books replaced the priest's Latin chant, and even after Hooker himself conceded the importance of the auditory faculty in the work of transmitting religious conviction, Puritans were hardly satisfied. "That which offendeth us," Hooker remarks, is "the great disgrace which they offer unto our custom of bare reading the word of God." On this point he peppers his commentary with outbursts against their truculence: "*Sermons* are not *the only preaching* which doth save souls."

> Unless . . . clear contrary to our own experience, we shall think it a miracle if any man acknowledge the divine authority of the scripture, till some sermon have persuaded him thereunto, and that otherwise neither conversation in the bosom of the church, nor religious education, nor the reading of learned men's books, nor information received by conference, nor whatsoever pain and diligence in hearing, studying, meditating day and night on the law, is so far blest of God as to work this effect in any man; how would they have us to grant that faith doth not come but only by *hearing sermons?*[17]

The Puritans rarely gave an explicit answer to this question. They offered instead a continual refrain about hungry multitudes going unfed—"blockish, ignorant people" adrift without the preached word that must be "fit both for the peoples understanding, and to expresse the Maiestie of the Spirit." In New England they would institute regular weekday lectures, a sabbath of which six or seven hours might be devoted to preaching, and a range of supplementary sermons on fast and election days—to which the populace was summoned by drumbeat. Yet in both New and Old England most of their comments about the value of sermons (as opposed to prescribed homilies or "the bare reading" of scripture) were brief and tautological. To William Bradshaw, for example, the indispensability of the preaching elder was a self-evident fact on a par with faith itself: "A man," he declared at the turn of the century, "may as well call into question the whole New Testament, as doubt whether there ought to be a Pastor in every congregation." Such claims for the sanctity of pastoral preaching must be read in the context of a time when curates throughout England could be lower in the social scale than agricultural laborers, and when incumbents continued to resort, although in diminished numbers, to plural livings. Much of the clergy was undereducated and only marginally self-sufficient; nearly half the livings in England were held by lay patrons "who collected the tithes and usually only passed a proportion of this income on to the incumbent." At the turn of the seventeenth century, the Anglican church was simply not supporting a literate and married clergy.[18]

In this context, Hooker readily found confirmation for his suspicion that the Puritans' fascination with the power of oratory concealed a deeply antiauthoritarian impulse. Richard Bernard, Puritan author of the clerical handbook *The Faithfull Shepheard* (1607), judged that it was Satan who "stoppeth the *Eare* from hearing," and went on to give a more developed sense of the preacher's holy function: "Such as in the Pulpit pray for themselves in the singular number, as thus; I pray thee, open my mouth, &c, doe therein breake off the course of their publique Function, and make it a private action, untuneable, without concord to the rest, as a jarring string." Such preachers were throwbacks to the days when it was common for chantry priests to murmur daily mass in their patrons' chapels with no one in attendance. The Puritans' revulsion at such an onanistic clergy was at the heart—as Hooker sensed—of their half-articulate program to wrest authority from all surpliced priests appointed by absentee authority, and to convey it instead to a local ministry that would be answerable to the laity as "*Gods Mouth* to the people."[19]

Beneath these disputes over preaching was a still deeper confrontation between two sectors of a dividing culture, neither of which quite possessed the vocabulary for expressing its alienation from the other. One was committed to religion as the visual representation of hierarchy ("pedagogy in [stained] glass," it has been called), the other to the scriptural literacy of the hitherto unlettered—as instructed by preaching ministers who were as likely to address such issues as enclosure and poor laws and debtors' obligations as they were to dwell on traditional biblical topics. One was organized in the service of the supreme authority of the church; the other was engaged in persuading Englishmen that they must participate in their own reconstruction as members of linked, but distinct, Christian communities. If "argument," for the Anglican, "end[ed] in adoration," argument for the Puritan threatened to end in the expulsion of an unresponsive minister, or in the separation of certain members from the main body of a parish church, or, as Hooker seemed to prophesy, in the wholesale destruction of the national church in favor of self-governing groups of visible saints.[20]

The Bible remained the central text in this program—especially in the translation rendered by the Genevan exiles—but to hear it "opened" by a fervent minister was to be offered truth that would be complete only when grasped and put to use by the individual believer. "Christians," John Cotton explained in one of his early Lincolnshire sermons, must "never . . . rest in any Scripture they read, or Ministers they hear, before they have examined things by the testimony of the Spirit."[21] For the Anglican, "spirit" was suspect, especially when it became a presumed possession of the people. For the Puritan, even the most learned commentator, if he were without the requisite spirit of discernment, would find the Bible a dark and unyielding book.

One can sense these differences at work by listening to two opposing views of the meaning of the sabbath. According to the Anglican John Prideaux, writing in the 1630s, "Wee are permitted Recreations (of what sort soever) which serve lawfully to *refresh* our *spirits*" on the sabbath because the scripture does not contain a clear set of prohibitions or prescriptions for sabbath observance. To this sort of mind the Bible was a kind of reference book which, in this particular case, did not furnish much data. To "search into the *Veiles* and *Shadowes* of the *Old Testament,* to finde this *Institution* [of the sabbath is to] fall, with the Ebionite . . . into the Toyles of *Judaisme.*" By this remark Prideaux means that the full authority of the fourth commandment, like that of any other Jewish ceremonial law, has been abrogated by the incarnation, but that it retains some validity as a Mosaic precept. Thus the sabbath should be observed, but not with Judaic strictness. In taking such a middling position he was consistent with Calvin, who had made "the Mosaic Law and the Gospel of Grace parts of one unbroken covenant" through the device of typology, and had thereby rescued the sabbath from total extinction—but had nevertheless "bowled on Sunday and was buried on a Lord's Day afternoon." There were, as well, other than hermeneutic reasons for Anglican resistance to strict sabbatarianism. Rigorous observance of the sabbath was inconsistent with the festive traditions of saints' days and the seasonal rhythms of rural labor (harvesting cannot be suspended on Sunday), but was a highly serviceable institution for the incipient business culture in which Puritanism was taking hold through the weekly submission of laity to ministerial instruction. Thus Thomas Shepard recognized when he came to New England a bitter irony in the fact that the stringent Sunday for which he had fought in England was now coming under assault from the very class for whom it had once been a convenience. The greed of merchants and employers, Shepard believed, had outgrown the enforced respite of a day's rest. By means of a rampant typology that opposed the continuance of Old Testament institutions (on the grounds that they had been abrogated as literal injunctions by their fulfillment in the spiritual truths of the New Testament), these greedy typologists were seeking to "spiritualize the sabbath out of the world." Theirs was an exegesis in the service of mammon. Yet for Shepard the legitimacy of the sabbath rested not on its social utility or on any specific Old Testament passage that might be construed as carrying it over into the Christian age, but rather on the general spirit of its scriptural sanction:

> Look, therefore, as when man hath run his race, finished his course, and passed through the bigger and larger circle of his life, he then returns unto his eternal rest, so it is contrived and ordered by divine wisdom, as that he shall in a special manner return unto his rest once at least within the lesser and smaller circle of every week, that so his perfect blessedness to come might be foretasted every Sabbath day.[22]

For this Puritan the Bible was a divine poem to be experienced perpetually. The Sabbath was for preaching. And preaching, at its effective best, was a communal meditation on the beauty of the word.

In considering the audience to which such Puritan ministers were offering the spoken word, Hooker had observed that "most labour hath been bestowed to win and retain towards their cause them whose judgements are commonly weakest by reason of their sex . . ." Already in the 1590s Hooker saw the importance of a female constituency to the ongoing zeal of the Puritan movement, and he would not have taken exception to a modern historian's judgment that "Puritanism was not only a lay movement" but also "a women's movement." Hooker also knew that certain forms of zeal depend on the pride of the persecuted, and so he recognized in Puritanism (in ways that Shepard was ruefully to confirm) the inevitability of its attenuation. "To themselves they draw all the sentences which scripture hath in the favour of innocency persecuted for the truth," but they forget (and will be reminded) that although "with thieves was the Lord himself crucified . . . they, who were matched in the pain which they suffered, were in the cause of their sufferings disjoined." When the first flush of piety waned in the isolation of the New World, John Cotton came to agree that "*Paul* accounteth it a folly to make boasts in comparisons, even of sufferings," and women were among the first to take note of the slackening: "Not well lik[ing the] Doctrine and grave pollished Church order," women especially, according to Samuel Gorton, regarded the exiled Puritan community as "much decayed and allmost worne out" even in its infancy.[23]

The chief challenge to Puritanism in America was that it found fewer opponents than it had in England. It had once been possible to say with more pride than anger that "the word Puritan in the mouth of an Arminian, signifies an Orthodoxe divine; in the mouth of a drunkard signifies a sober man; and in the mouth of a Papist signifies a Protestant." But in New England the Puritans heard mainly the carping of their own dissidents. Hooker knew that the concept of Puritanism had been invented and sustained by its detractors. To follow the development of the very word "Puritan" from the 1560s into the early seventeenth century is thus to follow its transformation from a resisted insult—"a soule-killing Nick-name," as one indignant minister called it early in Elizabeth's reign—into an acknowledged title of honor. That process of legitimation could proceed no further in the New World. "[We should] reject the society," Cotton declared in his Lincolnshire years, "of such men as inwardly loath the name of *Puritans;* alas, if they cannot endure the name of purity in poor weak Christians how would they hate the purity of Christ? If they cannot endure the brightnesse of a candle, how will they endure the brightnesse of the sun?" "Reject the society" was what some of them did, as Hooker had known they would. The trouble was that when the candle burned not as a rebuke to the profane and outraged world but only for the benefit of the sequestered faithful, when the "stimulating experience of persecution" subsided into a remembered ache from across the ocean, then these Puritans could no longer evade the question of who they were. In their departure they were fulfilling another of Hooker's prophecies: "Yea, I am persuaded," he had written forty years before the Winthrop fleet set sail, "that of them with whom in this cause we strive, there are [those] whose betters amongst men would be hardly found, if they did not live amongst men, but in some wilderness by themselves."[24]

People of any color seldom run unless there be something to run from.
Abraham Lincoln, 1862

2 Errand out of the Wilderness

Just as the terms "Anglican" and "Puritan" may have outlived their usefulness as unmodified categories for understanding Elizabethan and Stuart England, it has become increasingly clear that the word "Puritan" can no longer serve alone as a description of the people who came from Old to New England in the fourth and fifth decades of the seventeenth century. A certain kind of composite portrait of these people has lately begun to emerge through the painstaking work of a number of social historians. Some have stressed the essential homogeneity of the New World immigrants, noting that from Rowley and Ipswich in the north to Dorchester and Hingham in the south the settlements were "primarily a transplantation of families," in which husband and wife were likely to be in their mid-thirties, with young children and a servant or two. It was not an especially youthful migration—a fact with which the emigrant ministers (who numbered about one in every two hundred migrants) had to contend as they continued to pronounce the conventional Puritan notion that God worked mainly upon the young. Other historians have stressed diversity, denying "any uniform set of reasons" behind the phenomenon. Some communities transplanted themselves from Old England almost intact under the sway of a powerful clergyman who was being harassed by the authorities; others virtually dragged their unwilling

minister along, only to see him return to England at the first opportunity. Some communities replicated the open-field system of strip-
farming with its relatively egalitarian land distribution and the communal requirements of collective ploughing and harvesting. Others
adopted a system of much more individualized agricultural enterprise,
with sharp differences in the size and value of land grants. Some
farmers raised hemp and flax along with grain, and thus reproduced
the cottage industry of weaving that had supported them in the Old
World. Others were primarily dairy farmers, whose experience with
long days of field work was minimal. In certain towns the selectmen
were essentially agents of the town meeting; in others an oligarchical
leadership of prominent families quickly emerged. Some towns were
settled by sermon-drenched East Anglians, others by "Yorkshire natives [who] were likely to attend services [in England] only when
extraordinarily induced." And perhaps most important, some towns
were composed of families who had been close neighbors in England,
others of people who had lived miles or even parishes apart and had
known each other, if at all, from occasional meetings at market.[1]

There was, in short, a good deal of vocational and regional diversity
among the migrants; a substantial number came from market towns
where they had been shoemakers, coopers, joiners, weavers, or most
generally, carpenters, who of all trades were deemed "most needful."
But there is one negative generalization that seems to fit them all:
"The families that went to New England had largely avoided the
serious [economic] setbacks that afflicted many of their countrymen."
These were not a desperate people, if by desperation we limit ourselves to the idea of physical want. In this connection it is important
to recognize that it was by no means cheap to transport one's family
to New England; some could afford the outlay for passage and equipment while managing to retain at least some landholdings in England;
others had to convert their goods and homes into liquid funds; still
others, including some young men of not inconsiderable social rank,
had, in order to finance the trip and resettlement, to commit themselves to a term of indentured service. The one social group barely
represented at all was that of beggars, scavengers, and vagabonds—
England's visible poor.[2]

It is a kind of tribute to this mixed multitude that their most recent
and scrupulous students have tended to confirm their own explanations of why they came. "That which is our greatest comfort," wrote

Francis Higginson after his arrival at Salem in the late 1620s, ". . . is, that we have here the true Religion . . . plentie of Preaching . . . and good and commendable orders to bring our People into a Christian conversation." One recent scholar, after exhaustive computer-aided research into the surviving evidence of the immigrants' motives, comes to the similar conclusion that "religious motivation is the only factor with sufficient power to explain the departure of so many otherwise ordinary families." But if we are to grasp what "religious motivation" finally meant to those who left their homes on its account, we must widen and complicate our sense of how religion worked in their lives. There can be no doubt that "the traditional either/or dichotomy— either religion or economics—makes no sense."[3] The question becomes, therefore, how can these explanatory categories be brought together?

An answer can be found in Hooker's analysis of Puritanism, whose hallmark, he knew, was its insistence that the obligations of piety knew no bounds. Religion was to infuse rather than degrade the activities of daily living. To be certain that this remained so, the emigrants to America brought with them a preaching ministry. "Gods Servants . . . have alwayes a Teacher within them," Cotton had remarked in England, "they carry a Prophet about them, a Minister about them." Many of those who came to America were commited to making Cotton's metaphor literal. Some would never have embarked without the fellowship of the brethren with whom they had formed a church or conventicle, and others made the decision to leave in consultation with the particular man whom they hoped would be a Moses to his flock in exodus. When "our teacher Mr. Cotton . . . [was] put down," said Anne Hutchinson, of Alford, Lincolnshire, "there was none in *England* that I durst hear." "I never so much as heard of New-England," wrote Roger Clap of Devonshire, "until I heard of many godly persons that were going there, and that Mr. Warham [minister of Exeter] was to go also."[4]

As for the ministers, they sometimes had little choice, or at least felt themselves to be choosing among silence, conformity, and exile. Something like half the emigrant clergy had already encountered serious trouble from their episcopal superiors. Though in the 1620s there arose some support for the procuring of Puritan lectureships through such agencies as the Feofees for Impropriations (a group of London lawyers, merchants, and ministers who raised funds for buying the right of clerical appointment from lay patrons) the prospects for dissenting ministers grew dimmer with Archbishop Laud's increasing power. Laud and his ally the Earl of Strafford—that "Black Tom Tyrante" as some called him—were full of fury in the 1630s; lecturers were, to Laud, merely "the people's creatures [who] blew the bellows of their sedition." Yet it has been suggested that he actually conducted his attack on the Puritan clergy with "an administrator's, rather than an ideologue's" mentality, and tended to be grudgingly disarmed once he elicited outward conformity from an offending minister. He was a man of complicated convictions: he had fined, pilloried, and cropped the ears of the insolent William Prynne, but even as he sent him to the Tower he considered it unchristian to deprive him of books and writing materials. Still, to his enemies Laud became virtually Antichrist incarnate, outdoing all his predecessors in what Bishop Jewel had called "scenic apparatus." He had at least as large a commitment as Hooker's to the power of ceremony. He was openly Arminian and determined to restore the centrality of the sacraments to the church—literally to bring every altar in England out of the dark corners to which Puritan congregations had banished them. Most important, he seemed entirely capable of carrying out King James's thirty-year-old threat to "harry [the Puritans] out of the land." Here is Thomas Shepard's account of his own day of reckoning before the fearsome Laud:

> As soon as I came in the morning about eight of the clock, falling into a fit of rage, [Laud] asked me what degree I had taken in the University. I answered him, I was a Master of Arts. He asked me, of what College? I answered, Of Emmanuel. He asked how long I had lived in his diocese. I answered, Three years and upwards. He asked who maintained me all this while, charging me to deal plainly with him, adding withal that he had been more cheated and equivocated with by some of my malignant faction than ever was man by Jesuit, at the speaking of which words he looked as though blood would have gushed out of his face and did shake as if he had been haunted with an ague fit, to my apprehension by reason of his extreme malice and secret venom. I desired him to excuse me. He fell then to threaten me and withal to bitter railing, calling me all to naught, saying, You prating coxcomb! Do you think all the learning is in your brain? He pronounced his sentence thus: I charge you that you neither preach, read, marry, bury, or exercise any ministerial function in any part of my diocese, for if you do, and I hear of it, I will be upon your back and follow you wherever you go, in any part of the kingdom, and so everlastingly disenable you. I be-

sought him not to deal so, in regard of a poor town. Here he stopped me in what I was going to say. A poor town! You have made me a company of seditious, factious Bedlams, and what do you prate to me of a poor town? I prayed him to suffer me to catechise in the Sabbath days in the afternoon. He replied, Spare your breath; I will have no such fellows prate in my diocese. Get you gone, and now make your complaints to whom you will![5]

2

"In this world," Shepard had written while still in England, "there grows a secret satiety and fullness upon our hearts, and it grows common, and blessings of greatest price are not so sweet as the first time we enjoy them; they clog the stomach and glut the soul." By "this world," Shepard meant not just Laudian England, but the whole expanse of man's temporal existence, yet the terms of his description are recognizably local. They are, for example, essentially the same terms John Donne employed to describe the sinful feeling of "stupefaction": "You feele nothing . . . your soule it selfe is become a carcasse . . . Oh, slowness is our punishment and sinne." By the second decade of the seventeenth century English Protestants—by no means only those whom we call Puritan—were more and more lamenting a blasphemous form of satiety, a kind of low-grade nausea that shuts down the appetite and replaces it with bilious fatigue. Such a notion of moral evil as its own penalty—a condemnation of the sated self to languor—is very far from what we might expect in Calvinist imprecation; far from a savoring account of "*odious . . . detestable* . . . and also pernicious, fatal and destructive . . . depravity." As reported by its Puritan soul-physicians, Stuart England was not acutely ill, but in a kind of collective sedation—a "sleepy, sluggish, stupid, benummed senselessnesse."[6] Sin was dissolving from something active into a seeping thing—a silent, slow narcotic. It had once been different.

It had been different for the Puritans of Hooker's time, who tended to conceive of sin as a menace external to the self—a bad neighborhood, a painted woman, the rattle of dice. "As it is the nature of a Canker, or Gangreene," Robert Cawdray had explained around the

turn of the century, "to runne from one joynt to another, from toe
to the foote, from the foote to the legge, from the legge to the thigh,
till it have wasted and destroyed the life of the body: Even so, if we
give Sin but an entrance, it will soon overspread the whole man."
Sin, in this typically late-Elizabethan formulation, had been an entity
with a life of its own, something greedily alive, a "concupiscence," as
another preacher called it, ". . . the roote and fountaine, out of which
groweth & floweth al evill that is committed in the world." Through
the 1580s and 1590s scores of Puritan guidebooks had taken as their
chief targets such pastimes as bear-baiting, cock-fighting, and, of course,
that "Sathans Sinagogue," the theater. The recoiling imagination of
Philip Stubbes had found England in the 1580s in the midst of an
epidemic of sensual indulgence—to which his response was essentially to recommend moral quarantine, to turn the country's dance-
halls into sexually segregated discotheques: men should "daunce by
themselves & women by themselves," or there will be "provocations
to lust and venery."[7]

Twenty years later such therapies had not worked—a predictable
outcome according to opponents; a failure of enforcement according
to devotees. With their civic indignation unabated as the century
turned, Puritan moralists were chiding as vigorously as ever the "covetous . . . and voluptuous" sons of the gentry, privileged brats who,
according to the terms of the indictment, were by no means "benummed," but still "too quick to act in the flesh." To say, as the
Puritans incessantly did, that there was too much heat in the boys'
blood was not to snipe at far-away libertines, but to bend close to
one's tempted neighbor, to coax him feelingly out of hell. There was
angry intimacy in this tutorial relation—the kind of resentment that
accompanies sibling obligation. Only a "permeable membrane" as one
historian puts it, divided the leisured gentry from the main Puritan
constituency of the "industrious sort"—a barrier that was constantly
being traversed: "careers in trade or the professions . . . constituted
a kind of social oscillation of many younger sons of the landed gentry,
a way of retaining . . . the place and 'port' of a gentleman by means
other than the undisturbed possession of the land." More than any
other religious force in Stuart England, Puritanism held out the promise of reversing one's slippage in status; it gave voice to those who
felt discarded from lives of property and ease. "A poor servant here
that is to possess but fifty acres of land," promised Francis Higginson
as he waited at Salem for the main force of the Great Migration, "may

afford more wood for timber and fire as good as the world yields than many noblemen in England can afford to do. Here is good living for those that love good fires."[8]

The audience for this kind of reassurance was, in part, one class squeezed out of its traditional way of life by scarcity and primogeniture and learning to behave like another. When Shepard, during New England's difficult first decade, declared (out of Hebrews 12) that "chastisement is part of the portion of sons, not of bastards," or William Stoughton announced somewhat later that New Englanders were "surely the Lord's first-born in this wilderness," they were not conjuring up some remote Levitical parallel in the minds of their hearers, but were speaking directly to a first-hand emotion. They were contending with the sore frustration in a younger brother's displacement—a feeling already at work in England and intensified for those who eventually migrated to the American outland.[9]

Perhaps the most vivid representation of the theme of virtue endangered by the oppression of youth comes not from a disenfranchised gentleman but from a young apprentice tailor of modest means named John Dane. Writing of his flight to New England nearly fifty years after the fact, Dane tells of a stern and disapproving father from whom he flees into a wandering life at age eighteen; he writes of leering tavern women who meet his blushing self-restraint—"Mis, I am troblsom to you," he manages when lured into one busy bedroom—with scandalous invitations: "No, sayd she, you are welcum to me." Temptations to succumb to harlots and join with thieves and vagabonds are swept away in a moment of deliverance that vindicates not only Dane the pilgrim but also Dane the son:

> When theas stormes ware a lettle over, thare was a great cuming to nu ingland [around 1637] . . . [and] I was mutch bent to cum [and] I went to starford to my fatther to tell him . . . My fatther and motther showd themselfs unwilling. I sat close by a tabell whare thare lay a bibell. I hastily toke up the bybell, and tould my fatther if whare I opend the bybell thare I met with anie thing eyther to incuredg or discouredg that should settell me. I oping of it, not knowing no more then the child in the womb, the first I cast my eys on was: Cum out from among them, touch no unclene thing, and I will be your god and you shall be my pepell. My fatther and motther never more aposd me, but furdered me in the thing; and hasted after me as sone as they could.[10]

Many among these first New Englanders, as if embarked on "a personal exodus . . . from the limited future of a youngest son," sound

like children fretting to catch the attention of their elders by advertising their self-taught virtue. We find even Shepard retorting as if
to an off-stage scold: "Out of men fallen [God] picks out usually the
poorest and vilest, the younger brother less loved out of a family . . . and this is strange that the Lord should choose thus, but this
he doth to blur the glory of all the world." According to one recent
portrait of mid-century New England, these exiled juniors turned
rather quickly into stern immigrant fathers—bristling at the first signs
of independence in their own children. Deputy Governor Dudley,
who spent his teens pouring the wine and laying the gaming-tables
as a gentleman's page in Northampton, ended his life in Massachusetts
proclaiming himself "NO LIBERTINE." There is something general in
this particular, a proud inflexibility, something of the tightness of the
arriviste who has put his green years behind him—with a vengeance.[11]

Nathaniel Hawthorne represented this New World mixture of pride
and stringency in Governor Bellingham, who, anticipating that "the
exigencies of this new country" would transform him from a lawyer
into a soldier, brought across the ocean all the emblems of his rank:
"a head-piece, a cuirass, a gorget, and greaves," and built himself a
house of a "brilliancy [that] might have befitted Aladdin's palace."
Hawthorne's is a portrait of a people stalled in preening adolescence—
in a time of life devoted to conformity, when mercy has not been
learned. Many less allegorically minded writers have confirmed the
presence in early New England of such a huge and unreflective
pomposity, and some have proposed specific reasons for its shriveling
effect on those whom Cotton Mather called "Criolians"—the American-
born children of the emigrant generation. Remarkably soon after the
establishment of the first settlements, land scarcity within the borders
of New England's towns compelled younger sons to migrate west and
south, and the ministry added greed, disloyalty, and filial impudence
to its growing catalogue of declensions.[12] New England, in unexpected
ways, was duplicating Old.

Long before such ironies of repetition played themselves out in
America—before restless English sons turned into fierce New England fathers—the Puritan ministry in England had placed at the center
of its pantheon of sins the breakdown of filial discipline. Young men
of wanton self-indulgence had been the *bêtes noires* of Elizabethan
Puritanism, and the writings of moralists like Stubbes (along with
many others like John Downame and Richard Bernard) lend some

support to the Puritans' reputation as tongue-clucking prudes. They spoke from a spirit of reaction against the dissolute life, and did so, one often suspects, in a mood of resentment at being excluded. Theirs was a literature of witness to decadence, written by those left out of the revels. If this were the end as well as the beginning of their social critique, the movement would represent nothing more than a fleeting reflex at a moment of high social tension. It became, of course, much more—in large part because it did what reactionary movements rarely do: it attached an intellectual program to its emotion. That program was the doctrine of preparation.

"Beginnings of preparation," explained one of the architects of the theory, "are such as bring under, tame, and subdue the stubburnnesse of mans nature, without making any [gracious] chaunge at all. Of this sort are the accusations of the conscience by the ministerie of the law, feares & terrors arising thence, compunction of heart, which is the apprehending of Gods anger against sinne." Puritans, however, were careful to divide this spade-work (furthered, if not begun, by human agents) from God's uncoerced planting of the seed of grace: "Beginnings of composition [that is, gracious change], I tearme all those inward motions and inclinations of Gods Spirit, that follow after the works of the law and rise upon the meditation of the gospel; that promiseth righteousnes and life everlasting by Christ: out of which motions the conversion of a sinner ariseth and of which it consisteth."[13] Arminian notions of self-reliance were thus kept at a remove—though very much within hailing distance.

Within these general categories of preparation and composition the Puritan divines made many fine distinctions: Shepard, for instance, spoke of conviction, compunction, and humiliation as stages in the preliminary work of achieving a true sight of sin; and of justification, reconciliation, adoption, sanctification, and glorification as sequential elements within the process of composition. Thomas Hooker preferred the scriptural image of ingrafting or implantation into Christ as a metaphor of composition, which, along with the preliminary preparatory work, required eight stages—not so much of growth as of radical pruning.[14] Such elaborate treatises on the theme of preparation challenged the most diligent transcribers (Hooker delivered his sermon series on the *ordo salutis* at least three times, and published it twice), but represented less a theological innovation than an expansion and restatement of orthodox Calvinist doctrine. Although new notions of the autonomous self lurked within the Puritan elaboration of Calvinist teaching, methodical preparationism was, like most popular ideas, more a recapitulation of old structures of thought than a departure. Yet it was also a historically inseparable part of the social landscape of prerevolutionary England.

Preparationists spoke only with utmost care of windfalls that might descend from the father's sudden generosity; they taught that anyone who counted on a "rightful" inheritance was self-deceived. In marking a step toward filial independence, the doctrine was an advance toward the abrogation of prevailing status relations—a religious recourse not so much for the poor and dispossessed as for those who resented reward without labor, who felt the sharp presumption of those above them. For English Puritans generally, even the millennial prophecies of Isaiah and Revelation were welcomed for their promise of a universal reordering in sibling relations—especially for those who felt cast aside by history. The obligations of paternity and the privileges of legitimate sonship were to be reestablished: "the *Israelites* as a firstborne shall be chiefe" among nations.[15]

As part of the groundwork for this anticipated change, preparation was an important element in what has been called "the culture of discipline." Conversion, its proponents declared, "is not wrought all at one instant, but in continuance of time and that by certain measures and degrees." Strictly speaking, reformed dogma held that "the individual is transformed instantaneously by the act of God," but the believer's apprehension of the change had several stages which theologians regarded as "causally related." This ascription of deliberateness to the holy spirit in revealing itself was an emotion as much as an idea—an appeal to repudiate the impulsive, to document a stately rhythm in the life of the reborn soul. Especially in the early phase of its development, the doctrine denied the "strict predestinarian dogma that the sinner was taken by storm," and tended to soften rather than emphasize "the trauma of regeneration." Even some who grew skeptical of its most rigorous applications agreed that "sometimes grace is so low in the heart as that you cannot discern it. This is true, but it is but for a time." According to one of its leading spokesmen, although the act of justification itself "has no degrees, and is completed at one moment and in only one act, yet in manifestation, consciousness, and effects, it has many degrees." William Ames's statement makes a fundamental distinction between divine act and human perception. Justification is a slow sunrise; there may be a moment when, in some absolute sense, the sun has risen, but men do not have the epistemological equipment to say, "the moment is now." Ames was willing to admit a wide range of experience—sometimes steadily ascendant, then falling into discouragement and doubt, then surging again—but his open-mindedness had a limit: he drew the line at cataclysmic possession by the holy spirit. God may dispense his gift of renovation in an instant, but that flash is always diffused and scattered for the human recipient into a lifetime of tantalizing subtleties. "He stuns you," as a later New England writer was to put it, "by degrees." The human recipient experiences God's nod of generosity as a long procession of hints, of interpretable suggestions: apprehensions of beauty, feelings of renewal, but above all for the preparationist, a new capacity for self-control.[16]

The doctrine of preparation may be seen, then, not so much as a mitigation of the fear in which men were left by pure Calvinism, but as a way of discounting the prestige of impulse in the progress toward salvation. It was as much a response to the threat of disorder as were the poor rates and the laws of settlement. It was an endorsement of regularity in the itinerary of the soul as well as in the household and the street. Recommending "the ensample of the gravest Ministers," preparationists taught gravity in all things; they identified the chief pastoral problem of late Elizabethan England as the need "to keepe order and to exercise discipline."[17] Theirs was the heart and triumph of Puritan conservatism, a central contribution to the emerging culture of stamina and rigor. In the last analysis, preparation was not so much a doctrine as a style.

Yet even as they helped to remake the rhythm of English life, the avatars of discipline recognized in their new religion of order their most dangerous temptation. Perkins warned that one must heed the "follie of that man who, having a costly clock in his bosome never extolleth or thinketh on the wit and invention of the clocke-maker but is continually in admiration of the spring or watch of the clocke by whose meanes all the wheeles have their swifter or slower, their backward or forward motions, and by which the whole clocke keepeth his course." (One thinks of Benjamin Franklin setting out to read the deists with the intention of refuting them, only to be seduced.) Perkins felt the pull of the same deist siren. He saw in the installation of order as the standard of value a both necessary and alarming achievement. Within thirty years of his death, he was being proven right on both counts. The prestige of order—notably in what Edmund Morgan describes as the increasingly formulaic "morphology of conversion"[18]—had overwhelmed the older notion of conversion by divine shock. This reinterpretation of the idea of grace, which took many decades to complete, may be glimpsed (at a moment somewhere past its midpoint) in this act of "misreading" by Thomas Hooker:

> Thus it was with *Paul* when he was running along to *Damascus;* and had gotten a lusty Steed to make haste, suddenly there did shine a light from heaven, and he heard a voice from heaven saying unto him, *Saul, Saul Saul, why persecutest thou me?* He mervailed at the matter and yet hee did not know what the matter was, and therefore he saith, *Who art thou Lord? What wouldest thou have me doe?*
>
> As it was with *Saul,* so it is most commonly with us all; it may be a poore man drops into the Church, and the Lord lets in a light, and the Lord doth compasse him about with some threatnings of the Law . . . and [the man] retyres home, and thinkes thus with himselfe, Surely the Preacher spake strange things today, if all be true that he spake, then certainly my condition is naught, surely there is more in sinne than ever I thought of . . . [and so] hee resolves to heare the Minister againe.[19]

This is hardly the blinded Saul of scripture, trembling in the presence of God. Nor is it Caravaggio's Saul, thrown down in terror, remade from the calculating enemy of Christ into his most passionate apostle. Hooker's Saul is perplexed, bemused by an event he cannot quite explain; a man who has lived without reflection and now begins to think; who, with a mixture of curiosity and caution, comes back to church to hear a little more.

This, by the 1620s, was the Puritan Paul—though there were, of course, many variations, and some dissent from the gradualist paradigm. His mystery, indeed his power to inspire, has slackened— "hearing, and reading, and conferring, he seeth the thing he doubted of is too certaine, and that the thing he questioned before, is without all doubt: the Law is just, the Word is plaine, if God be true, this is true."[20] Hooker's Ramistic singsong has no crescendo; it makes its appeal to mind, not to heart. One way of understanding those Puritans who fled to America is to think of them as wondering if their rationalism had come too far, if it was robbing them of their sense of miracle. Their doctrine of preparation had been the intellectual product of a historical moment when sin meant surrender to appetite. For this reason it began to lose its force as a religious idea when sin became

the *absence* of appetite. It had once been a solution. On the eve of
the Migration, it became a problem again.

This shift—from the representation of sin as corrigible excess to its
association with system and lassitude—may be detected both in doctrine and in the changing symbolic texture of religious language. It
may also be connected to specific social change. In the linked evolution of these social and intellectual processes, William Perkins was
a pivotal figure because he treated sin not as Stubbes and Cawdray
and Gifford had done—as discrete, actionable charges in a ledger of
indictment—nor as the unnameable deficiency that would later be
evoked by Sibbes and Preston and Cotton. For Perkins, sin was something midway between those poles, a presence in the soul, though a
blurred and elusive one: "A man that commits . . . murder," he had
written in the 1590s, or "fornication, adulterie, blasphemy, etc., albeit
he doth so conceal that matter that no man living know of it, yet . . . he
hath a griping in his conscience and feels the very flashing of hellfire." The effect is vivid, the causative agent unclear. Perkins exemplified, in E. R. Dodds's well-known schema, the almost imperceptible
shift from a shame culture to a guilt culture: sins were becoming, for
him, if not quite the psychological state of blurred indolence that
seemed to afflict the next generation, then secret acts that festered
in the memory—acts whose consequent guilt he was beginning to
evoke as a private burden more than a public scandal. This account
of sin as a corrosive internal anxiety marked an important shift away
from its representation as outward crime, and toward a conception
of sin as inward incapacity.[21]

As the seventeenth century moved on, the representative sinner
in Puritan discourse tended no longer to be the rapacious youth who
needed to be tamed, but the joyless man who toiled grimly at his
trade, who ate the bread of carefulness. This was an extremely important change of emphasis because it entailed a shift of admonitory
anger from the dissolute "brother" to the disciplined self. "Though
you may have a godly man," wrote Cotton in the 1620s, "busie in
his calling from Sunne rising to Sunne setting, and may by Gods
providence fill both his hand and head with businesse, yet a living
Christian when he lives a most busie life in this world, yet he lives
not a worldly life."[22] Cotton was preaching in the thriving seaport
of Boston, where the pews of St. Botolph's church were filled with

merchants whom we may safely imagine chafing in their Sunday idle-
ness—as likely to be thinking of tomorrow's cargo as of today's sermon. To this kind of audience, which was increasingly characteristic
of Puritan congregations, the ministers were speaking now less often
about lewd university lads and fornicating dandies, and more about
a peculiar emotional numbness associated with the acquisitive life—
days spent over balance-sheets and nights full of planning. Into this
world where the prestige of the rational was reaching new heights,
where the illusion that one might control one's destiny was furthered
every time an investment paid off, the Puritan ministry spoke increasingly against what had once been the cornerstone of its ethics—
the virtue of self-control.

The Puritan achievement in early seventeenth-century England had
been to make control a social and sexual virtue as well as a religious
one, an accomplishment that helped to bring about enormous change
in the tone of English life. By 1600, when "sex had gotten the upper
hand over death" (at least in Essex county) "illegitimacy . . . reached
a temporary peak" throughout the land. Pregnant brides were common, as were abandoned mothers; "great-bellied wenches" was the
term of contempt. Sexual exploitation of servants by masters, or of
socially inferior women by "gentlemen," was, as it always had been,
part of the disorderly story. Most illegitimacy, however, involved
couples who hoped to marry, but whose plans were thwarted by
economic hardship, dislocation, death, or sometimes by neighbors
who feared the resulting children would become a burden on the
town and refused therefore to sign the banns. Yet despite such discouragements to marriage, the rate of illegitimacy continued to drop—
an extraordinary fact that cannot be attributed to contraceptive im-
provements at least until after the Restoration. In general, English
men and women still married late, and though sexual contact after
betrothal seems to have been a less than grievous crime, female celibacy before marriage was more and more expected—a social phenomenon that amounted to what one historian calls "largely
unconscious . . . demographic rationality." Population growth was thus
being kept in check, a process in which famine, plague, and war had
always played a part, but in which they were now being joined by
abstinence.[23]

Still, Englishmen continued to feel the pressure of numbers in
their lives; they felt themselves to be living in "a land overburdened

with people, [where] many . . . perish for want of sustenance and employment; many others live miserably [and] all . . . complain of the burden of poor people and strive by all means to rid any such as they have"—a recoil from the tumult of too many bodies that went together in the Puritan mind with the values of celibacy and fidelity. "The sin of adultery or wilfull desertion," declared William Whately with full indignation around 1620, "dissolveth the bond [and] doth annihilate the covenant of matrimonie." By the time Milton took up this theme it had become more a complex moral idea than a strategy for preventing the birth of bastards. But long before the argument of the divorce-tracts or the marriage-poetry of *Paradise Lost* (1667), Puritans were attacking England as a "hive . . . too full," and were counseling self-restraint: "As soon as ever thou awakest in the Morning," advised Lewis Bayly, using a prudent metonymy, "keep the door of thy heart fast shut, that no Earthly thought may enter," especially no "fleshly desires." England was becoming, if not a chaste nation, at least a modest one.[24]

Between the 1590s and the 1630s, then, Puritanism can be regarded as a Freudian model of the making of a superego for an entire people. First came the threats of divine retribution for dissolute behavior—"when a man is most lively in the life of sense, it is but the action of a dying man"—then the force of community pressure to conform to respectability—"the more you walk in good duties and a Christian conversation, the more you feel Fellowship with God"—and finally the voice of repression: "The last night a filthy dream and so pollution escaped me in my sleep," confessed Michael Wigglesworth in the 1650s, "for which I desire to hang down my head with shame and beseech the Lord not to make me possess the sin of my youth and give me into the hands of my abomination." For Wigglesworth, who learned his preparationist lessons from Thomas Shepard at the American Cambridge, the work of conversion continued to involve the traditional first step of putting aside the cards and dice and withholding himself from the wench. This had long been the formula for clerical memoir and biography; an astonishing number of the black-frocked preachers in Samuel Clarke's Puritan hagiologies are described as having once been Godless gambling boys.[25] For Wigglesworth, however, the struggle has moved entirely into the realm of imagination; he was contending not with daytime debauchery, but with nocturnal emissions.

For the generation of John Downame and Richard Bernard (born when Elizabeth still reigned) the idea of sin as lust had had some highly visible proofs—alehouses, brothels, the free use of maidservants—the kinds of vices Puritanism helped to bring under control. For Wigglesworth's generation in New England, however, these had become mainly pornographic legends from the old country—shadows that had no force in daylight, but that might invade the mind at night. "I lived in a country seven years," reported Giles Firmin, who returned from New to Old England in the 1640s, "and all that time I never heard one prophane oath [nor] did [I] see a man drunk in that land." Other New Englanders expressed candid nostalgia for some of the dissipation that Firmin had proudly noted as missing: "We will not dispute [with those who complain that New England's water] is not so wholesome as the good beer and wine in London."[26] The point is that if self-discipline had once been the centerpiece of the soul-physicians' apothecary, for those who fled to New England it had become the too-constant tonic in every pious household. Saturated by the habit of self-rebuke, the typical sinner was no longer in need of a remedy for passion, but for torpor. Even before the embarkation for America, Puritan sermons contain fewer and fewer catalogues of sinful excess, and more and more demands that a sleeping people be roused. "General spiritual malaise," is how one student of the migration describes the characteristic condition of those who were hoping to make the trip. This sense of chronic numbness—the state that American antinomians from Anne Hutchinson to Emerson would identify with radical evil—was one reason that, "when a wide doore was set open of liberty," many young Englishmen stepped through. This was, moreover, something long anticipated by those who had mastered the techniques for promoting colonization. Sir Ferdinando Gorges, in "shewinge the benefitt of Planting in Newe England," had stressed the possibilities of landowning for younger brothers of the gentry who felt locked out of their rightful inheritance. "My burden is taken off," said one Essex youth as he contemplated the voyage, "my soul is refreshed." America held out more than the promise of acreage; it furnished the prospect of personal awakening.[27]

Once in New England, the Puritan leadership confirmed—still with an accent of anticipation—that "true grace never fills, but puts an edge on the appetite." Already by the 1620s Puritanism was not so

much stressing watchfulness over the senses as it was promising
arousal—a promise, however, that carried a stringent demand. "Take
heede," Preston had warned, against "refusing the acceptable
time . . . there is a certaine acceptable time, . . . (as we say to you,)
when *God* offers grace, and after he offers it no more . . . take heede
of deferring; it is an exceeding dangerous thing." The last thing these
sentences may be said to attempt is to soothe the anxious soul. They
do not allay anxiety; they feed it. Addressed to a people in debilitating
rest—in the sleep of depression, the kind of sleep that only fosters
more sleep—they are efforts to induce wakefulness, to inspire a feeling that one blink can mean disaster. The tantalizing quality of Preston's preaching is that while he prodded his audience into sentry-
alertness, he never quite identified the signal that would mean the
transforming moment had come. Moving back and forth between the
Court and Lincoln's Inn (one of the legal guilds in which attorneys
were trained and certified), he was lobbying on one day of the week
for royal aid to the Elector Palatine; the next day he might be in the
City inciting merchant opposition against monopoly. Yet his movement between Court and City only partly explains his obliqueness,
because it does not tell us what this kind of preaching did to those
who heard it. In reading Preston and his fellow preachers of the
premigration years, one feels in the pace of the sentences an extraordinary tension with no promise of imminent resolution:

> [God] will heare thee, but it may be, thou art not yet fit for the mercy:
> not because hee doth not heare thy prayer, and tender thee in that
> case thou art in, but thou art not yet fit. Herein God deales with us as
> the Physician deales with his Patient; the Patient earnestly desires such
> and such things; the Physician wants not will to give them him, but he
> resolves to give them as soon as he is fit: and therefore he makes him
> stay till he have purged him and made him fit for it, till hee be fit for
> such a Cordiall, for such a Medicine, that it may not hurt him: it may
> be *God* staies thee for this end. So . . . *God* deferres long: What if thou
> fast and pray, and God doe not heare thee? yet conclude with thy selfe,
> that thou art not yet fit. There is somewhat more that must be done.[28]

This kind of prose, coiled into implication but never relaxing into
statement (a style Perry Miller emulated, perhaps in conscious homage), is a barometer of the mood of pre–Civil War England—a mood
to which not only the Puritan ministry responded with deliberate
disturbance. "It is [the ministers'] duty," wrote John Donne, "to

preach on till their Auditory wake." The usually serene Richard Sibbes agreed: "If we looke to the generall temper of these times," he wrote in the late 1620s, "rouzing and waking scriptures are fittest." When the war itself had broken out, John Rogers rattled off precedents to Parliament for the ministry's long insistence on the dangers of sleep: "*Aristotle* used to sleep with a Bullet in his Hand ore a Bason, that by the fall it might wake him: *Pythagoras,* with a threed that tied his hair unto a Beam; that with a Nod it might Check him."[29]

Much of the pastoral literature since the twenties, then, suggests that the once-nervous professional men to whom Puritanism had appealed were becoming familiar with something akin to lulling pride. The reconstruction of the Puritan ego had gone well, perhaps too well—for, according to ministers like Preston, the sense of arrival posed a greater danger to "heart religion" than did the fear of deferral. It was that insight which Edward Taylor (born in England) would again find slipping away in the wilderness of western Massachusetts later in the century. Here is the essence of his argument for keeping the Lord's Supper closed to the unconverted: "When a Carnall Person hath attaind to a Full state & the Highest attainments in Gods house of Visible Fellowship, how ready is the heart to beat off all calls to the unconverted, all convictions & Exhortations & to say, I am in a full state & Conformity of the Gospell."[30]

When this alarm was sounded in Stuart England against the danger of prematurely felt achievement, it was more likely to be expressed through the Aristotelian doctrine of the potential than through Taylor's brand of sacramental exclusivism. "You may see a good man sometime unlike himself," Preston explained, "yet it is at that time that when the flesh prevails, for now grace though it be there, yet sometimes it is laid asleep, it is not always acted, as the Philosopher was wont to say." Summoning Aristotle as his authority, Preston believed that "that which 'is' has two senses . . . [that] everything changes from that which is potentially to that which is actually." It was a version of this doctrine upon which Elizabethan Puritanism had grounded its nonseparatist opposition to the established church: "it is right and lawful to remain in communion with the Church of England," Thomas Cartwright himself had argued, because it possessed "the *esse* of a church, if not yet the *bene esse.*"[31] It is not hard to see why this kind of thinking found congenial the accelerating pace of a developmental typology that predicted the imminent flowering of the seeds God had sown at the start of history. It is this same tradition that Jonathan Edwards revived in a later time and place when he, too, thought too many people judged themselves fit in the eyes of God: "Let the most perfect union with God be represented by something at an infinite height above us; and the eternally increasing union of the saints with God, by something that is ascending constantly towards that infinite height, moving upwards with a given velocity, and that is to continue thus to move to all eternity." This ecstatic geometry—whose beginnings are present in Preston's and Cartwright's scholasticism—proclaimed itself to be permanently incomplete: "the time will never come when it can be said it has already arrived at this infinite height." An idea of progress was always at the heart of the Puritan dynamic—a world-view that could never finally accommodate the sense of arrival. Entelechy promised both the culmination and the extinction of the Puritan spirit. As its most intelligent opponents always knew, the Puritan movement could flourish only if it had an enemy and an agenda. For this reason it readily adopted the idea of America; it found purpose in the New World as long as it remained new and unattained; it faltered when that world became an achieved reality, a possession with a lengthening past.[32]

3

By all accounts, the population that spilled from Old England into New in the fourth decade of the seventeenth century had long been restless. The mobility of Englishmen within their own country was, according to one authoritative writer, "startling," and between 1620 and 1642 nearly 2 percent left Britain altogether. Something like half a million English men and women left the country between 1630 and the end of the century, of whom only a very small percentage settled in New England. With the outbreak of civil war, the literature of controversy—army sermons, ecclesiastical tracts, parliamentary speeches—expressed a feeling of exhilaration that the moment of direct action had come, precisely the moment those who emigrated to America had grown tired of waiting for. Such a feeling is everywhere in theological writing by the forties; in Joseph Mede's contempt, for example, for the "kinde of Saint-worship, wherein prayers are not made unto them directly, but God is prayed unto in their names." Puritans were fed up with brokerage—with clogged ecclesiastical courts, with petitions and admonitions and the mediation of saints. "God stands at the doore and knocks . . . his locks are wet with waiting," wrote Samuel Ward in paraphrase of Revelation 3:20; his brother, Nathaniel, was eventually to join the migration.[33] These Puritans craved (and got) bluntness, confrontation, which is to say that they found release from what they themselves were becoming— arbiters, litigators, men of the busy world.

It has become virtually received doctrine that the Puritans led the introduction of legalist thought into English culture in the seventeenth century; the proposition has been essentially unchallenged since Max Weber and R. H. Tawney first proposed it. More recently, Christopher Hill has given us vivid accounts of the Puritan as parsimonious foreman—a "small merchant or craftsman or farmer who was beginning to give employment to a wider circle than his own family and an apprentice or two . . . [whose] surplus was produced by hiring labour and selling the products of its workmanship." The Puritan was a man who carefully guarded his means, for whom "the amount of [his] surplus depended on his ability to keep wage rates down." By 1610 John Cotton was preaching to the import-export merchants of Boston that "virtue consists not in a mean between two degrees, but in a mean between two extreams."[34] Some who heard him doubtless took this as sanction for paying thrifty wages to their employees.

But despite their flavor of tough entrepreneurship, and despite their constituency at Lincoln's Inn and in the trading companies, Puritans also produced a powerful critique from within the early capitalist mind. There is some suggestive evidence, for example, that the Puritans of Elizabethan England can be distinguished from their conforming neighbors as "young conservatives" who stipulated in their wills that their money bequests be loaned at "reasonable" rates of interest rather than at those maximum rates allowable by law. John Winthrop, while pressing one of his sons to come home with a law degree in the 1620s ("think not of seeing England till you may bring a hood at your backe"), at the same time heaped contempt upon "the multitude of Atturnies" at Westminster. This kind of ambivalence went much deeper than a discomfort with lawyers as a caste: some "men boast in themselves," remarked Preston, that "I shall receive [eternal life] as wages . . . No, saith the Lord." There was a double assault in this thundering *no*—first against the presumption of worthiness, but also against the unseemly association of God's constancy with his coughing up of grudging pay. "Wage labor," which was considered by "many . . . as little better than slavery," was sporadic, unreliable; those who depended on it in seventeenth-century Britain tended to live "in one-room cottages . . . with little furniture . . . on a diet of bread, cheese, lard, soup, small beer and garden greens." "The life of the labourer," in one historian's summary, "was a constant battle for survival."[35] The wage relationship was hardly an exalting model for the relation between God and man; it carried at least as many associations of niggardliness as of generosity.

As the imagery of finance invaded Puritan discussion of the covenant—in a world where "status was [being] replaced by contract as the juridical foundation of society"—it brought with it a sense of degradation as well as of power. Even as they helped to work out England's future as a commercial society, Puritans remained resistant to the ideas of legal obligation, with its attendant penalties and profits, as the basis for relationships of exchange. In the Essex village where Shepard had once been vicar, "loans" (often interest-free) were regarded not as a means for increasing capital but as "a way of storing money in the absence of banks." A man loaned money not to a good credit risk, but to a neighbor who needed it. The idea of formal contractual relation remained deeply suspect to the Puritan mind even as it became a part of its theology. "The best assurance," complained one preacher in the 1640s, "that men can have of the enjoying of the Mannors or Lands, which they purchase . . . is but an evidence under the hands and seales of mortall men." Even "the copyholder for life could never be sure his children would inherit; [and] had to face an uncertain fine at each demise."[36] Living by the law of contract in Stuart England was a guarantee of only one thing: insecurity.

With such anxieties in mind, it is appropriate to question whether the Puritan drift toward covenantal legalism—the argument that God had bound himself to fulfill his obligations to those men who honored theirs to him—meant an upsurge in confidence about God's intentions. Preston's God, for example, remained much closer to the generous seigneur touring his estate and dispensing uncoerced favors to his tenants, than to the capitalist who drafts an exchange of monetary reward for labor. The Puritan still craved intimacy with such a God— the kind of intimacy a tenant might feel for a master to whom his family had been connected for generations. In fact, as the experience of the Puritan emigrants will reveal, the encroaching doctrines of covenant and preparation—even as they placed more and more responsibility on God's human partner in the transactions of grace—produced in America a generation not of rationalist presumption but of morbid anxiety.[37] The Puritans had surrounded their God with the most impersonal and demeaning innovations of the modern world—the world they were helping to create, and from which they were also in flight.

This condition of self-estrangement is enormously difficult for any human being to acknowledge; only the most courageously honest confessions can contain it. Though muted and in some ways displaced, the various presence of such a confession helps to explain the peculiar power of the literature of American settlement. "As necessity was a taskmaster over them," wrote Bradford about his years at Leyden, "so they were forced to be such, not only to their servants but in a sort to their dearest children." Bradford's pilgrims did not like what they were becoming. "Why meet we so many wandering ghostes in shape of men," asked Winthrop in similar anguish, "so many spectacles of misery in all our streetes, our houses full of victuals, and our entries of hunger-starved Christians? Our shoppes full of riche wares, and under our stalles lye our own fleshe in nakednesse." There is self-indictment in Winthrop's choice of pronoun; he does not distance the sins of greed and indifference from himself; he expresses his horror at the irrational outcome of what is supposed to be a rational way of living. "Dog's flesh," remarked one of his Lincolnshire counterparts in brisk articulation of the same disgust, "is [now] a dainty dish."[38]

Winthrop himself was never in urgent economic distress; his concern, while other men fell upon dog meat, was not to keep hunger from his door but to tend his soul. He was, to be sure, less than sanguine about his family's prospects for maintaining its social standing: "Though his means," he wrote, characteristically referring to himself in the third person, "be sufficient for a comfortable subsistence in a private condition here, yet the one half of them being disposed to his three elder sons, who are now of age, he cannot live in the same place and calling with that which remains." Two of his sons—hardly "hunger-starved"—had wandered the Levant and the

Mediterranean as prolonged adolescents with no evident aim; a third, heavily in debt in Barbados, sent home "evill-coloured tobacco" in a pathetic effort to please his father.[39] Such generational problems—national as well as personal—had long been building.

Already in 1604, during the ominous plague that struck in the first year of James's reign, when "the living lived as if the world were ending on the morrow [while] the sick and dying, maddened, sought to . . . drag all into the darkness with them," Nicholas Bownde, author of an influential sabbatarian tract who had long maintained that "though every man hath some grace of God's spirit in himselfe, yet it is *greatly increased by conference*," now pleaded for a kind of concert of prayer to bring Englishmen together: "When we have suites unto Princes or great men, we desire those that are in favour with them, to further our suites, and those especially that are most gracious with them; and wee rest not in our selves, though we be well knowne unto them . . . Why should wee not then much more speak unto others, that they would pray to God for us, and commend our suites unto his high Majestie?" This plea is made in the hope that God himself might be impressed by a resurgence of "neighborlinesse" among Englishmen. It was sorely needed. Life was full of the emblems of disconnection: with the plague at high pitch, business was transacted in London by dropping money "into a tub of water from which it was taken out by the seller. No hands touched." In the impersonal city the "minimum standards below which a neighbor fell only at the risk of losing the benefits of local good will" were themselves dropping—or, what was worse, the loss of "good will" was becoming increasingly affordable in a society that ran on another currency. Only a rebirth of community, Bownde thought, might persuade God to spare a penitent people from death in this stinking city:

> as in the naturall bodie all parts doe need the mutuall helpe one of another, as the eyes of the feete, and the belly of the hands, and doe in a sort seeke unto them for it, and by a naturall instinct, as it were begge and crave it . . . all experience teacheth us, that in all other things none of us is sufficient of our selves, and therefore we crave the help of others, as in counsell, in labour, and in all worldly affaires; why then should it not be so in praier also?

Bownde was aware that such a structure within the body politic was teetering. "Such accounts," as one historian puts it, "portrayed society as it *ought* to be . . . Even its most enthusiastic protagonists knew very well that it was an ideal, an aspiration." And yet Bownde tried, perhaps naively, to rescue aspiration from the mockery of the actual: "If the king would have his subjects pray for him, he must pray for them." James, of course, had nothing but scorn for such pleas for royal humility: the more he was urged into concession—symbolic or otherwise—the more he pressed his case for absolutism: "God gives not Kings the stile of Gods in vaine."[40]

James's attitude toward his subjects has been nicely imagined by the novelist Mary Lee Settle: "the new King James pass[ed] by, all swaddled up like a great baby, his full armor underneath his state robes, because he had a deadly fear of assassination . . . [He was] a surly man and when he saw the gaping crowd, growled in his foreign Scots' tongue, 'By God's wounds, what would they have of me? Must I pull down my breeks that they may see my arse?' " Yet the early 1620s saw a revival of hope in the Puritan party that this iron-swaddled king might still look upon them with favor. When James recoiled from those he deemed capable of speaking "the language of Ashdod," of conniving to "un-king a King . . . and . . . give him the stab," he was still likelier to be speaking of Jesuits than of Puritans. The Puritan party hoped to keep it that way.[41]

A good deal of their hope was focused on the person of Preston, who in 1621 became Prince Charles's chaplain, and who seemed for a while to rival Buckingham in having the king's ear. James preferred, according to unflattering gossip, his four-legged to his two-legged companions, and Preston had been a favorite with him ever since he was selected at Cambridge to argue the affirmative side of the royally chosen question "whether dogs can make syllogisms." With full enthusiasm, the brilliant young scholar (of whom it was said that "what broke others teeth was nuts to him") argued that any dog could, and clinched his point with this illustration: "an Hound . . . had the major Proposition in his mind, namely, the *Hare is gon either this or that way;* smells out the *minor* with his Nose: namely, *she is not gon this way* and follows the Conclusion, *Ergo this way,* with open mouth." The king was highly pleased. But his personal affection for the man Clarendon was to call "the perfect politician," came finally to nothing in the larger conflict between Court and City. When Preston rode with Charles in the funeral coach after James's death, he was at the peak of his prestige. With the rise of the Laudian party, he began to lose his place as royal confidant and advisor, and the Puritan cause was in retreat.[42]

Surely more ingenious than ingenuous, Preston's gift for flattery was, once again, typical of the style of Puritan leadership in the 1620s. The aldermen of John Cotton's Boston responded to the threat of new taxation on the traffic of their port not with outrage and indignation but with evasion—claiming that "silting had decreased the size of ships that could use the port," despite the fact (which they themselves recorded) that the average tonnage of ships had nearly doubled in the two decades after 1610. Puritans had less appetite for confrontation than they tended to claim. As with their Lollard forebears, martyrdom did not occupy a high place in their list of compulsory virtues—the Boston aldermen were more rule than exception. When the Earl of Lincoln, enraged by the Forced Loan and the king's indifference to the plight of the Palatinate, threatened to raise troops and lead them to the Elector's aid, his steward, Thomas Dudley, efficiently talked him out of it. Puritans, especially those who emigrated, tended not to be open or daring in their dissent. By the mid-1620s their press was risking only "moderate criticism of the standing order," and even after Preston's death, the main Puritan effort was concentrated on persuasion at court.[43] They were, said many of their opponents, duplicitous connivers. Retreating into "policye," capable of making any statement to achieve their consuming objective, they were ostracized as devotees of an ideology that supposedly authorized deceit as a form of service to their cause.

Oliver Ormerod, an Anglican of considerable acerbity, expressed his distrust this way: "The painting of a *Puritane* is so hard and difficult, as that the joynt skil of *Appelles, Pyrgoteles, Praxiteles,* and of all the cunning Painters in Saint *Chrisostoms* time, will scarce reach this object." This is not a friendly recognition of human variety breaking the bounds of a reductive category. It is a charge of evasiveness—a charge that the Puritan was a man of changeable aspect and voluntary disguise. Preston himself, with the country buzzing over the rumored marriage between Charles and the Spanish Infanta, made a clandestine trip abroad in order to smoke out the true Spanish intentions, posing in "skarlet cloak and gold hatband" as a potential convert to Catholicism. To unsympathetic contemporaries, such deceivers seemed engaged in perpetual domestic espionage, hiding enmity behind obsequiousness: "Stand bare before him," was William Bradshaw's published advice to those who had a grievance with the local magistrate, "bow unto him . . . kneel down before him, and in the humblest manner . . . censure his faults; so that he may see apparently that [there is not] the least spice of malice against his person, but zeal of the health and salvation of his soul."[44]

The recurrent charge of Puritan hypocrisy ("all professors," declared a woman in the village of Elmstead, "are dissemblers or liars") was sometimes seasoned by obscene innuendo. Here is Ben Jonson's Subtle baiting a man whom the audience would recognize immediately as a Puritan hypocrite: "Nor shall you need o'er night to eat huge meals, / To celebrate your next day's fast the better: / The whilst the Brethren, and the Sisters, humbled, / Abate the stiffness of the flesh." Not all critiques of Puritan dexterity slipped to (or reached) this level of comic slander, so not all are so easy to dismiss with a laugh. "A Puritan," explained one commentator near the end of Elizabeth's reign, "is such a one as loves God with all his soul, but hates his neighbour with all his heart."[45] There was something to all this noise of derision. The Puritan invited it.

Perkins, who was popularly called "Painful," acquired the epithet not so much for the heat of his hellfire preaching as for his skill at splitting hairs, for his cutting precision at guiding his audience through the niceties of moral choice. He was a consummate casuist. In performing that service, he—along with scores of lesser ministers—was occupied with questions ranging from the rights of enclosure to the worth of astrology. This was not intellectual diversion, but urgent assistance for men and women for whom the old resorts—chiefly auricular confession—had become inadequate or unavailable. One feels the intimacy of family conference when Perkins proposes a typical problem: If a father and son are simultaneously sick, and "the son dieth first, the father asketh whether his sonne be dead or not; if it be said, no, an untruth is told; if yes, then the fathers griefe is increased, and his death hastened; therefore silence is the best." Such tight-lippedness was not so easy to maintain when confronted by the inquiring agents of Bishop Montaigne, but some managed it. John Cotton, before he had fully worked out his distinctive intellectual architecture of holy paradox, impressed (and, it seems, irritated) one colleague by his skillful toeing of the line: "Of all the men in the world," said Samuel Ward, "I envy Mr. Cotton, of Boston, most; for he doth nothing in way of conformity, and yet hath his liberty, and I do everything that way, and cannot enjoy mine." The elasticity of the Puritan mind attracted simultaneous envy and contempt; nor was it confined to those of the "Independent" way. John Paget, who tangled with Hooker in Holland and later instigated a long debate with Davenport over baptism, somehow managed to claim for himself both episcopal and congregational ordination.[46] Though joined by only a few such diffident Presbyterians, the early New England settlers were not to be outdone in intellectual flexibility: Plymouth, after all, might never have been settled if John Carver and Robert Cushman had not kept the sort of silence that Perkins excused—composing their "Seven Articles" with an obsequiousness toward bishop and king that they knew the London-Virginia company expected.

With this kind of groveling in mind, Perry Miller credited the founders of the larger enterprise at Massachusetts Bay with a "genius . . . for finding ways to reconcile irreconcilables." Thirty years before the Bay was settled, that talent was already anticipating its ultimate challenge: how to reconcile three thousand miles of ocean with the claim of "non-separation." "Whether a man may break Prison," was Perkins's most prescient test case, and his answer was tellingly provisional:

> Popish schoolmen answer that he may; if the cause of his imprisonment be unjust. And suitable to this assertion is the common practice of Papists. We on the contrary say, and that truly, that no man beeing in durance, may use any unlawfull or violent meanes to escape; for we may not, at any hand, resist the magistrate in our sufferings. Servants are commanded, to subject themselves with patience, unto the unjust corrections of their masters (1 Peter 2:19). And this reason is given; *For it is Thankworthie, if a man, for conscience toward God, endure griefe, suffering wrongfully.* The Apostels beeing in Prison, used no means to deliver themselves; but when the Angel of the Lord had opened the prison doores, then they came forth and not before, (Acts. 5:19) . . . When God in his providence, cuts off all Lawfull meanes and waies of flying, he doth then (as it were) bidde that man stay and abide.

Perhaps it was the secret of casuistry that, when all was said, anything could be done. For those who eventually left England ("ambidextrous theologians," as they have been called) there was good news in Perkins's answer; and they prudently took their "Lawfull meanes"—the Charter—with them. The genius of casuistry was that there was equally good news for those who "used no means to deliver themselves," but chose to stand and wait.[47]

For the emigrants, moreover, the casuistic habit not only remained vital but grew stronger. Twenty years after the Charter was obtained one New England leader was defining conversion itself not as the infusion of grace but as the acquisition of the casuistical idea. We know, he declared, that the Indians have made great strides toward godliness, because "there have been many difficult questions propounded by them":

> First [for example] suppose a man before hee knew God, hath had two wives, the first barren and childlesse, the second fruitfull and bearing him many sweet children, the question now propounded was, *Which of these two wives he is to put away?* if hee puts away the first who hath no children, then hee puts away her whom God and Religion undoubtedly binds him unto, there being no other defect but want of children; if hee puts away the other, then he must cast off all his children with her also as illegitimate, whom hee so exceedingly loves. This is a case now among them, and they are very fearefull to do any thing crosse to Gods will and mind herein.

It has been remarked that "the social group whose interests were most directly advanced by the spread of Protestant doctrine . . . [were] the preachers themselves." One of the first achievements of the Puritans who came to New England was to teach the Indians to ask questions which only ministers could answer.[48]

For those who were skeptical that the fate of the soul depended on asking and answering such questions, there was great offense in the Puritan penchant for "cases of conscience." But if seen in a more sympathetic light, the outpouring of casuistic debate—both before and after the migration—may be judged a creditable effort to cope with overwhelming ethical confusion. "It will come," Albany had prophesied in *King Lear,* "Humanity must perforce prey on itself, / Like monsters of the deep." Thirty years after that line was written, John Cotton declared to Winthrop's departing fleet that just such a prophecy was being realized in England: "Tradesmen no longer live one by another, but eate up one another"—an expression of revulsion at much more than merely hard times. Every wool-merchant knew that a warm winter could thin the coats of his sheep, that selling his undyed cloth depended on peace and weather and decent crops in Flanders. A good business year, of which there were few in the 1620s, required the lucky convergence of favorable circumstances. But Cotton in 1630 was speaking about much more than the unpredictabilities of the market: he was describing a deep cultural shift from a system of exchange to one of aggrandizement, "from a hierarchy of communities to the agglomeration of equal competing individuals." "Each man," agreed one of the Leyden emigrants, "is faire to pluck his means, as it were, out of his neighbor's throat." Yet there was no articulated response—only new versions of Lear's "Fie, fie, fie! pah, pah!," more of Jonson's recoil from Sejanus's rapacity, a response that was "choric and denunciatory merely, representing no positive values."[49]

The special dilemma of the Puritans, who, unlike Jonson, had committed themselves to England's Protestant future, was that they were caught in a paralyzing mixture of aspiration and revulsion toward the same thing. The "chattering and chaunging" merchant, for example, came in for harsh treatment in early Puritan tracts—with his "counterfait balances, and untrue waightes." And yet his was clearly the way of the future—a future in which many Puritans were literally invested: "The good Merchant," wrote Thomas Fuller in 1642, "is one who by his trading claspeth the iland to the continent, and one countrey to another. [He is] an excellent gardiner, who makes England bear wine, and oyl, and spices." In coming uneasily (and therefore shrilly) to such defense of "merchandize," the Puritans were speaking for English culture as a whole—which was everywhere split by the same ambivalence. Pamphlet after pamphlet rolled off the London presses in the twenties, proclaiming "it an additament and encrease of honour, to deale in the way of Marchandise," a propaganda flood whose very volume indicates the size of the resistance to it. Groping for a definition of "the good merchant," Puritans chastised themselves by negative example, trying to stir up the "feare to doe any wrong, so that if a poore childe or silly woman should lay him downe a groat or a tester more than his commodity is worth, he dares not take it, but give it backe againe." As one astute biographer has remarked of Winthrop, himself a Gray's Inn–trained lawyer and a candidate for the Court of Wards, "he was ambitious . . . and yet . . . repelled by the sinfulness of his ambition."[50] The distinction between selling oneself and selling for oneself remained a subtle one.

The most poignant concern, however, which Puritans felt in their manifold confusion was not for themselves, but for their children.

This has often been noted in Bradford's *Of Plymouth Plantation* (1630–1650), which records the Plymouth "pilgrims' " sense that their "posterity [had been] in danger to degenerate" in Holland. Partly because of later remarks by Edward Winslow and Nathaniel Morton, this theme in Bradford has been explained—indeed explained away—as the fear of living in an alien land, where a child's sense of his Englishness and even his attachment to his mother tongue were threatened. It is less often remarked that the same kinds of fears afflicted those who had never tried Holland. "There is nothinge in this world," wrote Winthrop, "that can be like cause of private comfort to me as to see the wellfare of my children."[51] This father, and many like him, had no alien language as an objective correlative for their dread. They were strangers at home.

Solomon Stoddard's remark that his emigrant fathers feared less for themselves than for their children fits well not only the scattered surviving statements of those who made the journey, but also the systematic findings of recent social historians. "Most of the emigrants," T. H. Breen has concluded about some who are well enough documented to have been closely examined, "were grouped into relatively small nuclear families." Other historians (well before the computer became central to the practice of social history) have gone so far as to assert that "it was the transfer of Puritan families, whole and intact, that explains the uniqueness of New England." As we learn more about the piety of ordinary men and women, there seems more and more reason to agree with these judgments that the moral welfare of children stood high among the motives for emigration. One Dedham woman, at first "unwilling to come" to New England, "yet thinking that her children might [there] get good," concluded for that reason that "it would be worth the journey." Her minister, John Wilson (future pastor of the First Church of Boston), encouraged her to think so: "Maybe," he suggested, "the Lord thou dost deny to do good" to your children, "till [you] come thither." For a woman whose own parents had "kept her from gross sins," this was a conclusive piece of advice.[52]

One who did not leave, Robert Harris, nevertheless felt the same pressures that drove his brethren to do so, and warned in the 1620s that "our children [may] fall in the streets for bread . . . they [are] ready to eat up us, we ready to chop them to the pot." Though the hunger was real, the cannibalism was by now conventionally figurative—another version of Lear's vision of the world gone carnivorous. England was become permanently monstrous, or so it seemed, and Harris understood that the characteristic response to such rapacity was to search for a resting place outside the self in which to place the blame: "tis long of Corne-masters who hold-in corne, that theres such scarcitie, therefore downe with them; tis long of Inclosers, therefore downe with them: tis long of hard Land-lords, and therefore down with them; long of Merchants . . ." These were dislocations of blame from where it was most deeply felt—in the self—a strategy known and condemned by the Puritans' own spokesmen: one "shift," remarked Thomas Hooker after he had settled in America, "whereby a carnal heart comes to lighten the hainousness of his evil [is] *Because he can put off the blame from himself . . . upon his Companions . . .* It was the fault of such & such, I am free."[53]

In the decades, then, before it found outlet—in colonization as well as in rebellion—a gathering anger was overtaking English Puritanism, whose leaders, despite their own warnings about self-deception, strained for a way to deflect it from themselves. One can feel this in the restraining appeals of the ministry:

> they [landlords and enclosers] deale unjustly with you, they robbe you, wil you deale therefore unjustly and robbe others? It is very like that God doth use them as meanes to chastise you, to make you knowe your selves . . . you must not therefore . . . avoide this crosse, which God layeth upon you by these wealthie oppressors, but rather you are to bear it with patience, till such time as God shall deliver you; praying to God (if it be his will) to soften the hearts of these hard hearted men.[54]

This Pauline admonition not to kick against the pricks (Acts 9:5) became, to more adventurous minds, a way of organizing all experience:

> Let a man taste of salt water in the sea, and it wil be brackish and unsavoury, but let it be sublimated by the Sun, and taken up into the Clouds, and then it is sweet and fresh; so is it in this case, looke at your afflictions as they run along by the sea shoare of this world, take them as deserts for thy sin, and they are salt and unsavoury; but by faith looke at them, as coming out of Gods hand in his speciall favour, and then they wil breed you much joy & consolation.[55]

To accept this view (in a much later formulation of the same conviction) is to "thwart the . . . elemental impulse [of protest and despair] for the sake of the higher unity of experience; as when we rejoice in the endurance of the tragedies of life." That has always been an ultimately stringent demand. If we are to understand the Puritans, we must try to sense how deeply they felt this idea not as an abstraction but as an ethical imperative pressed upon them by their experience and by their faith. We may, thereby, appreciate why James Truslow Adams insisted that they had "the type of mind which . . . preferred to exchange the simplifications of unpeopled America for the complexities of . . . England."[56]

The single work that most clearly states this kind of exhaustion with life in England is Winthrop's lay sermon aboard the *Arbella*, *A Model of Christian Charity*. Enshrined as a kind of Ur-text of American literature, it has received an enormous amount of commentary, which usually includes a nearly ceremonial invocation of its closing image of the "city upon a hill"—the phrase from Matthew 5 that Peter Bulkeley, Edward Johnson, Urian Oakes, and other Puritan leaders subsequently used to evoke the meaning of New England.[57] Focusing on that image, most interpreters of the sermon have stressed its celebration of what lay ahead, rather than its judgment of what was being left behind. Perry Miller, for example, allowed that high rhetorical moment to govern his sense of the whole work, which is the centerpiece of his theory (in "Errand into the Wilderness") that the founders hoped to make of New England a beacon for the world. And Winthrop's sermon, along with Cotton's farewell sermon at Southampton, has taken an important place in more recent arguments for the millenarian impulse as the chief impetus behind the Great Migration.

The *Arbella* sermon is, in fact, considerably more focused on what was being fled than on what was being pursued. Not only does Winthrop lay small stress on the exemplary value of New England (and when he does, it is for "succeeding plantations," not for England), but he actually expresses a desire for anonymity. The scriptural image of the visible city is followed by a crucial conditional phrase—"if wee shall deale falsely with our god [then] wee shall be made a story and a by-word through the world." Winthrop had more fear of notoriety, of "shipwracke," of being revealed as leader of "a perjured people," than he had appetite for fame.[58]

Winthrop's statement was not only an expression of anxiety about the prospects of dissension and conflict in the new settlement, but an impassioned attempt to make retrospective sense of the world he was leaving. Its definition of the Christian church is framed in terms of rectifying a general bodily disorder: "The several partes of this body, considered aparte before they were united, were as disproportionate and as much disordering as soe many contrary qualities or elements, but when christ comes and by his spirit and love knitts all these partes to himselfe and each to other, it is become the most perfect and best proportioned body in the world." This is not a plan for New Jerusalem, but a lament that the severed elements of the Christian body (the church) had not been restored to unity in England. That lament is the engine of Winthrop's eloquence:

> the way to drawe men to workes of mercy, is not by force of Argument from the goodness or necessity of the worke; for though this course may enforce a rational mind to some present Act of mercy, as is frequent in experience, yet it cannot worke such a habit in a soule, as shall make it prompt upon all occasions to produce the same effect, but by frameing these affections of love in the hearte which will as natively bring forthe the other, as any cause doth produce effect.[59]

Couched in a language somewhere between physics and legal advocacy, this is a repudiation of the utilitarian ethic that Winthrop sensed was coming to dominate English life. The soul, he insists, is beyond the reach of reason. To bargain with it is to settle for an ethics of exchange—for a gesture of generosity now and then, in return for social approval. A real transformation of the soul from calculation to mercy can be attained only if the affections are ignited with love— an event that is, in the last analysis, nothing less than the experience of conversion.

Winthrop, who shouldered the chief responsibility for managing the inevitable problems of enterprise and regulation in the new colony, was presenting to his fellow passengers a series of imperative questions: "What rule must wee observe in lending," he asked, and "what rule . . . in forgiveing?" To such questions he gave essentially a single answer: the rule of charity. By this he meant more than a demand for case-by-case attentiveness when it came to setting interest rates, or loan qualifications, or the timing of repayment. He meant that those who were coming to New England had to enlarge the most basic of their motive forces—their capacity for self-love:

the ground of love is an apprehension of some resemblance in things loved to that which affects it. This is the cause why the Lord loves the creature, soe farre as it hath any of his Image in it; he loves his elect because they are like himselfe, he beholds them in his beloved sonne. Soe a mother loves her childe, because shee throughly conceives a resemblance of herself in it. Thus it is between the members of Christ. Eache discerns, by the worke of the Spirit, his owne Image and re-semblance in another, and therefore cannot but love him as he loves himself . . .

If any shall object that it is not possible that love should be bred or upheld without hope of requittall, it is graunted; but that is not our cause; for this love is allwayes under reward. It never gives, but it allwayes receives with advantage; first, in regard that among the members of the same body, love and affection are reciprocall in a most equall and sweete kinde of Commerce. Secondly, in regard of the pleasure and content that the exercise of love carries with it, as wee may see in the naturall body. The mouth is at all the paines to receive and mince the foode which serves for the nourishment of all the other partes of the body, yet it hath noe cause to complain; for first the other partes send backe by severall passages a due proportion of the same nourishment, in a better form for the strengthening and comforting the mouthe. Secondly the labour of the mouthe is accompanied with such pleasure and content as farre exceedes the paines it takes. Soe is it in all the labour of love among christians.[60]

In this remarkable passage, before it veers from the sexual to the alimentary metaphor, Winthrop proposes—perhaps with I Corinthi-ans 15 in mind—a transformation of bodily into spiritual desire. In the instant before the metaphoric shift, we may catch Winthrop at his least meditated: he gives us a glimpse of his hope that man can truly be remade from a creature of onanistic self-delight into an image of a generous God; from a consumer into a partner, from one who lives by sexual appropriation into one who delights in mutuality. Though it is only God for whom self-love and love of the other are not in conflict but mutually necessary and enhancing, this mutuality is a miraculous identity that man—Winthrop briefly believed—could emulate. His *Arbella* sermon is the first great communitarian statement in American literature—a "pre-libation," as the Puritans would have called it, of Edwards, of Melville, of Whitman in their hortatory modes. And it shares with such successors the fact of its fleetingness, which is why it is the best measure of how quickly and how far the Puritan aspiration fell. One historian has even spoken of Winthrop's "putting himself on trial" after the Antinomian crisis for his failure to husband and protect the original promise.[61] There is a sense in his American career of grievous imaginative loss.

His disappointment had long been building. Men of Winthrop's rank had found themselves in England in a devilish moral dilemma: since leasehold rents (which were often fixed for generations) had fallen far below the real market value of their land, it had become economically wise—and sometimes urgent—for the landlord to raise fees wherever he legally could, mainly from leasing his demesne. To those who lived through the relentless rise in rents during the late sixteenth and early seventeenth centuries, such "rackers of rent" seemed to be doing nothing else than grinding the faces of the poor, forcing them into "plain servitude and misery." But once-great families who refused to take such measures and continued to honor the ancient traditions of nominal fees and manorial largesse found that there was simply no way to avoid financial collapse. The de Veres, for instance, "watched a sizable portion of their estate pass into the hands of the Harlackendens, their former stewards." (Roger Harlackenden was a patron of Thomas Shepard.) Many of Winthrop's counterparts among the gentry (who, although only a fraction of those who emigrated to New England, were its first holders of authority) faced in England the choice of pressing their advantage over those dependent on them, or slipping into dependency themselves.[62]

All the leaders of Massachusetts Bay had faced such quandaries while still in England. Among the first laws they proclaimed upon securing their New World settlement was that "all our lands and heritages shall be free from all fines and licences upon Alienations, and from all hariotts, wardships, Liveries, Primerseisins, yeare day and wast, Escheates, and forfeitures, upon the deaths of parents or Ancestors, be they naturall, casuall or Juditiall." Other Old World problems had required more dexterous management, as, for example, when John Davenport explained that his parishioners at St. Stephen's Church in London could not kneel for communion because the pews were so crowded that they had to stand close together with arms pressed to their sides. In Cotton's Boston the question of reclaiming cropland out of swamp had become an issue less readily disposed of. Financed by such magnates as the Earl of Lindsey, the project aroused hot opposition, especially among scavengers whose gaming rights were threatened. Many of the poor lived, however meagerly, on what they could extract from the unrestricted wetlands. Cromwell himself, who would be known as "Lord of the Fens," was soon to gain considerable popularity among the poor for his reputed opposition to those who would drive their livestock off the grounds that had traditionally sustained them. And yet—there was always such a proviso—the drain-works provided short-term jobs, helping to relieve the chronic problem of unemployment.[63] Whether it was gentlemen like Winthrop trying to balance realism with generosity, or yeomen trying to stay free of usury, or the Boston aldermen trying to measure hardship for some men against benefit for others, there seemed always to be an excruciating choice to be made. More often than not, the choice one did make appeared despicable when made by another man. What seemed sound to the intellect felt like poison in the heart.

Winthrop's response to this world was both a bitter valediction and a preemptive attempt to keep it from replicating itself in America. (Hooker, who came over three years later, went so far in his will as to "forbid my sonne John . . . from marrying and tarrying" in England.) Winthrop's strategy—eventually to be codified by Cotton and Nathaniel Ward in *Moses his Judicials* (1636) and *The Body of Liberties* (1641)—included explicit prohibition against the rule of the market: "Thou arte to walke by the rule of Justice . . . if [a man's] meanes of repayeing thee be onely probably or possible then is hee an object of thy mercy thou must lend him, though there be danger of looseing it (Deuteronomy 15:7)." This was to be a world not only free from outright greed of the moment, but also from speculation on future demand: "a man can have no right to more than he can subdue." This was Winthrop's country-conservatism; the voice of repugnance at those who manipulate nature and men's need for their own gain. It is the early American voice that Gordon Wood has in mind when he speaks of the relation of American revolutionary ideology to its Puritan inheritance as "an updated, reactionary effort to bring under control the selfish and individualist impulses of an emergent capitalistic society." It is also, however, Winthrop's voice of retrospective self-chastisement—a curse upon what he and other propertied men had become in England: enclosers, rent collectors, speculators in land. Like Bradford, Winthrop was publicly dissociating himself from "newfangledness and other such like giddy humor."[64] He conceived of the act of migration as a holding action against the evident future.

It was, perhaps, predictable according to the Puritans' own estimate of human appetites that within less than half a decade Winthrop was to judge this effort a failure. Newcomers, he was lamenting by 1634, "will be forced to go far off for land while others ha[ve] much, and [can] make no use of it, more than to please the eye with it." The founding gentry of Boston acted quickly to reestablish their wealth in land; grants of hundreds of acres were made by a committee of "allotters" to such leading families as the Haughs and Bellinghams and Hutchinsons and Keaynes. Pastor Wilson of the First Church was soon in possession of a six-hundred-acre tract (even as he declared that "a man that hath competency, may not pray for more enlargement in the world"), and Winthrop himself obtained an expanse of outlying farmland which can only be explained by the prospect of speculative gain, or perhaps out of concern for his sons' inheritance. At the same time, he grew disgusted with his deputy, Dudley, for hoarding corn and lending it out at times of scarcity against promises of a return with interest upon the next good harvest. Such behavior was especially offensive because maltmaking, illegal export, and engrossing of grain had been common offenses in East Anglia in the lean years preceding the migration.[65]

Endorsement by word and disdain by act for the founding ideals were never matters exclusive to a single class. John Dane, the half-literate tailor who upon his emigration became, like most craftsmen, a small-scale farmer, recalled his early New England experience in the accents of Biblical parable: "Thare came a naibor to me and said he had no corne. He made great complaints. I tould him I had on[e] bushill and I had no more, but he should have half of it. And he had; and after I herd of sartain that at the same time he had a bushill in his house. It trubled me to se his dealings, and the dealings of other men."[66] It needs to be remembered in the face of this unanswerable indignation that for every such instance there were others to suggest that the communitarian ideals were not entirely chimerical. The early New England records are filled with stories that illustrate the persistence of Winthrop's original vision: William Brackerby, formerly a baker, now, in 1639, a man of means, sells his Charlestown house to another baker by trade, and agrees (in exchange for the continued right to walk his cattle across their accustomed grounds) that he "shall not bake or cause to be baked any sorts of bread to sell except only for his owne familie during the time the said partyes live in Charlestowne together, except the magistrates shall find a necessity in regard of his or his wifes poverty or in regard of the townes want." Civil

issues were, as such compacts show, by no means distinct from the
moral concerns of the church—just as Winthrop had intended. Early
in the second decade we find the Dorchester elders intervening in a
dispute between an aggrieved carpenter from Boston and the local
ferryman who hired him—and who then reduced the agreed compensation because his hired craftsman had "received some smale comforts . . . [such] as houseroome in an outhouse" while completing the
job. There is both comic animosity and deadly earnestness in such
bits of compromise effected by the church authority in civil disputes.
The first New Englanders did not give up their ideals without a fight.
But the fight itself was a measure of cost.[67]

What Winthrop, as much as Bradford, had hoped to recapture in
the New World was a "delight in each other," an ability once again
to "make other's conditions our own, [to] rejoice together, mourn
together, labour and suffer together . . . as members of the same body."
There had been some in England who tried, without leaving, to keep
the same hope alive: "Every particular Grace is part of a Christians
Beauty. But as they use to say, *Pulchritudo non est partis, sed compositi;*
so the perfection of Beauty ariseth from *all Graces,* and a *Perfection
in all.*"[68] This statement (by Anthony Tuckney, Cotton's successor at
old Boston) is a genuinely integrated vision of morality and aesthetics,
which calls attention to itself because of its increasing rarity in the
descriptive literature of the period. "An Animal," Tuckney continued,
"exceeds that which is Inanimate [because] together with *bonum* it
can *appetere pulchrum,* which the Inanimate skills not of; let it never
be that, in which a Christian shall be inferiour." Such "skill" is precisely what T. S. Eliot judged to be passing when he spoke of a
"dissociation of sensibility" in seventeenth-century England, of a lamented time when a man could "feel [his] thought as immediately
as the odour of a rose." One way of understanding Puritanism (which
Eliot found so culpable in the fragmentation of early modern Anglo-
American culture) is to think of it as a failed attempt at shoring up
the ruins of such a unity. The Puritan knew that what he thought ran
counter to what he felt, and he tried, with growing desperation, to
find a way to restore the congruence. Those who stayed, and some
who left, struggled to retain their belief that through the intervention
of grace the human soul could still incline toward unfractured beauty.
They tried to believe that sin is not a constituent part of the self, or

even an invasive poison that saturates the soul, but at worst a noxious breath that could be, with God's help, exhaled.[69]

Such a faith was ultimately incompatible with the doctrine of preparation—with its call for a relentless, graduated assault upon the self, but more important, with the fundamental ideas upon which it was based: that "the imperious will . . . drives one into vice," and that sin is a palpable thing that must be located and arduously dug out of the soul.

> A man that is troubled with the tooth-ach, when the Tooth-drawer comes to apply his Instrument, and hee findes hee hath hold of him, he saith, that is it, pull it out, leave nothing behinde: So when the soule is under the power of some violent lust, when the Word comes home to the conscience, and meets with that distemper, the soule saith, Lord, pull it out all, that I may never see that pride more, nor that covetousnesse more; leave not a stumpe remaining Lord, but free me wholly from this vile accursed condition . . .

"He that will be clear of sin," Hooker announced as he readied himself for leaving the sins of England, must "fly far enough . . . soon enough . . ." The business of the godly was to maintain "a sequestration of the soule from . . . sin," as if sin were a poison or a place. For many who demurred at this prospect of the Christian in flight from pursuant, particular evils, there could be no literal escape, only what Michael Walzer has called an "internal emigration." "This committing of our souls to God," said Richard Sibbes, who was one of those who counseled against the idea of sin as entity, and against literal emigration, "must be our ship to carry us through the waves of this troublesome world to the heavenly Canaan of rest and peace." This was the vision of those Puritans who resisted the impulse physically to migrate—"shall we leave God's children for this or that fear?" There was, they said, no earthly refuge, no truly New World. The process, they believed, by which the penitent sinner might find rest was not so much a war against or flight from isolable sin as a lifting of the self in place toward beauty—"the first beginnings thereof . . . [are] as the falling of the dew, or 'the blowing of the wind.' "[70] Some who remained were still able to speak in this scriptural (John 3:8) voice. Those who left for America yearned to hear it again.

The journey to America was in part an effort to conserve what was left of the conviction that sin, rather than being an entity implanted in the soul, was something more abstract: a temporary estrangement from God. Behind (in the double sense of impetus and abandonment) the Puritan journey lay an utterly un-Calvinist hope—not quite articulated, yet never fully suppressed—that Englishmen were not so much depraved as victims of a distorting experience. The Puritan social critique, as Richard Hooker had understood, carried a wistful hope that the fault lay not with man but with what had been done to man. The Puritan in England felt forced into pettiness. He felt ashamed. He was likely to be a family man at midlife—"most . . . in their middle Age . . . and many . . . in their declining years"—a tested adult who had found that day-to-day life in Essex or Lincolnshire or Yorkshire or London was killing his spirit. For this man or woman, as has been said of a later immigrant generation (with more in mind than physical dimension), "space was the stuff of desire."[71] The Puritans' emigration from England was undertaken not as a confident journey toward the millennium but as a flight from chaos in their once-hospitable world, and in themselves.

Our people went to America because that was the place to go to then.

Ernest Hemingway, 1935

3 City on a Hill

In 1609, speaking to those about to sail in Lord de La Warre's Virginia expedition, William Crashaw (father of the poet, editor of Perkins) conferred a series of blessings on the venture. In the course of his benediction he carried the Jonsonian indictment of English society out of satire and into soteriology: "Seest thou a Merchant or trades-man that deceives? . . . a father, a wife, a childe . . . that are negligent or unfaithfull? . . . The cause is, they are unsanctified." This explicit equivalence between a man's spiritual estate and his behavior—as approved or condemned by social consent—is one that more radical Protestants refused. "Cannot a man be religious to himselfe," demanded Robert Bolton in the 1620s, "except he hang out his flag and let all the world know it?" As this kind of exasperation attests, Crashaw was being entirely conventional, even formulaic, in proposing social up-rightness as the test of sainthood. The Lord, one Puritan spokesman had already declared in the 1570s, has "bought with his blood a zelous addicting of ourselves to Christian conversation." What was new was that Crashaw offered the act of migration as a way of passing the test of zeal.[1]

As suspect as this idea would eventually become to those who stayed behind, there was nothing outlandish in Crashaw's argument, even as it moved with gathering velocity toward authorizing departure

from corrupt England. Of the "threefold kinde of physicke," he insisted—he was the author also of *The Parable of Poyson* (1618)—,
"the first is purgative." The first step to health, that is, is to separate
patient (emigrant) from poison (Britain)—again a convention, a metaphor drawn directly from the language of Galenic medicine. In one
of its dimensions, the doctrine of preparation itself was a theological
analogue to this old therapeutic idea, a kind of moral bloodletting.
The physician, armed with purgative laxatives and the blood-sucking
leech (after which he was named), spoke a language that the minister
gratefully borrowed: "You must be empty, if ever Christ fill you."

> Yea further, if any man beeing afflicted with . . . outward calamities
> have only a worldly sorrow, that is, if hee mourne not for sinne as it
> is sinne, but for the punishment of sinne, hee is not by and by to bee
> comforted, but first this sorrow is to bee turned into that other sorrow,
> which is according to God: as is the counsell of Physicians in the like
> case. For if a mans life be in danger, by reason of blood gushing out at
> his nose: they commaund also that blood bee let out in his arme, or in
> some other place as the case requireth, that they might stay the course
> of the blood which rusheth out at the nostrils, that so they might save
> his life, who was readie to yeeld up the ghost.[2]

In the science of the soul, however, the language of purgation was
coming under stress. And so it was in the science of the body. By
the turn of the century English medical practice was being revised by
the influence of Paracelsus, whose followers had begun to subvert
time-honored therapies: "the common practice of bloodletting," they
said, ". . . only diminish[es] the vital heat." To make such impudence worse, the new-minded physicians bolstered their novelties
with the authority of the Holy Word: "Scripture teaches that 'the life
dwells in the bloud,'" which therefore should not be drained away,
but should be medicinally restored to healthful balance. Crashaw,
possibly sensitive to such revisionist currents, conceded that "when
a sicke man is purged . . . it helpeth not if he be not also restored to
strength." To renounce disease, in other words, was not enough—
separation was at best a preliminary step in the restoration of the
patient's health—and thus the prophetic significance of his sermon
was that he found completion for this unfinished therapy in the act
of migration. If trading and fathering, he implied, are activities that
can reveal not just a rascal but a reprobate, then shipping for the
uncharted wilderness as agents of the gospel is a restorative act that

certifies permanent sainthood: "inasmuch as . . . Christ commands him that is *converted to strengthen another,* it appeares (by a necessary implication) of what an excellent nature godlinesse and holiness is; namely, of a large, a liberall, a communicating and diffusive nature."[3] Crashaw was not quite brazen enough to assert that the *only* way for an Englishman to express his "diffusive nature" was to sail for Virginia, and thereby to spread the gospel. This would have been psychologically improbable for him, since he himself (like Cotton at Southampton twenty years later) had no intention of going anywhere. Still, he was proposing the idea that those who shipped for America were uniquely virtuous—an entitled people.

Delivered at a moment when dissenting English Protestants felt variously constricted and colonization had just begun, Crashaw's sermon centered on Christ's command to propagate the faith. It was reticent on the commercial interest of the venture, but relentless on the aim of converting the savages: "Whosoever is of abilitie; and knowes the true grounds and ends of this voyage, if hee assist it not, discovers himselfe to be an unsanctified, unmortified, and unconverted man, negligent of his owne and other men's salvation." Crashaw's mind was not especially penetrating, and much of his sermon is murky with imprecise implication—but through it one feels a growing pressure on Englishmen to look for signals, to complete the unfinished instructions they were receiving from such as Preston, and to identify a directive from God as meant for them. English eyes were peeled for what Puritans called an "overvaluing providence," for the beckoning gesture from God by which he would make clear his will. The appeal of the Puritan ministry, which was fast growing in 1610, had always been its insistence that there exists a relation between God and men in which not even the minister can forceably intervene. "Go home and consider," Cotton advised his parishioners, "whether the things that have been taught [by your minister] were true or no." Puritan hostility to Catholicism—"that colliers faith of the Papists, that put out his owne eyes to see by another mans"—was focused on its failure to grant such a liberty to the individual judgment.[4]

The idea of emigration, then, was anchored deep in a complex of analogous ideas—in a mix of medical and theological notions about purification, and in an atmosphere of expectancy that God would make clear to attentive men what he required of them. This was both an intellectually pedestrian and an emotionally urgent idea—the idea that the act of renouncing England might have a cleansing effect on those who dared.

Twenty years after Crashaw's sermon, the first minister of the Naumkeag colony delivered himself of similar sentiments. "Many that have been weak and sickly in old England," declared Francis Higginson, "by coming hither have been thoroughly healed and grown healthful and strong." America, it seemed, was proving to be the "transformational terrain" for which Englishmen yearned. Although skeptical voices from Thomas Elyot to Raphael Holinshed had warned against the ill effects of New World imports ranging from red beans to tobacco, by the time colonization began in earnest the prestige of America as a place of cure was soaring. Higginson himself, with a touch of delicious satisfaction, felt "freed from [the] pain and vomitings" that had plagued him in England. There is perhaps an emblematic irony in the fact that he survived barely a year after announcing his restoration to health.[5]

In both his hope and his disappointment, Higginson was typical of many who sailed toward what Spenser had called "fruitfullest Virginia" and fell with almost desperate delight upon its bounty. Even the more northern region (named New England by John Smith) was expected, according to its literary previews, to be a succulent retreat where one could tap the "source of . . . silver streames of wealth"— the sea—from which the fish, of which "each hundred you take here, is as good as two or three hundred in New Found Land." The shortest (and sweetest) accolade was Thomas Morton's: "The more I looked, the more I liked it." And though Morton's Puritan neighbors shuddered at his lascivious use of Indian women, at his pimpish salesmanship of his heathen paradise, they finally shared his delight: "I was soon cloyed," admitted Higginson, "with [the] plenty of skate and thornback and abundance of lobsters . . . They were so great and fat and luscious." This was in part a calculated confirmation of Smith's prediction that New England would pay for itself in fish, and an early form of all-you-can-eat salesmanship carried on with a snicker of challenge to the consumer's capacity. But it was also a genuine exclamation of delight. "Everything that is here either sown or planted prospereth far better than in Old England," wrote Thomas Graves, ". . . the grass and weeds grow up to a man's face."[6]

Soon after settlement this language of carnal allure began to disappear. "Bread was so very scarce," recalled Roger Clap about his first months at Dorchester, "that sometimes I thought the very crusts of my father's table wd. have been very sweet unto me." Yet the switch from celebration to lamentation was not unanimous. Thomas Welde was still using the language of plenitude when he exclaimed (around the time of Clap's complaint) that "I am fully contented [with] . . . such groves, such trees, such aire . . . and desier no better while I live." Apparently unembarrassed a year later by their continued good circumstances, the General Court ordered "lettres of thankefullnes" to be sent to several "benefactors to this plantation," among whom was William Wood, whose *New Englands Prospect* described for English audiences the "very large . . . strawberries . . . some being two inches about," as well as the "gooseberries, birberries, raspberries, treackleberries, hurtleberries, [and] currents" that sprang from New England's soil. As the thirties went on, unseemly boasts receded before the sound of advertised hardship, and by the end of the decade New England's public tone was becoming more uniformly somber, even calculatedly grim.[7]

Higginson, who died before this change was complete, never lost his capacity for reading providential consistency into what might, to others, seem discrepant events. The first life to be lost aboard the *Talbot* was that of his own four-year-old daughter, born deformed, whose death by the pox—"the first in our ship that was buried in the bowels of the great Atlantic Sea"—was a sign that it had "pleased God to remember mercy in that child, in freeing it from a world of misery wherein otherwise she had lived all her days." Next to die was "a notorious wicked fellow that was given to swearing and . . . bragged that he had got a wench with child before he came this voyage and mocked at our days of fast, railing and jesting against Puritans."[8] One perished through God's mercy; the other through his wrath. To Higginson's ear their deaths made a chord; there was no dissonance.

Others had more difficulty forcing experience into a shape that would confirm the imperative sense of divine sanction. Even as the people of Charlestown "were necessitated to live upon clams, and mussels, and ground-nuts, and acorns, and these got with much difficulty," Winthrop assured his wife by letter that "the Lord . . . mixes so many mercies with His corrections as we are persuaded He will not cast us off." John Pond, a farmer whose wife had been a servant in the Winthrop family, was not so sure. "People here are subject to disease," he wrote to his father in England, "for here have died of scurvy and of the burning fever two hundred and odd, besides many layeth lame, and all Sudberey men are dead but three and the women and some children . . . We do not know how long this plantation will stand, for some of the merchants that did uphold it have turned off their men and have given it over." According to Winthrop, those who died of scurvy were generally those who pined for home.[9]

Shivering a few miles north of where the Leyden separatists had come ashore ten years before (accidentally, since their intended destination had been much farther south), these members of the Massachusetts vanguard openly envied the earlier settlers' good fortune in having landed "by the favour of a calm winter, such as was never seene here since." Yet it is striking, considering the assaults of winter and disease, how stubbornly the vernal images linger in the first reports—as if the newcomers were clinging to the idea of a tropical haven. When they did renounce it, it was without qualification: "If any come hether to plant for worldly ends that canne live well at home," warned Dudley, "he committs an errour, of which he will soone repent." Witnessing this retrenchment, the prickly Thomas Morton thought it peculiar that life in New England had turned suddenly spartan—for which he had a less than respectful explanation: "I have observed how divers persons . . . out of respect to their owne private ends, have laboured to keepe both the [religious] practice of the people there, and the Reall worth of that eminent Country concealed from publike knowledge."[10]

If such alternations between hope and discouragement yield no immediately clear pattern to us, it is because at first they yielded none to the emigrants themselves. The colonists had not yet found a common voice, a way to read the changeable events of their newly shared history. There was incipient division within their self-conception, and it was not a cleavage that ran cleanly between classes. It could be resolved into a tentative consensus only when the clergy began to supply New England with the language that has ever since been associated with its (and America's) founding—the language of heroic struggle and deliverance patterned on the story of the Old Testament Jews.

There had, all along, been warnings about the rigors of the enterprise—even from those who looked to New England for health and plenty. "Payment of the transportation of things," Higginson had warned, "is wondrous deare, as 5£ a man and 10£ a horse and commonly 3£ for every tunne of goodes." And Higginson's figures were lower than most. This was, as Dudley reiterated, not a place for "the poorer sort . . . For wee have found by experience that they have hindred, not furthered the worke." But the most striking feature of this modulation from Edenic fantasy into chastened realism was its identification (here in the voice of Peter Bulkeley) with the people of Israel: "God hath dealt with us as with his people Israel; we are brought out of a fat land into a wilderness, and here we meet with necessities . . . If we look to number, we are the fewest; if to strength, we are the weakest; if to wealth and riches, we are the poorest of all the people of God through the whole world."[11]

This appeal to the precedent of the Jews was not an invention of the emigrants; it had been put to long and complex use in recent English political rhetoric, and it carried a high degree of apocalyptic expectation. For many literate Protestants an intimate connection had long been established between the "Israel" of Romans 11 ("Even so then at this present time also there is a remnant according to the election of grace . . . And so all Israel shall be saved"), the "New Jerusalem" of Revelation 21 ("the holy city . . . coming down from God out of heaven, prepared as a bride adorned for her husband"), and the unfolding history of England itself. It was a connection so firmly made that by the 1620s Laud was already "appalled" by what he deemed to be the growing fanaticism of certain of his countrymen who felt themselves explicitly referred to by the Hebrew and early Christian prophets. Drawing on ancient eschatological tradition, English dissenters had for at least a century been promoting a view of history that incorporated the vision "of a true and a false church operating in inexorable opposition" throughout recorded time. John Bale, who had found in the 1530s that Revelation made refreshing reading for Christians in exile, established the identity of Rome with the whore of Babylon (Rev. 14:8), and that of the New Jerusalem (Rev. 21:2) with the emerging church of Christ's elect.[12] The pilgrimage of the English church from one to the other was, according to Bale's Puritan heirs, not yet complete even after a century's progress.

By linking the covenant promises of Genesis with the prophecies of Daniel and the apocalyptic visions of Revelation, the typologist could reveal a continuous stream of sacred history— with Christ "at the center . . . casting His shadow forward to the end of time as well as backward across the Old Testament." The great themes of this continuity were the identification of God's elect in scripture with an enduring "Israel" of true believers in the world, and of antichrist not only with the papacy but with all Romish corruptions that had survived the Reformation purge. The first decades of the seventeenth century saw the application of these ideas sharply expanded until every conformist in the Church of England stood accused of being "a limb of Antichrist." As Laud acted to shore up the imperiled ceremonies and hierarchy of that church, the rhetoric of his Puritan opponents became increasingly militant and even apocalyptic. The repulsion of the Armada in 1588 had given impetus to those who imagined that God was offering his servants literal as well as spiritual swords, and Laud, by the 1620s, clearly sensed that another outbreak of militant action was building. A relentless new typology seemed to be infecting the radical Protestant mind, a fantastic hermeneutic that not only linked the Testaments around the life of Christ, but insisted on pressing forward into the Johannine prophecies as guides to the imminent future—to next year's, next week's events. One eulogist of Queen Elizabeth asserted, perhaps with her touted virginity in mind, that she was none other than the woman of Revelation 12, who was traditionally taken to be Mary herself, appointed to bring "forth a man child who was to rule all nations." Bale, Laud knew, had read the life of Wycliffe as the pouring out of the sixth vial (Rev. 16). A century later, the spilling of the seventh and last vial seemed—to some— overdue.[13]

All this was not entirely eccentric within the mainstream tradition of Protestant hermeneutics; even conservative Anglicans were willing to construe Isaiah 10:21—"The remnant shall return, *even* the remnant of Jacob, unto the mighty God"—as referring to a remnant of Jews who would be saved at the second coming, as well as to God's newly chosen. But the important change by the 1620s and 1630s was that such texts were becoming engines of fantasy about the salvation of whole nations, which would be divided into saved and damned by a "great threshing." This "is a strange Jerusalem," Laud exclaimed as he saw the Israel of Isaiah becoming a type of England—a nation that replicated, according to its self-appointed Puritan prophets, the paganism of the inconstant Jews.[14] As Puritan millenarianism and the national identification with Sion converged, there was no telling where such a conjunction might lead.

Those who came to America in the early 1630s did not wait to see. Some among them had postulated the approaching desertion of England by God, and had chosen to bear further witness to that event from across the sea. Once there, they found themselves within a decade witnessing, not the wholesale apostasy which they had predicted, but precisely what Laud had feared: the expropriation of the biblical parallel and the millennial promise by the new political ideology of the revolutionary movement from which they had just broken away. "Some think," Thomas Shepard preached soon after his journey over in 1633, "that all this time may be the days of the coming of Christ, wherein . . . we ought to live in a daily expectation of his coming." Shepard's "some" was uttered in more alarm than sympathy; he was talking, as Laud himself had done, about a fanaticism with which he wanted nothing to do; and once in New England he worked to dampen whatever apocalyptic expectation the people had carried with them. We are not yet, he reasoned, in "the latter part of those last days." Compared with the high pitch of millenarian enthusiasm in England, "the American quest for the Fifth Monarchy," as James Maclear has said, "was low-keyed."[15] Yet despite the efforts of Shepard and others at containment, the fever would arise again in the 1640s, fueled by such rousing performances as Cotton's sermons on *The Powring out of the Seven Vials,* through which rekindled millenarianism became a propelling force in the reverse migration back to England.

By 1645, a critical year for the fledgling New Model Army, New Englanders could read, fresh from the London presses, renewed proclamations that "in the state of the *Jewes* . . . our own Condition [is] every way answerable thereunto, as face answers face in the water." These were not the words of some Massachusetts minister making the connection (as Bulkeley had done) between chosen peoples in exile, but an impassioned call to arms by John White (member of the Feoffees and ardent supporter of "root and branch" extirpation of bishops) delivered to the House of Commons in wartime. White went on to point out what every reader of scripture already knew (and should have known in 1630) that "the time of delivering *Israel* out of *Egypt* was . . . a time of heavie bondage," by which he meant that to pay a price in blood was among God's demands of his steadfast elect.[16]

In sermon after sermon the Puritans who had heeded such calls *in England* reclaimed the prophetic warnings of the Old Testament: "For the Lords sake," declared Stephen Marshall, also before Parliament, "take care to keep him with us; if hee goe, all goes; we can never light our Candle, if this Sunne bee set: wee shall never fill our Buckets, if this Fountaine bee shut up. All your counsels and advising will bee nothing, if God say, *I will stay no longer in* England." By then, Marshall's refrain had been current for decades: "Tell mee not," Robert Harris (the same Oxfordshire minister who had preached on the plight of children) had proclaimed in the late 1620s, that "theres no danger; the Word of God is against us . . . Oh England, looke to it that wee drinke not up the dregges." For Thomas Hooker, whose own sermon of dire alarm, "The Danger of Desertion" (1631), included similarly ringing phrases—"Look about you, I say, and stop him at the town's end, and let not thy God depart!"—the trials of the times became reasons for departure. For Harris and Marshall and White they were nothing of the sort.[17]

This kind of militant identification with Israel was one with which the emigrants to America were necessarily uneasy. Governor Winthrop was at pains to dispute it, because he recognized its power as an argument for remaining in England. "Since Christ's time," he insisted, "the church is to be considered as universal without distinction of countries." This was one of the many questions on which the leaders of the "non-separating" Bay colony were in full agreement with their Separatist predecessors:

> Neither is there any land or possession now like unto the possession which the Jews had in Canaan, being legally holy and appropriated unto a holy people. . . . Now there is no land of that sanctimony, no land so appropriated, none typical, much less any that can be said to be given of God to any nation as was Canaan . . . Now we are all in all places strangers and pilgrims, travellers and sojourners, most properly, having no dwelling but in this earthen tabernacle; our dwelling is but a wandering, and our abiding but as a fleeting, and in a word our home is nowhere, but in the heavens . . .[18]

This defense of Plymouth's territorial claims (made by the colony's agent, Robert Cushman, in 1620) was based on a traditional reading of Genesis 1:28—"replenish the earth and subdue it"—which all English colonists, Puritan or otherwise, regarded as a sanction for wresting "unused, and undressed" lands from heathens who roamed and wasted them. To this standard scriptural citation Cushman added a brief footnote: legal agreements with the Indians had been duly drafted. Ten years later, in order to answer the charge that "we have no warrant . . . to enter upon that land which hath been so long possessed by others," Winthrop used exactly the same argument in the form of three rebuttals: (1) Genesis authorizes those who will "possess and improve" the land to supplant any by whom it "hath never been replenished or subdued." (2) Legal agreements have been made with the Indians. (3) God has providentially "consumed the Natives with a great plague." Winthrop said nothing, directly or by implication, about apocalyptic expectation.[19]

Cotton had said not much more in his farewell sermon to Winthrop's fleet—which was in some respects an even less resounding endorsement of colonization than Cushman's had been. Intending to salve the hesitant conscience of his audience, Cotton spoke in order to "satisfie," in the words of one who heard him, "the Godly-minded of our Removal out of *England.*" His mode was reassurance, not militance. He offered a highly general statement of the principle of colonization into which the particular case at Southampton might be made, with effort, to fit. "When wee doe withall discerne, that God . . . maketh comfortable provision as well for our soule as for our bodies . . . then doe we enjoy our present possession as well by gracious promise, as by the common, and just, and bountifull providence of the Lord."[20]

Some scholars have judged that this distinction between promise and providence expressed a belief that "God had appointed America as the place where he would . . . establish the throne of David's kingdom," but in fact Cotton took pains to define the limits of what he meant when he spoke of a "land of promise": "It is a land," he said, of "provision for soule as well as for body . . . When God wrappes us in with his Ordinances, and warmes us with the life and power of them as with wings, there is a land of promise." In this respect he was in perfect agreement with Thomas Hooker, who argued "that God is generally present, as once with the Ark, whenever and wherever his ordinances are rightly observed." These definitions include no eschatological and certainly no geographical content. For one thing, there was "more traffic between East Anglia and Holland than between East Anglia and New England"; for another, the wings in Cotton's formulation are those of Ruth 2:12, signifying the father's embrace of a buffetted child, not the eagle's wings of Revelation 12:14. The land of promise was any place of intimacy with God (some Puritan leaders placed their hopes on a tiny island off the coast of Nicaragua), and Cotton, when he preached at Southampton, still hoped to find that promise fulfilled in England. A full two years later he "was [still] not attracted to New England as a refuge." On the dock at Southampton he attributed no more eschatological importance to the settlement of Massachusetts than did the Earl of Warwick ten years later when he favored Trinidad—a plan for relocation that Winthrop scuttled not by reminding his comrades of any role they might play in hastening the millennium, but by asserting that they "were in better condition [in Massachusetts] than they could be in those parts." In 1645 one New Englander suggested that the Delaware River Valley looked like a better settling place than stony Massachusetts.[21]

When Cotton's Southampton sermon was published four years after its delivery, its preface (written by a John Humphrey, of whom there were two connected to the Massachusetts Bay Company—one who never left England, and another who returned from Massachusetts after a short stay) promised the reader "a larger declaration of the first rise and ends of this enterprise . . . a clear and full . . . justification of this design." That "declaration" was *The Planter's Plea*, published the same year as *God's Promise:*

> the undertaking to plant a Colony, needs no extraordinary warrant . . . *Abrahams* undertaking was extraordinary in many things, and therefore needed an immediate direction from God.
> 1, *He was to goe alone with his family and brethren.*
> 2, *To such a certaine place far distant.*
> 3, *Possessed already by the Canaanites.*
> 4, *To receive it wholy appropriated to himselfe, and his Issue* . . .
> Now none of these circumstances fit our ordinary Colonies; and consequently *Abrahams* example is nothing to this purpose . . .

It was to be a very long time before New England came to think of itself as more than "ordinary" in this sense. Even its most celebratory historian, writing in the 1650s, echoed not only *The Planter's Plea,* but also Cushman's and Winthrop's caveats about the typology that Bulkeley had seemed to invoke: "Let all men know the admirable Acts of Christ for his Churches and chosen, are universally over the whole Earth at one and the same time."[22]

It was, then, in Old England, not New, that the idea of a new chosen nation supplied a basis for militance. It gave solace in times of military misfortune. "As *Moses* hastened on that work [of deliverance], that yoke [of Egyptian bondage] was made heavier upon them," and "when God . . . by strong hand brought them out of the Land of *Egypt* [they faced] forty yeares troublesome travaile in the wildernesse." This wilderness was figurative—but certainly not to be taken as signifying the forests of a distant continent. Some New Englanders did read their scriptures typologically, though not usually as prophetic of a corporate antitype, but as foreshadowing the preparatory afflictions of the individual wayfaring soul: "There must be Contrition and Humiliation before the Lord comes to take possession [of the soul] . . . [which] was typified in the passage of the Children of Israel towards the promised Land."[23]

The Puritans in America were hearing from England that the national struggle should have been, for the truly faithful, sweet, not bitter—a point with which Shepard collided when he declared (in 1648, while explaining his departure of fifteen years before) that "wee might easily have found the way to have filled the Prisons," but chose exile instead. Nor was Shepard's response an adequate answer to his own beloved teacher, Preston, who had declared shortly before his death in 1628 that "to suffer imprisonment and disgraces for good causes . . . is a good worke," but not quite the best of all possible works. We "must," Preston had insisted, "be men of contention . . . My brethren, *Contend for the faith once delivered to the saints*." The fact is that the Puritans who came to America had fled *from,* not toward, the prophesied moment of Revelation 15:2, when the "sea of glass [would be] mingled with fire."[24]

And so when Peter Bulkeley, in the late 1630s, imported to New England the traditional Puritan identification with the Jews, he was tapping a source of doubt about the enterprise as much as a source of assurance. To replicate the history of the Israelites was not only to experience a renewal of God's promise; it was also to risk repeating their refusal of the proffered Messiah.

To some the Messiah was acquiring a name—that of the Lord Protector. But even those who doubted Cromwell's legitimacy shivered in the shadow of the revolution he led. Well before Cromwell's rise to power, as Cotton was preaching imminent chiliasm in New England, God's attention seemed more and more focused on Old; by the mid-forties Winthrop had to recognize that men were remaining in and returning to "*England* in expectation of a new world." "In this

Century," Edmund Calamy declared before parliament in 1641 (the second year of the Long Parliament, and the year of Strafford's execution), "God hath multiplied deliverances upon deliverances; wee have had our 88 and our Gunpowder deliverances, but as *Benjamins messe* did exceed all his brethrens, and as Josephs sheafe was lifted up above the *sheaves* of his brethren; so the mercies of these two last yeares doe farre exceed all the mercies that ever this Nation did receive since the first Reformation."[25]

Here, by contrast, is William Bradford's imaginative reconstruction of the birth of Plymouth Plantation, a passage composed at about the same time, but in a state of chilled abandonment made worse by his sense of history passing him by:

> Being thus passed the vast ocean, and a sea of troubles before in their preparation . . . they had now no friends to welcome them nor inns to entertain or refresh their weatherbeaten bodies . . . It is recorded in Scripture as a mercy to the Apostle and his shipwrecked company, that the barbarians, when they met with them (as after will appear) were readier to fill their sides full of arrows than other wise. And for the season it was winter, and they that know the winters of that country know them to be sharp and violent, and subject to cruel and fierce storms, dangerous to travel to known places, much more to search an unknown coast. Besides, what could they see but a hideous and desolate wilderness, full of wild beasts and wild men—and what multitudes there might be of them they knew not. Neither could they, as it were, go up to the top of Pisgah to view from this wilderness a more goodly country to feed their hopes; for which way soever they turned their eyes (save upward to the heavens) they could have little solace or content in respect of any outward objects.

This famous passage can be sharply illuminated by a document that had been composed two decades closer to the actual landfall (and thus well in advance of the hurtling events of the thirties and forties), a work that Bradford himself may have partly written, and that reports the landing not in the language of scripture but with "eyewitness" economy. In *Mourt's Relation* (no one knows the identity of its putative author, "G. Mourt,") no forests loomed: "Our greatest labor will be fetching of our wood, which is half a quarter of an English mile" away. No savages descended: "What people inhabit here we know not, for as yet we have seen none." And there was no shortage of "solace" or "content in respect of . . . outward objects": "A very sweet brook runs under the hill side . . . and in this brook much good fish in their season." These features of the landing have not made their way into our national mythology.[26]

Bradford's version has. Through it he anticipated the imaginative effort of every New England historian—at least from Edward Johnson to Thomas Prince—who was to apply himself in the coming century to the same natal moment. It was an imagination devoted to the quest for meaning—initially for dignity—in the American exile. It had an element of insolence as well, for even as they laid claim to a heroism that was perforce unavailable to those who had declined to join them, the New England historians insisted on their role in guiding the fate of Old England. Sixty years after Bradford, Cotton Mather (just before beginning his work on the *Magnalia,* in which he was to coin the word "American") was still pleading for recognition that the "lives [of his grandfathers] bear no little Figure in the *Ecclesiastical Histories* of our *English Israel*." The idea of history that the generation of Mather's grandfathers had learned from Bale (and more directly from Foxe's *Book of Martyrs*)—had thoroughly accustomed them to think of England as a specially covenanted nation. Though it is true that the future of English Protestantism (which, in the mind of such a Puritan, did not include the likes of Laud and Charles) looked bleak in 1630, it is also true that the emigrant Puritan believed with all his heart that a long night must, by God's decree, precede the final dawning of the light. "There shall be as terrible Signs and Presages fore-running the erection of the *New-Jerusalem,*" wrote William Hooke, "as there were before the Destruction of the *Old. Hinc illae Tenebrae.*" In this eternal "vicissitude or enterchange [between] good and evil times" there was more reason to risk repatriation than to stay with the safety of exile. Some, including Hooke, took seriously from afar the "signs and presages" that were emerging out of England—and returned to see for themselves."[27]

Only if we keep in mind these manifold tensions between New English emigrants and Old English revolutionaries can the effect, if not the intention, of Bulkeley's remarks about "his people Israel" be understood. Bulkeley was (unwittingly, perhaps, since he first made the statement in the thirties) implicating New England in a tangle of ironies, of which they would soon and persistently be reminded from home. By recasting the New Englanders' sense of themselves into an exemplary martyrdom patterned on the history of the Jews, he was trying to find some dignity in their situation by calling up the militant idea that they had, in practice, abandoned. Yet nothing is so destructive of the Puritans' reputation for stolid determination as a reading of their literature of emigration. It is a literature without poise, flustered, knotted into embarrassed contradiction. It gives us insight, for example, into why the Indian wars, when they came, were not crusades or even products of calculated policy, but conglomerations of error—reactive gestures of revenge, the excess of brutal malcontents (the Pequot War was triggered, if not "caused," by the Indians' murder of a coastal trader whom the Puritan authorities had charged with drunkenness and sexual offense). Quarreling among themselves, and alternately revolted by one another's bloodthirst or squeamishness, the New England warriors were no more secure in their role as conquerors than they had been as exiles. To read the early documents is to follow a record of vacillation between mission, conquest, coexistence, and even humility before the native inhabitants of the land into which they had so uncertainly come. If these people sought to read their destiny in the Bible, they were affected less by the clarity of scripture than by its ambiguities.

Winthrop himself had spent his last months in England trying to turn the inevitable charge of desertion from his English brethren into a claim of solidarity: "The departing of good people from a country doth not cause a judgement but foreshew it, which may occasion such as remain to turn from their evil ways that they may prevent it." Yet in the same year we find him demanding to know "why [God's ambassadors] constantly denounce wrath and judgement against [England] . . . Why doe their soules wepe in secret? and will not be comforted, if there be yet hope that our hurt may be healed?"[28] At one moment, England's hope lies with those who leave her. At the next moment, England has no hope. Somewhere between these oppositions a rationale for emigration has been lost.

Accordingly, one of the best ways to feel the depth of uncertainty among the emigrant leaders is to notice their habits of scriptural selection. "Our dear mother [England]," Winthrop declared, "findes her famyly so overcharged, as she hathe been forced to denye harbour to her owne children . . . [a] condition [for which] no remedy appeares." Winthrop's correspondent (whose letters have unfortunately been lost) has been pummeling him with scriptural examples of self-denial and constancy to one's imperiled people. A Christian should, he has been saying, look in perilous times to the example of David who, despite his raging thirst (II Samuel 23:16–18), refused the drink brought to him at great risk to themselves by three heroic soldiers. God disdains personal relief in times of community peril. Winthrop's reply is more than a little testy: "As for those allusions resembling David's longing for a draught of water to this action, the things are so unlike, as need no answer; your similitudes must have more legs if you will have them stand upright or prove anything."[29] These are not the words of a man about to embark on a scripturally sanctioned journey. Their petulance is self-convicting. Why, one may ask, did Winthrop (who knew his Bible) not counter with Psalm 63: "O, God, thou *art* my God; early will I seek thee: my soul thirsteth for thee, my flesh longeth for thee in a dry and thirsty land, where no water is." To have declared themselves well rid of this English desert— truly to make of England an antitypical Egypt or Babylon—was an emotional impossibility for the Puritan emigrants. It was also a prerequisite to their making an Israel or a New Canaan of New England. They left not only without such an idea, but with the nagging sense that those who rebuked them for leaving at all might be right.

2

It was out of this internal debate within Puritanism, and within the minds of individual Puritans, that the strategy of rendering New England as a colony of heroic sufferers emerged. This project faced many obstacles, some of which we have seen, but there was nevertheless reason to hope that it could be carried out. An expectation of purgative pain was built into the preparation for every Atlantic crossing. "The yarns of sailors," as one historian puts it, "contained rich ingredients for nightmares." Bradford's pilgrims had embarked with vivid awareness of what had happened not long before to one Francis Blackwell—an Amsterdam separatist who, in Cushman's words, had sailed "towards winter" in 1617. His crew and passengers numbered nearly two hundred; fifty survived. Even as early as 1610, when Crashaw gave his blessing to de la Warr's fleet, the prospect of any Atlantic crossing was heavy with daunting precedents. Not only was there the recent memory of the short-lived colony at Sagadhoc (Maine), but all mariners knew that "like an hell of darkness," storms could—

and often did—arise to "beat all light from Heaven." Those who survived their contests with the sea gave vivid accounts of sloshing about with bailing buckets under the light of St. Elmo's fire, as the ocean "covered our ship from stern to stem like a garment." Winthrop, who carried such accounts in his head, kept a passage diary that grew into his full-scale journal, but that began, like Higginson's, as a record of providential events at sea—a record kept in the hope that in it would be revealed God's blessing.[30]

There was reason for such a hope. The ships of Winthrop's fleet were a far cry from the *Sea-Venture* that foundered off Bermuda or the *Speedwell* that was leaking by the time it had reached Land's End. Mostly "sweet ships"—well-caulked vessels built to carry wine— Winthrop's heavily provisioned fleet made an uneventful crossing. "Three of the four ships were usually within sight and hail, so that boats passed back and forth in calm weather, dinners were exchanged [and] there was plenty of fun aboard . . . Games and horse-play with the seamen kept the young people's minds off their stomachs, and they [in Winthrop's phrase] 'gave themselves to drink hot waters very immoderately.' " The darkest word the Governor used to describe the ocean wind was "handsome." Once arrived, he and his contemporaries made few direct references to the crossing itself, possibly because it did not fit their emerging self-definition as a suffering people. When their children reconstructed the experience, it became, of course, an instance of the superintendence of God, who had "safely led [them] so many thousand miles / As if the journey had been through a plain."[31]

Soon after such calm crossings the first New Englanders were vigorously reminded of the political and ecclesiastical storm they had left behind. Already in 1629 Robert Ryece had written to Winthrop that "the church and common welthe heere at home, hathe more neede of your beste abyllytie in these dangerous tymes, then any remote plantation." While still in Lincolnshire in the fall of 1630, Cotton himself (in a letter later copied down by Richard Mather) had written to Samuel Skelton of Salem demanding to know on what grounds he was denying communion to new arrivals. Cotton, in fact, knew the reason—that the newcomers were members not of covenanted churches but of the "false" Church of England—and he was taking the opportunity to express his disapproval. "Neither a false nor a tyrannical government (as [Skelton] calleth it) of the prelates . . . can disanull the being of a church"; and in virtually the same phrase he had used in his farewell sermon to Winthrop's fleet, Cotton accused the Salem covenanters of short memories and ingratitude: "reject not the wombe that bare you nor the paps that gave you sucke." Six years later, when he himself had made the trip, Cotton reversed himself in his famous Salem "confession," by which time he was supporting a compulsory profession of faith for all who wished admission to the churches of the Bay. In his long dispute with Roger Williams he continued to deny that he had ever favored "divorcement" from the English church; but his denials were always more tense when Williams retorted that he was rejecting in theory what he was performing in practice: "What is that which Mr. *Cotton* and so many hundreths fearing God in New *England* walk in, but a way of separation?" It was a stinging accusation because it had the feel of truth. The leading spokesman of the "New England Way" was on the defensive throughout his American career—and the sensitivity of his position was heightened by the fact that his opponents spoke in the voice that had once been his own.[32]

Knowing this, and exasperated by "the rocky flintinesse of [Williams's] self-confidence," Cotton threw up his hands at Williams's insistent application of the principle of separation. Attributing a piece of wit to his colleague Thomas Hooker, Cotton offered to the wondering world a homely illustration of Williams's mad consistency:

> [Mr. Williams] made complaint in open Court, that he was wronged by a slanderous report up and downe the Countrey, as if he did hold it to be unlawfull for a Father to call upon his childe to eate his meate. Our reverend Brother Mr. *Hooker* . . . being mooved to speake a word to it, Why, saith he, you will say as much againe, (if you stand to your own Principles) or be forced to say nothing. When Mr. *Williams* was confident he should never say it: Mr. *Hooker* replyed, If it be unlawfull to call an unregenerate person to take an Oath, or to Pray, as being actions of Gods worship [this was one of Williams's controversial claims], then it is unlawfull for your unregenerate childe, to pray for a blessing upon his own meate. If it be unlawfull for him to pray for a blessing upon his meate, it is unlawfull for him to eate it, (for it is sanctified by prayer, and without prayer unsanctified, 1 *Tim.* 4.4, 5). If it be unlawfull for him to eate it, it is unlawfull for you to call upon him to eate it, for it is unlawfull for you to call upon him to sinne.
>
> Here Mr. *Williams* thought better to hold his peace, then to give an Answer.[33]

The point of this conceit is to show how easily Williams's thought was subject to *reductio ad absurdum* because it was already close to

being absurd. But if one lingers for a moment over Hooker's little
satire, it discloses what sometimes lies beneath the satiric voice—a
sympathy for the victim as anachronism, a farewell to a once dignified,
now stodgy way of thinking. What Cotton had unwittingly done through
this citation of Hooker's sarcasm was to mock the syllogistic logic not
just of Roger Williams but of the Puritan mind itself. The burlesque
risked wider application than Cotton had intended. Designed to elicit
a laugh at the expense of one extravagant man, it was really an attack
from within on the coherence of scholastic thinking, to which Puritanism still owed a great deal. The Anglican charge, after all, had
always been that Puritan docrine made it impossible to lead a man-
ageable life in this world because "precision" was destructive of social
custom, and without custom the world cannot function. Custom, it
was true, had never had a place in the Puritan universe; it was a human
invention that obscured God's intent. Was there really such a gulf
between condemning the misuse of the communion table and the
supper table at home? The tragedy of Roger Williams was his antipathy to one idea: the idea of pragmatic compromise. The tragedy of
New England, he said, was its surrender to that same idea. If the
Puritan synthesis was failing, it was because it led to conclusions
uncongenial to reason. One had, after all, to eat.

Not all the stress on New England, however, was a matter of internal
tension. For one thing, a flurry of questions out of Old England
hounded the founders—awkward, needling questions. Already in 1636
a group of English ministers were not just politely inquiring how
things fared with their New England brethren; they were charging
them not merely with inconsistencies or uselessness to those at home
but with inflicting damage on their cause. "You know how oft it hath
been objected, that Non-conformists in practice are Separatists in
heart . . . How shall your brethren [in England] bee able to stand up
in the defence of their innocencie and the uprightnesse of their cause,
when your example and opinion shall be cast in their dish?" John
Davenport, who was assigned the task of responding to this charge,
did not have much of an answer: "It was not an easie thing," he
explained, "for all of us often to meet together to consider of these
Questions."[34]

  More questions followed—thirty-two to be exact—and this time
Richard Mather was chosen to reply. An interesting feature of his

published rebuttal (which reprints the question along with his answers) is his careful avoidance of a phrase that the interrogating ministers consistently employed—"Old England." He wanted, one suspects,
nothing to do with this dangerous adjective. It carried a taunt: have
you put us behind you? Are we, to your minds, obsolete? Have you
not noticed something changed, something new about "old" England?
Mather's book was published in 1643; a year later Thomas Coleman
delivered this news at the start of the Westminster Assembly: "Oh,
here is a change of late . . . God hath established Sion [in England],
and as for his people, there is a new world with them."[35] "Old," in
the forties, was the verbal equivalent of a sneer.

By 1645, one of the leaders of the Presbyterian party, John Bastwick, who had been branded and mutilated by Laud, could speak with
immense contempt for those New Englanders who were reevaluating
their original decision to depart:

> Let a Venison Pasty be the Text, foure Independent Ministers shall
> open and devide it better and more accurately handle it then any eight
> Presbyters in the City of London . . . There is not any man that shall
> seriously thinke of them but will say they have very acute senses, that
> can out of the Americans and out of the Low-Countries smell the good
> cheere and plum-pottage into England, which was indeed one of the
> chiefest causes that made these men leave their charges and flocks there,
> and choose rather to live among Wolves, Beares, Lyons and Tygars,
> (for so they tearme us) . . . [36]

Indeed, with the outbreak of war in England, irritable questioning
had turned increasingly to righteous anger. English Independents
were more and more driven into fanciful defenses of their New England allies as charges of intolerance were pressed by the Presbyterians: "I think," explained Katherine Chidley in 1641, "it was because
they [the New Englanders] had (here in *England*) taken upon them
an oath of conformity . . . and because the tyranny of the Prelates was
so mighty . . . that they were fain to go away privately, and so had
not time or opportunity publikely to disclaime this their Oath; and,
then there might be feare, that upon complaint made for suffering
disorder committed there [in New England] . . . they might have been
sent back by their Ordinaries."[37]

Meanwhile, Judges 5:23 became a favorite text of the parliamentary
preachers: "Curse ye Meroz, said the angel of the Lord, curse ye
bitterly the inhabitants thereof; because they came not to the help

of the Lord . . . against the mighty," a text rarely invoked by the Puritans in America until Davenport used it twenty years later to thrash those who faulted him for aiding the regicide judges. "There are [some] . . . who stand as *neuters*," declared Stephen Marshall in the House of Commons, "who stand aloofe off, shewing themselves neither open enemies nor true friends" to the soldiers of the Lord. Though the Puritan warriors under Cromwell had in mind a variety of malingerers, mainly domestic, their exegesis carried specific embarrassment for New England. "I could never learne," Marshall added, "whether *Meroz* were a *Citie* or a *Province* . . . If they were a *Province*, their Land proved a *desolate Wildernesse*."[38]

Charges from England tended to be less circumspect than acknowledgments from America: "Some," wrote Henry Whitefield from Guilford (Connecticut) in 1651, "are heard to question the affections of New-England towards the Parliament and the present state [but we] have been faithful and cordial to the Parliament from the first, and do own this present Government." That same year the General Court tried to express its devotion more warmly: "since the first beginning of your differences with the late King and the warre that after ensuied, we have constantly adheared to you . . . by our fasting and our prayers for your good success." But even these modest claims stretched the credulity of some in England. Governor Winthrop had, after all, greeted what he called the "ill news" of civil war with something less than zealous solidarity, and such an upstanding New England spokesman as Nathaniel Ward (who called the English revolutionaries "young spaniels") had roundly scolded Parliament for its impudence toward the king well before anyone contemplated killing him. In fact, the revolutionary attitude never really took hold in New England, which did not experience anything resembling an uprising against royal power until Sir Edmund Andros was clapped into jail in 1689. "It is not a gospel spirit to be against kings," observed John Norton in a carefully worded election sermon delivered soon after the Restoration. By then Norton's was hardly a novel moderation; he spoke for the whole founding generation when he prayed for "God [to] make us more wise and religious than so to carry it, that they should no sooner see a congregational-man, then to have cause to say *they see an enemy to the crown*."[39]

Such dissociations from the "Puritan" revolution echoed through the century, culminating when Peter Bulkeley's grandson inveighed against the "Oliverian republic," and declared that "we may sorrowfully remember the years in England from 1642 to 1660." But fifty years before Gershom Bulkeley expressed this retrospective disgust—when Stephen Marshall stood in the House of Commons and offered his parallel to the people of Meroz—New England was feeling the challenge of events in England not merely as a frightening precedent for democratic excess, but as a devastating reprimand. There was, in short, reason from the start for New Englanders to wonder if their claims for themselves were coming back to haunt them: "It shall not be with us there as it is with the wicked Israelites," Shepard had announced on the eve of his departure for America, "who when they came into the good land of rest, they then forgot the Lord and all his works past . . ."[40] It was to be another quarter-century until Peter Folger would ridicule his countrymen with his "New England they are like the Jews / As like, as like can be." Such a mocking reply, before the Puritans had been in America for fifteen years, was already ringing in their ears.

As charges and countercharges accumulated, English Puritans grew brusquely impatient with those who had evaded their "duty." "I thought it base," wrote John Milton in 1654, remembering his own journey to Italy at the end of the thirties, "that I should travel abroad at my ease for the cultivation of my mind while my fellow citizens at home were fighting for liberty." Those among Milton's contemporaries who traveled to New England cannot be—and were not—said to have gone in search of leisure. But their advance-party had made the mistake of advertising their destination as a country of ease where nature was thrillingly rampant. Not until the generation of Americans who came of age in the 1860s would our literature again be comparably afflicted with "the sharp alternations of anxiety and hope [of] those who spent the long years of the civil war in foreign lands."[41] It was out of just such a combination of hope and fear—which produced for the exiles more than a little of the onlooker's guilt—that the New England founders began, in a rather strained voice, to speak of themselves as martyrs to the same cause for which their brethren were fighting at home. The accolades to America as Eden simply had to stop. One could not describe this place of refuge as a playground, and at the same time lay credible claim to the tradition of Protestant martyrdom.

Puritans on both sides of the Atlantic associated the language of heroic struggle, if distantly with Israel, then more immediately with the Marian exiles—those scholars and churchmen who, during Queen

Mary's Catholic reign, had, in Geneva and Zurich and Frankfort, worked out the basis for a continuing English Reformation. "Blame," wrote Cotton in 1648, in a revealingly defensive phrase, "was not attached . . . to those pious witnesses who in the days of Mary betook themselves to foreign parts." More strident appropriation of the Marian precedent was made by Edward Johnson in the years immediately following the execution of the king: "Oh all yee Nations of the World, behold how great is the worke the glorious King of Heaven and Earth hath in hand . . . Counsellors and Judges you shall have as at the beginning to fight for you, as Gidion, Bareck, Jeptha, Samson, etc. . . . Then judge all of you (whom the Lord Christ hath given a discerning spirit) whether these poore New England People, be not the forerunners of Christs Army . . ." Others spoke in similarly justifying retrospect, associating the sedentary with indifference to the work of the Lord: "Had this [refusal to venture outside the boundaries of home] been the course in the primitive time, the Gospel had been pinfolded up in a few cities, and not spread as it is." The pressure on New Englanders to vindicate themselves from the charge of shirking their duty may be measured by their strategic shift in self-definition—Higginson, after all, had also listed the virtues of the New England adventure with a taunt at those who stayed behind: "those that love their own chimney corner, and dare not go far beyond their own town's end shall never have the honor to see these wonderful works of Almighty God." Embarrassingly enough, however, the "wonderful works" to which he had been referring in the early thirties were not the works of gospel-teaching in the wilderness, but "ripe strawberries and gooseberries and sweet single roses" which those who stayed in England would never taste or smell.[42] By the later thirties, and certainly by the forties, this kind of explanation could not be sustained. It would have been vulgar in the extreme, tantamount to sending travel brochures to soldiers at the front. New Englanders had now to speak—and speak they did—of their travails.

There was, nevertheless, when they explained their presence in America, an occasional slip into the old candor. "We thought it our safest course," admitted the General Court in 1651, "to get to this outside of the world, out of [the] view and beyond [the] reach" of the bishops. And, after expunging the language of ease from their public declarations, New Englanders seemed for one alarmed moment to have done too good a job of convincing the Lord Protector that they really were living in a crucible from which rescue would be welcome. To deflect Cromwell's plan for colonizing Ireland by draining off some Massachusetts men—who were now describing themselves as battle-weary warriors—the Court reverted to the old language of Edenic plenitude: "God hath blessed the countrey with plentie of food of all kindes . . . insomuch that there are many thousands of bushels of graine, and other provisions, of beef, pork, &c. yearly transported to other places [and] we know not a more healthie place in the whole world . . . There can be no ground of removing for want of health."[43] This was the language of a people betrayed by their own rhetoric. If it had once been possible to believe that the saints were those courageous enough to leave England, they now seemed more likely to be found among those who had remained.

The need for self-justification did not, therefore, abate. It grew. And as it grew, it placed a new premium on the missionary purpose, which some (notably Roger Williams) knew to be a very shaky foundation for the colonial venture. In the early 1650s Williams reports an "eminent [English] person's" remark that "We have Indians at home—Indians in Cornwall, Indians in Wales, Indians in Ireland." The missionary motive had of course always been an element in the rationale for colonization, but it carried no special endorsement of the American enterprise. England itself was full of "dark corners"— Wales, Lancashire, Yorkshire, Devon, Hampshire—which were badly in need of illumination. It is true that Richard Hakluyt himself had made the missionary purpose a central feature in his argument for New World colonization as early as the 1580s: "with discretion and myldenes [we should] distill into their [the Indians'] purged myndes the swete and lively liquor of the gospel." The same appeal was at work in Crashaw's benediction in 1609. Cotton, too, urged it upon Winthrop's company: "Make [the Indians] partakers of your precious faith." But it was by then a public motive with a long history, and it ran the risk of seeming a grace note for purposes of embellishment. By the forties, with war under way in England and New England in the grip of economic depression, the missionary motive had urgently to be rehabilitated. It had to be because, in effect, the order to do so came from home: "We hope," declared a group of English ministers about (and to) their counterparts across sea, that

God will make their distance and *estrangednesse* from us, a meanes of *bringing* many near and in to acquaintance with him. Indeed a *long time* it was before God let them see any *farther* end of their comming over [to America], then to *preserve* their consciences, *cherish* their Graces, *provide* for their sustenance: But when *Providences* invited their return, he let them *know* it was for some farther Arrand, that hee *brought* them thither . . ."

To say that there is an edge to these good wishes is to put it mildly—but however mordant their tone, the effect was to place a new burden on "the prosperous *success* of their endeavours upon those *poor* [Indian] *outcasts.*"[44] There was, both sides were genially agreeing, no other reason to remain in America.

Things had not gotten off to a good start. Something between one- and two-thirds of New England's Indians were killed by disease introduced by Europeans *before* 1620—a fact that was celebrated more than mourned. "The good hand of God favoured our beginnings . . . in sweeping away the great multitudes of the Natives by the Small Pox." For those Indians who were left when the colonists arrived in force, "discretion and myldeness" gave way to warfare and massacre. Recent historians have strenuously corrected the traditional account of peace-loving religious refugees facing redskinned marauders (a tradition invented by Bradford: "these savage barbarians . . . readier to fill their sides full of arrows than otherwise"). We know now that certain Puritans had considerable appetite for carnage; John Endecott displayed an attitude toward war that foreshadowed General Sherman's, and John Underhill (a principal in the Pequot War of 1637–38) expressed disdain for the almost gingerly military techniques of his foes: "They come not near each other, but shoot remote . . . [as if] more for pastime, than to conquer and subdue enemies." Yet the historiographical pendulum has swung too far; the Pequots (whose name was the Algonquin word for "destroyers of men") had effected their eastward expansion from the Hudson Valley "by force of arms," and were dreaded by the less aggressive tribes they had overwhelmed. They hardly constituted a refutation of the Puritans' doctrine of original sin. Yet the "causes" of the Pequot War remain in dispute (as surely must the very concept of limited causation in any human conflict) as historians attempt to secure the moral high ground for one side or the other.[45]

Some accounts stress the colonists' efforts, however heavy-handed, to identify and punish those Indians responsible for the assassination of English traders who had been ambushed while plying their trade (which may have included kidnapping and various forms of extortion) on the Connecticut River and in Long Island Sound. We get a story of bungling Puritan negotiators with nervous trigger fingers, hoping to obtain some account of the sordid events, while resisting the pleas from other tribes to make war while time allows upon the savage Pequots. Undefended English villages come under attack; children, women, and men are killed without discrimination. Other historians, of at least equal authority, give a very different account of the same events: the first English murder victim, whose death becomes a pretext for premeditated imperial conquest, was a "trader-cum-pirate" and a "known freebooter." The Pequots are driven to extreme recourse by the Puritans' systematic policy of extorting ever larger quantities of wampum (which the colonists valued as currency, since its workmanship made counterfeiting difficult) in exchange for trade, and for diplomatic intervention with other tribes. The Pequots, their tributary system violated and disrupted by demands that they hand over suspects from tribes they are committed to protect, are caught between English and Dutch designs on the fertile Connecticut interior. The rest is inevitable. Whichever combination of such factors we prefer as historical explanation, it is clearly as inadequate to speak of Puritan "imperialism" as it used to be to speak of Indian savagery.[46]

What we do know is that the Pequot war was regarded by at least some of the Puritan leadership less as a holy crusade than as a divine judgment—and a judgment that was at least as much upon themselves as upon the natives. "The Lord awakened us by the Pequot hornet, yet what use is there made of it?" asked Shepard before 1640. The shift from conversion to conquest was by no means considered an acceptable change of tactics to fulfill a scriptural destiny; looking back on it was not a matter for resigned equanimity. It was nothing less than the collapse of a major, if belated, justification for their venture. "By the close of the colonial period," as James Axtell has written in an influential essay, "very few if any Indians had been transformed into civilized Englishmen. Most of the Indians who were educated by the English—some contemporaries thought *all* of them—returned to Indian society at the first opportunity to resume their Indian identities. On the other hand, large numbers of Englishmen had chosen to become Indians—by running away from colonial society to join

Indian society, by not trying to escape after being captured, or by electing to remain with the Indian captors when treaties of peace periodically afforded them the opportunity to return home." Most of Axtell's evidence comes from eighteenth-century and later sources, but the trend of failure, and even of "Indianization," is already detectable in the early years. The one-way inclination extended even into the sexual realm. The candid evidence suggests that while the colonists found the "black-hair'd, high foreheaded . . . out brested, small wasted" Indian women very alluring, Indian men generally regarded English women with indifference. Mindful of continuing English curiosity about all aspects of colonist-native relations, and fully aware that it was more badgering than disinterested, Roger Williams inflamed his fellow emigrants in the early forties by remarking that it "is the great Inquiry of all men what Indians have been converted?, what have the *English* done in those parts? What hopes of the *Indians* receiving the Knowledge of Christ!"[47]

As an explanation of their weak record as missionaries, the claim has been made that the Puritans soon "unequivocally identified [the Indians] with the doomed 'dark brothers' of Scripture—Cain, Ishmael, Esau, and above all the heathen natives of the promised land, who were to be dispossessed by divine decree of what really belonged to God's chosen." This was only partially true; the colonists made distinctions, for example, between their Narraganset allies and their Pequot enemies. In the 1650s New Englanders who returned to England were generally not boasting of Indian losses as a measure of their military prowess on behalf of the Lord. They were still talking about Indian "harvests," assuring their hosts that the project of conversion was going well: "My eyes did gladly see," reported Marmaduke Matthews, "several of those naked natives . . . fervently praying to God, and feelingly preaching of Christ on a solemn day of Humiliation, and that in the presence of not a few hundreds of Christian Auditors." (It is a tribute to Matthews's honesty that he could do no better than "several.") Much later in the century Increase Mather was still not finding in the outcome of English-native hostility a deserved Indian doom, but, on the contrary, a very dark meaning for the colonists:

[the] work of *Gospellizing the Indians,* [was once] one of the peculiar Glories of *New-England* . . . But since the Death of that Apostolical

man, Old Mr. *Eliot,* how has that Glorious work been dwindling and dying? . . . The greatest Number of *Indians* who have given clear Evidences of a real Conversion to Christ, were in *Martha's Vineyard* . . . but God has sent Sickness amongst them which has swept away most of those in that place . . . As for many . . . who now make a Profession of Christianity, [they have been] Debauched . . . with Drink, and so made . . . more Brutish, and *Inglorious Creatures;* yea, more the Children of Hell then they were before the Light of the Gospel came among them.

Failure with the Indians was one among many reasons that led Mather to conclude that "*God has not seemed to take pleasure in the* American world," and that "*that which some have thought was the special design of Providence in bringing a choice People into this part of the world, seems as if it were now over.*"[48]

There was much more here than embarrassment at the Puritans' failure to proselytize. The project of converting the Indians had long been associated, if not securely identified, with the doctrine of the conversion of the Jews—considered by virtually all Protestants to be an essential prelude to the advent of the millennium. As with every other apocalyptic expectation, there was a wide range of learned opinion on just what was meant by Romans 11:26: "All Israel shall be saved." Some English commentators, like Andrew Willett and later William Prynne, interpreted this phrase as referring to an act already accomplished in apostolic times, namely the conversion of a small Jewish "remnant." Others, like Thomas Thorowgood, considered it a prophecy that the entire Jewish nation would be called to God as the immediate prelude to the reign of the saints. And in a speculation of obvious attraction for those already settled in New England, Thorowgood added the tantalizing notion in his *Jewes in America* (1650), that the Indians might be descended from the lost tribes of Israel. How large a role this idea played in very early New England remains a matter of debate, but Thorowgood certainly did not invent it in 1650; it had been present from the start: "They separate their women," reported one of the original patentees, "in the times appointed by the Law of *Moses,* counting them and all they touch uncleane during that time appointed by the Law [and] the name of the place, which our late Colony hath chosen for their seat, prooves to bee perfect Hebrew, being called *Nahum Keike,* by interpretation, *The bosome of consolation.*"[49] Such linguistic clues encouraged those who saw eschatological importance in American events from the beginning. There were, after all, precious few Jewish candidates for conversion in all of England (barely twenty Marrano families in London)—whereas, if the theory of Indian descent were true, there might be thousands, indeed whole nations, of potential "Jewish" converts in America.

Until the late forties, however, with Indian conversions few and far between, the leadership tended less often to speak of the natives as Jews, and more as "American Gentiles." In his sermons on Revelation (c. 1640), Cotton associated the Indians with other non-Christian gentiles, and, by arguing that their conversion must await God's call to the Jews, "made any major missionary undertaking pointless." John Eliot did not launch his first Indian mission until 1646, and he did so unconvinced that he was preaching to anything other than ordinary heathen. Still, the idea of Jewish origin persisted as a sort of underground eschatology. While some conceded that it was merely a hopeful hypothesis, others continued to maintain that "the *Jewes of the Netherlands* (being intreated thereunto) *informe that after much inquiry they found some of the ten Tribes to be in America,*" and that "those sometimes poor, now precious *Indians* . . . may be as the *first fruits* of the glorious harvest, of *Israels redemption.*" Eliot followed a tortuous course from skepticism to full belief in the theory and then back to a quasi-endorsement, concluding that the Indians were actually descendants of Eber (Gen. 10:21–24) which entitled them, if not to first place in the salvific procession, then at least to ultimate inclusion in the covenant promise that God had made to Abraham.[50] The idea of the Indians' Jewish origin was, then, a short-lived and tentative element in New England's search for purpose. It flourished only briefly, under the pressure to find something with which to match revolutionary events at home. The decline of the idea followed upon its practical collapse—not the other way around.

One exemplary case is that of Harvard College. In 1651, a lively year for tart exchanges between New England and Old, President Dunster solicited funds for an Indian College. Morison remarks that "the failure of this enterprise was so complete as to raise among modern readers the suspicion that it was merely a blind to get a new building for Harvard." Daniel Gookin, who saw the resulting structure in the 1670s (while compiling his *Historical Collection of the Indians in New England;* 1674), noticed that it "hath [not] been much improved for the ends intended, by reason of the death and failing of Indian scholars. It hath hitherto been principally improved for to accommodate English scholars, and for placing and using a printing press." Compounding such failures was, once again, England's success—or at least the growing prospect of success during the Commonwealth years. "Since there was a promise of [the Jews'] conversion," Cromwell patiently explained to those who balked at his plan to admit Jews to the London merchant trade, "means must be used to that end, which [is] the preaching of the Gospel, and that [can] not be done unless they were admitted where the Gospel [is] preached." And so the barriers against Jewish immigration into England (which had held since the expulsion of 1290) began to come down, a fact that generated what one scholar demurely calls "great interest" in New England. New England had nothing to compare with this, nothing whatever to show. To make matters worse, Menasseh ben Israel himself, whose messianism waxed rather than waned with the disastrous pogroms of the late 1640s, dedicated his *Hope of Israel* (1650) not to some "missionaries" in America who might once have hoped to bring his scattered people to God, but to Cromwell's government, "whose appearance on the scene [he] saw as a portent of the messianic world."[51]

As the idea of Jewish Indians declined into a crackpot theory and the claims surrounding it proved spurious, an enervating effect could be felt upon New England's collective morale. By the end of the century lists of possible Indian genealogies were still being compiled, but with hardly a mention of the theory of Jewish origin. There was, moreover, no compensation for the failure of conversion in reverting to the idea of Indian savagery—"What God will do for the future with *America*," remarked Increase Mather, "is not for us to determine . . . but . . . the Lord has not hitherto seen meet to shine upon this so as on the other *Hemisphere*. The greatest part of its Inhabitants are Pagans. Most of those that have any thing of the *Christian* Name are really *Anti-Christian* . . . a Scandal to any Religion." This is not a righteous call to arms. It is a confession of abject failure. And it goes some distance (along with the many other portents of disaster) to explaining why second-generation Puritans attended to predictions from England that America was likely to become "one of the dolefullest spots of Ground on the face of the Whole Earth."[52]

Long before Mather's discouragement, the Pequot war may have "called forth in its most vigorous form the Puritan culture's sense of itself as an armed band of the Lord," but it rapidly degenerated from

crusade into carnage. "It came," says Larzer Ziff, ". . . to be a matter
not of capturing and executing the Pequots who had committed crim-
inal acts, but of exterminating the tribe altogether." Captain John
Mason burned down an entire village with hundreds of men, women,
and children trapped within; those who ran for their lives were picked
off by Puritan muskets. But even as the army tallied its vile victories,
a shift can be detected in the Puritan battle cry from the declarative
to the interrogative mood—a shift that persists into the later seventeenth century and beyond. "Thus we Marched on," reported Mason,
"in an uncoath and unknown Path to the *English,* though much fre-
quented by the *Indians.*" And though he was speaking here of literal
trails through the underbrush, there lurks everywhere in his bloody
History (w. 1637) a question Cotton Mather would pose more explicitly at the end of the century. Were the colonists being "Indianized"? Were they, in their felt distance from England, in their appetite
for flesh-and-blood enemies, giving vent to a compensating zeal for
conquest? There is more than a hint of self-doubt even in the crude
mind of Mason as he winds up his self-exalting chronicle with a
question: "Was not the Finger of God in all this?"[53]

Was it indeed? From England there came not reassurance but indifference. "I thinke," said John Archer in 1642, as he speculated on
Christ's descent to judgment, that the destruction of all the wicked
"shall not be now, but at his third and last comming . . . Now he will
onely ruine the Armies of them . . . as the ruine of the Egyptians at
the red Sea was not of every one, but of them that were in Armies
combin'd against the Israelites." The engine of destruction Archer
had in mind was Parliament's army, not the Massachusetts militia.
The enemy were not Pequots but royalists. To add to New England's
embarrassment, some emboldened Baptists among them were, by the
mid-forties, proclaiming that "no servant of Jesus Christ, hath any
liberty, much less authority to smite his fellow-servant." The orthodox
rushed to dissociate themselves (with an English audience in mind)
from such pacific sentiments: "As for you (most Noble Sir)," wrote
Thomas Cobbett to Cromwell, eagerly dissociating himself from the
Baptists' charge, "who in your Military way, have had so many Military
disputes for the Causes of the Lord, if it be vile to be for Jesus Christ,
be you yet more vile." Aware with equal discomfort that New England's "armies" were being overshadowed by their counterparts in

England, Edward Johnson found in Anne Hutchinson an even more "cunning Devill" than were the Pequots, and drenched his *Wonder-Working Providence* in frank delight at her suppression. Here was, he thought, incontrovertible proof of New England's militancy, proof that New England was "zealous to stand for the truth of [the Lord's] Discipline [and] not to give ground one inch." But one who disagreed, William Coddington, quietly pointed out to the General Court that there was disproportion between Hutchinson's acts and her punishment: "I would entreat you to consider whether those things you have alledged against her deserve such censure as you are about to pass."[54] What Johnson exemplified, and Coddington understood, was that in order to ratify its godliness New England had had to find its local Satans.

With what, then, were they left? With a sense, as Nathaniel Ward had said, that the true church had never been stationary. (Ward's wanderings turned out to be circular; he ended his life back in England, only a few miles from the Suffolk village where he had been born.) When New Englanders looked back into the tradition from which they had emerged, they could at least find precedents for Ward's assertion: the early church, John Knox had written nearly a century before the Great Migration, "was compelled to fly from citie to citie, from realme to realme, and from one nation to another; and yet so wonderously was it preserved, that a great nomber of those whom the wycked pryestes, by their bloody tirannye, exiled and banished from Hierusalem, wer kept alyve til God's vengeaunce was powred forth upon that most wicked generation." Here the Scottish reformer had presented the faithful in disciplined retreat, as buffeted witnesses from afar to God's fury on their behalf. When he turned from surveying history to reporting it, Knox's acuity was on full display, in an almost baroque combination of pain and joy: "When I call to mynd and revolve with myself the trubillis and afflictionis of God's electe frome the begynning . . . thair is within my hart two extreme contraries; a dolour almaist unspeakabill, and a joy and comfort whik by mannis sences cannot be comprehendit nor understand."[55] This was an authentically Calvinist vision of the saints as suffering instruments of God's will—and one the Puritans in America would dearly have liked to apply to themselves.

They were not able to. Knox's sentences have a candor that is alien to the expression of the exiles to New England. What he is confessing is a psychic dependency on persecution—something continually hinted at by those who came to America—"we shall find in times of persecution, never such assurance as then"—but rarely indulged in, savored. It simply could not be. To make such a point about the utility of pain, Shepard had to find his text in the safely historical Book of Zechariah; he could not hold high the examples of Prynne and Bastwick, who were branded and mutilated in the London pillory for acts of treason; he could not turn to such as them because there was reproach in their wounds. Most of all, the New England Puritans could not follow Knox because they were caught in a contradiction of their own making: in order to explain their presence in America, they were telling a tale of woe and righteous struggle—yet at the same time, as they noticed the slackening of fervor, they lamented the absence of "enemies to hunt you to heaven, chains to make you cry . . . sour herbs to make the lamb sweet."[56] To borrow some terms from current literary discourse, it may be said that the Puritans in America had privileged a narrative of pain (first for their foreign audience, then for themselves), while simultaneously deconstructing it. It was a situation in which many could not bear to remain.

And so in the forties some acted to resolve these contradictions by returning to England—a story of defection that remains to be told (having largely disappeared as a tale unfit for our national mythology.) The return migration of the 1640s dealt a further blow to New England's already fragile self-confidence, and even when the "deserters"—Vane, Hooke, Firmin, and many others—had been expunged from the historical record, a continuing sense of drift among those who remained had still to be explained. Toward that end, Cotton Mather rather shrilly maintained that the founders' pain was not so much in the physical deprivations of their settlement or journey— their "passage . . . was attended with many Smiles of Heaven"—but in the fact of displacement itself, something their sons could never duplicate. As if still coaching the founders on how to answer the queries from home, Mather insisted again and again that their flight had been "a *Banishment,* rather than a *Removal,*" an inflicted event borne with holy passivity. "Sometimes *Dropping* and sometimes flocking," they had been spasmodic migrants—quickening their pace with bulletins of New England harvests and Laud's rage, slowing with news of endless winter and promises of Laud's restraint. In Mather's filiopious history, it was of course the timorous who stayed behind and the brave who ventured out. The founders "were driven out of that *Island,* into an horrible *Wilderness,* meerly for their being Well-willers unto the *Reformation.*" And yet the same contradiction that troubled Mather's grandfathers still obtained for him. Savoring "the precious odour" of martyrdom, Mather proclaimed that "adversity makes the best Christians," and yet, despite the many impressive disasters of his own time—smallpox, fire, revocation of the charter, witchcraft—he spent most of his life searching for ways to recapture what he imagined as the militant spirit of his immigrant fathers. "Security, a sleeping sickness," Shepard had prophesied, "will be the disease of others." But the idea of piety under pressure never proved itself in the New World.[57]

It had, however, been vindicated, at least briefly, in the Old. Or so it seemed to those who watched the revolution from afar. For those who elected to stay at their spectator-distance, the voice of English Puritanism—even before it became openly conscriptive and defiant—was always a voice of indictment. Before New England had been named, John Dod (whom Mather revered as one of the towering Puritan patriarchs), declared that "those that have but a glimpse of Christianity in them, would rather have the society of others, than live alone in the middest of the earth." Dod, whose long public life spanned from Elizabeth's reign to the civil wars, was, in effect, answering Richard Hooker's charge that Puritans would never be able to "live among men" but only "in some wilderness by themselves." In an equally predictive mood, he was saying that Hooker had seen only part of the future (New England's part, as it happened); that the real Puritans (real Christians) will not be separatists; that the faith will be contended for in "societie," not alone. Most painful of all for the spiritual leaders of New England, they themselves knew that they had said the same: "When Christians are disjoynted they lose all their heat, as when a man means to put out the fire, he layes one brand from another, a signe he means to go to bed and sleep; so when Satan would put out the life and heat of grace . . . he disjoynts Christians, and . . . all their heat is quite extinguished." The cruelty of such superseded words lay in their accuracy. Not only was the act of migration a violation of Christian "societie," but God's plantation in New England was itself "disjoynted" from the start.[58]

A few years into the colony's formative period, Winthrop had had to report that the first "dispersions" were not enough: "it was alleged by Mr. Hooker [who arrived in 1633], as a fundamental errour, that towns were set so near each to other," and soon thereafter the General Court was trying to restore by statute what was all too clearly slipping away—the sense of New England's voluntary fellowship: "Hereafter, noe dwelling howse shalbe builte above halfe a myle from the meeteing howse, in any newe plantacon . . . without leave from the Court (except myll howses & fferme howses of such as have their dwelling howses in some towne)." To the many ordinary men and women who crossed the sea in search of community, New England was becoming not "just a disapointment, [but] a positive setback."[59]

New Englanders had no answer to such historical opponents as Richard Hooker; nor to their teachers, like Dod; nor to their former selves. It was left to their children and grandchildren to formulate some sort of reply on their behalf. One begins to sense the return of the dormant heroic theme from the founders' sons: from John Winthrop, Jr., for example, who declared in the 1640s that his fathers had "had all things to doe, as in the beginning of the world." Yet even these zealous children, whose jeremiads have lately been interpreted not as dark laments but as reaffirmations of an older millennial promise, were, like their parents, far from confident of their place in the scheme of sacred history. Increase Mather, whose father, Richard, had crossed the ocean in 1635 with passionate praises to the Lord for sparing him from shipwreck, and who is often cited as a relentless spokesman for New England's sacred mission, took careful note that

Mr. [Joseph] Mede conjectures . . . that the *American Hemisphere* will . . . not be concerned in the Blessedness of the renovated World, during the Thousand Years, and that *Gog* and *Magog* will come from thence; that the Devil will suggest to [the People there], *Your World is a miserable world compared with that on the other side of the Earth: You die and never rise again, but they on t'other Hemisphere live again after they die, and are an happy People: Do you invade their land, and you shall be like them, you shall be like the Gods* . . . Mr. *Medes* Conjecture is ingenious, and may probably prove true.[60]

After twenty years of being American, the first-generation leadership managed only to protest that they had not fled England like "mice from a crumbling house." They were, like many immigrants after them, more bewildered than revived; they would leave it to their children to make sense of their uprooting. And even those among their children who developed the theme of chosenness—what Charles

Olson has expressed in a nicely oxymoronic phrase, "We Americans are the last first people"—did so with a candid sensitivity to their need for a solacing idea. Here, again, is Richard Mather's son:

> Such of us as are in an exiled condition in this wilderness . . . are under special advantage to understand [the] mysterious truths of God [concerning the coming apocalypse]. God hath led us into a wilderness, and surely it was not because [he] hated us but because he loved us that he brought us hither into this Jeshimon. Who knoweth but that he may send down his spirit upon us here if we continue faithful before him?[61]

These tentative, interrogative phrases are full of self-persuasion. They remind us that the myth of America, if it still persists at all, has always rested on a precarious foundation. It is precisely its fragility, not its audacity—the proprietary worry of its believers, not their arrogance—that has made it something different (dare we still say, something better?) than just another version of nationalist pomp.

Whenever the pulpit is usurped by a formalist, then is the worshipper defrauded and disconsolate. We shrink as soon as the prayers begin, which do not uplift, but smite and offend us. We are fain to wrap our cloaks about us, and secure, as best we can, a solitude that hears not.

Ralph Waldo Emerson, 1838

4 *The Antinomian Dissent*

"Persons are very ready," wrote Jonathan Edwards a century after the first New England settlements, "to be suspicious of what they ha'nt felt themselves." This is the most unanswerable of dismissals. It is a rhetorical gesture that can be invitational or exclusionary depending on the spiritual confidence of the addressed; a statement that claims the ineffability of grace while declining to describe it. Within a remarkably few years after the landing of the *Arbella,* New England's religious life had become divided over just such a conundrum: What some considered a taunt others felt as a beckoning. Grace, John Cotton was insisting (still with the voice of authorized leadership), was a "mystery" open only to those who already had experienced it—but was virtually inexpressible to everyone else. Yet by 1637 Cotton's disciple Anne Hutchinson was on trial for heresy, and Governor Winthrop himself felt compelled to intervene to keep the court's attention fixed on her alone—"Mr. Cotton is not called to answer anything but we are to deal with the party here standing before us." "I [have] found soe much strangeness, alienation, and soe much neglect from some whoe would some times have visited me with diverse myles going," wrote Peter Bulkeley in 1637 to Cotton (who had declined to attend Bulkeley's installation as teacher of the Concord church), yet now they "passe by my doore, as if I were the man that they had not knowen." New England had ruptured over the meaning of grace.[1]

One way to begin to understand how this could have happened is to consider the first dominant, then precarious position of Cotton in the Bay Colony—a position he had, in effect, successfully transferred from Old England to New. Cotton's English parish, the Lincolnshire town of Boston, had been a thriving seaport during the years of his vicarship in the first decades of the century. Traveling there today from London, one can take a detour for purposes of comparison and pass through the Essex village of Earle's Colne, where one of Cotton's New World opponents, Thomas Shepard, preached in his youth. Shepard's modest stone church looks like a hundred country churches. Fieldstone pathways lead to it from the village. The fenced field in which it sits stops a few yards from its doors and becomes a grave-yard, where names on the gravestones match the names of benefactors chiseled in the interior walls. The whole arrangement has a domestic air, as if a familial traffic had moved for centuries between village, church, and burying ground. By contrast, Cotton's church, planned at the end of the fourteenth century when Boston was England's second port and merchants from all over Europe made it a cosmo-politan town, "was the largest . . . in England which has always been a parish church." Though his "livinge [was] very small and his paines in preaching very great," he worked in England among the symbols of his consequence; preaching from a massive pulpit (installed for him in 1612) that dominated the nave, under a vault that rose to nearly one hundred fifty feet. This tower of St. Botolph's was "reck-oned," according to one eighteenth-century visitor, as "the high-est . . . in Europe." It touched sublimity: "All the Country thro' there are very fine Churches . . . but this ore looks them all like a proud Dame sensible of her beauty and scorning the mener Croud about her."[2] St. Botolph's steeple is as good an emblem as any of two facts that have a special salience for understanding religious strife in New England's first decade: first, that John Cotton was closer than anyone in England to being the Puritans' "bishop"; and second, that his col-leagues—Shepard, Hooker, Bulkeley, and the rest—knew it well. When they brought Anne Hutchinson under attack in the late 1630s, it was something like assaulting the prime minister by calling a vote on an issue to which he was committed.

Cotton preached voluminously at old Boston, preaching of which the first substantial record is a sprawling, formless book called *A Practical Commentary upon the First Epistle Generall of John,* a book through which one hears a young man still very close in time, and so in vivid memory, to the day he had publicly abandoned the artistry of Anglican pulpit eloquence. As a rising star at Emmanuel College, Cotton had drawn large crowds to his sermons—performances that were earning him a reputation for oratorical wit. But under the influence of Richard Sibbes, Fellow of St. John's College, who preached with melting simplicity in another part of town, Cotton repented his crowd-pleasing manner. According to a traditional story, he threw away the tropes and showmanship one afternoon so suddenly and so completely that "the schollars [who] came generally with great expectation to heare a more than ordinary learned Sermon from him . . . soone [were] pulling their hats over their eyes, thereby to expresse their dislike" of what they heard. In the *Commentary upon John* the young vicar was still close enough to his stylistic reversal to be defending it. He had, he said, abandoned the "mode of the university" in favor of the "plain and profitable way [because] . . . a velvet scabbard dulls the edge of the Sword, [and] the Word deckt over with Human eloquence . . . hinders the power of it." Refusing now to be a "minister [who] fits [the] itching ears [of his parishioners] with New-fangled Doctrin," Cotton was making public witness— sometimes haltingly—to his personal Puritanism. "A man is not judged by a step or two, but according to his walk." This was the man of consolation for whom many of his parishioners, who felt themselves more and more to be stumbling Christians, would soon relinquish their town offices, sell their goods and land-deeds, pay off their debts and call in their loans, and make a journey across an ocean.[3]

If this seems a difficult loyalty to comprehend, we may perhaps begin to grasp it by recognizing that at a time of increasing social disorder (when all could see, but not prevent, "the secret comeing in of poore people out of other Townes into this Towne to dwell") Cotton reassured them that their sense of panic might not foretell doom as old certainties—known neighbors, the predictable poor— began to become unstable. His was a voice of counsel at a time when one's social responsibilities and, indeed, one's personal prospects seemed less and less clear. It was, moreover, a voice of self-exoneration for having assented to practices in which many no longer believed: he was, himself, toeing the line between prevarication and conscientious doubt in matters of church ceremonies; he had sworn fealty to the Book of Common Prayer, had knelt before bishops, had worn the surplice, and thereby kept his Episcopal overseers satisfied that there was no heresy brewing in Lincolnshire. Like all his fellow ministers who made the decision to emigrate, Cotton lived with (and shared with his parishioners) the pressing questions of his time: what was conformity, and what holy compromise? "Take heed," he exhorted them (from James 1:6–8) and perhaps himself, "that you be not of a wavering double minde."[4]

This self-questioning is clearest not so much in passages of explicit wavering, as in his Ramistic technique of mediation between opposites. Christ, for example, was sent by God "that hee might bee a middle person, or of a middle nature, between the persons offending, and the persons offended." Christ as mediator was of course an unexceptionable description to a whole range of Christian opinion, but there is something here of a disinterested bargainer, the neutral go-between. This is a functional Christ, the middle term of a bloodless syllogism. Cotton had mediation on the mind when he preached these sermons early in his Boston career, and, having just spent "much time in Schooles, and Universities," he clearly had been especially impressed by the balancing aesthetic of the *Nichomachean Ethics:* "Virtue consists not in a mean between two degrees," he preached with scholastic neatness, "but in a mean between two extreams." The heart of Cotton's early sermons is their sense that virtue amounts to the avoidance of excess: "In our Callings we must be diligent, . . . but we are never to desire more than we may have good use of." There is a residue of stoicism here, a pride in self-denial.[5]

The young Cotton was, however, liberal with his learning. He peppered his sermons with Greek quotation, exhibiting Epictetus and Aristotle as a preparative to dismissing the church fathers for being insufficiently literate: "Few knew the meaning of the Scripture in the originall, none knew the Hebrew, but *Jeremy* and *Origen*." Such gestures of learned impatience were the first elements to drop away as Cotton faced the necessity of making and recommending to his flock a choice of devotional style—a choice for bookless faith over the polish of learning. This becomes clear in his massive *The Way of Life; or Gods Way and Course, in Bringing the Soule into Life and Peace*, the longest of his works, which shows very early his new hostility to the trappings of erudition, and a new concern for spirit liberated from the library: "Use Books as young swimmers use Bladders; the spirit of Grace will help thee beyond what thou wouldst think, and thereby thou wilt more sweetly tell God thy mind, and therefore labour chiefly for a spirit of Grace." This is the Emersonian Cotton—prescient of the sentiment that "books are the best of things, well used; abused, among the worst . . . They are for nothing but to inspire"—who may be said to supply a new first term for Perry Miller's celebrated sequence, "from [Cotton to] Edwards to Emerson."[6]

If the secret theme of the *Commentary upon John* had been the need to construct a place of compromise where the individual conscience might reside without shame, *The Way of Life* no longer centers on the individual so much as on a whole social faction: "if . . . Gods people fall out with their brethren, or neither higher nor lower persons suffer them, nor favour them, then see what a division God makes." Cotton by the 1620s was beginning to speak less as a studious clergyman of pressured conscience and more as a spokesman for "God's people" (he had already organized a "conventicle" of "godly persons in Boston [who] entered into a covenant with the Lord, and one with another"), and his critical need was to find a means of retaining and expressing their solidarity without splintering the society of which they regarded themselves as the elect part.[7]

So it was that Cotton the high Calvinist cast his lot with England even as the breakdown of English social order drew near, and even as he took steps toward leading the elect out from among what his predecessors had called the "mixt people." Despite his increasingly sharp division of the world into spiritually distinct halves, Cotton still embraced England's collective fate as his own, mustering for this commitment all his eloquence and not a little of his ingenuity. The problem was to offer a rationale for a people's interdependence while it was clear to the world (and to themselves) that they were becoming sundered. *The Way of Life* makes a brave attempt at such a feat: "In Gods ordinary estimation of things, the practice of his people, is the Act of the whole State in which they live." It is impossible to know whether Cotton pronounced that word "ordinary" from the pulpit of St. Botolph's or whether it is an American interpolation, but in either case it carried an enormous burden. For the thrust of a hundred sermons from the twenties to the forties—"God is packing up of his gospel, [saying] farewell . . . England"; "if God say, *I will stay no longer in* England: Wee shall then bee a spoyle to any enemy"—was that things were not "ordinary" anymore; and Cotton's effort to forestall agreement with such prophecies begins with *The Way of Life:* "So long as Gods people keepe themselves free from the pollutions of the time, and mourne for the sinnes of the times . . . all that while, all that which is the act of *Families,* is the act of Countries, Kingdomes, and Nations." He longed for union, albeit a paradoxical one, between dissent and loyalty, and it was in the service of such a unity that he tried to induce in his hearers a revulsion from the ways of the world while forbidding contempt for those still mired in it. For him, the tendency of dissent was never toward secession, but toward protection of the wayward commonwealth:

> Though there were many branches of the Vine dead yet if but a cluster of Grapes, the Vine shall not be cut up, till that he gathered: When God shall see his faithfull servants bring forth Clusters of sweet fruits unto him, they shall be a blessing to others; implying, that where ever Gods servants are, because of his Covenant with them, where ever they crave a blessing, and mourne for the want of it, God will provide it shall be stretched forth upon the whole Country they live in.[8]

The function of the saints was to restore the commonwealth to social health, never to abandon it.

Such a politics could take shape in Cotton's mind only if a certain vision of society preceded it, and that vision was built in turn on some basic assumptions about man. If godly men were to leave England, he warned, it would be a kind of amputation: such a departure "implies something more" than a reduction of number from an ample human supply. "As to expresse it from what Surgeons are wont to say; They say, all piercing of a member, is piercing of the body that is compact together . . . the heart and braine are the vessels of life, and as soone as one of these vessels are broken, the life of man runs out like water spilt upon the ground." This view of the human creature—that a wound to part of him is a wound to all of him—was the foundation of Cotton's ministry, and the cardinal belief that he carried to New England. It was, moreover, the essential principle underlying the Puritan concept of the self as well as of the church; the individual version of what John Coolidge has called a "principle of harmony among the members of the communal body." One feels, to borrow another of Coolidge's phrases, a hostility in Cotton "not merely to disorder but, more significantly, to a non-living kind of order" in the self as well as the community. This can be felt, for example, in the first sermon of *Gods Mercie Mixed with His Justice,* where Cotton takes pains to explain how scripture can call the heart the "inmost closet of the soule," and yet, without inconsistency, call it in the next breath the soul's "door." He feels no confusion of sequence, because for him there is finally no distinction between the inner and the outer man.[9]

Such an organicism explains as well why it is to music that he turns in search of adequate expression for his ideal of social cohesion:

> We are all one mystical body: and I cannot tell how better to compare it, than to a musical instrument, wherein though there be many pipes, yet one blast of the bellowes puts breath into them all, so that all of them at once break forth into a kind of melody, and give a pleasant sound to the ears of those that stand by; all of them do make but one Instrument, and one sound, and yet variety of musick.

However embryonic, this delight in the fusion of discrete sounds into choral harmony was part of an insistence that writings "do not prosper to conversion," while preaching can. This, of course, was hardly an exceptional premise—Puritans (as their opponents were never tired of complaining) were sermon-drunk. Their intoxication with preaching, which is perhaps the closest thing to a usable definition of their movement in the opening years of the seventeenth century, had already in the 1590s, as we have seen, been the sharpest source of Richard Hooker's exasperation. Their passion for sermons—fleeting, unrecorded utterances, "sermons without book, sermons which spend their life in their birth and have public audience but once"—involves a refusal to submit to the documented authority of the past, a rejection of institutional structures as the tested products of time, and a sanctioning of every moment as a potential repository of grace. It regards experience itself not as an accumulation toward wisdom, but as an ungraduated assemblage of discrete moments, any one of which may deliver grace with sudden power. As Coolidge puts it (borrowing some terms from Windelband), the Pauline spirit within Puritanism may best be understood as a "mysterious reconciliation" of the Hebraic or "idiographic" conception, which places "the significance of any item or event . . . in the relationship between it and all the others in [a] continuum," with the Hellenic or "nomothetic" interest in general laws as freed from their particular expression in a unique historical pattern. Puritanism was, in these terms, a liberation from history, a reversion to the moment when time itself had been halted and re-commenced by the incarnation: "The *First Age* was the Golden Age: To return unto That, will make a man a *Protestant,* and I may add," says Cotton Mather, looking back to his grandfathers' day as a re-capitulation of Christ's, "a *Puritan.*"[10]

One way to understand John Cotton's centrality in New England's spiritual life is to notice that he devoted his ministry to fostering the psychological conditions that would enable his listeners really to *feel* that such a "return" was possible and imminent. "When this vail shall be removed," he promised, " . . .then shal you see the stars of heaven . . . you shall see . . . the sons of God . . . blameless, harm-lesse . . . without rebuke, shining as lights in the world." A state of anticipatory excitement had to be maintained, a mood in which one could scan experience for clues to the soul's condition while at the same time disallowing past experience as the ultimate measure of spiritual possibility. It was a frame of mind opposed to the idea of stepped progress and open to the hope of sudden illumination. There were, for such a mind, no beginnings and endings in the topography of the body any more than in the career of the soul: "Give God the heart, and then you give the whole soule and body too." This is not a slow adjustment of a complex apparatus, but a concentration of all personal history into one transforming moment; an "*inhabitation*" of the spirit. Cotton was, in his psychology of regeneration as well as in his polity and politics, always an organicist.[11]

It was for this reason that the migration was the crisis of his life, and inevitably, a challenge to the very social ideal it was undertaken to preserve. Cotton's mentor, Sibbes, had preached in the weeks just before his death that "Josuah was much cast downe when he saw it went not well with Israel: but get thee up Josuah, saith God, what doest thou lying here? Up and doe thy duty; consider what is amisse." We hear Cotton, in the same vein, speak longingly of England (from New England) in the 1640s, as if we have eavesdropped on an intimate dream: "It is a fit season to return to our Native Countrey . . . when every Ordinance of God is settled in peace and purity . . . when con-course of providence giveth fair opportunity . . . [and] Winter is over." He could not give up the idea of a collective English destiny. Always a poet of what he called "member-like union with our brethren," he insisted that the polity of New England's Churches be called "Con-gregationalism," not "Independency," and rejected the vocabulary of separatism, however abstract. He therefore urgently required a sense of paradox that would enable him to imagine New England unsevered from Old. "So long as Gods people keepe themselves free from the pollutions of the time," there is hope; but that hope is dashed if they become "Families apart, or Congregations apart."[12]

Where *The Commentary upon John* had demanded an uncomplicated, even pagan ethic of moderation, the later sermons of *The Way of Life* (published nearly ten years after his flight to the New World, but first delivered in England) transform the caution—"never to desire more"—into something much more complex: "Though you may have a godly man busie in his calling from Sunne rising to Sunne setting, and may by Gods providence fill both his hand and head with businesse, yet a living Christian when he lives a most busie life in this world, yet he lives not a worldly life." In this description, which inaugurates a New England genealogy that eventually yields the consecrated industriousness of Thoreau, it is plausible to detect something less exalted—a rationalization of greed, or at least of parsimony. It is not hard to see why Cotton was popular with pious entrepreneurs, for he seemed to be inviting a juggling of opposites—charity and profit—just the kind of mental gymnastic at which every Puritan merchant had to be practiced. But such oppositional structures were built in, not merely appended to his speech—"the life wee receive from baptisme, is death unto sin"; "when a man is most lively in the life of sense, it is but the action of a dying man"—and are deployed not to confirm habits of mental evasion, but to drive the listener from surface contradictions to a deeper harmony. They constituted an intellectual strategy for dealing with a series of almost unbearable contradictions—high among them, love and abhorrence toward the native nation. For Cotton it was a strategy that became a thoroughgoing way of looking at the world:

> It is true, should a man offer his house full of Treasure for Christ, it would be despised, Cant. 8.7. and when *Simon Magus* offered to buy the gifts of the Holy Ghost for mony, it was rejected with a curse . . . And yet thus much I say, that many times without laying out of mony, he [Christ] cannot be had, with out parting with money we cannot get him, the case so stands that sometimes, the holding fast a mans mony lets go the Lord Jesus Christ . . . so that though Christ cannot be had for money, yet sometimes without expence of mony he cannot be had.[13]

This is not a frivolous delight in paradox; it is a way of circling the unsayable—of communicating the incompatibility of greed with grace, but without saying that grace is obtainable through the charitable gesture.

The experience of conversion, then, involves a totally reorganized perception of the world, which in turn requires a new mode of expression: "The truly regenerate they see a great change . . . he is borne of God to a Spiritual life, is become a *new Creature, and old things are past away, 2 Cor. 5:17.* He hath a new mind and a new heart, new affections, new Language . . ." Gracious language is, moreover, always embroiled in contradiction: the saint is "inlarged with . . . joy" at God's generosity and "full of grief of heart that ever he should have so much displeased." "In the worshipping of God" he feels both "joy and feare"; he is "full of much patience, but without all forbearance." He combines "gentlenesse and meeknesse with much austerity and strictnesse, . . . modesty . . . with . . . magnanimity," and is capable, above all, of "love of enemyes." The monotone saint of the *Commentary upon John* has been transformed into a being of manifold imaginative capacity—the capacity to hold oppositions in his head. He is no longer a compromiser, but a paradoxist—"if you have therefore found your joy mixed with sorrow it is right"—and takes delight in God's power to contravene the logic of nature: "The clouds sometimes are so full that one would thinke they would burst through the aire, and fall upon the earth, but God having set the aire to be a Firmament or expulson between the waters above, and waters below, though of it selfe a very liquid thing, yet it stands like to a wall of brasse."[14]

It is thus possible to sense how close Cotton brings his search for gracious feeling to the Catholic mysteries themselves: 'If [a man] be a Christian . . . he feeds upon Christ. Christ is turned into his nature, or which is more, his nature is rather turned into the nature of Christ . . . so then consider, do I feed upon *the flesh of Christ, and drinke his blood,* and do I finde a spirituall appetite to the Lord Jesus raised up in my soule?" Indeed the entire history of reform dogmatics on the question of the Lord's Supper had oscillated between an essentially commemorative view of its efficacy—Zwingli's rationalist claim that the reenactment of the supper is a "representation and memorial of his body and blood"—and the more stridently pietistic claim (derived from Luther) that the body and blood of Christ are simultaneously ascendant and present in the "material signs," that is, in the bread and wine, of the sacrament. For the Puritan inheritors of this dual tradition, its legacy was, not surprisingly, "a common ambivalence about sacraments." On the one hand the taking of the sacrament remained an event of enormous gravity, commended as the "seal" of faith by Christ himself, and standing as the central ratifying ceremony of the community of believers. On the other, it retained an air of exclusive mystery and even menace as a ritual historically administered by an initiate clergy who controlled access to it. Generally, Puritan utterances tend toward the Zwinglian side of the spectrum; John Dod, for example, soberly explained that "when we see the bread broken, and the wine powred out, we must consider of the bitter passion of Christ Jesus, who was wounded for our transgressions." Yet, as the most scrupulous student of this aspect of Puritan piety has argued, "the study of the Puritans is also a story of their resistance to their own antisacramental impulse." In Cotton we sense exactly this self-division. There is, of course, no secret adherence to transubstantiation in his "do I feed upon the flesh of Christ, and drinke his blood," but there is an unslaked appetite for mystery; the break from Catholic doctrine is more subtle than abrupt. Cotton rejects the Catholic meaning of communion (by which he means to rebuke the lingering sacerdotalism of the Anglican church) not because of its irrationality or superstition, but because it is too fixed, too anchored in ceremonial occasion. This was the essence of Puritan iconoclasm: "To make a crosse with reference to Christ, is to respect a crosse superstitiously," wrote one of his fellow emigrants, "and yet to honor the Lord Christ in ones heart upon the occasional sight of the crosse, whether natural or artificial, may be lawful." Ritual sacramentalism constricts the communicant's passion; the Puritan would see it diffused through the activities of life. The Catholic routine, according to the Puritan critique, confines the spirit to regular seasons; the true Christian would make it rampant.[15]

  More than an attack on priestly control, Cotton's discussion of transubstantiation manifests his highest hope in England, which is finally a social version of his aesthetic standard. The real failure of Catholic practice is that it shackles the imagination. To conceive wine and bread literally as blood and body is not an imaginative triumph, but a failure:

> Not that you should here look at the naturall body and blood of Christ, for that were a Canaball eating and drinking . . . Had a company of *Roman Souldiers* fallen upon Christ, and either out of wrath against him, or love to themselves, had pulled him in peeces and eaten him, goblet by goblet, it had profited them nothing . . . had men eaten the reall

body of Christ and drunk up his blood, and joyned with others in so doing, and left none of him, all this had profited nothing, and therefore our Saviour so confesseth, that it is no part of his meaning, that they should eate and drinke his reall body and blood: but hee meanes the breathing of the spirit in the Ordinances, if you can rellish, and feed upon that, and grow to be such as Christ was in this world that was the meate and drinke of his soule, if you grow humble and meek, and be transformed into the spirit of Christ, if you see your spirits conformable to the will of Christ, it is a signe of the life of holinesse in your soules, which God hath given you through Christ.[16]

To be a Christian is to grasp the essence of metaphor (which Cotton defined as a "short similitude"). It is to avoid confusing figurative with denotative language, to escape what has been called the encroaching "empirical temper" of Stuart Puritanism. "The study of nature," Cotton insisted, "healeth not the sinfull defects of nature in our own spirits." Some persons simply cannot grasp the idea of metaphor, which, in its melding of disparate ideas, is a form of paradox: "Diligence in wordly businesse, and yet deadnesse to the world [is] such a mystery as none can read, but they that know it."[17] One imagines Cotton's audience dividing between riveted assent to such riddles and resentful bewilderment (the latter was the emotion that gripped the challenged clergy during the Antinomian crisis). The meaning of any act, the "antinomians" were saying—acts of interpretation, of obedience, of commerce—derives only from the spirit in which it is performed.

More than any other, the act of journeying to New England put the principle of holy paradox to the test of experience. Every man and woman who had come to the Bay Colony had heard restraining voices, had left behind something irrecoverable. Someone—a family member, a neighbor, a creditor, the self—had summoned them home. The storefronts and street signs of London remained markers for a range of transactions: "I William Hudson of Boston Junior do acknowledge my selfe indebted to Lewis Kidbie of London mariner in the just summe of twenty fyve pounds sterl to be paid unto him or his Assignes at Mr Joshua ffootes shopp at the Cocke in gracious streete in London by fyve pounds a yeare, yearly uppon the 28th of ffeb." Holding in mind the "lovely countenance" of the wife he had left behind, Governor Winthrop arranged more frequent and more personal reversions: In "griefe for thy absence," he resolved by letter that they should "meet in spiritt till we meet in person all mundayes and frydayes at 5:." Edward Johnson, giving vent to a more abstract but still visceral ambivalence about his presence in America, set the scene in his *Wonder-Working Providence* for "Friends and Acquaintance . . . [to] expostulate" with their departing brethren even as the gangway is pulled back into the pilgrim-laden ship:

> Will not the large income of your yearly revenue content you, which in all reason cannot chuse but be more advantagious both to you and yours, then all that Rocky Wildernesse wither you are going, to run the hazard of your life? . . . may you not here as pithily practise the two chiefe Duties of a Christian (if Christ give strength), namely Mortification and Sanctification, as in any place of the World? What helps can you have there that you must not carry from hence?

Cotton, too, who had incorporated a restraining voice into his premigration sermons—"Be not unmindful of our Jerusalem at home . . . forget not the wombe that bare you, the breast that gave you sucke"—had gone so far as to excoriate the separatists: "Run we not . . . from the Church because of her blacknesse, but runne to her, and embrace her in her most sad defections." Thomas Hooker pronounced with higher indignation that "all that are fearfull to suffer, [will] flie into the low countreyes"—and shortly thereafter made the flight himself.[18]

Such appeals to hold fast by speakers who could feel their own resolve slipping were, in part, self-directed commands. "Schism," declared William Ames (who did not live quite long enough to weigh the choice of emigration for himself), "is a most grievous sin." Only in severe "oppression," he said, "or persecution [may] a man be compelled to withdraw himself " from the church. And so the question became: what constitutes a sufficiency of oppression? As for Cotton, he knew that even as he lobbied against departure a personal reckoning was drawing near. By 1632 Laud's police had hounded him into hiding, and he had nearly died of a fever that carried away his wife. Already in the mid-twenties there had been a sense of foreboding in his sermons at the approaching need for binding choice. *Christ the Fountaine* proceeds by an almost paralyzing pattern of proposition and retraction: "A thing may move in its place, and yet move from some kind of outward respects; as a Watch, or a Clock, it moves, but it is from the weight that lyes and hangs upon it, and so it is rather a violent motion then a naturall." It was deeply necessary for the Puritan mind to obliterate this distinction, and for every suc-

ceeding generation that claimed the name "Puritan," the Migration
had equally to be understood as "a *Banishment,* rather than a Removal"—an act in which the "violent and the naturall" became one.
The idea of the secessionist self had to be repelled.[19]

2

Though by 1700 Cotton Mather was still trying to protect himself
from the return of that idea—by describing his grandfathers' generation as a "little knot of Christians," "a Flock of Kids," "forced,"
"harried," "driven"—but also willing to fly—into the desert wilderness, such a syntactic fusion between internal wants and external
pressures had already begun to break apart during New England's
first decade. The colony's first half-dozen years had been a variously
arduous test of Winthrop's dream. It was by no means clear how
stable the enterprise was to be; it began, after all, as little more than
a movable encampment—first at Salem, then at Charlestown, then
scattered into the towns of Watertown, Roxbury, Dorchester, Med-
ford, Saugus, and the peninsula of Shawmut, renamed Boston. These
collections of huts, cellars, and a few wooden houses left unpainted
against the weather did not include a brick structure for at least two
years, and the very fact of the main town's existence—its retreat to
a cramped piece of land protectively bordered by swamp, river, and
ocean—suggests that the first grand intentions were failing under the
pressure of necessity. The dispersions from Charlestown, which Dudley and Winthrop lamented, had been responses to "problems of
defense and disease"—a reluctant effort to stop the contagion that
was debilitating the underfed settlers, and the result of a decision that
security against French or Indian attack more likely lay in scattering
than in consolidation. "Many of our people," wrote Dudley, "are sick
of fevers and the scurvy, and . . . thereby unable to carry up our
ordnance . . . we were forced to change counsel, and for our present
shelter to plant dispersedly."[20]

Winthrop's first response to the various threats of dissipation was
a bold one: he extended the franchise. At one of the first meetings
of the General Court (the periodic assembly of freemen stipulated
by the Charter) in late 1630, he seems to have altered the terms of

the Charter, or rather, to have taken advantage of its latitude. As the idea of a consolidated colony made up of literal neighbors became elusive if not fantastic, he moved to draw the populace into greater political interdependence than a small cadre of large investors could enforce. At two successive meetings of the Court he proposed that freemen should have the power to choose Assistants, and that the Assistants in turn would elect the Governor and Deputy Governor from among themselves. This proposal, in itself, was nothing new; it was, indeed, a redundancy since only a handful of freemen (investors in the original Massachusetts Bay Company) had made the journey, and they could be expected to rotate the Assistantships among themselves. But it was then that Winthrop made a truly startling move: he called for "the people's" approval, thus implicitly enlarging the meaning of freemanship to widen the right of franchise in the election of Assistants. By this action, as Edmund Morgan puts it, "the assistants were transformed from an executive council into a legislative assembly," and a "trading company [transformed] into a commonwealth." Although freemanship was subsequently limited to church members, Winthrop's decision was more enlarging than restricting. At the Court's next meeting more than one hundred persons were admitted to freemanship, and "the implied hope was that the whole body of male inhabitants exclusive of servants would eventually be freemen."[21] Even indentured servants were eligible for membership in the church.

These developments did not, to be sure, signify the onset of some democratic fever. They were instead a pragmatic strategy for holding in check the colony's literal dissolution. First calling themselves Justices of the Peace, then Magistrates, the Assistants were "clothed in the mantle of their generally accepted superiority in the communities," and became, in effect, agents of the original central authority within the developing towns. They "empaneled juries . . . tried felonies and misdemeanors, heard civil suits, conducted probate and coroners' hearings, . . . regulated wages and prices, taverns, trade, apprenticeships, and defense, and even determined liability in cases where one man's cattle wandered into another man's corn." Perhaps most important, they "assumed the direction of the impromptu distribution of land within the towns." What Winthrop had reacted to were the first evidences of the overwhelming centrifugal forces that would test the colony's coherence. By 1634 his and the other Assistants' authority was under challenge from the very body of freemen they had created; Winthrop himself was only narrowly elected that year to the land commission (after Cotton's intervention to show "that it was the Lord's order among the Israelites to have all such businesses committed to the elders"). But the first, and in some respects the deepest, upheaval that eluded political adjustment—and thus required the exercise of raw power—was the crisis over "antinomianism."[22]

Anne Hutchinson, the "masterpiece of woman's wit" who became identified as leader of the heretics, was the wife of a prosperous cloth dealer whom Winthrop thought "a man of very mild temper and weak parts and wholly guided by his wife." Whether or not this portrait of henpecked subservience had anything to it, William Hutchinson was soon in possession of a thriving mercer's trade, an interest in Boston's busiest pier, an island in the harbor, and a large farm in Braintree. Struck by such evidences of his commercial amplitude, historians have tended to associate his wife's radical religious opinions with the economic interest-group to which he belonged. To some extent, contemporaries agreed: "They," wrote Thomas Shepard, meaning the faction that would come to be known as the antinomian party, "prefer tradesmen before those whom God has gifted." This sort of indignation, which Winthrop shared, has been described as a symptom of the colony's rupture into two economic factions—one of urban manufacturers and tradesmen with capital to invest, to whom high prices for the goods they made or imported were welcome, and another of the governing gentry (and ministry) who sensed and shared the resulting discontent within the farming communities in which most of the emigrants had hoped to make their new lives. It was in this atmosphere that William Hutchinson's wife began to attract a group of attentive admirers. She seems to have begun by presiding at gatherings in her home—reminiscent of the outlawed "prophesyings" of earlier days in England—mostly of women. At about the same time Thomas Lechford reported that "the confession or speeches made by members to be admitted [to the Boston church] have beene by some held prophesying." For Hutchinson's "double weekly lecture, which she kept [according to Winthrop] under a pretence of repeating Sermons," the constituency ranged from the respectable milliner's wife Mary Dyer to the socially marginal midwife Jane Hawkins, a notorious purveyor of aphrodisiacs. Soon they were joined by a panoply of emphatically substantial men: prosperous merchants, the local inn-keeper, officials of the docks.[23]

The resort of these men to Mrs. Hutchinson has been explained as a flight from the reproaches of clergy and magistrates—whose medieval antipathy to usury and whose insistence on honoring the principle of a "just price" were in conflict with market realities. In contrast to these reactionaries—so the story goes—Mrs. Hutchinson was a charismatic promoter of a more elastic religious style that left room for self-aggrandizement. Eventually her followers constituted not just a faction but a majority of the Boston church. The immediate issue between them and their alarmed opposition within the church and the Court was the continuance as pastor of John Wilson, whom they accused of degrading the gospel promises into a covenant of works whereby men could earn God's favor by demonstrating sanc-tified (that is, socially approved) behavior. In the fall of 1636 Mrs. Hutchinson's newly arrived brother-in-law, John Wheelwright, was put forward as a candidate to join Cotton as second teacher to the church. The insult to Wilson—and the implicit challenge to orthodox clergy throughout the colony—was now open.[24]

And so, in a number of long and tense sessions, the General Court began to bear down on the radical Boston faction. Rancor grew on both sides—inflamed by Wheelwright's fast-day sermon, in which he divided the colony yet more sharply into those who would build their assurance upon the evidence of sanctified works and those who knew the ravishment of the Holy Spirit as an event immeasurable by any standard external to the soul. Contention for power continued for months within the Court, and when Winthrop finally broke the deadlock (Vane, for a time, had replaced him as Governor), a synod of the churches was called, at which Cotton himself, whose under-standing of conversion as an "illuministic and . . . noetic awareness of union with the Holy Ghost" had been the darling doctrine of the offenders, became the center of attention. Such remained the case even into the late stages of the controversy, when Mrs. Hutchinson was brought before the court for trial.[25] The charge against her was sedition.

"Let us state the case and then we may know what to do," Winthrop declared as the Court moved to deal with her conclusively in the fall of 1637, barely six years after the founding of the colony—"She hath said the ministers preached a covenant of works and Mr. Cotton a covenant of grace." This was as stark a discrimination as could possibly have been made, and it came from a woman who claimed to know the difference between "the voice of [her] beloved and the [lesser] voice of Moses." She had, furthermore, ratified such a distinction again and again—not only for herself, but for others, and so often that "it began to be as common here to distinguish between men, by being under a covenant of grace or a covenant of works, as in other countries between Protestants and Papists." At her trial Hutchinson spoke about true and false voices, continually aware that she and her accusers were not only fighting an ideological battle but were *speaking* differently: "I bless the Lord, he has let me see which was the clear ministry and which the wrong," she said, with unacceptable defiance. "How did you know that that was the spirit?" demanded Mr. Nowell (who had stayed at Charlestown when the First Church had moved to Boston), to which she barked back a question of her own: "How did Abraham know that it was God that bid him offer his son, being a breach of the sixth commandment?" Deputy Governor Dudley was eager to answer: "By an immediate voice." "So to me," she replies, "by an immediate revelation." It was then that the murmuring must have risen to a buzz of horror, and Dudley seized his chance: "How! an immediate revelation." After this, Hutchinson's qualifications came too late: "By the voice of his own spirit to my soul. I will give you another scripture, Jeremiah 46:27–28—out of which the Lord showed me what he would do for me and the rest of his servants."[26]

However ill-advised her statements may have been as strategies of self-defense, Anne Hutchinson was saying absolutely nothing at odds with Puritan biblicism (which is perhaps why historians have been hard pressed to identify her heresy, and quick to align it with clear social factions). She was in fact speaking firmly within the Pauline tradition; faithfully applying Cotton's principle that there

is more than the Letter of the Word that is required . . . [for] spiritual grace [to be] revealed to the soul . . . there is need of greater light, than the *word* of it self is able to give; for it is not all the *promises* in Scripture, that have at any time wrought any gracious change in any soul, or are able to beget the *faith* of Gods elect: true it is indeed, whether the Father, Son, or Spirit reveal any thing, it is *in* and *according* to the *word*; but without the work of the Spirit there is no faith begotten by any promise: the word of God, and all his works, may beget you some knowledge, if you be not mistaken in them, but to beget the *faith* of Gods elect, that may be able to stand against all the powers of darkness, and to crush all the temptations of that wicked one, it is not all the *works* of God, nor all the *word* of God, of it self, that is able to beget such *faith*: if there be any, it is but an historical faith, a dead faith that is not able to bring the soul nearer to God.[27]

Some scholars have suggested that Hutchinson's heresy was in essence to subvert the authority of the Bible—which was, indeed, one of the charges leveled at her: "By advancing the Spirit, and revelation by the Spirit [she] destroy[ed] or weaken[ed] the revelation of the Scriptures." Yet the fact is that she produced an array of biblical texts— from Hebrews, Jeremiah, Isaiah, Daniel—in support of her discrimination between the true ministry and the false. To her accusers what was always most audible in her speech was not some antiscriptural impudence (she sometimes embarrassed them by correcting their quotations, usually citing the Geneva translation, which she preferred for its Christocentric marginal glosses) but her blunt charge that New England was slipping into spiritual death. Her emphasis on the spirit of discernment over the prescriptive content of scripture did, to be sure, carry an implicit challenge to the ministry as authorized interpreters for the Puritan community. But the truly astonishing thing at her trial was finally not her claim of having heard an "immediate voice." It was, instead, the ministers' furious reaction. Hutchinson might have pointed out, since she apparently knew Hooker's sermon on the "danger of desertion," that he had spoken in much the same way not long before—"What if I should tell you what God told me yesternight that he would destroy England and lay it waste?" She knew, in other words, that an idea was being lost in New England: the idea of a spirit that works within scriptural or sermonic form, but which nevertheless has precedence and superiority over the agents of its delivery. In this attenuated state, scripture could still be a source of religious knowledge and a repository of ethical principles, and so it remained. But once its partialness without the spirit had been forgotten—once, in Emerson's phrase, "men have come to speak of the revelation as somewhat long ago given and done"—then it could no longer be the occasion, furnished by the living God, for a felt experience inspiring worship. To speak of the immediacy of God's voice in New England was, Anne Hutchinson discovered, to blas-

pheme. To feel intimacy rather than obeisance toward Him had become an offense and the distinction had become suddenly stark:
"first you [must] conceive and understand a thing," insisted her opponents, "secondly, you will and choose it."[28] For Anne Hutchinson,
the acts of understanding, volition, and desire remained indistinguishable in their divinely effected fusion.

In Hutchinson's trial we are thus able to glimpse the moment at
which the idea of a suprarational spirit was beginning to be beaten
down in New England. Cotton had attempted to preserve such an
idea from the pressure of experience, and it did survive here and
there. One place was in the mind of Anne Bradstreet:

> The spring is a lively emblem of the resurrection: after a long winter
> we see the leafless trees and dry stocks (at the approach of the sun) to
> resume their former vigor and beauty in a more ample manner than
> what they lost in the autumn; so shall it be at that great day after a long
> vacation, when the Sun of righteousness shall appear; those dry bones
> shall arise in far more glory than that which they lost at their creation,
> and in this transcends the spring that their leaf shall never fail nor their
> sap decline.[29]

There is much more here than conventional Christian punning. This
is the contemplation of the world by a perception *created,* but not
limited by the apprehension of scripture; the Lord's promise through
Ezekiel (37:4), "Behold, I will cause breath to enter into you, and
you shall live," has an immediacy for Bradstreet that is quite as visceral
as the warmth of a New England thaw. There is no division here
between text and world. The divine books of scripture and nature
(registered through a mind also steeped in the classics) are utterly
fused in Bradstreet's imagination. Bradstreet was no less enraptured
by her discovery of correspondence between nature and spirit than
was Jonathan Edwards a century later in discovering that "the whole
outward creation, which is but the shadows of His being, is so made
as to represent spiritual things." She was able to accommodate an
epic simile—"after a long winter we see the leafless trees . . . so shall
it be at that great day"—to her felt belief in Christian eschatology:
"the Sun of righteousness shall appear." Her confident "we," denoting
the community of regenerate perceivers, functions here to hold the
vision together.[30]

But what from Anne Bradstreet was a moment of unified devotion
was from Anne Hutchinson a public rebuke—a challenge to her

opponents to produce some experience of equivalent value. One imagines the punitive ministers lowering their eyes in avoidance of what Henry James called (in reference to a later New England dissident, Margaret Fuller) "the glare of her understanding." In disciplining Anne Hutchinson, they declined her challenge. She had, therefore, to be muted, or, in Winthrop's well-chosen word, "reduced": "we have thought good to send for you to understand how things are, that if you be in an erroneous way we may reduce you that so you may become a profitable member here among us." The Latin force of *reducere* (as of *errare*) remains primary here—Hutchinson has wandered from and must be led back to the truth—but beneath its root meaning one feels the pressure of the modern sense of the word: to lower, to diminish, to cut down. In reducing Anne Hutchinson from her spiritual height, the Puritan community was repudiating not so much an external threat as an uprising part of itself. It was not incidental, as we shall see, that that part was female.[31]

To identify the antinomian dissent as the mischievous work of an intemperate woman whose "tongue wagged incautiously" is as reductionist as to judge it a veneer for certain men's greed. Yet the facts are that it began among women (in a culture where the "good wife earned the dignity of anonymity"), and that it took hold among Boston's men of means. If it was, in one scholar's phrase, "an authentic locus of Puritan fragmentation," its historical meaning has eluded our full understanding. This is in part because in one of its dimensions it was the culmination of a long debate within Puritanism over nothing more or less than religious style—an issue from which the modern observer has trouble sensing the seventeenth-century heat. Style seems to us too slight a matter to have torn a community apart. Yet the conservative response to Puritanism itself had always prominently featured a stylistic critique. To the ears of their enemies, the Puritan clergy, unawed in the hushed caverns of the English church, had committed an acoustic sin: they had broken the reverent silence of sacramental worship with the sound of the unfettered human voice sounding God's praise. "Some called [us] raylers, and worse," said John Knox in proud understatement already in the 1550s. This was an ironic preview of how Hutchinson would be described: as leader of a mob of "ignorant and unlettered Men and Women [who sought] praise for their able Tongue."[32] Through the 1630s the value of religious decorum continued to be invoked by the Anglican party of "moderation"—a subject on which the Puritan leadership made searing comment: "Oft we see a false spirit in those that call for moderation, it is but to carry their owne projects with greater strength, and if they prove of the prevailing hand, they will hardly shew that moderation to others, they now call for from others." As if in confirmation of this remark, Archbishop Laud's way of insulting Thomas Shepard was to call him "prating coxcomb" to his face—a phrase in which the participle was as nasty as the noun. The virtue of decorum was of course never entirely relinquished by the Puritans themselves, who sometimes turned it against the ecclesiastical establishment. They likened prescribed prayer to cacophony: "It is a Babilonion confusion," wrote William Bradshaw, "for the Pastor to say one peece of a prayer & the people with mingled voices to say another," as if these were the "vaine repetitions [of] the Heathens, which thinke to be heard for their much babbling." In the end each side was claiming that it was the other that sounded barbarous; each claimed to be making the holier noise. And one way of expressing the Puritans' bewilderment in New England is to say that they found themselves becoming there the party of "moderation."[33]

Some among them objected: "Are the people and ways of God under reproach?" asked John Davenport, resisting the prestige of decorum: "Ah! but they are called fools and fanaticks? *Ans.* When was it otherwise? . . . *Augustine* describes the scoffs and frumps of luke-warm professors against the zeale of those that were *fervent in spirit* . . . [just as] the present temptation of this time . . . is the reproachful titles put upon the people of God, whom prophane men call *Phanaticks*." Samuel Gorton, who was banished to Rhode Island not long after Hutchinson, agreed: "Whereas you charge me with *passion*," he wrote to Nathaniel Morton, "I know not your meaning in that word, it is an ambiguous phrase, but through god's goodnesse I know the passion of Christ, and the apostles saying, that he fulfills the rest of his passion in his flesh, and his being in a multitude of passions. And I know that Elijah was a man of passion yet he was strong in prayer."[34]

Despite such qualifications as Bradshaw's, and long before Gorton's self-defense and Davenport's appeal to the maligned history of God's fervent chosen on behalf of present "phanaticks," the Puritan ministry had reached agreement that their major task was to awaken a sleeping people. This remained the first commitment of those ministers who came to the New World. There is very little suggestion in the early sermons (or in the conversion narratives or letters home) that the New England ministers judged their transplanted flock to have been sufficiently awakened before or by their ocean voyage: "It is not sin," preached Thomas Shepard in Massachusetts in 1636, "but a privy peace with sin, and a secret quietness in sin, which overthrows Christ's kingdom." As long as Shepard and others believed that complacence remained New England's basic spiritual affliction ("you have the pillow of peace to lie on"), the pressing need would remain a language efficacious for awakening. What they discovered (a discovery best reflected in the early sermons of Shepard's *Parable of the Ten Virgins*) is that there were risks in both imprecation and stimulation; that to rouse a wilderness people in a country without "pinching persecutions," a minister had not only to address the understanding but also to appeal to the sensory appetite: "If the Lord would but open your eyes to see him, this would win your heart . . . to Christ, whose dominion is from sea to sea, from sun to sun, who sets up and pulls down kings like counters, [who] is set down on the right hand of God on high, clothed with endless glory." There is a wonderful irony here in Shepard's proximity not to Perkins or Ames or Preston but to Bishop Hooker—who had long before pointed out that "men are edified . . . [by] sundry sensible means . . . especially the means [that appeal to] the eye." In their willed absence from stained glass and pipe organs, Shepard and his colleagues inevitably had recourse in the New World to what may be called the language of ceremony (which would be brought to its height later in the century by the poet-preacher Edward Taylor). Presenting Christ as God's vice-gerent clothed in light, Shepard typically builds to a pitch of sensory excitement by describing the relation between man and God in highly erotic terms, with the posture of the saint usually that of a woman: "Taste the all-sufficiency of the love of Christ. A woman that is not content with her husband's love, she will not love him as it is fit . . . Do but sit down and think what this is: if once he loves thee, whatever he can he will do for thee; he will order all thy life . . . so as thou shalt say his denials are better than his gifts, his blows better than smiles, his withdrawings better than his presence . . . O, taste this!"[35]

Shepard's program in the early New England years was not so much a disciplined preparation of the soul or a sequential training of the rational faculties as it was an anticipatory relaxation induced by highly sensual, even sexual language that went well beyond the metaphors of betrothal and marriage as conventionally applied to the union of the soul with Christ. In his memoir Shepard thanked God for giving him "the heart to receive Christ with a naked hand, even naked Christ." In the later commentary on the *Ten Virgins* he distinguishes between the five wise and five foolish sisters by invoking an *a priori* knowledge of the bridegroom for the elect, who are, in effect, sexually experienced before their initiation. Still virgin, they have nevertheless felt, as if by dreaming it, the intromission of Christ— and, most important, the ministers knew that they themselves were complicit in fostering such a feeling. This was a good deal more than the brokering "function of the ministers to serve as the 'friends' of the bridegroom . . . to arrange the match." "Consider he makes love to thee," says Shepard, reaching back to Isaiah for his imagery, ". . . it is constant and continual; there is not a moment, thou dost not so oft breathe, as thou mayst see and taste [his] love."[36]

The more they risked such orgiastic language in the service of awakening, the more the New England ministers were subject to unwelcome warning from their English critics: "Errour," they were reminded with increasing frequency, "is very fruitfull and will spread apace." Here is Winthrop's estimate (made for an English audience) of the essence of Hutchinson's heresy; the striking thing is that it is equally apt as a description of Shepard's early New England preaching:

> They would lift up themselves, so also their Opinions, by guilding them over with specious termes of Free Grace, glorious light, Gospel truths, as holding forth naked Christ: and this tooke much with simple honest hearts that loved Christ, especially with new converts, who were lately in bondage under sinne and wrath, and had newly tasted the sweetnesse of Free Grace; being now in their first love to Christ, they were exceeding glad to imbrace any thing, that might further advance Christ and Free Grace; and so drank them in readily.

Winthrop expressed "wonder how [the heretical opinions of Anne Hutchinson] should spread so fast and suddenly amongst a people so religious and well taught," and it is not difficult to see why those who had worked so long to make hard hearts supple were horrified by the extent of their success, particularly when the women of the Bay began to seem ravished by their own homiletics.[37]

There is a clue here to one of the more mysterious passages in the literature of the first generation—John Cotton's report that Mrs. Hutchinson "disesteem[ed] generally the elders of the churches (though of them she esteemed best of Mr. Shepard)." Most historians have tended to agree with Perry Miller that Shepard was among "Mistress Hutchinson's most vindictive persecutors." And so he was. But Anne Hutchinson knew as well that Shepard's zeal to "reduce" her had its roots in a felt knowledge of what she represented. "I heard of Grindleton," Shepard reported about his youth in England, "and I did question whether that glorious estate of perfection might not be the truth and whether old Mr. Rogers' *Seven Treatises* and *The Practice of Christianity* [tracts that emphasized self-discipline in a regimen of trained faith], the book which did first work upon my heart, whether these men were not all legal men and their books so . . ." One might risk a displaced platitude here and say that Shepard confirms the dictum that there is no anti-antinomian like an ex-antinomian. "I account it no small mercy to myself," he confessed in a phrase that suggests more temptation than revulsion, "that the Lord kept me from [her] contagion." And, indeed, we find him in the late thirties coming again to terms with his past affinity for those he now despised: "I am weary with speaking," he announces in the midst of his series on the *Ten Virgins,* turning away from "those doctrines which in show lift up grace," and declares his "desire rather to go aside and mourn." His fatigue was not, as the subsequent flood of sermons confirms, with speaking itself, but with the particular style—the Cottonesque style—that he had helped bring into the New World: "If ministers do preach any things which are not about the person of Christ, or the excellency of a Christian in Christ, or the emptiness of the creature to prepare for Christ, (which are, indeed, of great use,) and press to any work or service of Christ, they are legal preachers, and bring people under a covenant of works."[38]

There was nothing in these words with which Mrs. Hutchinson disagreed; yet Shepard was soon asking, "what meaneth these . . . golden dreams of grace. Who would think that ever any should so fall by a simple woman?" New Englanders, it was turning out, were less afflicted by complacence than by anxiety; they were a people locked in fear, which on the one hand was deepened rather than relieved by the preparationists' relentless demand for hewing and hammering the corrupt self, and which, on the other, created conditions for spiritist hysteria. There was an appetite in New England, pent up and building even as most continued to believe that "that ministry which doth not ordinarily humble the soule, and breake the heart for sinne, doth not convert." And so some, like Shepard, chose to speak differently. When he did employ the language that Hutchinson approved, he sounded very like such "fanatics" as Gorton: "He who takes upon him to be an interpreter of the word of God and brings not eternity into the thing or matter whereof he speakes, that man is a false prophet or interpeter of the word of God, and hides and covers Christ that he appeares not in the Church."[39]

As we approach the moment of Anne Hutchinson's expulsion for her own celebration of Christ's nakedness, Shepard seems to be groping toward an explanation for why God has led a whole people into a panic of doubt: "It was the speech of one to me," he says, that "next to the donation of Christ [there is] no mercy like this, to deny assurance long—and why? for if the Lord had not, I should have given way to a loose heart and life." This kind of anecdotal report (Shepard is here presenting the case for the fruitful connection of spiritual doubt to one's chance for election) works together with dramatic dialogue to reinforce the point that anxiety itself can be a sign of grace:

> Objection. But many a Christian that retires hither [to New England] hath no peace; and so have I done, yet find none.
> Answer. . . .you have faith, but you imprison your faith, you put out the eyes and shackle the feet of faith; for faith will conquer and trimph over all sins and fears of the world, if at liberty . . .
> Obj. But he [God] is angry with you.
> Ans. If he be angry for my departure from him, I will not provoke him more by staying here; who knows but he may repent?
> Obj. But you can not go to him with all your heart.
> Ans. True; yet I'll look to him to draw me.
> Obj. But you feel nothing.
> Ans. Yet I will wait.[40]

One hears in this almost Beckettian exchange the voice of a newly chastened minister as he comes to realize that the demands of preparation have reduced at least some New Englanders to the condition of paralyzed dread, and thereby authorized any form of solace. The sinner's will has, sure enough, been broken; but instead of leaving him in a state of pliancy, it has made him a terrified seeker—ripe for seduction by those who offer, in Winthrop's words, "a faire and easie way to Heaven." The preparationists (to whom Shepard was less securely allied than has often been assumed) had done their job too well: "What art thou but a sad spectacle," he asked in his severest voice, "hung up in thy chains in this world, for angels in heaven to see and tremble at, and for devils, sins, and eternal sorrows, like fowls of heaven, to prey upon?" The consequence of such preaching was not a willed self-discipline under the minister's management, but a desperate expectancy for rescue. "O how did men and women, young and old, beg for Christ in those days," remembered Roger Clap. "And it was not in vain."[41]

Of all New England's ministers, it was certainly Cotton who had most encouraged such an expectancy by broadening the terms in which it could be recognized as authentic:

> You have heard of many that have attended to Revelations, that have been deceived. It is true; for the devil himself will transform himself into an Angel of light: he will be foisting in delusions, yea, many times when the soul waiteth for the revelation of God's mercy, the Devil will be apt to foist in such revelations, from whence many delusions may grow. But yet on the other side, let not men be afraid, and say that we have no *revelation* but the *word;* for I do believe, and dare confidently affirme, that if there were no revelation but the word, there would be no spiritual grace revealed to the soul.[42]

Cotton was insisting (as Edwards was to do a century later at the height of the Great Awakening) that the liberty of God to work wonders in the soul was being abridged by those whose doubt about some kinds of religious excitement was becoming a constitutional skepticism about all.

The antinomian outburst touched the tenderest nerve in New England's leaders because it spoke to their sense of their own spiritual diminution. If the merchants endorsed it, it was not because they calculated its value as a doctrine that sanctioned the making of unseemly profits, but because it helped to alleviate their growing anxiety as they stood accused of replicating the carnivorous world from which New Englanders had fled. The moral quandaries of Old Boston were back with a vengeance. "Something keeps on not happening; I shrink" is the phrase that John Berryman astutely assigns to Anne Bradstreet, who, though her father and husband sat in unappeasable judgment on Anne Hutchinson, reported that she had fallen "into a lingering sickness like a consumption together with a lameness" after her arrival in the New World, and was "after . . . perplexed that I have not found that constant joy in my pilgrimage and refreshing which I supposed most of the servants of God have . . ." The ministers (and many among the laity) knew that the antinomian outburst was neither unprecedented nor inexplicable, that it grew out of a long foreground of spiritual disappointment—"eyes dim, hearts hard, consciences asleep, ears deaf, breath gone, life lost, God departed"—and their awareness of this intractable fact played a part in the ferocity of their reaction. New England had been doubly embarrassed; on the one hand the events of 1636–1638 seemed to confirm the oldest of charges against them, that *all* Puritans were really antinomians at heart. (Oliver Ormerod, writing twenty years before the Migration, had compared the Puritans of his day to "certain Hereticks called *Begnardini,* who held, that *a spirituall man is not subject to humaine obedience.* Now let it therefore be judged with indifferencie, whether you Puritanes have not some touch of this Heresie, who will not submit your neckes and soules to the yoake of humane obedience in things indifferent.") By 1636 Richard Hooker's prophecy that the Puritans' contempt for reason would eventually turn them all into fanatics appeared on the verge of wide adoption. Here is Zechariah Symmes, minister of Charlestown, who had crossed with the Hutchinsons in the *Griffin* and sensed in them "a secret opposition to things delivered":

> I am much greved to hear that soe many in this Congregation should stand up and declare themselves unwillinge that Mrs. Hutchison should be proceded agaynst for such dayngerous Errors. I fear that if by any means this shold be carried over into England, that in New England and in such a Congregation thear was soe much spoken and soe many Questions made about *soe playne an Article of our fayth as the Resurrection is,* it will be one of the greatest Dishonors to Jesus Christ and of Reproach to thease Churches that hath bine done since we came heather.

The "antinomian" crisis was thus simultaneously a danger and an opportunity for New England to clear itself of the charge that "Puritan" and fanatic were synonymous—a process of self-exoneration that would continue through the century. Berryman establishes a causal relation between his verses: "Arminians, and the King bore against us; / Of an inward light we hear with horror."[43]

With horror transmuted into satisfaction, Winthrop reported in 1639 the hanging of one Dorothy Talbye, who had been "possessed with Satan [until] he persuaded her (by his delusions, which she listened to as revelations from God) to break the neck of her own child, that she might free it from future misery." This was only a few months after he had taken equally careful note of the stillbirth to Mary Dyer of a deformed "woman child" (the news of which he charged Cotton with trying to suppress) with "a face but no head, and the ears stood upon the shoulders and were like an ape's . . . [and] over the eyes four horns." Punitive providences rained down upon the malefactors: Anne Hutchinson herself "brought forth not one, (as Mistris Dier did) but . . . 30. monstrous births or thereabouts, at once," an event which has been given a name by modern medical commentators—a "hydatidiform mole"—and offered as evidence that "Mrs. Hutchinson's behavior during this crucial period can be explained largely in terms of menopausal symptoms." For Winthrop these were sensible judgments. For the modern mind they are biological malfunctions. The two explanations have little in common except the conviction that Mrs. Hutchinson's behavior was pathological. On that point they are cordially agreed.[44]

Years later Shepard was writing that those who were banished have had "some strange hand of providence against them; either delivering them up to vile lusts and sins, or to confusion amongst themselves, or to some sudden and terrible deaths, for their obstinacy against the light." By the early fifties, the Baptists' proposition *"that every Believer ought to improve his talent, both in and out of the congregation,"* could still be instantly refuted by conjuring up the memory of wicked Anne: "May not a gifted believing sister, upon whom as a hand-maid a gift is powred out . . . preach and adminster the seales in a Church? . . . Then what become[s] of the rules, *Let your women keep silence in the churches,* I Cor. 14, 34. *I suffer not a woman to teach,* I Tim. 2, 13." Edward Johnson elaborated on Winthrop's reports with righteous glee: "the Lord had poynted directly to . . . the sinne [of the antinomian women] by a very fearfull Monster, that [one] of these women brought forth, they striving to bury it in oblivion, but the Lord brought it to light, setting forth the view of their monstrous Errors in this prodigious birth." Twenty-five years later Thomas Shepard's son asks whether God "hath not . . . blessed the coercive power of the civil magistrate [as in] . . . the case of the heresy of the familists, which brake out of old among us."[45]

Despite this range of celebrations, the immediate resolution of the crisis left New Englanders feeling they had paid a very high price for their victory. It was, they knew, a victory dependent on coercive power, not a reclamation of lost spiritual cohesion. "Mrs. Hutchinson's Repentance," as Dudley said, "is in a paper . . . [but] *not in her Countenance,* none can see it thear I thinke." Cotton, whom Winthrop now thought of as her "stalking horse," tried to put the best face on things by insisting that "all the strife amongst us was about magnifying the grace of God; one party seeking to advance the grace of God within us [justification], and the other to advance the grace of God towards us [sanctification]." He tried to protect Mrs. Hutchinson from her own self-incriminations: "I am in the hands of the eternall Jehovah my Saviour," she claimed,

> I am at his appointment. The bounds of my habitation are cast in Heaven, no further doe I esteeme of any mortall man, then creatures in his hand, I feare none but the great Jehovah, which hath foretold me of these things, and I doe verily believe that he will deliver me out of your hands, therefore take heed how you proceed against me; for I know that for this you goe about to doe to me, God will ruine you and your posterity, and this whole State.

To this scandalous impudence Cotton offered mitigation, distinguishing between the "satanicall" fantasy of escape by supernatural or magical means, and the scriptural faith that God can miraculously heal all breaches and save both prosecutors and prosecuted from the hell of spiritual blindness. In the end she would not recant her charges or her claims, and Cotton was compelled to officiate at her excommunication. He stood at last with her accusers; but after passing sentence, he very nearly reversed himself by voting with his feet.[46]

He gives us a glimpse of his newly somber mood in his great sermons on Ecclesiastes, preached in the forties: "Now contrary things being divided one against another, make the whole body of short continuance, one wasting another, till all faile. Mat. 12:25. Heat against cold, and moysture against drinesse, work continually one against another, till all be consumed." One expelled "antinomian," writing much later, agreed: "Your understanding reacheth not," he told those of his banishers who were still alive, "the things wherin God excerciseth his people." What was once the mark of sainthood—the capacity to live with unresolved contradiction—had been obscured. New England had once been the place where piety and discipline were to be held in holy equilibrium; by the second decade, its chief spiritual spokesman was making valediction to the possibility of contraries existing in transcendent balance—to metaphor itself. This is the relinquishing experience that American writers have chronicled in one way or another ever since; and it is expressed as well as anywhere in Berryman's *Homage to Mistress Bradstreet*:

> Now Mistress Hutchinson rings forth a call—
> should she? many creep out at a broken wall—
> affirming the Holy Ghost
> dwells in one justified. Factioning passion blinds
> all to her good, all—can she be exiled?
> Bitter sister, victim! I miss you.
> —I miss you, Anne,
> day or night weak as a child,
> tender & empty, doomed, quick to no tryst.
> —I hear you. Be kind, you who leaguer
> my image in the mist.
> —Be kind you, to one unchained eager far & wild[47]

Berryman's point has great historical fidelity. Puritanism was a movement that arose out of a sense that the available language of official religion could not give adequate expression to the complexity of experience. That expression, in its Puritan revision, had always prominently included the voices of women—who were now saying that New England, like Old, had turned to prescription and rote. Anne Hutchinson, even as she was banished, was beginning to be missed.

Marke the severe command that the Apostle gives his Scholar Timothy, *I charge thee before God, and the Lord Jesus Christ, who shall judge the quick and the dead, preach the word, be instant in season, out of season, reprove, rebuke,* (as if he had said) the stubborne hearts of men neede this specially *reproving,* and therefore doing this, is the maine thing that God requires, and the maine end for which the Word serves. *Sharp reproofes makes sound Christians.* He that heales overly, hurts more than he heales; Are there not many lusts raigning in the hearts of men and women? Let us therefore throw away this shamefull hiding, and make our Ministery knowne to the soules of those to whom we speake.   Thomas Hooker, ca. 1628

[Satan] suggests any word that may terrifie them, and presents to their memory and thoughts former sins, to amaze them . . . He presents . . . unto them . . . the comforts of God, in a diminishing glasse . . . and . . . their sins in a multiplying glasse.   John Davenport, ca. 1661

5 *The Founders Divide*

Anne Hutchinson was missed, Winthrop implied with almost obtuse bitterness, because "most of her new tenents tend to slothfulnesse, and quench all indeavour," by which he meant that she pandered to the spiritually lazy, who believed that "Christ was all, did all, and that the soule remained a dead Organ." Winthrop did not have quite the ministers' defensiveness, but he associated the antinomians' prostration before God with a proportionate haughtiness toward human authority, including, specifically, his own: "Upon the election of the new governour [Winthrop], the serjeants, who had attended the old governor [Vane] to the court, (being all Boston men, where the new governor also dwelt,) laid down their halberds and went home; and whereas they had been wont to attend the former governor to and from the meetings on the Lord's days, they gave over now, so as the new governor was fain to use his own servants to carry two halberds before him; whereas the former governor had never less than four." Wihthrop's statement about "indeavour" appears even more striking if we bear in mind that he, as a Calvinist, was expected to believe that man is wholly passive in the reception of grace. This contradiction did not give him pause, nor did he make any conscious connection between the kind of preachers New Englanders had brought with them (preachers who believed salvation to be not only a "work" but

a work of "unconceiveable difficulty") and the sort of behavior he
observed in the spring and summer of 1637:

> A man of Weymouth (but not of the church there) fell into some trouble
> of mind, and in the night cried out, "Art thou come, Lord Jesus?" and
> with that leaped out of his bed in his shirt, and, breaking from his wife,
> leaped out at high window into the snow, and ran about seven miles
> off, and being traced in the snow, was found dead next morning. They
> might perceive, that he had kneeled down to prayer in divers places.

Winthrop reports this event in the midst of, but not as a digression
from, his account of the antinomian troubles. A more famous incident
follows a little later in his Journal:

> A woman of Boston congregation, having been in much trouble of mind
> about her spiritual estate, at length grew into utter desperation, and
> could not endure to hear of any comfort, etc., so as one day she took
> her little infant and threw it into a well, and then came into the house
> and said, now she was sure she should be damned, for she had drowned
> her child . . . [1]

Somewhere Winthrop, like Shepard, knew that a spreading desperation was creating conditions for "antinomian" release. Complaining that Anne Hutchinson saw "the Spirit act[ing] most in the Saints,
when they indeavour least," he conflated their spiritual passivity with
civic irresponsibility. Noting that Cotton had preached from Chronicles and Numbers on the obligation of rulers to consult with ministers
"upon occasion of any war to be undertaken," he began to associate
the antinomian disruption less with spiritual need than with the failure
of the citizenry to turn out for the Pequot War:

> whereas before . . . there was a peaceable and comely order in all affaires
> in the Churches, and civill state, &c. now . . . All things are turned
> upside down among us . . . it spreads into the families, and sets divisions
> between husband and wife, and other relations there, till the weaker
> give place to the stronger, otherwise it turns to open contention: it is
> come also into Civill and publike affaires, and hath bred great disturb-
> ance there, as appeared in the late expedition against the Pequeds; for
> whereas in former expeditions the Towne of *Boston* was as forward as
> any others to send of their choyce members, and a greater number then
> other Townes in the time of the former Governour [Vane]; now in this
> last service they sent not a member . . .[2]

Still others among Hutchinson's critics echoed with more sneer than
sympathy Winthrop's accusation that she preyed on the hopes of the

weak: "Come along with me, sayes one [of her followers in Johnson's *Wonder-Working Providence*], i'le bring you to a Woman that Preaches better Gospell then any of your black-coates that have been at the Ninneversity, a Woman of another kinde of spirit, who hath had many Revelations of things to come . . ."[3] If, as a variety of historians beginning with Winthrop have argued, Anne Hutchinson did pose a manifold threat to the ecclesiastical, sexual, political, and even economic stability of New England, then she was surely challenging the *idea* of order as much as its social manifestations. Her notion of conversion, or at least what can be sensed of it from her few preserved words, had nothing to do with the regulation of the self, and everything to do with the sheer miracle of invasion by the spirit.

We venture, perhaps, into untestable speculation by pursuing further the question of why this threat to "order" seemed so often associated with women, and why it seemed suddenly so dangerous that women had found a theological voice: "You have stept out of your place," declared Hugh Peter at Hutchinson's trial, *"you have {acted} rather like a Husband than a Wife and a preacher than a Hearer; and a Magistrate than a Subject."* Looking back on these years of gender-confusion, Samuel Gorton was to recall in puzzlement the "threatning of a widow one Ellin Aldridge" by the elders of the Plymouth Church, "whom they said they would send out of the Collony as a vacabond . . . when as nothing was laid to her charge, only it was whispered privatly that she had smiled in [the] congregation." In the years following the antinomian upheaval, when charges were still being made openly (in this case by a female churchmember) that "Mrs. Hutchinson neyther deserved the Censure which was putt upon her in the Church, nor in the Commonwealth," yet further expulsions of women were triggered by such infractions as "disturbing the Congregation by her disorderly singing . . . and refusing to hear the counsel of Christ." Winthrop had early on noted with dismay that the antinomians "commonly laboured . . . first upon women, [who are] more flexible, tender, and ready to yeeld [and] . . . if they met with Christians that were full of doubts . . . they would tell them, they had never taken a right course of comfort." The wrong course, no doubt, had been the course of preparationist self-discipline, for which an imagery of wrestling, self-bruising, horse-taming, and the like had become standard pulpit fare. It has been suggested by one student of the phenomenon that "Hutchinson and her associates [were asking] that the priesthood of all believers be body-blind." Their language, however, was not so much sexually neutral as emphatically evocative of experiences unique to women. We should attend in this regard to the insight of Patricia Caldwell, who points out that some English Puritans consistently employed an imagery of childbirth to describe "the culmination of [their] movement away from (Old Testament) father, husband, and all the other elements of . . . ordinary life before 'birth,' " and that the frequency of this alternative metaphor (along with the sense of restored self it expressed) slackened with the migration. Anne Hutchinson, in other words, may have been stepping into a cultural breach, speaking on behalf of those—not just women— who inclined in their spiritual lives to a more "feminine" apprehension of grace than that which the ministry expressed.[4]

As Cotton acknowledged in his moving address to the "Sisters of our owne Congregation" during Hutchinson's church trial, she had been a much valued advisor, especially to women in distress: "you have . . . receaved much good from the Conference of this our Sister and by your Converse with her: and from her . . . you have receaved helpes in your spirituall Estates, and have bine brought from Restinge upon any Duties or Workes of Righteousnes of your owne." Her fame, and later her notoriety, had everything to do with her position as counselor to women, many of whom must have felt with her that they had been transported into a place of "meanness" and discouragement. Her daily activity centered on childbirth and childrearing; her talk and counsel had necessarily to deal with the fears of mothers for their children—born, expected, and hoped for.[5]

One such woman was Anne Bradstreet, who recalled in a letter to her children the dual sorrow of her own first months in the New World: "It pleased God to keep me a long time without a child, which was a great grief to me and cost me many prayers and tears before I obtained one, and after him, gave me many more of whom I now take the care, that as I have brought you into the world, and with great pains, weakness, cares, and fears brought you to this, I now travail in birth again of you till Christ be formed in you." In this remarkable sentence we see again how Bradstreet, like Hutchinson, fused idea and felt experience, describing her children (sons as well as daughters) as seeded vessels in need of nurture, not unruly beings in need of control. There is nothing here of conversion as a process of bodily elimination, nothing of the question "how shall we shake off Selfe," which the preparationists so liked to pose. When Hooker, for instance, turns to the women in his congregation, he tends to address them sternly—"look as it is with a woman's conception, those birthes that are hasty, the children are either still borne, or the woman most commonly dies"—and he uses sexual tropes that are more brutal than evocative of mutuality: "the soule now submits itselfe, and saith, Lord, doe what thou wilt." The volatility of women was nothing new to Hooker; he had spent months as spiritual advisor in the Surrey manor house of a distracted gentlewoman who was alternately in transport and sorrow, frequently suicidal, and convinced that her psychic and physical pain were being exacted by God as penance for her having sinned against the Holy Ghost. Hooker's prescription seems to have been essentially that she should take hold of herself and diminish her expectations. Her problem, he thought, had been an overheated desire for spiritual satisfaction, resulting in inevitable disappointment—"I never found it, I feel no such thing"—and then to despair.[6]

Bradstreet's metaphors, by contrast, are much closer to Cotton's, who had himself "lived with [his first wife], *childlesse* for eighteen years," and who, even when he spoke of the strain of conversion, was likely to use the language of labor and fruitfulness rather than that of self-combat: "Labour daily to see what need you have of the blood of Christ . . . set faith awork . . . and you will be more fruitfull in your age then ever heretofore." There was in Cotton's discourse something of special sustenance for women:

> Women, if they were not Mothers, would not take such homely offices up, as to cleanse their Children from their filth; why if God were not of the like affection to us, hee would not cleanse us from our filthiness, wee count it an homely office, to sweep Sincks, and scum pots, &c. this is Gods office, if hee did not sweep the Sinck, and scum off the scum of our hearts, it would never bee done; and therefore it shews the tender affection of God towards us, in that hee is willing to take such an office upon him, to cleanse us from our filthiness, hee powres clean water upon us; all other means will do no good without him; it is with us as it is with young Infants that would lye in their defilements, if their Mothers did not make them clean, and so would wee even wallow in the defilements of sin, if God did not cleanse us, therefore admire Gods love and mercy toward us.[7]

This is as close as Cotton comes to the language of sin as indelible stain, and even here he encloses it within an envelope of maternal analogy. The idea of grace as infusion was always corollary for Cotton to the idea of sin as *absence;* God as Father introduces the spirit into an empty self: "Let his abundant graces fill our empty soules." This punitive God is nurturing mother too. "The Ambassadors of so gentle a Saviour," Richard Sibbes had taught, "should not be over masterly." Preachers who honored that tradition were less corrective authorities than "nursing fathers" who should "be full as the honey-combe dropping out of it selfe, [and should] preach sweet doctrine as honey, and wholesome as milk, for the nourishment of Christs lambes." Even Cotton's eschatology builds on the vocabulary of "deliverance" and "appointed time" as he applies his account of divine insemination to the *Powring out of the Seven Vials:* "The Lord will send forth . . . a bright & cleare knowledge of his Christ."[8]

These were much the same convictions that Bradstreet taught her children: "And could I have been in heaven without the love of God, it would have been a hell to me, for in truth it is the absence and presence of God that makes heaven or hell." This was, in its purest form, the Augustinian language of privative evil—a language shared by the two Annes, who differed more in the mode of their address than in their convictions. (It should be noted that Bradstreet felt the weight of some of the same dismissals that Hutchinson incurred: "I am obnoxious to each carping tongue / Who says my hand a needle better fits, / A Poets pen all scorn I should thus wrong, / For such despite they cast on Female wits"). Perhaps Anne Hutchinson's brother-in-law, John Wheelwright, summed it up best when he declared in his fast-day sermon that some people "do principally and above all seeke for blessings to be procured and evills removed, and this is that, they are first caryed unto, this is not the mayne matter, the mayne matter is the absence of the Lord." Here was the core of the antinomians' dissent—their insistence that there was a very large difference between noting the presence of "evills" and feeling the absence of God.[9]

In the end, Anne Hutchinson was expelled from Massachusetts Bay because she taunted the ministers for missing the truth of Wheelwright's indictment. They were, as Increase Nowell pointed out at her court trial, in no mood to be disparaged: "I do hear it affirmed, that things which were spoken in private [between ministers and congregants] are carried abroad to the publick and thereupon they do undervalue the ministers of congregations." Hutchinson nevertheless refused to soften her accusation that most New England ministers were preaching reward rather than grace: "I seek not for promises; but for Christ; I seek not for sanctification, but for Christ; tell not mee of meditation and duties, but tell me of Christ."[10] Some among her sympathizers went with her to Rhode Island, while others undertook journeys of their own: back to England, or (like Wheelwright) to New Hampshire, or to a place that has not usually been considered in this context, New Haven, which provides an illuminating instance of the faltering effort to sustain the "feminine" spirit of the Great Migration.

By the summer of 1637, John Davenport—formerly minister of St. Stephen's on Coleman Street in London, only recently arrived in the New World—was straining to explain why it would not be possible for him to linger in Massachusetts. To remain, he declared, would require removal "beyond Watertowne," where "a Boate cannot pass from the Bay thither, nearer then 8 or 10 miles distance . . . [which would not be] Commodious for our familyes, or for our friends." Complaints of overcrowding had already become as much a New England refrain as they had been in England; the inhabitants of Newtown, for instance, were grumbling about "straitness for want of land, epecially meadow," as early as the spring of 1634, and were en route to the Connecticut Valley two years later. Now, after making his own explanations, Davenport chose a tiny trading village on the Connecticut River which the Indians had called Quinnypiac. He renamed it New Haven, thus telling the world it was a place of rescue—but it has never been entirely clear from what. For one thing, though Winthrop thought that Davenport "clearly discovered his judgment against the new opinions" shortly after his arrival in the summer of 1637, the minister's own remarks at Hutchinson's church trial do not confirm Winthrop's view; they are much more coaxing than hostile. Here Davenport guides her away from "error"—from her notion that the soul dies with the body, and that the body does not rise at the Last Judgment:

> Mr. Damphord. . . . Now the Curse is this, that Missery is annexed to Immortalitie. Immortalitie was a Gift to the Spirit from thear very Beinge. *The soule cannot have Immortalitie in itselfe but from God from whom it hath its beinge.*

Mrs. Hutchison. *I thanke the Lord I have Light.* And I see more Light
a greate deale by Mr. Damphord's opening of it.[11]

It is clear from such exchanges that Davenport had a great sensitivity for Hutchinson's refusal to consent to any doctrine unless she
could feel its contribution to God's glory. He responds to her hesi-
tancy by stressing not the socially disruptive implications of her beliefs
(which were uppermost in the minds of most of his colleagues) but
the fact that immortality is a gift of God—and must not be scorned
as such. Hutchinson was flirting with a brand of mortalism—the belief
that the soul died, or "slept" until the general resurrection of bodies
and souls at the Last Judgment. This was a doctrine in ill repute among
orthodox Protestants of all stripes. It had originally arisen in reaction
against Catholic purgatorial teachings (with their attendant option of
buying propitiatory indulgences), and it smacked of eschatological
extremism: if history was soon to end, then the endurance of the soul
lost much of its meaning. In an aspect more relevant to the antinomian
affair, the mortalist heresy was also associated with belief in the an-
nihilation of personal identity by the indwelling of the holy spirit.
But most generally it was a doctrine that "subverted discipline by
displacing the afterlife as a common sanction for ethics." "We are
dead to the *Covenant* of the Law," Cotton had explained in England,
"but not to the *command* of the Law." That was the fine distinction
Hutchinson was accused of obscuring.[12]

Davenport nevertheless understood that to treat her as some sort
of licentious hysteric (which is how she was regarded by Bulkeley
and Dudley and Wilson) was a travesty of pastoral duty. He saw,
instead, that her doctrinal waywardness was an expression of the
intensity of her piety: that she was made nervous, in this case, by the
doctrine of the immortal soul—which orthodox Puritans believed
"passed instantly [upon death] to an unspecified region where it remained in a . . . felicitous state, praising God and anticipating the
resurrection of the body at the end of time"—because she feared it
might glorify man at the expense of God. But Davenport's clarifi-
cations, psychologically acute and generously intended as they were,
did not clear away her doubts. As the trial goes on, Mrs. Hutchinson
seems on several occasions to offer a distinction between soul and
spirit—the former dying with the body, while the latter (which only
the faithful possess) achieves eternal life in its immediate union with

Christ. Even here, Davenport was at pains to correct, not condemn: "The Spirit is not a Third Substance but the Bent and Inclination of the soule and all the facultis thearof. Now this is not a substance differing from the soule, and that Spirit in *Ecclesiastes is ment of the Soule.*" (At other points Hutchinson wavered on whether "union with Christ" means the moment of conversion or the resurrection at the Last Judgment.) To most of her examiners all this was dispensable detail; she was merely raising the specter of "foule, groce, filthye and abbominable opinion[s]" such as the belief that conversion abrogates all antecedent human relations—leading to such appalling possibilities as indulgence in "the Communitie [that is, free intercourse] of Women" by the "saints." Such lascivious visions had become a hideous reality a century before at Leyden, which had been turned by the "Familists" into a city of orgiastic delights—an episode in which all the New England ministers were deeply read. "Oh it pleaseth Nature well," said Winthrop, "to have Heaven and their lusts too."[13]

With John Wilson thus proclaiming her guilty of "Sadducisme and Athiisme and therefore to be detested," and Peter Bulkeley calling her an "abominable" Familist, Davenport continued to strike an entirely different note—one of patient explanation. Yet he has somehow been allowed to slip into the gallery of her denouncers. It is true that his refuge, New Haven, developed an aura of austerity and that it exhibited, in Cotton Mather's words, "a yet stricter conformity to the *word of God,* in settling of all matters, both *civil* and *sacred,* than he had yet seen exemplified in any other part of the world." There is also reason to credit Winthrop's implication that Davenport was fleeing from "differences among Christians," and, that having just left England under duress, he was keen on peace. But there are equal grounds for believing that he had developed a good deal of sympathy for the person and temperament of Anne Hutchinson, if not for her doctrinal positions.[14]

For one thing, it is simply not possible to piece together his motives for departing Massachusetts Bay from his letters or even his later political tracts, in part because he honored what Perry Miller called New England's "tribal reticence," and rarely aired internal differences in public. His resolve in this regard eventually cracked, but not until twenty-five years later, when he agreed to lead the bitter fight against the Half-Way Covenant, which sanctioned baptism for children of noncommuning church members. He was, to be sure, a man of stringent standards—incredulous, for instance, that during his years in Holland he had been required to "conforme unto a particular custom of the dutch Church for the unlimited Baptising of all infants, which were presented in the Church . . . although that either of the parents were christians, was no otherwise manifest, then by their (all) answering yea, at the reading of the leiturgy of baptisme publickly, or by nodding their head, or some other gesture." But he was also a man committed to a special kind of internal toleration, a commitment that can be sensed not only in his performance at Anne Hutchinson's trial but also in his efforts to admonish rather than excommunicate another Anne, Anne Eaton, whose anabaptist opinions brought turmoil to the New Haven Church in the 1640s. "For your incouragement," he continually preached to the spiritually uncertain, "consider . . . that you are not excluded from the Fellowship of [grace], unlesse you exclude yourselves." Davenport always spoke with such a consolatory note: "Sometimes a dejected discouraged Christian thinks he hath so much to say against his comfort, as will put to silence the best and ablest Ministers." One can hear in this remark that his basic understanding of the minister's function was to provide reassurance. And like Cotton, he insisted on grace as something entirely outside the sequences of ordinary experience. He was impatient with those who would cheapen the currency of religious expression: there are some "presumptuous professors, who are confident, without a good ground, that they do believe in Christ unto salvation. To discover the vanity of this their confidence, I demand . . . How long have you thus known Jesus Christ? Ever since you can remember? Suspect it, For all that know Christ in a right manner, can tell, that there was a time when they did not thus know Christ as now they do." For Davenport, conversion was subject to an experiential standard; it was not an assumable birthright, but a transforming event. His hints on the nature of the transition from the insolent to the dependent self are unmistakably in the comfort-preaching tradition of Sibbes and of Cotton: "As the needle in the Compass, being touched with the Load-Stone, is in continual motion till it points to the North . . . so the soul being touched by the spirit of Faith, is in continual motion, till it points unto God in Christ, that living Rock and tru Load-Stone, who draws believers to him by a spiritual sympathy which they have with him."[15]

Davenport coupled this language of allure (the language that

Hutchinson rightly said was waning in the Bay) to images of organic nature—"as naturally as beams come from the Sun, and branches from the root; so, by spiritual discourse, one truth issueth from another," and thus began to tell the tale of his continued migration: "Look not so much with the eye of sense downward, and round about you, as with the eye of faith upward, and into the scripture-promises." Like Cotton, he continued to celebrate "the comfort in knowing . . . that there is an *Aliquid Ultra,* something further to be sought after, besides what we have found in ourselves." And like Cotton he maintained his sense of an unfractured social whole: "the holy seed are . . . the props that shoar up the places where they live." Regeneration for Davenport, as for Cotton, meant a willing submission to paradox: "Yours [are] unwarranted expectations of good, without mixture of evil; of peace, without trouble; of health, without sicknesse; of ease, without pain; of joy, without sorrow; of prosperous successes, without crosses; which God hath no where promised; but hath foretold the contrary everywhere in his Word."[16]

But most important for understanding Davenport's dissent from the hardening Massachusetts orthodoxy are his comments on the nature of sin itself: "The schoolmen," he declared, "do rightly define sin to be an aversion of the soul from the immutable God, and turning of it to the mutable creature." Sin, for Davenport—who stands in this respect as an exemplar of the post Hutchinson exiles—was always a blindness, a wrong inclination, what Emerson was to call (with a similar intensity of conviction) "a diminution, or *less* . . . [a] shade, absence of light . . . no essence." Standing with Cotton (with whom, as a successor to the ministry of the First Church, he was to be buried in a shared tomb), he affirmed that sin has no independent existence, that the normative condition of men and women is one of expectancy and openness; that the meaning of hell, in the words of one English Puritan who did not make the journey, "[is] to bee turned to the gulfe of nothing, from whence wee came." We find him defining grace in a curt disagreement with Lear that sums it all up in a phrase: "something is made of nothing."[17] He was obsessed not with the regulation of sin, but with the miracle of rebirth out of nothingness.

2

Perhaps the briefest way to encompass the earliest years of the New England spiritual experience is to say that that reverent obsession came to be regarded as untenable. Sensing this, Roger Williams wrote that Cotton had considered joining Hutchinson in exile as a rebuke to the "legall" Massachusetts churches; Cotton denied the charge, but conceded that he had thought of removing to New Haven, "as being better known to the Pastor" there. For those arrayed against Davenport and Cotton and their disciples, reactions ranged from discomfort to satisfaction at their "reduction." No one, however, was entirely easy in victory.[18]

We may begin with Thomas Shepard. New England's leadership, he knew, was dividing intellectually (and in some respects geographically) between those who saw the world as inhabited by rapacious creatures in need of constraint, and those who thought that the community of saints was still a realizable possibility soon and near. The prospect for balance between the two seemed increasingly illusory. With Hutchinson silenced and Davenport gone to New Haven, Cotton himself nearly decided to follow, though in the end (perhaps because of the spiritual trial attendant upon his first emigration) he remained. He did give vent to an *ubi sunt* emotion: "If men be weary of the Country and will back again to *England* because in heart they are weary, and can goe to the west part of this Country without Ordinances, I feare there is no Spirit of Reformation, at least, not of Resurrection" in the land. There were many others for whom the decision to emigrate had been a personal trial that would not easily admit of either recantation or repetition. All of Anne Hutchinson's leading prosecutors had endured some comparable perplexity in reaching their initial decision to leave England; we have seen Winthrop retorting to charges of desertion even as he made plans to sail, and Hooker attacking "those fearful to suffer" a few years before his own flight to Holland. Among them, the most personally candid was Shepard, who recounts several painful "removals" in his *Memoir,* beginning with his flight as a child (the "youngest and best beloved" of his parents) for safety to his grandparents' home, from an epidemic that was soon to kill his mother. These were events that Shepard could barely have remembered; reconstructed for him by guardians and family friends, they shaped a patterned expectation in his life that sorrow always follows hard upon "removal." It was a pattern that his adulthood confirmed. Embarking for America prevented him from attending the funeral of his first-born son, who "was buried at Yarmouth, where I durst not be present lest the pursuivants apprehend me and I should be discovered, which was a great affliction and very bitter to me and my dear wife." His wife, like other women who made the trip weakened from childbirth, lived only a short while after becoming ill aboard ship, dying of what he considered a sea-borne consumption. So it is less than surprising to find him troubled a few years later when Hooker (father of his second wife) urged another move upon him—south to Matabeseck: "When there was a church meeting to be resolved, I looked upon myself as poor and as unable to resolve myself or guide others in any action as a beast . . ." There were good reasons to go: in October corn had been declared legal tender; creditors, growing as nervous as they had ever been in Earle's Colne, were seeking authority to seize house, land, and cattle in fulfillment of unpaid debts. But "I saw myself," Shepard confessed as he felt the temptation to move again, "in respect of Christ as a beast is in respect of a man."[19] This time he stood still.

There was a countervailing element in the idea of flight itself, which Shepard now found himself resisting. Puritans had always regarded themselves as a people in motion; their leaders had "the experience of exile as the crucible" of their doctrines, and the first hard years in America did nothing to suggest that the age of exile was over—though some wished it were so: "We Inn at a place in our passing by," wrote Hooker after his own third migration (he had gone first to Holland, then to Massachusetts Bay, and finally to Hartford), "when we take repast only, and bait, but depart presently, intending not to stay; but where we dwell, we settle our abode, we take up our stand there, and stir no further." There was a bound sense of finality and commencement in New England's founding. Hooker had imagined it (before he went) a "rock and a shelter" for God's righteous ones, and though some New Englanders still lived in an atmosphere of charged expectation that the final stage of history was about to begin, most of their intellectual leaders, as we have seen, were skeptical and wary of the social effect of such radical millenarianism. "Men's wits in imagining types and allegories," said Shepard, "are very sinfully luxuriant."[20]

England, in Shepard's view, had been a madhouse of debtors fleeing creditors, an image out of which he made a recurrent simile for sinners fleeing Christ: "If the Lord of hosts can catch you, you . . . shall feel with horror of heart that which you fear a little now." In the New World one could run not in tawdry panic, but as God's people had always run, "as upon Eagles wings"; one could speak not of a flight from obligation, but of flight "into the Wildernesse from the face of the Dragon." Thus Shepard in New England began by speaking in the spiritist mode: "I do not cry the temple of the Lord," he preached shortly after his arrival, "nor idolize order and churches; but I tell you what your privilege is . . ." In those early New England years he had echoed Cotton on the insufficiency of the letter: "Saints do not only see things in letters and syllables and words, but see things as they are in themselves . . ." There had always been an impulse in Shepard to disdain the rustle of pages, to play the raw, untutored enthusiast: "Jesus Christ," he had declared in England, "is not got with a wet finger"; and he had allowed himself an almost mystic expression on the eve of his departure from England:

> Consider the glory of the bodies of the saints in [the third heaven]: the Lord shall change our vile bodies, which are but as dirt upon our wings, and clogs at our feet . . . It shall be [there] an incorruptible body: it shall never die, nor rot again . . . it shall be a glorious body: it shall "rise in honor," saith Paul; and what glory shall it have! Verily, it shall be like "unto Christ's glorious body, . . . which, when Paul saw (Acts ix.,) did "shine brighter than the sun;" and therefore here shall be no imperfection of limbs, scars, or maims, natural or accidental deformities; but as the third heaven itself is most lightsome, (Gen. i. 1,2,) so their bodies that inhabit that shall exceed the light and glory thereof, these being more compacted, and thence shining out in greater luster, that the eyes of all beholders shall be infinitely ravished to see such clods of earth as now we are advanced to such incomparable beauty and amiableness of heavenly glory.[21]

Within a short time, however, he was speaking differently during the long months of the antinomian crisis—almost shyly, as if to a former intimate who had once coaxed him into such reveries: "Quest.: How do the soul see [Christ] as he is? Ans.: I, in this case, rather desire to learn than teach . . ." (At Hutchinson's trial he would reflect that "the vilest errors . . . are . . . brought in by questions.") In America the language of ecstasy gave way in Shepard's mind to a language of discipline. He began to put in interrogative form what others were casting in declarative sentences: "if faith close with the person of the

Lord Jesus, the same faith must first see that person . . . Did you ever see any espoused together that did not first see and know each other?" The antinomians, Shepard was coming to see, were jumbling the orderly picture of the mind. This was, for him, the first intellectual step to overthrowing all social hierarchies—in favor of a world, as one of New England's benefactors ominously described it, "where every man is master, and masters must not correct theyr servants." Shepard's new father-in-law, Hooker, had already in England associated such upheavals with "some malapent, saucie, domineering women [who] marry men not to make them husbands, but their servants." And so Shepard reasserted a vision of order among the faculties: "The eye or mind of a man sits like a coachman, and guides the headstrong affections." This is why his preaching changed, why the appeal to affections faded from other New England pulpits as well—and gave way to a newly American contemplation of sin as the affections run wild: "A man's master-sin may be changed; those sins that are his master-sins in his youth are not in his old age; those that are at one time, in one place, are not in another . . ." What is expressed here, and throughout the context of this passage, is an acutely heightened sensitivity to the invasive and chameleon nature of sin. It had changed its tactics. In the old world it had been icy complacence; now it was the hysteria of evangelical pride—and, most important, in its new face Shepard was able to see his own.[22]

The plant-root metaphor—sin offers boughs for excision while its roots remain concealed—joins the imagery of invasive disease, and with it a corresponding interdependence of the violated sectors of the soul: "He that escapes one sin, another shall slay him." We find Shepard returning to the comforting metaphor of reason as groom and coachman for the unruly but breakable affections. "Sudden work," says the man who had once burned in Preston's converting fire, "is superficial." His metaphors, chiefly of hollowness and rottenness, mix: "It is with the soul as with water, all the cold may be gone, but the native principle of cold remains still. You may remove the burning of lusts, not the blackness of nature, from a carnal heart, and the ground holds, nature is not changed." This is a man who cannot decide between the metaphors of cold and heat, water and fire; or, more likely, a man who cannot bring himself to pronounce his decision whether cold is an absence of heat or a positive property—a "native principle."[23]

It was thus a Shepard of chastened expectation who received in November of 1640 the letter from his father-in-law inviting him to lead his congregation on another journey. With immigrants scarce and money scarcer, Massachusetts was entering full-scale depression, and Shepard's journal records a sore temptation to move again. The explanation for his resistance lies in the startling self-abuse that fills the pages of his journal around the decision to remain. It is a language suddenly reminiscent of his account of his youth before conversion; he calls himself, as we have already seen, a "beast," a "brutish" lout for whom the will of God is obscure. "My heart," he reports, "began to withdraw itself from my brethren and others." Spiced by his felt absence from old England on the edge of revolution, this self-hatred left Shepard in a mood of bilious contempt for what we may call his previous self:

> Are these abstracted notions of a Deity (into the vision and contemplation of whose amazing glory—without seeing him as he is in Christ—a Christian, they say, must be plunged, lost, and swallowed up, and up to which he must ascend, even to the unapproachable light) the true and only Sabbath? . . .must the new light of these times be the dreams, and visions, and slavering of doting and deluded old monks?

Though John Saltmarsh, with his "mere new-nothing and dream" that "all believers [could] burn their Bibles" and still possess the "ministry . . . of Christ from within" is the unnamed adversary here and a kind of proxy for Cotton, Shepard had once felt washed by the same light.[24] The final vision of his *Sound Believer* had been very close, sadly close, to what is now being mocked. From the last years in England to this New World scorn is an intellectual distance commensurate with the miles.

Shepard's central discovery in the *Theses Sabbaticae,* a tract that probably began as sermons delivered shortly after the antinomian crisis and that was later expanded into a series of Harvard lectures, was that the sin of greed had adapted itself to new conditions, to "the counsels of lawyers . . . or the herring trade of fishermen." It had made the ocean journey as a stowaway, awaiting the right moment to step forth and be welcomed. Making an extra day's profit was not, perhaps, the conscious motive of those among the "spiritists" who believed that every day was equally a sabbath, and that the ordinance of weekly rest was a vestige of Hebrew superstition. But there were those who would gladly balance their books on Sunday. The still larger significance of the *Theses* lay in its newly American tone as it set forth this discovery of irrationality in the service of greed. Conciliation creeps into the ministerial voice; the ring of debtless authority is fading; one feels that Shepard is laboring in his exertion to satisfy his quizzical Harvard audience—their chins resting on their fists. Many of them were making a vocational choice between ministry and marketplace, and before them Shepard felt compelled to defend the institution of the sabbath (in terms that would be almost exactly repeated in another context by Benjamin Franklin more than a century later) as a law "commanded . . . because it is good . . . not . . . good because it is commanded." Utility, not scripture, was becoming the standard of last appeal. Thomas Shepard was still a relatively young man when he died in 1649, but he had lived to see the great age of the gospel minister come and he had seen it begin to go. Though his party emerged victorious from the Synod of 1637 and his antinomian enemies were in retreat, he made no celebrations.[25]

It was the management of these feelings of pyrrhic victory and unwanted solitude that became the first project of American literature. Only one of the founders fully met that demand: Roger Williams, who alone among the first generation made exile into an American aesthetic. Williams is often grouped with Hutchinson and other renegades, but in fact he had little sympathy for most forms of radical spiritism (a wariness he made explicit in his anti-Quaker tract of 1676, *George Fox Digg'd Out of His Burrowes*). His place within the colony's internal debate was entirely distinct. His aesthetic response to the condition of exile is most readily felt in the *Key into the Language of America,* the remarkable book whose "*Materialls* [I drew] in a rude lumpe at Sea, as a private *helpe* to my owne memory," a book that at first glance looks like an artless project in thoroughness, an attempt to register the facts about what he elsewhere calls "the very Americans & wildest Pagans." (Even Perry Miller thought that the *Key* had "no formal continuity, that it consists merely of a list of words and phrases punctuated by seemingly random observations.") Its table of contents contains thirty-two headings, ranging from "Parts of the Body" to "weather" and "winds," to "coyne," "debts," and "Painting"—but we suspect something more than an exercise in comprehensiveness when we hear Williams vent his respect for the Indians' gift for waiting: "Their manner is upon any tidings to sit round, double or treble, or more, as their numbers be; I have seene neer a thousand in a round, where *English* could not well neere halfe so many have sitten: Every man hath his pipe of their *Tobacco,* and a deepe silence they make, and attention give to him that speaketh . . ." The Indians, to this Puritan, are incomparable teachers of the virtue of attentive silence: If "the whole race of *mankind* is generally infected with an *itching desire* of hearing Newes," the Narragansets have made patience their hallmark.[26]

In the context of the spiritual crisis of the first generation, the *Key* takes on great interest as a text conceived under the impact of the migration, and one that could never have been created in the Old World. Its linked exhilaration and sadness perfectly express the immigrant emotion that we have been trying to grasp. Williams reserved, for instance, his greatest approbation for that aspect of Indian life that at the same time elicits sorrow—its transience. The Indians are a people in motion: "they breake up their fields, build their Forts, hunt the Woods, stop and kill fish in the Rivers." The halts are momentary, the movement constant. They recognize in this "wild and howling land" how illusory is the idea of stability. They make no sacred settlements: "In the middle of Summer, because of the abundance of Fleas, which the dust of the house breeds, they will flie and remove on a sudden from one part of their field to a fresh place . . . they are quicke; in halfe a day, yea, Sometimes a few houres warning to be gone and the house up elsewhere." There is something here in embryo of the later American image of the phantom savage who strikes by night and vanishes by day, and also an ironic hint of the Puritan fear of being "Indianized": "I once in travell lodged at a house, at which in my returne I hoped to have lodged againe there the next night, but the house was gone in that interim, and I was glad to lodge under a tree."[27]

But there is more here than the flattery of imitation. Williams is pressing the point (with, no doubt, the doctrine of the lost Jewish tribes in mind) that the Narragansets bear a keen resemblance in their attitudes and rhythms of life to the people of God. In their language he finds self-admonition—a call for American Puritans to remember themselves: "Their language is exceeding copious . . . They have five or six words sometimes for one thing." They are practitioners of exactly the kind of precision by which godly men distinguish themselves from the mass of mankind. "Precisionist" was in Williams's time a synonym for "Puritan;" and as if to cajole those who might doubt the parallel, he remarks that some among the Indians "cut their hair round."[28]

Much more a goad to the Puritan conscience than a dissident from it, Williams presented an intellectual problem in Massachusetts because his candor forced his opponents to recognize the full implications of their own thinking. What he was doing in his tactless rage when he announced that he would not "officiate to an unseparated people"[29] was to trace original sin through the churches as if it were a physical chain of infection. This was intolerable to most of the ministers because, for one thing, it was a political embarrassment in their struggle to maintain relations with English authority—but the deeper problem was that it was *not* intellectually at odds with their teaching. The worst of it was that Williams knew that—and they did too. There was no lessening of sin, they all agreed, by virtue of distance from its origin. "In Adam's fall we sinned all" would a few years later become the first sentence of the *New England Primer,* and for more than alphabetical reasons. Williams had learned that principle very well; the problem was that he drew from it an unacceptable application: if Massachusetts communicants, visiting England, took the seals or heard the word in an English parish church, and if a Salem church member then shared a pew with such a man, the taint was transmitted as surely as God was just. This was an authentic syllogism. Williams rubbed his colleagues' noses in it.

After using the Indians' precision as an analogue to such reasoning, and their natural piety as a measure of all that was going wrong with his own culture, Williams went on, in what was becoming an explosion of work, to produce the *Queries of Highest Consideration* and the great *Bloudy Tenent of Persecution*—spiritual companions to Milton's *Areopagitica,* in which we can see the general intellectual impact of the migration crystallized. In London in 1644 to see what he could do about influencing the Westminster Assembly, which was moving in a presbyterian direction (Williams was the most peripatetic of the founders, making many Atlantic crossings), he published his *Queries* in which he made his famous argument that "the Common-weale cannot without a spirituall rape force the consciences of all to one Worship." This was the prelude to the *Bloudy Tenent,* for he was sounding a theme that he would now orchestrate into a bewildering series of variations at which the *Key* had hinted: We must, he insisted, remember "the vain uncertain and changeable Mutations of this present evill world."[30] Men are unequipped to write the kind of divinely sanctioned platform the delegates at Westminster hoped to write, and should therefore write none at all. There is no scriptural sanction for synods, he said, or even for assemblies. There is nothing in the Bible that authorizes a national church after the passing of Israel. Stamping out heresies—for which the Westminster factions competed in congratulating themselves—was no sign of a true church. Rome, after all, did that better than anyone else.

Speaking with childlike clarity, utterly free of circumvention, Williams made the whole world nervous. With his characteristic directness, he leapt in the *Queries* to an attitude of incredulity: have we not learned by now, he asks, that the decisions of political and ecclesiastical assemblies are ephemera? "Although [in England] the fame and sound is great of Reformation," King Henry VIII, with all his thunder about papist crimes, "sate down himselfe in the Popes Chaire in *England* as since his Successors have done." This is the American Williams of the early forties, to whose imagination something brutal has happened: his alarm at the obtuseness of reputable men has developed into a feeling closer to revulsion. What he calls "this present evill world" in the *Queries* comes to dominate *The Bloudy Tenent* as an earthly hell. One feels, as he builds his case against civil involvement in religious affairs, that the argument has finally little to do with reasoned conclusions, but is instead an articulated emotion of overwhelming disgust. Such is the emotion that leads Williams to accuse the leadership of congregational New England of imagining itself in the process of fulfilling the scriptural promises within history: "Mr. *Cotton* having made a locall departure from Old *England* in *Europe,* to New *England* in *America* [imagines that] he hath obeyed that voice, *come out of Babel my people* . . . Doth he count the very Land of *England* literally *Babel,* and so consequently *Aegypt* and *Sodome, Revel.* 11.8. and the Land of new England *Judea, Canaan? &c.*" Recent scholars have answered this vindictive question with a ringing yes—imputing to Cotton exactly the fantastic arrogance with which Williams charged him. Cotton himself vigorously—and curtly—denied it: "I doe not count *England,* literally to be *Babel,* nor mystically neither."[31]

But Williams was not to be mollified. The particular emotion— the American emotion—of the *Bloudy Tenent* becomes a longing for the purifying inferno: "these *Heavens* and *Earth* are growing *Old,* and shall be changed like a *Garment,* Psal. 102. They shall melt away, and be burnt up with all the *Works* that are therein." History was leading nowhere except into conflagration; there was nothing to do but await the appointment of new apostles as prophesied in Revelation, who will "replant [true] Churches out of the ruines of the Antichristian Apostate." To Cotton this was utter folly, since "the new Testament acknowledgeth *Paul* and *Barnabas* to be the last Apostles," and makes clear that "when the New *Hierusalem* comes downe from Heaven" it will be "built upon that foundation which the Lambes twelve Apostles have already laid, Rev. 21.14." Yet Williams could put no faith in any present institution that claimed descent from the primitive church: "A thousand severall renewed Forms of Apparell, alters not the condition of a dead man," he had told the Westminster factions, as a commentary on their absurd deliberations about ecclesiastical form. In *The Bloudy Tenent* this theme fills the book with an almost Swiftian imagery of filth: "A chaste wife," he writes, meaning in this context a pure, separated church, "will not onely abhorre to be restrained from her *husbands bed,* as adulterous and polluted, but also abhor (if not much more) to bee constrained to the *bed* of a *stranger.*"[32] The question—and it was Cotton who mercilessly asked it—is, what makes the wife chaste? What is the nature of chastity? Or could it in Williams's mind be defined only negatively as freedom from pollution? Such a sense of virtue—as the absence of stain—is the most one can extract from Roger Williams, and that fact stands as his American dilemma.

The more acutely he conceived of sin in his New World isolation, the less he could imagine an immunity to it. "By the change of a chaire, chamber or bed, a sick or sleepie man, whore or drunkard are not changed, but they remaine the same still." And so we find him retreating from the possibility of a land of pure churches, first to the idea of a single pure congregation, then, in Winthrop's words, to the point where he "refused communion with all, save his own wife," and finally into utter solitude. In *The Bloudy Tenent* we feel the walls closing in, as Williams's negative concept of virtue is joined by his heightened sense of the positive nature of sin: "Evill cannot alter its nature, but it is alway *Evill,* as *darknesse* is alway *darknesse.*"[33]

What paralyzed Roger Williams in America was his overwhelming sense of sin in all its hideous permanence beside an increasingly abstract and elusive concept of the good. As Cotton understood with searing clarity (and as Davenport continued to insist in New Haven), such a disposition would lead inevitably to the paralyzing assumption that sin is strong and virtue weak. "It is an exorbitant Hyperbole to make every passage of spirituall whoredome, a sinne infinitely transcendent . . ." And finally in the late 1630s Cotton summed up the difference between them: "I doe beleeve," he wrote, that "the repentance of the Ministers (for sinnes knowne and secret) and the faith of the godly party, is more able to sanctifie the corrupt and uncleane sort to their Communion; then the corruption of the uncleane sort is able to corrupt the Minister, and Worship, and Church-estate of all."[34] With this statement, whose explicit intent was to justify the polity that Williams now decried—a compromise between radical separatism and presbyterianism that the Puritans called nonseparating congregationalism—we come once again to the heart not only of Williams's personal ordeal, but of that of all the founders. What Cotton was saying with his brave "I do beleeve" was that he still retained his faith that evil was a privation. It was not something rooted in man, to be eradicated only by the final conflagration. To believe as he did was, he knew, to defend a faith under assault. Even he had to fight within himself to retain it. But he knew that only by such a faith could he and his fellow emigrants continue to hope, without the intervention of a fire-bearing god, for the realized Christian community as the destiny of man.

4

Sensing that such an aspiration had shriveled in the aftermath of the Migration, Thomas Hutchinson remarked that "Mr. Winthrop, the father of the country . . . was of a more catholic spirit than some of his brethren, before he left England, but afterward he grew more contracted." This is more than a biographical *bon mot*. It hints at a paradigm for the experience of the entire first generation, and it is in the career of Thomas Hooker that this paradigm is arguably most fully exemplified. Hooker was author of "the most coherent and sustained expression of the essential religious experience ever achieved by the New England divines," and some scholars have already suggested that his expression underwent something of a detectable change between Old World and New. It has been remarked that his sermons (whose mesmeric rhythms Moses Coit Tyler compared to "the tramp of an advancing army") became, in the New World, increasingly "marked by . . . conscious formalisms."[35] But there is more to the story of Hooker's migration than this; he enacts more vividly than anyone in his generation the chilling effect of the migration upon the Puritan sensibility.

From the beginning of his ministry in England Hooker had been relentlessly concerned to dismantle the pretensions of the unregenerate self, to expose spiritual fraud, and to remind the spiritually arrogant of their need for a "cunning" ministry: "the Word is like the Ax, that must be lifted by a skilful and strong arm." If "men think that Christ will come suddenly from heaven into their hearts, at a beck," they are dreaming, allowing themselves a "foolish and sottish conceit." Hooker had a range of reasons for his scorn; he suspected the authenticity of sudden grace—if it comes quickly it will pass quickly—and such a view conflicted with his concept of the soul as glutted in its natural state with sin. Not even Christ "can . . . put good gold into a purse that is filled with stones before." Hooker's world (in New England as much as in Old) was populated by goat-footed men; a world of such depravity that we find him complaining that even "the Scripture never enough expresseth the love that is between sinne and the soule." Toward the essential end of making this infernal love clear, Hooker insists with special urgency on the sinner's dependence on the minister: Christ "*never* commeth into the soule of any unawares, or on the sudden, but he sends his messengers before him." "Harbenger," "messenger" are the recurring terms; the minister precedes, prepares, as God's necessary agent for "plow[ing] up the weeds of sin and corruption." As doctrine this was a standard expression of the Puritan concept of means, but Hooker's version had a special intensity and incessance. Consider this statement by John Norton: "There is not the like degree of humiliation in all those that are converted; for some feel a greater measure of trouble, others a lesser." Hooker is sparing with that sort of qualification.[36]

The England we see through Hooker's sermons of the 1620s is a place where the hard lessons taught by ministers have been imperfectly learned. His English pages are full of complaint that a contagion of self-reliance is in the land; excessive dependence on a sacramental religion has made the soul-shaking work of conversion seem trivial quick-work within any penitent's grasp. Men continue to believe that they can "snatch" Christ from the air, or they stand and wait, confident that grace will descend to them. The minister, in such a world of presumption, faces obsolescence. One finds in Hooker the clearest version of the general Puritan response to this problem—he counters the swelling self by pounding home the news of its insufficiency: "If thou hast found it easie, nay if thou didst never stand amazed at the difficulty of the work [of salvation] . . . thou never hadst the right discerning of it to this day." He follows such passages usually by some such invitation as this: "were it not better to confess your sins to some worthy minister now?"[37]

What happened to Hooker over time was that this rhetorical technique became less a method under his control than a mastering idea with a life of its own. What we see in his lifetime of sermons, and to some extent in the concurrent development of all Puritan discourse as it made the transition from Old World to New, is a surrender to the power of its own imagery. In Hooker's case this meant, among other things, a certain loss of discrimination between the physical and the spiritual. Spiritual laziness, for example, becomes confounded with physical infirmity: "If a man will transplant a tree, he doth not take an old withered rotten tree . . . but hee takes a young tender twigge." There is a note of the conventional here—a standard Protestant disgust for deathbed confessions mumbled by libertines who out of fear have summoned the long-shunned priest. This sort of Catholic insouciance raised Hooker's indignation very high, despite admonitions from older Puritan teachers that an "insolent carriage toward miserable persons . . . is unseemly," and that Christ's "tenderest care is over the weakest." Even beside the dourest preachers, Hooker's vitriol against the unrepentant elderly has a special bite: "It is marvelous hard to drive a nail into a knotty snarly post, especially when it is weatherbeaten and seasoned, and clung together." But there is more here than embarrassment for our notion of a filiopious New England; Hooker's animus against the aged, which begins in England as a rising theme, comes in America to a pitch of fury: "When . . . a man grows towards his grave yet the evil of his tongue grows lively and active . . . as it is with old Huntsmen when their legs fail that they cannot follow the game, yet they wil sit and hear the cry and lewr after the hounds, when they can do little else." There is a touch of prurience here, a young man's contempt for the impotent:

"Men are Neuters now a dayes, which stand and see which side is best"—a sentiment that celebrates the spiritual athlete. Hooker's instinct for the muscular inevitably leads to the presumption that the workings of the spirit must submit to the logic of the body: "A man [in his twenties or thirties] hath better Materials, as I may so say, wherein, or whereupon the frame of conversion may be erected." This little apology for putting it bluntly—"as I may so say"—is a typical flinch of Hooker's when he tests a sensitive assertion.[38]

Such sentences reveal the pleasure of the empiricist, his frank delight that God chooses vigorous bodies to contain the gift of grace. These are the seeds of Puritan literalism (a form of what we now call "reification")—of the sort that can confound an earthly wilderness with a scriptural one; an actual ocean with a biblical sea. Others objected that "in weakness of body some [mistakenly] think grace dyeth."[39] But already in England, and increasingly in America, physical experience was being granted the status of truth in Hooker's discourse; simile tends to become metaphor; and when the distance collapses between the elements of a metaphoric comparison—between "tender twigge" and young penitent, or between hounds and grace—analogy becomes identification.

The most affecting of Hooker's books, *The Soules Vocation* (three times the length of its companions in the English series on salvation), is an effort to arrest this incipient naturalism. "I know," Hooker declares, that "there is a wilde kinde of love and joy in the world, counterfeit coyne, but this is not the love and joy we meane, we will have garden love and joy, of the Lords owne setting and planting." Toward this end, *The Soules Vocation* contains an untypically enticing vocabulary: "The Gospell," it declares, will "allure a man to come unto the Lord . . ." Here is the climax of Hooker's foray into the language of ecstatic harmony:

> Take a burning glasse that will receive the beames of the Sunne, and heat and burne other things, the glasse of it selfe hath no such heat in it, but when it hath received the beames of the Sunne, it heats and burnes other things, as flax, and such combustible matter; but it is by the heat of the beames of the Sunne received, otherwise it could doe nothing. So it is with an humble sinner, hee lieth fit to receive the beames of Gods mercy, and waits when the Sun of righteousness will shine from heaven comfortably upon his heart; and being warmed with the beames of Gods love and favour effectually, hee is able to reflect the heat of love and joy backe againe.[40]

Hooker is an early American confirmation of Poe's judgment that "all excitements are, through a psychal necessity, transient." Even as he sang out his heart in *The Soules Vocation*—"Were my eyes made of love, I could nothing but weepe love; were my tongue made of love, I could nothing but talke love; were my hands made of love, I could nothing but worke love"—he was questioning the basis of his own inspiration: "Wee would faine live by . . . what we see with our eyes, and feele with our fingers, and have in our hands." He tried, like Winthrop, to turn his own naturalism to the service of a Platonic piety: "love in the soul is like touching in the body." His flight to New England can be understood as an effort to prevent the degradation of the spiritual life into its physical analogues.

> When a man cries, then there is . . . trouble upon him; and when he cries loud . . . it gives us to conceive of a kinde of admiration, and a kinde of wondering with himselfe, what the cause of it should bee . . . in [Christ's] agonie there were some inklings of Gods mercy, and now and then a starre-light, and a little flash of lightning to cheere him; but now all the sense and feeling of Gods love was gone . . . and that drives him to a wonderment, saying, *"My God, my God, why hast thou forsaken me?"*[41]

Christ bereft was Hooker's Christ. We find in Hooker's last English pages the weary and brutalized man much more than the resplendent God. The Christ who captures Hooker's imagination is an abandoned man; loneliness is the feeling made vivid, matching Hooker's mood on the eve of his departure from the England he loved:

> When Saint *Paul* was to goe away from them, and for ought hee knew should never see their faces more, why yet marke what hee saith to them: Brethren, I commend you to God, and the Word of his grace . . . *Paul* must depart, and *Paul* must be imprisoned, and *Paul* must die; so that now he shall bee with you no longer to teach, to informe, to direct you . . . I leave you in the hands of your Saviour . . . when the head of your Minister haply shall lie full low, or death overtake him.[42]

These last English sermons bespeak a new intimacy not only with Paul but (as in the previous passage) with Jesus—with his suffering, and above all, with his doubt. They suggest that Hooker did not leave England as a man possessed by a bursting faith, but that he was in pursuit of something he had not found there.

He left in a martial mood: "When [Christ] hath given us weapons, and taught us to fight, and made us conquerors, then he will crowne us." If *The Soules Vocation* had closed with a gentle prod that Christians should value others' joy as if it were their own—"You that have found it thus in your selves, be comforted; you that know it in others, rejoyce"—the *Soules Exaltation* (probably Hooker's final English sermon-series) ends with a call for vengeance: "Curse him all yee Angels . . . and all yee Devils . . . and let these curses bee sealed downe upon him forever . . . [for] you had Christ and mercy tendered to you once, and you would not receive it."[43] It was in this mood that Hooker headed for what Cotton was soon to call the "country of universal profession." On the first leg of his journey to America, he was clench-fisted, both hopeful and wary of peace.

In America Hooker found a new voice. It is a subdued voice, which can be heard best in immediate contrast with its English predecessor. "Conscience," he had preached near the start of his Chelmsford ministry, "bursts into the Alehouse, and into the Tavern upon [the sinner] like a Segeant." In the American revision the conscience comes in stealth: "he surpriseth the sinner in the midst of his Mirth and greatest Jollity." In England, the sinner had been "brought upon the rack, and then one joynt is broken . . . and then he roares again . . ." In America, "the stabs of Conscience make him bleed inwardly . . . [until] he becomes weary of his life." Punishment has turned inward; the tavern, the invading constable, the snapping bones, are gone.[44]

Of course there are commonsense explanations for such shifts in tone: taverns and debtors' prisons were a good deal scarcer in Connecticut than in Essex, but Hooker did not write only for an American audience, and fidelity to circumstance does not tell the whole story. There is also the problem that the editors of Hooker's posthumously published American sermons (the English Independents, Thomas Goodwin and Philip Nye) claimed that he authorized their publication expressly in order to correct errors in the "imperfect" transcriptions of his English sermons that had been published twenty years earlier. But many of the parallel passages in the two versions run so close together that the small differences that Hooker approved as he collated them can at least be taken to represent the general trend of his stylistic development. In one section of the *Unbeleever's Preparing,* for example, which is nearly duplicated in the later *Application of Redemption,* there runs a vivid tale for many pages about a rascal with a nagging conscience who begins to irritate his cronies with his scruples; into jail and out of jail he goes, welcomed after each release a little more suspiciously by "all the drunkards in the towne." They suspect that he is getting rehabilitated, seduced away from them—and this, Hooker teaches, can be the social price of a burgeoning conscience: distrust from those who remain rooted in their sin. Such didactic vignettes all but disappear from the later version, and those which remain lose their charm. "The loose mates [who] hang about" the English version (we can practically hear their muttering) become in America an "accursed crew."[45]

As these comparisons suggest, the Puritans' physical migration had, among its manifold effects, some linguistic consequences. Certain words were restored by the very act of migration to the "class of emotionally significant and concretely meaningful terms"—"fire," for example, which "means one thing to a person [in this case, Anne Bradstreet] who lives [in England] in a stone castle such as Sempringham, and quite another to one who lives [in New England] in a wooden house with a chimney of wattle and daub." Such heightened awareness of the concrete was a sort of linguistically enforced recognition of the power of the physical, which is precisely what Bradstreet, as one critic points out, "had rather heroically held out against in her early conservative work"—the highly derivative *Quaternions,* which are largely imitations of Du Bartas. A similar conservatism informs Hooker's American revisions of his English sermons, composed not long after Bradstreet's earliest American poems. His language becomes periphrastic, decorous; it betrays a new reluctance to sound homespun. Among its most evident changes is a hardened insistence on the necessity of the preparatory stage in the process of salvation—"They should have received the Word with sorrow first," he declares, possibly in direct response to the antinomians, "and then afterwards with joy." Hooker arrives at this infallible precedence of preparation through a subtle transition from the celebration of God's omnipotence—"if all the sins in the world . . . should meet in one Soul as Waters in the Sea, the Mercy of the Lord would abound much more"—to the presumption that this is *always* God's preferred way of working: "When the Disease is most deadly, he then cures." Like Davenport in this instance, Hooker was adamant against those who think "they had grace from their mothers belly," insisting that "if thou thinkst thou broughtest faith with thee into the world, it is an argument that thou never hadst faith." Others were more willing to concede that for some, "God hath delighted to show himself gracious . . . from their childhood." Hooker's logic could seem almost blasphemous, assigning as it did a motive of display to the merciful Lord: "It's the glory of the Physician when the Disease is most deadly, then to do the Case." God's arbitrary will is here being transformed into a predictable will. In England Hooker had more readily acknowledged the variety of avenues to grace—"we must not limit the Holy One." Some men, he knew, may be flooded in an instant, while others · labor upward with agonizing slowness. But in New England the antinomian challenge intervenes, and Hooker retreats into a snarling intransigence toward "those which slight [preparation] as a matter meerly superfluous . . . as an invention of some discouraged, and drooping melancholly persons."[46]

This is bitter and defensive talk. "We must not look for revelations and dreames," he had, to be sure, preached in England, "as a company of phantastical braines do," but he had always balanced such cautions with encouragements: "Ye cannot be drunken with the Spirit, as ye may with wine, therefore drinke abundantly."[47] As Massachusetts seemed to fall under the spell of "phantastical braines," Hooker in his reaction struggled to hold on to the second sentiment as it was overwhelmed by the first.

He was, of course, not alone in this regard. By 1636 Winthrop was reporting alarm that things at the Dorchester Church were getting out of hand—most of the candidates for membership "had builded their comfort of salvation upon unsound grounds, viz., . . . upon dreams and ravishes of spirit by fits." Such excitements were related, no doubt, to the cresting prestige of Anne Hutchinson, and in the *Ten Virgins* (after he had begun to put his former sympathies away) Shepard found it prudent to caution that "it is not fit that so holy and solemn an Assembly as a Church is, should be held long with Relations of this odd thing and tother, nor hear of Revelations and groundless joyes."[48]

Despite the plain fact that New England by the mid-thirties was experiencing a revival (with Cotton at its center), a notion has persisted among modern historians that the introduction of the "conversion relation" that preceded it was somehow dampening and restrictive. Winthrop did not think so—"More were converted and added to [Mr. Cotton's] church, than to all the other churches in the bay"—and he noted with a mixture of admiration and alarm that "divers profane and notorious evil persons" were among those being "comfortably received into the bosom of the church." Doors were opening in the Bay, not closing. "We refuse none for weaknesse," Cotton explained, "either [of] knowledge or grace, if the whole be in them, and that any of the Church can give testimony of their Christian and sincere affections." After Cotton had settled in, the Assistants found it necessary to move his Thursday lecture back from morning to afternoon in order to preserve at least part of the workday for those clamoring to hear him. The people of Boston seemed to sense that he would grant them the benefit of the doubt—a practice in which ministers in outlying towns concurred: "Churches must be open and forward to rescue all that flee from the avenger of blood: the way must be made easie to the cities of refuge."[49]

Yet in order to be "received," candidates in more and more New England churches had to make a public profession of faith. How are we to understand this seeming contradiction between the inclusive appeal of at least some of the preachers and the apparently restrictive structure of their developing ecclesiology? The separatists in Elizabethan England had, as Edmund Morgan has shown, already developed a theory of church-covenant before the end of the sixteenth century that demanded the closest possible alignment of the visible church with the invisible. But they had stopped short of fully devising a method for making the discriminations between souls that were necessary to gather such a church. An institutionalized solution for this problem (though its outlines had been established in England) was left to those in America—and some sort of procedure for assessing the spiritual condition of prospective churchmembers does seem to have become a part of New England church practice by about 1633. Cotton, who came over in that year, was its leading exponent. It is at this point, however, that the story as reconstructed by modern historians becomes confused, in large part because the notion of "a screening process" has become a controlling image for the conversion relation—an idea based less on evidence from the 1630s than on the modern notion that any "test" must be designed for the purpose of exclusion.[50]

Lately, the applicability of this assumption has begun to be fruitfully questioned: "A suggestion worth pondering is that the test for saving faith was added to the requirements for admission not in order to narrow but rather to widen the grounds upon which a candidate might declare, both for his own spiritual consolation and that of his auditors, 'the hope that was in him.' " Those who have taken up this challenge have found that the "test" did indeed have strongly communitarian purposes from the beginning: "Public profession of faith is not necessary to the individual but to the church—that is, it is necessary to link up the two halves of that living analogy, the invisible-visible church relation." The problem is further complicated by the fact of change; the "test" was applied with different degrees of rigor at different moments and in different places. There is good reason to believe, as one hostile observer of Presbyterian inclination suggested in the 1640s, that standards were stiffened after the antinomian affair. As Morgan has remarked, the English separatists as early as 1588 had envisioned a church that "consisteth of a companie and fellowship of faithful and holie people," and the "crucial question is what they meant by 'faithful' and 'holie.' "[51]

It is through an appreciation of the necessarily changeable answers to that question that we may detect the beginnings of a Puritan diaspora in the New World. It seems clear, to stay with Hooker as our example, that he treated conversion relations, which he defined as "the publike manifestation of our assent to the doctrine of faith," as a matter of less than ultimate concern: in Hartford, according to Cotton Mather, he left their administration "unto the elders of the church, as properly belonging unto their *work* and *charge*." And "usually [the candidate] only answered unto certain probatory questions which were tendered them; and so after their names had been for a few weeks before signified unto the congregation, to learn whether any objection or exception could be made against them, of any thing scandalous in their conversations, now consenting unto the covenant, they were admitted into the church communion." If Hooker was casual about this process of soul-examination, it was surely (as his relentless preaching attests) not because he treated the question of salvation with anything less than full urgency. He did complain in Massachusetts that too many were excluded, but his complaint needs to be placed in the context of a time when barriers were coming down rather than going up.[52] The only way of reconciling these seeming contradictions is to understand that Hooker was not, in the final analysis, concerned with how many candidates were admitted to the churches. He was concerned with what kind.

What Hooker expected in a Christian was a good knowledge of

"the morphology of conversion." He understood the conversion process, as we have seen, as a sequential accumulation of *rational* knowledge about the self—"faith may be strong, when a mans feeling may
be nothing"—and the first virtue of his tutored Christian was not
love of God, but an ability to concentrate on the internal spectacle
of festering sin. Lavish contrition—what Hawthorne was to call "an
anthem of sin"—and an acquaintance with the preliminary stages of
preparation were likely to satisfy him as the main features of the
supplicant's spiritual itinerary. It is therefore not surprising, as William Hubbard suggested after Hooker's death, that the atmosphere
of the Bay in the 1630s (not just the declining availability of land)
left him feeling increasingly restive. In England Hooker had insisted
on man's passivity in the work of redemption, though his language
betrayed him—"Faith jogs the hand of God"—and one acquaintance
remarked, "Mr. Hooker, you make as good Christians before men
are in Christ, as ever they are after . . . would I were but as good a
Christian now, as you make men while they are but preparing for
Christ." Now, in New England, he brings to his account of conversion
some razor-thin distinctions: "There is no Will in the first work of
Preparation, there is the Faculty of the Will, but not the act of Will."
Hooker showed a rising defensiveness on the questions of justification
by faith and man's ability to initiate the process of his own redemption.
His rancor, even sarcasm, against those who "judge [Christ] by sense,
and [by] some extraordinary sweetnesse," manifests a retrenchment
in the midst of the short but intense postmigration revival. He had
always recommended that men should "follow the path that God hath
chalked out," but now he was beginning to resemble a rule-monger.
One feels in his newly prescriptive tone the predicament of the provincial, which feeds by its very nature the felt need for propriety. What
happened to Hooker in antinomian America was the victory of experience over imagination. The empiricist who confused good bodies
with good souls has won the day. Although there is less "jingling and
tinkling" in his American accent, the grip of the similitude has tight-
ened. The language of self-exertion has undercut God's sovereignty
and the possibility of redemptive ecstasy. The idea of free grace has
become dangerous.[53]

One result (and a hint that Hooker sensed his own captivity to his
inhibitory language) was a tantrum against words themselves: "Our
words are . . . the panders and provokers . . . the evil [of which] is in

some regard . . . worse than the evil of thy heart." This invective holds a clue not only to Hooker's suspicion of the public, spoken "relations" that were becoming standard church practice in Massachusetts churches, but also to his flight to Hartford—a flight from "dangerous and infectious places." There is, moreover, a retrospective illumination here of all the Puritans' journey out of England: "The heart is like a dunghil of noysom abominations, but our speech and words let out the steem of it, which is able to annoy al that are in presence or pass by with [its] stench." Forty miles south, Davenport was still recommending "spiritual soliloquies . . . a man speaking within himself, to himself . . . communing with [his] own heart."[54] In a true church, a man could be alone with himself in public.

To get out of range, to find a quiet corner—these impulses had always constituted a theme in English Puritanism, but in New England they reached crescendo: "There is no greater hindrance to . . . holy Meditation than froathy Company and Companions, while a man is in the croud amongst such wretches there is no possibility in reason that one should search his own heart." Here we may catch a glimpse of what was perhaps the most profound effect of the Migration on Puritan devotion. The object of meditation—what Richard Baxter in England was soon to call "the Art of Heavenly-Mindedness"—has become in New England exclusively, obsessively, the self. "The soule," Hooker himself had written in England, "turnes it selfe wholly to that grace which is in Christ; it pores not altogether upon sinne and corruption, for then you goe off from Christ." In *The Soules Possession,* a series of sermons he delivered just before migrating, Hooker had even launched an extended tirade against self-absorption: "meditation warms sin" and "bestows our mindes upon it." And in England he had defined true meditation as "nothing else, but a settled exercise of the minde for the further inquiry of a truth, for the affecting of the heart therewith." But by 1640, in Hartford, "truth" has become "self"; the "Art of Meditation" has become "the follow[ing] of sin in a ful search and enquiry after it." "Grapling with the Heart," "following the footsteps of a corruption," "chew[ing] the cud," "stabbing . . . the heart through, and through again"—the self fills the picture, indeed it fills the world.[55]

To some extent Hooker was participating in a trend of modification in meditative practice that characterized English Protestantism generally. Catholic devotional treatises were commonly emended to reduce their emphasis on Eucharistic miracle, and as the topics of meditation came more and more to include personal dilemmas, along with significant and small events of the day, "the terms sermon and meditation became," as Barbara Lewalski has argued, "well-nigh interchangeable in Protestant theory." Joseph Hall, in an influential devotional handbook that went through many editions throughout the century, made a distinction between "deliberate" or traditional meditation on scriptural scenes, and "occasional" meditations called forth "by outward occurrences offered to the mind." Such occasions could "include the whole range of subjects which the natural world offers to us." Yet for Hall meditation remained "nothing else but a bending of the minde upon some spiritual object," and others who granted more room for self-reflection still kept it low on the list of recommended topics. Here is Samuel Hieron's hierarchy of permissible subjects: "1. Gods Maiestie: 2. Gods promises: 3. Our own vilenesse." Within the Puritan tradition Hooker was placing Hieron's primary meaning well below the upper register. The order of worship had been reversed.[56]

Davenport, in neighboring New Haven, seems to have sensed the change as he stepped up his attacks on the preparationist agenda as codified in Hartford. Preparation tends, he saw, to create not new chances but new snares: "Such is mens weaknesse, and Satans subtilty, that the contemplation of sin in the thoughts, though it be not done with any intent to commit it, but to avoid it, defiles the soul, before men are aware." Hooker likely never heard that sermon, but he had uttered similar caveats himself. "Wee turne the frame of the soule downward, and the frame of the heart inward, & shut down the sluce . . . after [our] dayly poring upon, and attending wholly to [our] sinnes." The telling thing is that this turning inward becomes, in America, a "mervailous circumspection." Whereas the English sermons describe the "holy violence" with which God breaks open the soul, the American revisions analyze the constituents of the soul in a loving/hating detail, with God at a permanent distance. In America the "sluce" to the divine is closing. The ultimate consequence of this New World isolation is a total absorption—albeit as an antagonist— with what is left: "As its said of darkness, it cannot be seen by itself but its light that discovers itself and darkness." The true sight of sin has become less a means to grace than an end in itself. Sin, not grace, has become the minister's consuming subject. This shift of emphasis—

sometimes subtle, sometimes stark—was among the central spiritual legacies of the Great Migration: these Puritans had discovered that America was the country of the isolated self; they had begun to miss what Cotton, in the 1620s, had called "something more and one step higher."[57]

"It is one thing to beleeve that there is a God," Hooker himself had preached in England, "and another thing to beleeve into God." What he lost in his passage to the New World was not the power of intellection but the sensory capacity fully to meet its demand. What makes his life, and those of his fellow emigrants, so compelling was their estrangement from their former selves: "it is impossible for a man to looke up to heaven steadfastly with both his eyes down to the earth, both at one time."[58] The transition from a religion of grace to a culture of discipline was appallingly advanced.

Ye say, why come not we over to helpe the Lord against the Mighty, in these sacred battailes?

I answer, many here are diligently observing the counsell of the same Prophet, 22.10. *Weepe not for him that is dead, neither bemoan him; but weep for him that is gone away and shall returne no more to see his Native Country.*   Nathaniel Ward, 1647

6 *Looking Homeward, Going Home*

Ever since the writing of romantic history collapsed under general agreement that "ultimate causes lie beyond our horizon," most historians have conceded in one way or another that theirs is a provisional activity. Proclaiming "*the* Truth, conceived as the one answer, determinate and complete," has properly become a mark of naïveté, and scholars now usually prefer to believe, with William James, that "truth grafts itself on previous truth, modifying it in the process," and that historiography is one index to the culture that produces it.[1] The recovery of the slave experience, for example, or of the public and private lives of women, are only the most obvious among recent achievements that have been encouraged by contemporary social change. The fortunes of the dead, it would therefore seem, depend not merely on the willed alertness of the living, but on a less voluntary devotion—on pressures and events that compel us to notice what we did not see before. With this in mind, it may be suggested that the activity of revising what we know about our earliest history is in part a matter of identifying human beings in colonial America who have lately had no constituency.

Those New Englanders who decided in the middle years of the seventeenth century that they would not remain in the New World are such a group. They have not fared well with historians—not as well, say, as the mob-tormented loyalists of the Revolution who were rediscovered in the 1960s. Perhaps because the Puritan re-migrants slipped back to England relatively quietly, and were not (for various political and psychological reasons) the objects of loud vituperation, they have not stirred much notice. Yet there can be no doubt that they constitute an important element in the experience of the founding generation that stayed—both in their own words and actions and in the complex response they elicited from those whom they left behind. "The currents of transatlantic migration," Oscar Handlin reminds us, "have always flowed in both directions"—a remark whose force is heightened by Handlin's estimate that "of the sixteen million immigrants who came to the United States from Europe in the three decades after 1900 almost four million went back home in the same years." Those among the Puritan immigrants who came, and saw, and turned back, do not match that astonishing percentage. But any treatment of New England's founding is incomplete without some account of them.[2]

By 1700 the re-migrants were already more or less invisible. "Some few suppose," wrote Cotton Mather in the *Magnalia,* that "Ten or a Dozen [ministers] . . . after divers years returned into England . . . but, by far, the biggest part of them continued in this Country, serving their Generation by the Will of God." Mather had to believe that numbers told the tale because—to put it bluntly—to think otherwise was dangerous to his sanity. The lure of England had touched him very personally: his father, as David Levin points out, "had often dreamed during the quarter century [after] his reluctant departure from England in 1661 . . . of returning one day to perform valuable services for the Lord in a theater worthy of his gifts." With the accession of William and Mary, Increase embarked on a diplomatic mission to England, and the younger Mather reacted with remarkable vehemence to his father's delay in coming home: "for myself, who am left alone," wrote Cotton, "in the midst of more cares, fears, anxieties, than, I believe any one person in these territories . . . I am sorry for my dear father too, who is, *entered into temptation.*" Increase's loitering stirred an ironic panic in his son—ironic because the utility and devotion of New England to Old had been the Mathers' theme for decades. This sensitivity is still frequently passed over even in comprehensive accounts of the Mather heritage: "The devotion of the two families [the Cottons and the Mathers] to the Puritans' Christian Israel [New England], meant that eight of Cotton Mather's closest male relatives were ministers: both his famous grandfathers, five of his six uncles—and of course his father." Of the five preaching uncles, it ought to be noted that two were ministers in Ireland (one of whom considered emigration to New England to be tantamount to desertion) and that one (after expulsion from his church in Plymouth) moved to South Carolina.[3]

The leadership of New England had never been free from temptations to defect, not just in the first dispersions west to the Connecticut Valley or north to New Hampshire, but farther afield to the West Indies, "a better place," thought Lord Saye and Sele, than Massachusetts, which had, after all, been "appointed only for a present refuge." Charles Andrews counts in the early years "at least four attempts from outside to persuade settlers to remove *en bloc* to other parts of the English world." The attempts mostly failed—but even the resulting trickle of what Winthrop called "weak-hearted men" was more than an irritant. From the beginning, the attitude toward mother England loomed large as a measure of the colony's spiritual success. "The Lord Jesus," recalled Roger Clap,

> was so plainly held out in the preaching of the Gospel unto poor lost sinners, and the absolute necessity of the new birth, and God's holy spirit in those days was pleased to accompany the word with such efficacy upon the hearts of many, that our hearts were taken off from Old England and set upon heaven. The discourse not only of the aged, but of the youth also, was not, "How shall we go to England?" (Though some few did not only so discourse, but also went back again,) but "How shall we go to heaven?"[4]

One could argue—and the Puritans who stayed with New England did so—that those who chose to make their lives elsewhere were a motley crew. They included the likes of Nathaniel Eaton, first master of the new college at Cambridge, who beat his students with "twenty or thirty stripes at a time," blamed his wife for their diet of "nothing but porridge and pudding," and left behind a group of empty-handed creditors when he fled for England in 1639: a man "full of pride and disdain," was among Winthrop's more moderate comments. There was George Starkey, author of *The admirable efficacy of oyl which is made of Sulphur-Vive* (1660), a notorious quack who put aside his medical treatises and launched a violent attack against the Puritan party in *Royal and Other Innocent Blood Crying aloud to Heaven for due Vengeance* (1660) before Charles II had been on the throne for a year. Even Winthrop's family—whose welfare had been a major factor in his own decision to migrate—was not free from blemish: his sister's son, George Downing, left his position as tutor at the infant college to become parliamentary leader of the movement to coronate Cromwell. Perhaps out of family loyalty, Winthrop pronounced Downing a man "of ready wit and fluent utterance" even as he headed home, but other New Englanders preferred Samuel Pepys's judgment that he was "a niggardly fellow." Before long it became "a proverbial expression [with his former countrymen in New England] to say of a false man who betrayed his trust, that he was an arrant George Downing." Whether they were Parliament-men like Downing or royalists like Starkey, those who returned were associated permanently with the idea of betrayal.[5]

Not all, however, could be so readily accused of an "unstayed spirit." Even the authors of a promotional pamphlet composed in the early forties, which extolled New England's "plenty of all manner of Food . . . of Venison . . . Fish . . . Fowle," and so on had to admit that "many are growne weaker in their estates since they [came] over." "Many that came over the last year," wrote one immigrant farmer, "which was worth two hundred pounds afore they came out of ould eingland . . . will [soon] be hardly worth thirty." Winthrop had only to look at his own brother-in-law, Emanuel Downing (father of the controversial George) to verify these statements: Downing, who came to New England as a gentleman of means, was reduced ten years later to selling his horse in a desperate effort to finance a liquor still, by which he hoped to recoup his losses. "Pray remember me," he wrote to Winthrop's well-traveled son, "about the German receipt for making strong water with rye meall without maulting of the Corne, I pray keepe a copie, in case the noate you send me should miscarye." There was fallen dignity here as well as fortune: a once-considerable gentleman begs his nephew to teach him how to make a salable brew. The recipe may have succeeded, but the business did not. "Most men," remarked Thomas Shepard around 1640, "have lost and sunk in their estates, and it is hard to live lower than we did."[6] In 1654 Emanuel Downing joined the eastbound traffic.

Most such defectors—even if it was conceded that some had weighty as well as flighty reasons—have been regarded by historians much as the New England leadership wanted them regarded: as signifying nothing more than a rash of personal aberrations or discouragements. There is, no doubt, a good deal of truth to that version; one scholar has recently suggested that among the first settlers there was some correlation between the failure to marry and the decision to return to England. That decision could be and was associated with immaturity and lack of stamina. "If it please God that I have my health," wrote one Watertown resident to his father in 1631, "I will plant what corn I can, and if provision be no cheaper between this and Michaelmas and that I do not hear from you what I was best to do, I purpose to come home."[7] Still, the reverse migration was much more than a winnowing of chaff, and everyone in New England knew it.

About one-twelfth of the original Watertown settlers, for example, had returned to England by 1660, and the citizens of other similarly diluted communities were stunned to realize that even their ministers might well be among those departing: "Both our teaching officers," reported Theophilus Eaton of the New Haven Colony, "have expressed their purpose of removing." One of these was John Davenport himself, who, in citing medical reasons, puzzled his fellow townsmen: "what his disease is, which it should be conceived curable in England, and not here . . . we understand not." The leading citizen of Guilford, Connecticut, whose "extremely beloved" pastor sailed for England in 1650, took note of widespread "harsh thoughts on almost all men yt. goe for England, as if they regard not this poore people here," and at the same time admitted that the impulse to pull up "stakes . . . from the Rocky sand pts. of this wilderness" was spreading.[8] By the mid-forties the dismissive indifference toward those who left was beginning to sound strained. Some were not so much thinking of the "counter-emigrants" as deserters, but of themselves as stragglers.

Accordingly, a new tone, hovering between explanation and excuse, begins to be heard in the forties toward those who went back. In 1642 the General Court declared, as one of the articles of the Body of Liberties, that "Every man of or within this Jurisdiction shall have free libertie, nothwithstanding any Civill power to remove both himselfe, and his familie at the pleasure out of the same, provided there be no legall impediment to the contrarie." "The scarcity of good ministers in England," Winthrop proposed three years later about the increasing number of Harvard men heading home, "and [the] want of employment for our new graduates here, occasioned some of them

to look abroad." Samuel Maverick, writing around the time of Restoration, held the reasonable opinion that Harvard College had been
founded explicitly (and, implicitly, as a temporary measure) to supply
the home country with preaching ministers during the time when
Cambridge under Charles I had been hindered from doing so. One
of Winthrop's correspondents did not think that even such straight-
forward explanations, however accurate they may have been with
respect to those who left, took account of the impact on those who
remained: "The irregular departure of some," wrote Samuel Symonds,
"causeth a deeper search of heart wherefore God hath brought his
elect hither."⁹ By the fifties, the reverse migration was leaving a
discernible trail in New England's literature of self-definition. It had
become more than a phenomenon for casual dismissal—it was a fact
demanding suppression.

2

One of the more interesting efforts to meet the demand for suppression was Edward Johnson's *Wonder-Working Providence of Sion's Savior
in New England* (pub. 1652). The first systematic history of Massachusetts Bay, it has usually been read as a celebratory work that
"catapult[s] the Puritan colonists into a position of unimaginable power."
It was composed, according to one critic, in the serene certainty that
"the outcome of [the Puritans'] mission—the New Earth itself—was
never in doubt."¹⁰ This view, however, fails to explain why it is that
the singular poignance of Johnson's work derives not from any building realization of millenarian fulfillment, but from an unreplenished
expenditure of rhetorical energy. The *Wonder-Working Providence* is
a book that winds down, wanes into monotony; it is one of those
works in which a proper ending feels elusive, in which precision of
intent (focused in the early chapters on celebrating the church militant) becomes toward the close a rambling catalogue of material pos-
sessions. Its closing chapters bear a formal relation to the main body
of the work much like that in *Huckleberry Finn*: the climb toward
fulfillment cannot be sustained, and the book is left in disarray.

    This rhetorical shortfall is especially costly because Johnson has
raised the expectation that, like any normative instance of Renaissance

historiography, his book will record and reflect the conquest of disorder under the aspect of providence. He opens with a drama—a spoken exchange in the give-and-take rhythm of objection and answer—and it is clear that his intent is to resolve this debate into harmony. The provoking question comes early:

> Can it possibl[y] be the mind of Christ (who formerly inabled so many Souldiers of his to keepe their station unto the death here [in England]) that now So many brave Souldiers disciplined by Christ himselfe the Captaine of our Salvation, should turne their backs to the disheartening of their Fellow-Souldiers, and losse of further opportunity in gaining a greater number of Subjects to Christs Kingdome [in New England]?[11]

This is the challenge that deploys Johnson's drama—just as the sentry's "Who's there?" initiates the theme of *Hamlet*. With his instigating question, Johnson has triggered a process he cannot entirely control; he has invoked the rules of aesthetic completion with a chord that cannot feel finished until its tonic is heard. The obligation to carry this first note through to a satisfying completion puts great stress on Johnson's linguistic decorum, forcing him at times to resort to an almost bizarre logic and leading him into a jarring repetition of the book's ironically central word, *England:* "for Englands sake they are going from England to pray without ceasing for England." This is a feeble answer to the original question—and precisely because of its inadequacy it informs the entire work:

> These brood of Travellers having thus through the good hand of their God upon them, thus setled these Churches, according to the institution of Christ, and not by the will of man; they now endeavour to be assisting to others. The reverend Hugh Peters, and his fellow-helper in Christ Mr. Wells [Welde] steered their course for England, so soon as they heard of the chaining up of those biting beasts, who went under the name of spiritual Lords; what assistance the Gospel of Christ found there by their preaching, is since clearly manifested; for the Lord Christ having removed that usurping power of Lordly Prelates, hath now inlarged his Kingdom there . . . by divers other godly Ministers of Christ, who have since gone from hence, both young Students and others, to the number of twenty, or thereabout, in the whole; besides some who were eminent in the civil Government here, both gracious and godly servants of Christ, and some who have been Magistrates here, to the number of five or six.[12]

This is Johnson's attempt to answer the charge that he himself has dramatized: that New Englanders had "turne[d] their backs to the

disheartening of their Fellow-Souldiers" in England. It is his best
response to his own initiating question, which nevertheless continues
to dog him, and which he now renders even more urgent by conceding
that something very like the capture of the dragon (Revelation 20:2)—
"the chaining up of those biting beasts"—is taking place in Old England. (One ex–New Englander put it even more clearly: it was "the
Parliament, and High Court of Justice, who slew the Beast.") Sometimes Johnson allows himself an outburst of expiation in response to
such far-away events: "The prayers of Gods people in New England
have had a great stroke . . . in [God's] great worke in England of
late." But to report efficacious prayers is one thing; to find the whole
meaning of New England in its mental reversion to Old England is
quite another. Even Cotton Mather was able to find more elegant
formulas for glorifying the eastward shift of God's attention: "From
that hour [the founding of Harvard in 1636] *Old* England had more
ministers from *New,* than our New-England had since *then* from Old."
And Cotton's father was franker still: "Since the year 1640, more
people have gone out of New England than have come hither."[13]

Written in vivid awareness that such a reverse pilgrimage had begun,
the *Wonder-Working Providence* ends not in resolved clarity or in open-
ended anticipation of the second coming, but with the language of
carnal accumulation:

> This remote, rocky, barren, bushy, wild-woody wilderness . . . [is] now
> through the mercy of Christ becom a second England for fertil-
> ness . . . First to begin with the encrease of food, you have heard in
> what extream penury these people were in at first planting . . . But
> now . . . good white and wheaten bread is no dainty, but even ordinary
> man hath his choice, if gay cloathing, and a liquerish tooth after sack,
> sugar, and plums lick not away his bread too fast . . . There are not
> many Towns in the Country, but the poorest person in them hath a
> house and land of his own, and bread of his own growing, if not some
> cattel: beside, flesh is now no rare food . . . This poor Wilderness hath
> not onely equalized England in food, but goes beyond it in some places
> for the great plenty of wine and sugar, which is ordinarily spent, apples,
> pears, and quince tarts instead of their former Pumpkin pies . . .[14]

This kind of supermarket inventory is Johnson's last resort as he
searches for a way to articulate the colony's purpose, and, more immediately, to stem the tide of defections. What makes the *Wonder-
Working Providence* affecting rather than merely grating is the historian's capacity to step back from his own degraded rhetoric and to

recognize it for what it is: "An over-eager desire after the world hath so seized on the spirits of many, that the chief end of our coming hither is forgotten; and notwithstanding all the powerful means used, we stand at a stay, as if the Lord had no farther work for his people to do, but every bird to feather his own nest." As the history winds toward an end, its celebratory verses—which Johnson has used throughout to enlarge the dignity of New England's civic heroes—turn admonitory: "Matthews stand up, and blow a certain sound / . . . Christs truths maintain, 'twill bring thee honors crown'd." Before the decade was out, Marmaduke Matthews (teacher of the church at Malden, and the recipient of this advice) was indeed standing up and garnering honors—but he was doing so back in England.[15]

Johnson knew, moreover, that Matthews was by no means an isolated case. Here, toward the close of the history, he meditates on the plight of the Old North church:

> the people gather[ed] into a Church-body, and [decided to] build a Meeting-house for their assembly, the which they have already done, but not as yet called any one to office; for since the people of Christ in some other places, both in England and elsewhere, have through the goodness of God obtained like liberty with our selves, the Ministers of Christ have had their labours taken up in other places as well as here, which hath caused this Church as yet to be destitute.[16]

If the destitution of New England and the consequent lure of Old begin as the submerged themes of Johnson's *Wonder-Working Providence,* they become, by its end, explicit. In both its intensity and its indirectness, it was a representative book for its time. England *redivivus* looms over the several apologetic tracts that flowed from the pens of New England's leading ministers in the forties: John Norton's *Answer to Mr. Apollonius,* Shepard and Allin's *Defense of the Answer made unto the Nine Questions,* Hooker's *Survey of the Summe of Church Discipline,* Cotton's *Way of the Congregational Churches Cleared,* all published in 1648, all straining to assert the exemplary value of New England's polity in the face of English hostility or indifference. Five years earlier, Cotton, Hooker, and Davenport had received invitations to join the Westminster Assembly, but all had declined. Though Hooker, according to Winthrop, "liked not the business, nor thought it any sufficient call for them to go 3000 miles to agree with three men" (a reference to the feisty minority of Independents led by Thomas Goodwin, Philip Nye, and Sidrach Simpson), he did go to the trouble of preparing treatises on catechism and the Lord's Prayer explicitly for consideration by the assembled divines. Hooker's most careful biographer tells us that "there is no indication that any parts of Hooker's works were directly transposed into the Assembly's finished products," and that his effect was "rather slim." Although it has been argued that Cotton's *Keyes of the Kingdom* (1644) had an important effect in converting other leading English ecclesiastics, such as John Owen, to Independency ("the Independent Churches [in Commonwealth England] were born of Mr. Cotton," said one contemporary), the overall effect of the Presbyterian victories at Westminster was clearly dispiriting to the New England leadership. In his Foreword to Norton's *Answer,* Cotton summed up the colonial mood in one exasperated question: "What, I ask, keeps you from regarding us not as traitors or deserters in a common cause, but in our measure, as defenders and supporters of our joint cause against the enemies of our common faith and our common church?"[17]

Despite, then, England's resistance to learning, such an assertion of New England's tutelary value was the only plausible answer to the ever-present question of purpose. "Our work," Cotton said in his sermons on the seven vials, "is to wrastle with God, that they [the Puritans in England] may not perish for lack of knowledge, nor mistake a false church for a true." The subtlest version of this answer was Bradford's *Of Plymouth Plantation* (w. 1630–1650), which has long been valued more highly than Johnson's for the beautiful linkages it evokes between cosmic and quotidian events. Yet despite its greater claim to aesthetic unity, it is also, like Johnson's, a book of fragments, a retrospective search for purpose:

> The boatswain . . . was a proud young man and would often curse and scoff at the passengers. But when he grew weak, they had compassion on him and helped him; then he confessed he did not deserve it at their hands, he had abused them in word and deed. "Oh!" (saith he) "you, I now see, show your love like Christians indeed one to another, but we let one another lie and die like dogs."

This is the first adumbration of what will become the great consolatory theme of Bradford's history: Plymouth as *exemplum* of Christian charity. Bradford's work was the *Middlemarch* of his time—an exquisitely wrought demonstration of the indispensable value to human kind of those who have "lived faithfully a hidden life and rest in unvisited tombs." Writing under the engorging shadow of Massachusetts Bay,

Bradford discovered in the very fact of Plymouth's obsolescence its vindication: "Out of small beginnings greater things have been produced by His hand that made all things of nothing, and gives being to all things that are; and, as one small candle may light a thousand, so the light here kindled hath shone unto many, yea in some sort to our whole nation." This passage has long been the center of scholarly dispute: did Bradford mean to say that Plymouth exported its polity to Massachusetts Bay? If that is what he meant, should we believe him?[18]

The fact is that such questions are unanswerable because the candle metaphor tantalizes more than clarifies. What is clear, however, is that Bradford's history was conceived and organized as a cosmology in which the Plymouth band stands as the shrinking center of an expanding sphere of infuence. As the Plymouth colonists emanate Christian charity, their range of effect expands to include Indians, Massachusetts men, ultimately England; while the core itself contracts with every expenditure of energy. This is a brilliantly conceived aesthetic idea; but it is always under stress: "The Indians came skulking about them, and would sometimes show themselves aloof off, but when any approached near them, they would run away." As the history concedes that Plymouth can repel as well as attract—its grace is resistible—it contends more and more with disruptive force. "Many," Bradford laments, "being aged, began to drop away by death," and he recounts the colonists' quickening attempt to replicate themselves by widening their embrace: "they resolved, for sundry reasons, to take in all amongst them that were either heads of families, or single young men, that were of ability and free (and able to govern themselves with meet discretion . . .)." As it proceeds, the texture of the history feels more and more like patchwork, and Bradford, as in the famous landfall passage, gives vent simultaneously to doubt about the future fealty of the young and to ringing certitude about his own national identity: "May not and ought not the children of these fathers rightly say: 'Our Fathers were Englishmen which came over this great ocean, and were ready to perish in this wilderness; but they cried unto the Lord, and He heard their voice . . .' "[19]

More than occasionally, the search for clues to Plymouth's place in history leads Bradford into wishful delusion: "Mr. Cotton's charge at Hampton was that, they should take advice of them at Plymouth, and should do nothing to offend them." Cotton had, to be sure, directed Winthrop's colonists to "offend not the poor natives"—but the natives he had in mind were Indians, not Plymouth-men. With more and more such lunges after forms of sanction, the history begins to chase illusory meanings, and its central exemplary idea inevitably falters before the reality of tolerationist England. Bradford's candle metaphor simply cannot sustain the weight it must carry, which is nothing less than the providential import of the Plymouth colony— and therefore the meaning of Bradford's own life. The unspoken problem is always England, which has become a chaos of competing polities—less a reflection of congregational Plymouth than an alien Babel. And so, where Johnson tries the language of Joshua with not much success—"these weak wormes instrumentally had a share in the great desolation" of the Bishops' Babylon—Bradford speaks the language of Job. In the end, he is forced to abandon the candle metaphor entirely and to replace it with the repetitive pattern of virtue generated by adversity.[20]

By this surrender of its organizing metaphor, the dominant structure of Bradford's history breaks into an aggregate of its many smaller structures—narrated instances of virtue forged in a crucible. The trouble is that this is not only a convention but a premise which, according to the history's own demonstration, has failed. For nowhere had there been greater stress upon the Pilgrims than in Holland— where adversity had been not purifying, but debilitating. Like all the historians who followed him, Bradford could not evade the fact that he had begun his narrative—a story lived as much as told—with a flight *from* adversity. It is for this reason that the reader of his history sees England at every turn: distorted, ubiquitous, as if in a funhouse mirror.[21]

3

The most direct way to exorcise the ghost of England was to go there; and some who went declined to do so quietly. Among them was William Hooke, minister of Taunton, whose published New England sermons show much the same rhetorical strain that is evident in Bradford and Johnson. In a fast-day sermon of 1640, Hooke was "overcast with griefe and sorrow, when the City of his Fathers was layd wast, and the gates thereof consumed with fire," but two years later his declaration of brotherly concern has become more a rallying cry: "Let us therefore, I beseech you, lay aside the thoughts of all our comforts this day, and let us fasten our eyes upon the calamities of our brethren in old *England,* calamities, at least, imminent calamities dropping, swords that have hung a long time over their heads by a twine thread, judgements long since threatned as foreseene by many of Gods Messengers." What had been in 1640 a call to some kind of transoceanic solidarity becomes shrill self-questioning by 1642: "are we not all the Voluntaries of Jesus?" The call to arms with which Johnson begins— "Attend to your commission, all you that are or shall hereafter be shipped for this service"—is preemptively amplified here by Hooke into frenetic conscription: "Though we have but a day, or two, wherin to joyne all our Forces in the Land together, and to give the Adversaries a broad side; Yet let us now and then make excursions by our selves in private, now that the Lord cals for help against the Mighty."[22] This is sound and fury but little else. One thinks of Churchill during the Blitz ordering guns from mothballed battleships to be fired from London's parks so that the populace might hear the sound of its own resistance. But symbolic noise is only a temporary measure, and Hooke knew it. He had dared to invoke the text so popular with parliamentary preachers, the uncited "subtext" of Johnson's history, the curse of Meroz—"they came not to the help of the Lord." There was simply no way, Hooke knew, to formulate in New England an adequate response to the imperative of that verse. Soon after the *Wonder-Working Providence* was published, with its own failed attempt to answer that imperative, Hooke was back in England.

His return had a remarkable effect on his rhetoric. In 1640 he had lamented civil war as "of all warres none so bloody . . . [a] *malum complexum,* a compound of Judgements, a mixt misery . . . commonly . . . the last of Gods Stroakes upon them that will take no warning." But in his later years, having spoken at Whitehall as Cromwell's chaplain, he was ejected from his pulpit and silenced as a brother-in-law of the regicide John Whalley. He spoke now of the prospect of holy conflict as if the opportunities of service to God—which *The Priviledge of the Saints* (1673), in consoling the disenfranchised ministry, is devoted to cataloguing—have been cruelly limited: "Let us expect no more Dayes of Tranquillity and Peace, but Wars, and rumours of Wars, Nation lifting up Sword against Nation, and learning of War, the confused noise of Battle, and Garments rolled in blood . . . That which concerns us is to be in a Posture of Humiliation and Preparedness, for the reception of these dark Dispensations. Here is the Faith and Patience of the Saints."[23] Composed in the atmosphere of suspicion that the second Charles would effect a rapprochement with Catholic France, Hooke's language undergoes a corollary transformation toward religious tolerance—a political exigency for any post-Reformation nonconformist, but nevertheless a change especially remarkable in view of the fact that Hooke had spent his final decade in New England as teacher to its "strictest" church, that of New Haven. "It doth not a little grieve my spirit," Sir Richard Saltonstall had written to Cotton in 1652, "to heare what sadd things are reported dayly of your tyranny and persecutions in New England, as that you fyne, whip, and imprison men for their consciences." New Haven was the bastion of enforced purity. News of such "sadd things" was part of the reason Saltonstall never rejoined his brethren in New England, as Thomas Dudley once had hoped: "The shipp now waits but for wind, which when it blows, there are ready to go aboard therein for England Sr. Richard Saltonstall . . . and many others, the most whereof purpose to returne to us again, if God will." The idea of toleration, then, which became the focus of bitter contention between New England and the Commonwealth, and a necessity for those returned New Englanders who lived out their days in Restoration England, never established itself in the minds of the first generation. It could not take hold because the Puritan rejection of *adiaphora*—their insistence that God's decrees are beyond pluralist interpretation—was too strong. It is therefore all the more remarkable to hear Hooke, after his return, relinquish the language of New Haven and take up that of *Areopagitica*:

> God's Heritage is unto him as a speckled Bird, which the Birds fly round about against her: But however let us not fly . . . against our selves . . . but let us bear with one another, as to particular Light and Darkness, so long as we are all enlightened with the saving knowledge of the Truth . . . In some things peradventure thou art in the Light, and I am in the Dark; in others, the Day perhaps shineth unto me, and not to thee.[24]

It was to be a long time before the New England orthodoxy could countenance this kind of sweet reason; and when such a time finally did come, it came not as intellectual capaciousness but as reluctant strategy (when, for instance, Cotton Mather decided that Presbyterians in Massachusetts were a lesser evil than Episcopalians). Nathaniel Ward was entirely representative of Hooke's New England generation when he declared that "he that is willing to tolerate any Religion, or discrepant way of Religion, besides his own, unlesse it be in matters meerly indifferent, either doubts of his own, or is not sincere in it." Yet even while shaking their heads at Old England's slide into sophistication—her "roses are turned to *Flore de lices*"—New England's intellectual leadership bore witness to England's increasing glamour (for which Ward used the code of women's fashions—"wherewith they are surcingled and debauched").[25] If history had once allowed New Englanders to feel bold, it was making them feel stodgy. Toleration was the wave of England's future; and the most biting reminder of New England's consequent archaism was the visible fact of compatriots heading home.

The most vocal of the defectors was one who came and went before the civil wars broke out. Henry Vane arrived in New England in 1635 on a mission to mediate conflicting land claims among the Saybrook settlers. Traveling with John Winthrop, Jr., and Hugh Peter (who was also soon to return), he was greeted by Governor Winthrop as "a young gentleman of excellent parts." It was well known that Vane, enormously precocious, had emigrated over the objections of his father but with the sanction of the king. Having already served as a diplomat in Vienna, Vane embodied both a political and a psychological lift for New England: here was a gentleman's eldest son who had refused for conscience's sake the comforts of his inheritance. He came to New England in a "giddiness which then much displeased . . . his father," and at a moment when any sign of youth's favor was gratefully received. He had, furthermore, the king's approval—and because relations with the crown had never been worse, he brought badly needed legitimacy. Just one year earlier Laud, having seized Massachusetts-bound ships in the Thames, had put a temporary stop to all emigration. "If you linger too long," one New Englander had long before warned prospective immigrants, "the passage of Jordan through the malice of Sathan may be stopped that you cannot come if you would." From the start the colonists realized that their prestige in England was low and sinking (they had, after all, whisked their Charter out of the country for fear it would be revoked), and though their reputation among enemies did not concern them in the same way as did the declining esteem of friends, certain practical problems persisted. By the mid-thirties invasion by royal troops was regularly expected, and with good reason, since a growing number of ex–New Englanders were petitioning the Privy Council for redress of grievances against what they considered an illegitimate Massachusetts government.

> Not long after haveing received a Report that his Majestie intended to send a Generall Governor over, and being informed by a Shallop that they had seen a great ship and a smaller one goe into Cape Ann Harbor about 8 Leagues from Boston There was an Alarm presently given and early in the Morning being Sabbath day all the Traine Bands in Boston, and Townes adjacent were in Armes in the streets and posts were sent to all other places to be in the same posture, in which they continued untill by theire scouts they found her to be a small shipe of Plymouth and a shallope that piloted her in. The generall and Publick report was that it was to oppose the landing of an Enemie a Governor sent from England, and with this they acquainted the Commanders.[26]

The "Enemie a Governor" never came (at least not until the 1680s), but the stream of returning discontents increased until it came to constitute a reverse migration of its own. Those who went were far from quiet about their disenchantment. Most notorious among them were Thomas Morton and his debauched followers, who, according to Bradford, had spent their New England days (and especially their nights) "dancing and frisking together like so many fairies, or furies," and who, when banished to England, wasted no time in making "infamous and scurrilous" charges against those who had thrown them out.[27]

Other scoundrels made matters worse. A man named Ratcliffe, who was probably no more than "a bondsman in a strange land . . . a coarse, crazy, homesick Englishman," had his ears cropped and was sent back to England as early as 1631 for "uttering mallitious and scandalous speeches against the government and church."[28] He too signed an affidavit demanding an end to self-sovereignty in Massachusetts. Such expulsions were becoming commonplace, but even when the Puritan authorities acted exactly as their counterparts in England would have done, and banished rascals and criminals at home, they created more trouble for themselves abroad.

Vane, then, was duly prized, and he rose quickly to dizzying prestige for a man of twenty-three. Admitted to freemanship in March

1636, he was elected Governor in May. He was worldly but pious, adept at "policye" but radiant with faith. Yet there was one very significant difference between his conversion and the kind of saving experience sanctioned by the New England Way: he insisted that he had been called directly by God, with no ministerial intervention. God had called him without the intervention of the preached word.

What Vane shared with the antinomian party was an almost mischievous sense of the sufficiency of the holy spirit. "If there were no revelation but the word," Cotton had declared in 1636, "there would be no spiritual grace revealed to the soul." To the less sober mind of Captain John Underhill, one of the military heroes of the Pequot war, "the government at Boston [was] as zealous as the scribes and Pharisees," and if "the Lord was pleased to convert Saul while he was persecuting, so he might manifest himself to him while making a moderate use of the good creature tobacco." Vane, who was similarly unimpressed with New England's "converting" ministry, clashed bitterly with Winthrop on election day in May 1637 when he tried to read before the court a petition on behalf of John Wheelwright:

> The governour [Vane] would have read it, but the deputy [Winthrop] said it was out of order; it was a court of elections, and those must first be despatched, and then their petitions should be heard . . . but yet the governour and those of that party would not proceed to election, except the petition was read. Much time was already spent about this debate, and the people crying out for election, it was moved by the deputy, that the people should divide themselves, and the greater number must carry it. And so it was done, and the greater number by many were for election. But the governour and that side kept their place still, and would not proceed.[29]

Winthrop, in due time, prevailed, and under his restored leadership the court issued an order "that none should be received to inhabite within this Jurisdiction but such as should be allowed by some of the Magistrates." The act was passed as a means of shutting off reinforcement of the antinomians, who, according to Winthrop, "expected many of their opinion to come out of England." The law had to be more broadly justified, however, and so Winthrop appealed to the conventional analogy of society and body: "the intent of the law is to preserve the wellfare of the body; and for this ende to have none received into any fellowship with it who are likely to disturbe the same." There is something here of the resort to quarantine in time

of trouble—the old Puritan strategy of isolating the uninfected self—
a technique that had ceased to work in the England of the twenties,
but that was now being revised by the ideologues of the thirties from
a strategy of retreat into one of righteous combat. Vane, soon to
plunge back into the fight for England, found Winthrop's premises
weak, and said so without tact:

> A common-wealth [says Governor Winthrop] is a certaine companie
> of people consenting to cohabit together under one government, for
> their mutual safetye and wellfare. In which description the maine faulte
> is founde. At the best it is but a description of a common-wealth at
> large, and not of such a common-wealth as this . . . The common-wealth
> here described, may be a companye of Turkish pirates as well as Chris-
> tian professors . . . And is this such a body politicke as ours, as you say?
> God forbid. By this law . . . it will come to passe, that Christ and his
> members will finde worse entertainment amongst us than the Israelites
> did amongst the Egyptians and Babilonians, than Abram and Isaack did
> amongst the Philistines . . . yea even than Lott amongst the Sodom-
> ites . . . Here by this law we must not entertaine . . . such strangers as
> the magistrates like not, though they be never so gracious . . . Christ
> commands us to do good unto all, but especially to them of the house-
> hold of faith.[30]

These words, a taunting echo of what Winthrop had expressed aboard
the *Arbella* only seven years before, carried a terribly personal rebuke
for Winthrop and for the youthful hopes of Henry Vane as well.
Winthrop had dreamed of a commonwealth governed not merely by
"the lawe of nature," which, among other deficiencies, "could give
noe rules for dealing with enemies," but by "the lawe of Grace or
the Gospell." Natural law, he had insisted in 1630, "propounds one
man to another, as the same flesh and image of god," while the Gospel
instructs him "as a brother in Christ allsoe." It was precisely this
language of Christ that he was now, according to Vane, relinquishing.
Focused on the lacunae of Winthrop's brief, Vane's reply was a lacerating explication of what he judged to be Winthrop's misleading
compressions. It dwelt on the absence of a vocabulary that had once
been indispensably present:

> The churches [says the Governor] take libertye (as lawfully they may)
> to receive or rejecte at their discretion . . . why then should the com-
> monwealth be denied the like libertye? . . . Churches, [however,] have
> no libertye to receive or rejecte at their discretions, but at the discre-
> tions of Christ . . . In one word, there is no libertye to be taken neither

in church nor commonwealth but that which Christ gives and is according to him, Gal 5:1.[31]

Two months after delivering this eulogy for the New England idea of holy commonwealth, Vane sailed for home.

In Vane's valediction and departure there was galling bitterness for those who stayed. Cotton himself was sufficiently disgusted with Winthrop's exclusionary law that even he "intended to have removed out of the jurisdiction to Quinnypiack, since called New Haven." But the worst of it was Vane's accusation that New Englanders had abandoned the purpose for which they had come. His was no dutiful jeremiad about the passing of a doddering generation; it was a charge of apostasy thrown into the faces of the emigrants themselves while they could still plausibly think of themselves as strapping pioneers. You have become worldlings, Vane was saying, and though his youth and extravagance gave him an air of manor-bred privilege, others from the opposite end of the social spectrum were soon saying the same thing. "The scope of [the magistrates'] doctrine," complained Samuel Gorton in the 1640s, "was bent onely to maintain that outward forme of worship which they had erected to themselves, tending only to the outward carriage of one man toward another, leaving those principles of Divinity, wherein we had been instructed in our native Country, tending to faith towards God in Christ . . ." Gorton, who also returned to England under duress, could be dismissed as a "high and palmy" fanatic, but in Vane the colony had lost a showpiece.[32] If the magistrates had hoped for political help from him, they were thoroughly embarrassed by his charge that they were usurping not only Christ's authority but the king's as well. Vane, like Gorton, touched New England's nerve by locating true piety in the *Old* World and doubting aloud whether it had been transferred without loss to the New.

4

Among those who decided that the migration had had spiritual costs, one hears more strains that bear a striking affinity to the antinomian style as it expressed its root meaning, *anti-nomos,* against the law. "Under the fifth Monarchy," declared William Aspinwall, one of Mrs.

Hutchinson's banished allies who followed Vane to England, "Christ alone shalbe Law-giver, and if he be the Law-giver alone, you may easily conclude that he will own no other Laws but what himself hath given." Aspinwall took with him a rekindled hope that in the time of Christ's authority there would be a revival of the communal spirit that had withered in legalist New England. "Things of a middle nature, which you carry this way or another way, without breach of any rule of righteousness (as for instance, to secure their fields by a common fence, or by a keeper, and many such like things)," he argued, "they are not to be regulated by Laws, but by Covenants amongst the neighbour-hood, for their mutual good." "Mutual good" sustained by the unregulated human will was an idea rescued from its disappointing career in New England, and carried back to England by some of the returning migrants, among whom were a disproportionate number from "the transcendental school of divines." One of its conservators was Marmaduke Matthews, the man whom Johnson had urged to "stand up" and maintain Christ's truths; here he explains himself before his departure to a wary General Court:

> Christ . . . affords unto [his believers] not only a single righteousness, or a righteousness of immitation, for the resembling of righteous ones in respect of outward conversation, which was all the righteousness that the Pharisee had . . . nor meerly a double righteousness . . . which were all the righteousnesses that Adam in Paradise had . . . but a trebble righteousness or a righteousness of imputation, witness 2 Cor. 5,21; Phil. 3:10; which is more than Christ himself either hath or doth need . . .[33]

However garbled doctrinally, this kind of refusal to relinquish the highest hopes for human renovation was at the heart of the reverse migration for many who joined it. Thomas Venner, who returned to England in the fifties and was soon implicated in a plot to overthrow the restored monarchy, believed fervently that "that beastlike and brutish nature, and principles (from whence has proceeded all Murders, Thefts, Rebellion, Violence, Oppression, Ravenning and Devouring his fellow creatures . . .) shall be in a great measure done away." How many participants in the reverse migration can be securely associated with this party of hope is a question for whose answer we shall have to wait. In the meantime, we must be content with the scattered hints. Women seem to have felt especially bereft by the suppression of the antinomian ministers—and it would be fascinating to know how many made the outward journey in the aftermath of Anne Hutchinson's defeat. "The female portion of [Matthew's] flock"—thiry-six women of the Malden church—affixed their names to a petition beseeching the court to permit his continued presence among them, "by whose pious life and labors the Lord hath afforded us many saving convictions."[34] If antinomianism had a special appeal for women in early New England, it was in part because they were less susceptible than their husbands to the charms of a religion that increasingly equated sanctification with worldly performance. Many of the exiled ministers spoke with uncommon ardor for those in New England who still thought of grace as a miraculous dispensation from a God who could not be courted or impressed.

Vane's *Brief Answer* was the manifesto of that party. What was most disquieting (and most prescient) in it was its sense that New England was stalled, a feeling that could not be denied even by those who assailed Mrs. Hutchinson for saying the same thing: "What came you into this wilderness to see?" asked Shepard—addressing a collective "you"—"more of the Lord Jesus [?] And will you now forget the end for which you came? . . . When a harlot seeks to satisfy her lusts, she cares not how far her husband be off, never desires his coming home; so here. Many a one commplains he can not desire the Lord Jesus . . . [and] where is the cause of it? O, they are running in another channel, and spent on other things."[35]

As the cry was raised against the reign of "things," in the ministers and magistrates was growing something of the desperation that can be the prelude to exorcism. Greed became the accusation of the times; the word was much closer then than now to neutrality; its pejoration inhered in the object, not in the emotion, of desire. By the late thirties, the New England ministry was losing its grip on the delicate ethical distinction it had struggled to maintain in the early days of settlement: the idea that the human will may be drawn into holiness or damnation according to the nature of its desired object. Once New England's oratory had been a rhetoric of ecstasy designed to incite holy intoxication in a "benummed" people. But if the ministers had once urged the people to "drinke abundantly" of the spirit, they spoke now less and less in the mode of invitation. "The great God of heaven and earth is up in arms against thee, he is upon the march to work thy destruction."[36] The New England ministry had once mainly beckoned; now it mainly attacked.

One of the consequences of this shift was a change in the ministers'

suasive strategy: if they had once tried to keep certain central words—
"greed" among them—in a sort of neutral transparency, they now
tended to avoid them. When a preacher, in the heady early days, had
used "bride" (situating it within the context provided by Canticles)
he did so in part to tease the mind into a brush with carnal meanings.
"O beloved, have you such a husband as Christ in heaven, that loves
thy looks, thy company?" One of the miracles of scripture was that
it could use profane language for holy purposes. Cotton, for instance,
had reminded the emigrants at Southampton that "the comparison
[in the parables] from the unjust Steward, and from the Theefe in
the night, is not taken from the injustice of the one, or the theft of
the other; but from the wisdome of the one, and the sodainnesse
of the other; which in themselves are not unlawfull."[37] The ministry
had once been willing to employ such a dangerous homiletics by
flourishing words like "bride," "bowels," "union," "greed." One way
of understanding what happened in New England in the late 1630s
is to notice that a shocked and chastened ministry came to the conclusion that this rhetorical practice had been a mistake. By 1640 they
were in visible retreat toward a concept of sin closer to its Elizabethan
form—as impulse, appetite, desire—and in the process the distinction
between holy and profane desire was being blurred.

Into this place of dissonance and truncated language, where ministers and magistrates were increasingly asserting order rather than
animating grace as the distinguishing mark of Christian society, the
stream of hopeful immigrants slowed to a trickle. By 1640 (as even
the Mathers conceded) it began to reverse itself. If Englishmen and
women had come to New England in quest of a foretaste of the
"GENERAL ASSEMBLY of the FIRST-BORNE," their hope, at least according to some who left, was turning to ash. "The exercise of church
discipline," as one historian puts it, "absorbed more of the church's
time than all other ecclesiastical activities combined." Winthrop himself had approvingly reported Cotton's opinion in 1639 that "when
magistrates are forced to provide for the maintenance of ministers,
&c. then the churches are in a declining condition," but that same
year the General Court found it necessary to pass a law assessing
those who did not voluntarily contribute. One of those who returned
to Old England in the 1650s uttered a retrospective judgment on
such a surrender of voluntarism: "To force the People of God to pay
tithes . . . [we] may as well by a civil Law require Bullocks, Goats,

and Lambes, &c. for sacrifices."[38] Winthrop's ideal of 1630 was in a shambles before the decade was out, and some had had the bad manners to announce its demise.

Most of the stresses were coming, as we have seen, from the religious "left." The radicals' argument, however various on matters of ecclesiology and doctrine, amounted collectively to the charge that the idea of grace was being debased into a tribal icon. Grace was not, they objected, a quantity that could be transmitted through the loins of gracious parents or through catechistic teaching (thus the case against baptising children before they have shown signs of gracious affections), nor could it be forced into the people by compulsion. The difficulty in answering these arguments was that they were very much the same as those which the mainstream Puritan leadership had made against the established church in England. Faced with the unassimilable historical irony that they were becoming what they had fled, the New England authorities acted in the forties with increasing severity to reign the "spiritists" in. In 1644 they passed a law against antipaedobaptists; in 1651 an outspoken opponent of infant baptism, Obadiah Holmes, was subjected to public lashing; in 1654 persons of "unsound" opinions were barred from teaching at Harvard College. There was trouble on the "right" as well—from those whose minds ran along "loose, large" Presbyterian lines and who raised questions about the scriptural basis of "exquisite examination" of candidates for communion. "Alas, alas!" exclaimed John Norton as he watched the cleavage widen, "Is there no medium between . . . Papacy and Anarchy, *Babylon* and *Babel*?"[39]

Civil disorder seemed equally on the rise. By 1642 Thomas Shepard was remarking on "that inundation of abominable filthinesses breaking in upon us," by which he was referring to a rash of incidents of bestiality and sodomy. Three years earlier one resident of the New Haven colony was executed for the unlikely achievement of engendering a piglet. In Salem, in the five years before 1640, roughly ten percent of its resident males (and a good number of women, too) appeared as defendants before the Essex quarterly court, a tribunal of magistrates created in 1636 to handle disputes that could not be settle by arbitration within the towns. "False weights, illegal sale of liquor . . . abuse of constables" were among the infractions with which individuals were charged, and in 1637 the evil of enclosure—an Old World sin if ever there was one—joined the list. One respectable townsman simply carved out a part of the common for his own use, and nothing could be done without a unanimous vote of the selectmen, one of whom demurred. Such local stalemates highlighted the impotence of diffused authority, and the General Court, clinging to "the lingering force of the communal paradigm" (which was more and more associated with an earlier day in England), began to move to consolidate its disciplinary power.[40]

In so doing, it found itself resorting to strategies that seemed— especially to those who ran afoul of them—reminiscent of the arbitrary powers that had hampered and enraged Puritan entrepreneurs in England. Among the king's most bitterly resented policies had been his efforts to limit and tax commercial activity by granting trade monopolies. By the 1640s the New England magistrates were issuing regional monopolies for the Indian trade and trying to bring the inflationary bidding for imports under control by determining which merchants could deal with which incoming ships. In the mid-thirties they had already attempted to regulate the distribution of land in order to counter the flight of labor from the towns and the resulting price explosion. But in general such regulatory tactics served only to create what the magistrates and their clerical allies began to regard as an ungrateful monster, a faction of rising entrepreneurs who, seeming to feed on shortages in foodstuffs and building materials, mounted a challenge for dominance in the Bay. When Vane described the magistrates as haughty absolutists, the merchants doubtless listened and agreed. But when the merchants turned to the ministers (or at least to most of them), they were likely to be rebuked:

> It is clear, then, thou lookest upon the things of the world as great things. O, to have such honor; such an estate; so many cows and goats; so much ground paled in; so many plows; lands, and oxen fit to labor; so much grain to come in every year; and such parts and gifts and duties to get me a name, to live before the best men, and to be good signs (to comfort me) of the favor of God . . . the very hopes heat and warm the heart.[41]

In this scramble for "parts," the mantle of representative villain fell to a Boston merchant named Robert Keayne, a man of solid Christian credentials who protested that the offense for which he was charged in 1639—overpricing a bag of nails—was "not only now common almost in every shop and warehouse but even then and ever since with a higher measure of excess, yea even by some of them that

were most zealous and had their hands and tongues deepest in my
censure." The behavior of Keayne, who was publicly admonished in
the First Church (he may have escaped excommunication by virtue
of being John Wilson's brother-in-law), was tested by Cotton against
the standard of I Corinthians—"if any man that is called a brother
be . . . covetous . . . or an extortioner; with such an one [you may]
not eat"—which raised the question of his eligibility to participate in
the Lord's Supper. Keayne had many companions in disgrace, of
whom Hutchinson, Gorton, and Williams (who continued to insist
through the forties that New England's churches must foreswear all
connection with the church of England) are only the best known.
New England had become practiced in expulsion and angry with itself.
Although historians have focused almost exclusively upon those who
arrived rather than those who left, we have nevertheless missed the
immigrants' sense (vivid already by the late thirties) that they were
coming into an imperiled place.[42]

One such immigrant, a hopeful English minister named Thomas
Tillam, recorded in passable verse his emotion "Uppon the First Sight
of New England" in 1638. His poem has become an almost hackneyed
centerpiece for the view that New Englanders—both new and established—were swelling with millenarian anticipation that "the come-
again Christ would reward his servants who had left English comforts
for this wilderness." The opening of Tillam's poem is indeed optative,
if not quite fulfilled: "hayle holy-land wherein our holy lord / hath
planted his most true and holy word." As the poem progresses, however, its force becomes much more hortatory than celebratory, its
pivotal verb is not "hayle," but "Come":

> come my deare little flocke, who for my sake
> have lefte your Country, dearest friends, and goods
> and hazarded your lives o'th raginge floods
> . . . . .
> Come yee my servants of my father Blessed.

These lines convey a notable sense of incompletion in a poem about
arrival. There is more journeying to do, and the turn of the verse—
the moment that gives it what sinew and tension it has—introduces
the prospect that this fortunate people, like the Jews, will squander
their God-given advantage:

heare I'le bee with yow, heare you shall Inioye
my sabbaths, sacraments, my minestrye
and ordinances in their puritye
but yet beware of Sathans whylye baites
hee lurkes amongs yow, Cunningly hee waites
to Catch yow from mee . . . [43]

This is a poet who had read at least a few love lyrics, who has grasped, if not mastered, the notion that a poem can come alive by hinting at the deficiency of its speaker as he rhapsodizes over his beloved. Tillam's little work is a stretched sonnet that piles the love-hope high and then—with a change that feels utterly expected—shifts into a minor key. Whatever the merits of its execution, it is not an entirely naive performance. It is, moreover, a poem less about hope than about betrayal.

While Edward Johnson and others were making Anne Hutchinson into their "Sathan" of "whylye baites," Tillam (who stayed in New England too briefly to have left any record of his activities) was doing precisely the opposite; he was confirming her spirit and her judgment. He exulted, as Anne Hutchinson did, in an ecstatic rhyming prose that expressed "the cleer knowledge of the great Mysteries of Godliness, the gracious flowings of love from life, and life from light— the sweet experimental breathings of a Christ within (in a more excellent manner than I am able to recite)." Tillam shared Hutchinson's conviction that the experience of grace was beyond verbal expression, and that no one in the Bay Colony (save, perhaps, Cotton, with his heavily scriptural recitations) was expressing it. He also shared her candor: "That *New-England* way of keeping persons upon trial many Months, my soul could never close with. The way of Christ, is to receive poor, wounded, thirsty, penitent souls, upon their earnest desires."[44] These words are a valuable clue not only to Tillam's particular experience but to the mood of many who returned with him to England in the aftermath of the antinomian crisis. Tillam is not so much a witness to the "apocalyptic emotion" of early New Englanders as he is an indicator that it was the most millenarian-minded of the Puritans who tended to give up on New England.

Tillam left in anger. "Godly pastors must be *patient* patterns, not self-willed, nor brawlers, but beseeching Ambassadors . . . bearing long with the infirmities of Christs Lambs." This is not the language of the synod of 1637, after which the injunction of I Timothy—that "a woman (must) learn in quietness with all subjection"—was more widely enforced in the churches. It was not the promise of "a word of terror to dash the hopes and sink the hearts of all haughty sinners"; it was, instead, a language of tolerance—a language fast becoming obsolete, spoken by the dwindling number of New England ministers who saw themselves "as doores to open a wide entrance for the people to come to Christ; not as . . . Port-cullises, yea, gates of Hell." More than anything else, the literature of repatriation confirms that New England was a place in which no deprivation was more keenly felt than the want of assurance. God "hath loved thee," said the ministry, trying to respond to this need, "when he might have passed by thee [for] men of greater place, greater gifts and parts, greater pomp in the world." But such words of reassurance were not enough. New Englanders, it was soon clear, were becoming restless, darting about in search of peace, pressing outward into the taunting wilderness.[45]

The only effective response to this pathology, as William Hooke discovered, was not militant language but purposeful exertion: a fact movingly declared in a letter to Winthrop in which Hooke called himself "still valetudinarious" but ready "to do . . . acceptable service [in England] before my great change cometh." The opportunity—any opportunity—of "acceptable service" was one of the leading impulses for the return migration. There is a vibrancy in its literature that was simply not possible in New England any longer. "The Beast or chief Soveraign," wrote Aspinwall, identifying King Charles with the beast of Daniel 23, "was slain or beheaded, v. 11. and his Body, that is, all reliques of royal power, which are as karkasses of royalty, all of them first or last must be demolished and destroyed." Aspinwall began his pamphlet (which predicted the fall of the Antichrist in 1673) with a nearly capering delight: "This is the doom of the little horn, or sovereign of 3 Kingdoms, and hath been fulfilled to a jot. And the karkasses of royalty have begun to be demolished, and more and more wilbe till they be utterly destroyed." His was, moreover, a widely shared delight: "Famous was our (*ever honoured*) *Cromwell, Lord Chancellor of England*," said Tillam, "for destroying *Babels* abominable *Monasteries,* whose visible ruines remain as a monument to the blessed memory of that renowned man." More than anything else, the literature of repatriation testified to the need for a visible enemy: If, wrote Hanserd Knollys (who returned in 1640), the children of God hope to witness a day when "professors of the gospel . . . will be much reformed," when "a pure language [and] the ministry of the gospel [and] the gifts of the Holy Spirit shall be restored," then "they ought to be . . . doing the work of their generation . . . bearing their witness for Christ, against antichrist, his ministry, magistracy, churches, worship, ordinances, and discipline; and in finishing their testimony of the kingdom." The New World held no adequate object for Knollys' preposition *against*. To find such an opposition, one had to go to England.[46]

If there was a truly potent enemy in the New World, it was not Indians, or May Pole misfits, but the self. The casualties of zeal in New England were not temples of the Antichrist but vulnerable seekers after assurance, people whose expectation of a blinding transformation of the self left every stirring of grace feeling too small. In New England's preparationism—which grew ever more stringent after the defeat of Anne Hutchinson—there was high human cost, and some of the most articulate of those who returned to England said so. The most candid among them was Giles Firmin, formerly deacon of the First Church of Boston. By 1651, as minister of Shalford, Essex, Firmin was attacking the New England preparationists, not with rancor, but with compassion. He expressed sorrow, for example, for a New England "Maid-servant who was very godly, and reading . . . *Mr. Shepherd's* Book . . . was so cast down, and fell into such troubles, that all the Christians that came to her could not quiet her spirit." The burden of Firmin's preaching was that the problem of assurance could not be solved by relentless examination of the quality of one's faith. The American preparationists, he suggested, had misdirected attention from the solace of Christ and had become obsessed with the inadequacy of the self. This was a theme particularly compatible with New England's corporate mood. "Some eminent Divines," Firmin wrote, "have . . . layed some blocks in the way, which have caused much trouble of spirit to loaden and afflicted Souls, who have been flying to Christ for Refuge." Unlike Solomon Stoddard, who was later to criticize the preparationist idea as a prop of pride (anticipating the spirit of Benjamin Franklin's remark that "if I could conceive that I had completely overcome [pride], I should probably be proud of my humility"), Firmin saw in it the curtailment of hope. Among the many "blocks" he identified he was especially exasperated by New England's demand that the "sinner [must answer] the question before you enter into the City, or close with Christ, *Is it the glory of Gods grace which you seek, above your own salvation? . . .* Good Lord, saith the poor sinner, how shall I know this?"[47]

New Englanders, Firmin implied, were torturing themselves with scholastic niceties, elevating "compunction" to a commandment. The elderly Richard Mather did nothing to refute that charge when he bade farewell to his Dorchester congregation in 1657:

> But what should I speak of comming to heaven? The truth is, without Compunction of heart & sorrow of soul for a mans sinns, he is never like to attain to any truth of saving grace upon earth . . . Is not the way to Canaan through the wilderness? . . . In like sort, a soul must go through a wilderness-like condition, that is, he must be afflicted with sight and sense of spiritual misery & sin, before he can attain to any state of saving rest & grace in Christ Jesus.

With "Zacheus," Firmin asked, "when he was converted . . . where were those legal sore Compunctions?" New Englanders had made pain a necessary witness to faith— the "true sight of sin," said Hooker, "is the onely doore to life and salvation"—the sort of assertion that was, according to Firmin, unsanctioned by scripture. "Where," he asked, "doth the holy Scripture (by which I must be judged) put that condition, *prepared,* into the Command, to make it my duty? . . . There is but one Rule to which all men must conform, who shall go to heaven, i.e. *Regeneration,* or *Faith in Christ,* or *Conversion.*"[48]

Though more specific and candid in his objections than any other writer on the subject, Firmin was by no means alone in associating New England's failing morale with the severity of its preparationism. Christopher Blackwood, whose reasons for leaving are made plain in the subtitle of his *The Storming of Antichrist In his two last and strongest Garrisons; of Compulsion of Conscience, and Infants Baptisme* (1644), also focused much of his post–New England preaching on the danger of finding sufficiency in the preparatory stage. "The efficient cause of Repentance is God," he insisted, as if to forestall any misunderstandings on that point. "Some look upon Repentance, as if it were nothing but a sorrow for sin . . . yet many a man . . . without a [divinely induced] change of minde and heart they will come to nothing."[49]

According to John Winthrop, however, who never liked to delve into such theological disputes, the economic and spiritual turmoils that were engulfing New England had a common external cause:

> The parliament of England setting upon a general reformation both of church and state, the earl of Strafford being beheaded, and the archbishop (our great enemy) and many others of the great officers and judges, bishops and others, imprisoned and called to account, this caused all men to stay in England in expectation of a new world, so as few coming to us, all foreign commodities grew scarce, and our own of no price.[50]

Winthrop was never a millenarian—not in the *Arbella* sermon, not now. As he shook his head at the excitements in England and the consequent collapse of New England's attraction as refuge, he understood that if there was a place where men and women felt (delusively, he thought) that they lived on the verge of "the new heaven and the new earth," it was Old England, not New.

For most who came over in the Great Migration, America was not a place where one might nurture a regeneracy that was already manifest to the self in England. It was instead a place where one could dare to hope that for the first time the spirit might make itself felt. The Puritan immigrant's question had not been merely, "shall *I* find Christ in America," but whether there could be in America a *community* of saints. The saint, as Blackwood explained in the language that Cotton had struggled to keep alive, is "a body of created graces," who must be "assimilating. He that changes his course, would have others to change with him; if a man change a principle or practice, he would have all the world to change with him." We have here once again the antinomian accent, which, like its Emersonian successor, is falsely accused of solipsism: "It is very certain that it is the effect of conversation with the beauty of the soul, to beget a desire and need to impart to others the same knowledge and love. If utterance is denied, the thought lies like a burden on the man." It is true that attendance at public testimony could have a discouraging effect by making the hopeful communicant shrink from his own inadequacy; "the intensity of experience [could seem] so much greater in others."[51] But the hope for living contagion was not easily given up.

By the mid-fifties, Norton summed up the mood of his generation this way: "Now our candlesticks cannot but lament in darkness, when their lights are gone; and the thrones of David mourn, that so many of our late worthies can be seen [in New England] no more. Our desiderable men that remain, remove from us, and few they are who return again."[52] The many who "removed" cannot be adequately understood within the categories devised by those who remained. They were not simply "weak-hearted men," nor could they be conveniently dismissed as tolerationists or familists or "palmy fanatics." If their diverse character defies summary, they nevertheless left a recoverable impression in the minds of those who watched them go. For New Englanders who wanted, in Christopher Blackwood's phrase, to change "all the world," it was impossible to remain in New England. For those who remained, the world's renovation had become a hope deferred.

We try to conjure out of the rescued fragments of forgotten time the historic memory that haunts us in dreams, in the residue of language, gesture and prejudice, traced to its genesis. There is a generation whose taproot was cut somewhere in each American past, whether by poverty, diaspora, or land enclosure. It is the generation that had to leave home. We inherited from it a sense of loss.   Mary Lee Settle, 1984

7 Fathers and Children

By the 1640s the first New Englanders were beginning to concede that some among them had made the journey to America "upon sudden undigested grounds, and saw not God leading them in their way." Such flighty ones, however, were not so much a burden as a happy explanation for the reverse migration; they were, after all, going back just as they had come—for "sleight, headlesse, unworthy reasons"—and they thereby gave to New England the chance to declare itself winnowed. It was an opportunity eagerly taken: "Though some few have removed . . . yet (we may truly say) thousands as wise as themselves would not change their place for any other in the World." This notion that the colony was being purified by the desertion of the weak was an attractive one, but the rhetoric with which it was put forward was frequently strained. Those who returned home were somehow "headless," yet "wise"; they left with no appreciation of what they were leaving behind, but once in England they "wished themselves [back in New England] again." For those who stayed, the restoration of monarchy and episcopacy would soon enough ratify their sense of having been deserted by all the world—of being left, as Perry Miller memorably put it, "alone with America."[1] The events of 1660 were, in this view, more a confirmation than a shock. In the whole literature of what we call Puritanism, stretching between the reigns of Elizabeth and Charles II, the distinctively American note is not the theme of chosenness, but of collective loneliness—the feeling of having been abandoned by both enemies and friends, of being consigned as a group to the world's indifference.

This note of abandonment contains the beginning of an answer to the question that sooner or later must be asked by and of all Puritan scholarship: Why is a grasp of Puritanism fundamental to an understanding of American culture? Lately, some historians have answered this question by denying its premise. A recent book by Francis Jennings, *The Invasion of America* (1975), proclaims by its title that what has usually been positively or neutrally styled—*The Transit of Civilization from England to America in the Seventeenth Century* (Edward Eggleston, 1900); *The Peopling of British North America* (Bernard Bailyn, 1986–)—was essentially a sustained act of violence by Europeans against the "savages" they found living there. Jennings's argument begins with a remark that is designed to shake up some old assumptions about the nature of our cultural inheritance: "Modern American society evolved from [the] web of interrelationship [between Indian and English cultures], and if much of the Indian contribution is not immediately visible nowadays, neither is very much of the Anglo-Saxon."[2] Intellectual historians have, of course, always given the latter a great deal of visibility, a fact that can sometimes distort our sense of more recent American cultural development and, ironically, obscure the experience of the Puritans themselves. They are in danger of becoming less human beings than manufacturers of an ideology for consumption by (and of) subsequent Americans.

The ideological legacy of the Puritans has, moreover, been peculiarly subject not only to culturally conditioned interpretations but to highly personal ones—a rule to which the present book is doubtless no exception. This is so because, no matter how estranged we may feel from their experience, to speak of them (whether with recrimination or with reverence) is still in some sense to speak of our nativity. In "Errand into the Wilderness," for example, Miller gave us a portrait of the founders embarking to the New World with a pathetically positive "sense of mission"—to erect exemplary churches—only to be forgotten by their battle-tested brethren back home. As powerful as this reading is, with its vision of the New World Puritans declining into compulsive material productivity and flabby moralism (their putative gifts to us), it manifested very deeply Miller's own bewilderment as a combatant in World War II. Writing in an injured spirit, Miller was reeling, with his Puritans, at the discovery that postwar Europe declined to embrace its American savior: "Thus early commenced that chronic weakness in the foreign policy of Americans, an inability to recognize who in truth constitute their best friends abroad." This was the Miller who felt friendless not only abroad but at home, who described himself as a "lone wolf," identifying with the variously abandoned figures of the pioneer generation. His "Errand into the Wilderness" was a great work of the historical imagination, but it was also an act of self-portraiture. One can readily imagine his growling assent to Leslie Fiedler's later remark that there have been many instances of "the shrinking on our shores from Brobdingnagian parents to Lilliputian children."[3]

Miller's drama has been periodically revised in the decades since it was composed, lately not so much for its extravagance as for its understatement. The leading variant was put forth about fifteen years ago—a version of the Puritans' undertaking their migration not merely for pedagogic purposes but as a journey "to the scene of Christ's triumphant descent to his New Jerusalem." This reading, chiefly associated with the work of Sacvan Bercovitch, was a deconstruction of what appeared to the mind of the 1960s to be a pernicious and fearfully compelling national myth. It disclosed in the colonial imagination a preposterous symbolism that contained the seed not only of Manifest Destiny but of Doctor Strangelove as well. "The Puritans," Bercovitch wrote in a sentence at least as angry as Miller's on our foolish choice of friends, "used the Biblical myth of exodus and conquest to justify imperialism before the fact." The unspoken question behind this statement was the pressing question of its day: "Why are we in Vietnam?"[4]

There is, to be sure, nothing startling about the fact that the Puritans have descended to us through time-bound interpreters. This has always been so. Isaac Backus, committed to the disestablishment of religion in Enlightenment America, saw in them the beginning of a lineage of Baptist martyrs. Peter Oliver, deposed as a colonial Chief Justice and hounded into exile by what he judged to be the upstart envy of rebel scoundrels, found in the Puritans a precedent for that "certain something in human Nature, let it be called Pride, [or] a Fondness for Superiority . . . which stimulates the Mind to act as a Bell Weather to a Flock." Daniel Webster, articulating the antebellum orthodoxy of the Whig party, imagined his Puritan forebears dreaming that their descendants would someday "whiten this coast with the canvas of a prosperous commerce." In the bitter aftermath of Appomattox, Sidney Lanier declared that "once upon a time there arose in the breasts of men a simultaneous desire for the formation of stock companies, and for the protection of their charters . . . hence . . . United States."[5] Such a catalogue can be endlessly extended. Yet no matter how relativistic our sense of history may be, we are always committed to the conviction that some readings of the past are truer than others.

With this in mind, I want briefly to retrieve an insight from what remains the single indispensable study of Puritan culture, Nathaniel Hawthorne's *The Scarlet Letter*. In that extraordinary book Hawthorne imagines a mid-seventeenth-century New England minister, places him before his flock, puts a candid and agonized confession on his lips, and tortures him with the impenetrability of his audience—an audience that will not comprehend the truth of the words he speaks to them: "People of New England . . . ye, that have deemed me holy!— behold me here, the one sinner of the world!"[6] If Hawthorne is to be believed—and he is at least to be listened to—the idea of sin had, with astonishing quickness, become an empty formula in Puritan New England. It had become precisely the kind of ritual incantation that had stirred the English Puritans against the Anglican church a century before. Confession (which was to play out its ultimate ironies at Salem, where the only hope for the innocent was to make an admission of guilt) has become a comforting familiarity—like blessings at Mass. Dimmesdale's audience is more reassured than troubled by his performance.

All the more desperate, therefore, to convey his unwelcome truth, and knowing that his only hope for doing so is to manifest his sin as materiality, Dimmesdale bares and mutilates himself. His self-humiliation remains, for all its vividness, an inadequate supplement to his words. His reverent people—from the infatuated "virgins . . . [who] grew pale around him" to "the aged members of his flock [who] believed that he would go heavenward before them"— still do not really see his brand:

> Most of the spectators testified to having seen, on the breast of the unhappy minister, a SCARLET LETTER—the very semblance of that worn by Hester Prynne—imprinted in the flesh. As regarded its origin, there

were various explanations, all of which must necessarily have been conjectural. Some affirmed that the Reverend Mr. Dimmesdale, on the very day when Hester Prynne first wore her ignominious badge, had begun a course of penance,—which he afterwards, in so many futile methods, followed out,—by inflicting a hideous torture on himself. Others contended that the stigma had not been produced until a long time subsequent, when old Roger Chillingworth, being a potent necromancer, had caused it to appear, through the agency of magic and poisonous drugs. Others, again,—and those best able to appreciate the minister's peculiar sensibility, and the wonderful operation of his spirit upon the body,—whispered their belief, that the awful symbol was the effect of the ever active tooth of remorse, gnawing from the inmost heart outwardly, and at last manifesting Heaven's dreadful judgment by the visible presence of the letter. The reader may choose among these theories . . . It is singular, nevertheless, that certain persons, who were spectators of the whole scene, and professed never once to have removed their eyes from the Reverend Mr. Dimmesdale, denied that there was any mark whatever on his breast, more than a new-born infant's.[7]

The beautiful conclusion of *The Scarlet Letter* gives us Dimmesdale in retreat from his function as soul-physician to this obtuse community. There is no longer any collective understanding about the nature, or even the existence, of sin. In the smaller circle of his family Dimmesdale is able to find rest in the "wondrous generosity" of Hester's heart—and, thus restored to tranquillity, to deliver his disordered daughter from incipient madness into womanhood. Such is the residue of his pastoral power. But one closes *The Scarlet Letter* with the sense that Dimmesdale, however complete his private purgation, has failed in his public office. "Majestic as [his] voice sometimes became, there was for ever in it an essential character of plaintiveness." After the election sermon, John Wilson, one of the surviving founders (and, as Hawthorne knew, a principal victor over Anne Hutchinson), notices "the state in which [Dimmesdale] was left by the retiring wave of intellect and sensibility," and offers him his arm. It is "decidedly repelled."[8] With the people of Boston in their own admiring swoon before him, Dimmesdale takes no satisfaction, and declines the laying on of a father's hand. The Puritan moment is over.

And yet in its termination Hawthorne finds a residue of a suppressed, but not entirely extinct, idea. He has dramatized a cultural conflict that was to remain central in the New World—a conflict between the struggle to preserve a sense of sin as what he explicitly called "alienation from the Good" (Dimmesdale's effort to complete himself with Hester's madonna love), and the community's more savage sense of evil as an entity with a dangerous life of its own (Hester as alien adultress to be expelled). By thus "creating romance," as Parrington put it, "out of the problem of evil," Hawthorne associated the dominant Puritan community with the latter impulse (characterized by a commitment to catechistic learning and forms of repression), while linking his antinomian dissidents (characterized by a released eroticism) with the former. (The preface to *The Scarlet Letter* was his preemptive effort to free this cultural paradigm from antiquarian quaintness, to connect it firmly with his—and his readers'—present. If we think of the burgeoning abolitionist belief in the 1840s that a slave-conspiracy exclusive to the whorish South was the whole measure of the nation's sin, and of the rising tide of disunion sentiment on both sides of the impending conflict, we may judge Hawthorne's linkage between the centuries a grim success.) In giving form to this fundamental conflict within the nation's moral imagination, Hawthorne littered *The Scarlet Letter* with suggestions that he was writing about the transition from a first-generation immigrant community to the world its children made. He takes care to register the death of Governor Winthrop, and emphasizes that the founders "possessed, by hereditary right, the quality of reverence; which, in their descendants, if it survive at all, exists in smaller proportion, and with a vastly diminished force." The founders, "had they followed their hereditary taste . . . would have illustrated all events of public importance by bonfires, banquets, pageantries, and processions." But "their immediate posterity, the generation next to the early emigrants, wore the blackest shade of Puritanism, and so darkened the national visage with it, that all the subsequent years have not sufficed to clear it up."[9] The reverent imagination, Hawthorne judged, was short-lived in America.

To demonstrate the captivity of subsequent Americans to this inheritance was among the leading purposes of others among the first writers whom we call major. Hawthorne himself treated the theme as forcefully in such tales as "Young Goodman Brown" as in the story of Dimmesdale's destruction. It became one of Melville's constant concerns—in the portrait of Captain Delano, who does not begin to examine his own pinched perceptions but is consumed by the effort to apportion sin between African and European satanic candidates;

in the monomaniac Ahab; in the "safe" lawyer who narrates "Bartleby, the Scrivener"; even in the tantalizing Satan-hunt that is *The Confidence Man* (1857). When seen (as he wished to be) in the same lineage, Henry James can be said to ratify this linkage between innocence and a fearful moralism: consider Ralph Touchett seeking to preserve the purity of an American girl by arming her against wooers with the means to be insular, or Olive Chancellor training Verena Tarrant in a separatist ideology, or John Marcher hunting everywhere but within the self for the obstacles to his fulfillment.

Such indictments of morally myopic Americans have been handed down by our most alert writers with a great deal of compassion; when the same judgment descends from distant witnesses, the judicial tone is likely to be angrier. Consider, for example, Graham Greene's withering account of evil as ignorance of the self, of *The Quiet American* (1954) as a man incapable of understanding the concept of complicity. There is a large literature (with, no doubt, an expansive future) that warns the world against this crusading American who finds Satan everywhere except in his own deficiencies. He wanders the earth, in Greene's terms, like a leper without his bell.

I have tried in this book to expound a related and perhaps even an originating theme: the transformation of the idea of sin from the self-critical Augustinian meaning that it briefly sustained in prerevolutionary England into the self-righteous form that it has chiefly assumed in Protestant America: sin as excrescence, disease—the threatening other—against which the community of purist selves builds barricades. Hawthorne understood that at the heart of the Protestant imagination as it developed in America there has always been a competition between these alternatives.

2

The process that Hawthorne cast in dramatic form as a generational decline in the New World had in fact begun with the rationalization of religious life in Elizabethan England. It was a century-long event that may be called the death of Catholicism. The Puritans naturally preferred a more positive terminology for it; they called it the substitution of a preaching ministry for a papist "dumbshow." They embodied it in the architecture of their chapels and meeting-houses, which were studies "in black and white etching," in which the chancel floor, if structurally separated at all from that of the nave, would be only slightly raised; the communion table of unpolished oak or pine; and the surrounding benches for communicants furnished with foot-rests rather than kneelers. The whole functioned to encourage an insular, "family-at-worship appearance" rather than as a public space to foster elevating mystery. Yet the leaders of the Elizabethan Puritan movement sensed a danger in their own affective and aesthetic renovations. They tried to discount the problem by turning it into a triviality: "Alas . . . what shall we now do at church," they asked in feigned sorrow, mocking the people's (especially women's) appetite for sensation and diversion, "since all the saints are taken away, since all the goodly sights we were wont to have are gone."[10] According to this view of condescension toward the people's taste for spectacle, the confiscation of "goodly sights" was not a grievous theft, but an act preliminary to the establishment of a truer, aural religion. The mind of the believer was now directed to roam among verbally delivered abstractions; the eye was sternly denied. What began as aesthetic discipline became a sensory deprivation that led to a stringent rationalism on the one hand, and, as Richard Hooker had predicted, to continual outbreaks of antinomian desire on the other. Those, like Perkins and Ames, who did much to dislodge the sense of grace as a miraculous apprehension of the holy spirit, and to replace it with an intellectually apprehended rectification of disorder within the soul, nevertheless felt the threat of loss overwhelming what they had gained. The displacement of visible grace by intellectual control as the paramount value of religious experience was a spiritually costly event.

This process of rationalization elevated discipline rather than reverent feeling to the first rank of devotional achievements, and became, in time, a psychological disaster. Some tried to cope with it by emigration which, as Edmund Morgan has remarked, "offered a substitute for revolution." In one sense both of these recourses were astonishingly successful: one nation was permanently altered, and another initiated as an essentially bourgeois "culture of discipline." Yet in a different sense both recourses ultimately failed as spiritual therapies for those who were uneasy with the historical transformation that they themselves were helping to enact. "Preparation and the fear it entailed," as one scholar has written, "became the special case for America."[11]

At least since the appearance of Tawney's *Religion and the Rise of Capitalism* (1938), we have all more or less subscribed to some form of the Weberian argument that the Puritans were born—or made— to be businessmen. Yet, as Christopher Hill has shown in a series of passionate books, the revolution that began to turn England into a business civilization was in many respects an aborted revolution whose hottest partisans had been committed to much different ends. The implied egalitarian principles of that radical revolution—the dreams of Diggers and Levellers—with their beatific vision of an earthly communion of saints, became the tenuous property of its lunatic fringe. Those Puritans who came to America brought that sense of communal possibility with them, and for a short moment remained intensely faithful to it. That is why Robert Keayne was pillaried for doing what he thought himself entitled to do—sell his product, with the calculation necessary to the functioning of a commercial society, at the price the market would bear. Keayne's "false principles" were summarized by Winthrop: "1. that a man might sell as dear as he can, and buy as cheap as he can. 2. If a man lose by casualty of sea &c. in some of his commodities, he may raise the price of the rest. 3. That he may sell as he bought, though he paid too dear &c. and though the commodity be fallen, &c. 4 that, as a man may take advantage of his own skill or ability, so he may of another's ignorance or neces- sity."[12] These are, in stunning clarity, the precepts of modernity. The Puritans who rebuked Keayne were trying to keep the modern world at bay.

The central question for any inquiry into the experience of these resistant emigrants (here posed by D. H. Lawrence) must be simply this: "What did the Pilgrim Fathers come for . . . when they came so gruesomely over the black sea?" This is Lawrence's own reply, which I cannot better: "Oh, it was in a black spirit. A black revulsion from Europe, from the old authority of Europe . . . But also, no more of this new 'humanity' which followed the Renaissance. None of this new liberty which was to be so pretty in Europe."[13] This is what we nowadays call a "push" theory of migration—though it is an extremely subtle one. Lawrence understood that the founding of New England was a retreat from the eruption of the modern self—the self as a disciplined being committed to vocation, to ambition, and to self-definition as an assertion of difference from some threatening other. I quote Lawrence's remark because it contains the essence of my argument—that the Puritan founders came to America not only to escape the authority of prelates and kings but also in flight from moral dangers that resided in their own "pretty" liberty. Upon their arrival they began—with pain and eloquent lament—to succumb to their sense of failure in their project of escape. They became moderns in the sense that their deference to the workings of a traditional society and to an all-disposing God receded before the ascension of their identities as self-governing individuals. "The settlements they made in a 'new world'," as Lewis P. Simpson has splendidly said, "were in one way or another responses to the dispossession of the integral and authoritative community of an 'old world' by modern history. If they sowed the New World gardens with the seeds of modernity, the initial makers of these gardens did so unwittingly."[14] Though they had put three thousand miles between themselves and the society their brethren were remaking at home, they could do nothing to forestall the triumph of the self.

3

The process by which we have lost sight of this complex of motives and experience in the founders can first be detected, as Hawthorne understood, in the consciousness of those who directly succeeded them. It was the founders' children who began to transform them from full and feeling human beings into simplified figures of inimitable heroism. In this filial reduction of the parents to static exemplars of virtue, the later Puritans may be regarded as initiators of a durable national tradition: American sons have periodically coped with feelings of smallness beside their pioneer fathers by exalting the fathers extremely, and by appointing themselves guardians of their patrimony against disloyal brethren. This was surely one of the therapeutic strategies adopted by those whom Cotton Mather called "Criolians" (and by Mather himself): "The families," wrote Samuel Sewall," . . . which first ventured to follow Christ Thorow the Atlantick . . . were so Religious; their End so Holy; their Self-Denyal . . . so Extraordinary;

that . . . the Plantation has thereby gained a very stong Crasis."[15] There is evident strain in Sewall's repeated intensifier, "so"; somewhere the celebrants knew that their fathers had been more stunned than vindicated by their experience. Embedded in the literature of this second generation—and in need of deeper burial—was a suspicion that the founders had proceeded not so much with certitude as with a tenuous grip on purpose. The task of the children was not merely to acknowledge heroism where they needed to find it, but actually to reconstruct a meaning for their parents' lives. The Puritan founders had done just what subsequent immigrant generations have done ever since: they had left it to the next generation to make retrospective sense of their act of migration.

If this was their first legacy, it was an onerous one. "I am affraid," confessed Michael Wigglesworth in 1653, "of my senselessness of my fathers death." This is one of the more direct expressions of what is everywhere whispered in the writings of the second generation—a feeling of widening distance from the immediate past. To fill that distance they performed what has been called "the invention of New England," "comfort[ing] themselves with an almost ritual elaboration of the names of the [parental] dead in elegy, anagram, and pun so as to retain mnemonically the meaning the departed persons held for the living." Yet the story of the second- and third-generation ministry is overwhelmingly the story of its fall from the fathers' position of authority—a fall that generated certain rhetorical evasions, notably in the fast-day and election sermons that have come to be known as the jeremiads. Riddled with internal contradictions, these sermons provide a field day for the deconstructionist. At one moment they vilify prosperity: "As the *heat* of the Sun in summer breeds a multitude of Insects, so does the *warmth* of Prosperity a multitude of Apostates." At the next moment the same Jeremiah prays for exactly that prosperous warmth—for the return of "that Comfortable Estate [we were] in but two years ago." If the jeremiads were designed to function as instruments of social control, the ministry quickly learned that bluntness, as when Samuel Torrey urged upon "the godly and religious Magistracy . . . direct subverciency unto the work of Christ," was becoming less prudent than the insinuated threat. With the new King Charles getting reports of unrepentant "murtherers of your royal father" strutting about his provinces, the ministers could only hint to their accommodationist government that if "the Axe of destruction" should strike the congregational edifice of New England, magistracy and ministry would fall together.[16]

Yet even as they muted the sound of their own alarm, the latter-day New England ministers were, within the tenuous political context of the Restoration, becoming an embarrassment to the civil authorities. From the point of view of the General Court trying to cope with an increasingly hostile English government, the preachers—including some of the most honored—were hurting more than helping: the elderly John Eliot tactlessly lectured his native country on its ecclesiastical errors, and published his admonitions as *The Christian Commonwealth* (1660); Increase Mather preached incessantly against toleration. Such eminences turned, not surprisingly, to an idealization of New England's intolerant past—an ancestral celebration in which the animating emotion was their sense of their own lost potency: "In the last age," lamented Mather, "in the days of our Fathers . . .scarce a Sermon [was] preached but some evidently converted; yea, sometimes hundreds in a Sermon. Which of us can say we have seen the like?" Twenty years later he answered himself with further questions: "Look into Pulpits, and see if there is such a Glory there, as once there was? . . . When will *Boston* see a COTTON, & a NORTON, again?"[17] The age of the fathers—as would again and again be the case in American history at moments of discouragement—was becoming the touchstone of all value.

Of course, fallible men had always labored at the preaching vocation, but for the sons and grandsons of the founders there is a new tentativeness in their self-monitoring, an uneasiness about their fitness to carry on. If Increase Mather had noted the decline in efficacy from his father's sermons to his own, his son demanded of himself in turn that not a word be wasted—"It must bee my Ambition, every where to speak *usefully*." "I could not get into the Pulpit," Cotton Mather exults on one occasion (which happens to have been an event with considerable popular appeal—a public execution), "but by climbing over Pues and Heads."[18] The minister's stature has become a function of how many tickets he can sell.

Despite the litanies of provoking sins that fill the jeremiads—"sabbath breaking . . . Pride in respect to Apparel . . . Oathes, and Imprecations in ordinary Discourse . . . sloth and sleepiness [at times reserved for prayer] . . . frequent Law suits . . . Back-bitings, hearing and telling Tales"—pastoral ferocity grew generally weaker as the century wore on. "There are some few, here and there," suggested one preacher in the late 1670s, in what was a rather tentative display of the precedent of Sodom, " . . . that keep them selves close to God and have a good measure of the Spirit breathing in them . . . But whether there be a sufficient number to obtain the sparing or saving such a place . . . as *New England* . . . may yet be a question." The failing competition for souls fed directly into the ministry's sense that "The Lord [who] took delight in our Fathers . . . hath forsaken us; they Walkt with him, we contrary unto him." The jeremiads relentlessly "contrasted present day 'contention' with the peace that once prevailed," and that peace, visualized, was a lone man at a pulpit with multitudes spread before him in reverent silence.[19]

The trouble was that the past had receded beyond recapturing. "Historical Christianity," we may say with Emerson, "ha[d] fallen into the error that corrupts all attempts to communicate religion." In trying to articulate their sense of what they were losing, the latter-day ministers had recourse, with almost unbroken unanimity, to images of quiet, calm, discipline—precisely the ideals their fathers had left England to transcend. There had been plenty of discipline in Laudian England, but now, in virtually Episcopal language Jonathan Mitchell proclaimed, "Keep Order, Keep in your places, acknowledging and attending the Order that God hath established in the place where you live . . . leave the guidance of the Ship to those that sit at Helm." When William Hubbard looked "into the Third heavens," he was not, as Thomas Shepard had been, "infinitely ravished" to feel "the indwelling of the Spirit of God poured out abundantly in us and upon us." He was not so much uplifted as he was relieved by his picture of the "royal Pavilion pitched by the Almighty," where the "Inhabitants . . . are . . . not all of one rank and order." Hierarchy had always been a part of the Puritan vision of the Chrisitan commonwealth, but never so dominant as now it was becoming. It infused every longing for an orderly alternative to the deficient present. "Order," Joshua Moodey quoted longingly from the Book of Numbers, "is Beauty and Safety." Where the essence of the congregational idea had once been "mutual brotherly help and communion one to another," the reigning definition now devolved into an ecclesiology of decorum: "There is a sweet *Temperament* in the *Congregational way*; that the Liberties of the people may not be overlaid and oppressed, as in the *Classical-way*; nor the *Rule* and *Authority* of the *Elders* rendred an *insignificant* thing, and trampled under Foot, as in the way of the *Brownists*; but that there may be a *Reconciliation* or *due Concurrence*, and a *Ballancing* of the one justly with the other."[20]

Even when the ministers quarreled among themselves over such questions as toleration, the break was over means, not ends. Hubbard shocked his counterparts by proposing appeasement of the Baptists in 1676, but he was finally suggesting only that suppression could be more disruptive than coexistence. He fully shared his opponents' appetite for "deliberation . . . peaceableness . . . and . . . moderation." Searching out the meaning of the Indian wars, he described a world where perception was everywhere obstructed—"so dark that an *Indian* could hardly be discerned from a better man." It was a chaos, he more than implied, of the colonists' own making—not in the old sense of divine judgment dispensed through human instruments, but in a much more materialist sense of causality:

> Many of these scattering Plantations in our Borders . . . were contented to live without, yea, desirous to shake off all yoke of Government, both sacred and civil, and so Transforming themselves as much as well they could into the manners of the Indians they lived amongst, and are some of them therefore most deservedly (as to Divine Justice) left to be put under the yoke and power of the Indians themselves.

The price of disorder was merely more disorder. Hubbard spoke barely at all of God. In such proto-deistic moralizing, as in their increasing worship of order, the sons were failing their own test of constancy to the fathers, and they knew it. In case they should forget it, they were periodically reminded: "It was another thing and a better thing [than prosperity and stability]," declared John Higginson in 1663, "that we followed the Lord into the wilderness for."[21] Higginson's "we" was an enormously prestigious pronoun, and the few who could still legitimately use it were doing so not for the purpose of reassuring their successors, but for rebuking them.

The astonishing thing is that despite this ocean of filiopiety, the later Puritan generation never really grasped what it was that they were missing in their fathers' experience. At the level of their deepest emotion, they were united in one desire—to hear from the fathers that they were keeping the faith. Yet the essence of that faith was becoming more and more an irrecoverable mystery. One may think in this regard, without much distortion, of a story written by Jerome Weidman more than two centuries later about another immigrant generation. Here is Irving Howe's summary of Weidman's "My Father Sits in the Dark":

> A son speaks, troubled that each night his immigrant father "sits in the dark, alone, smoking, staring straight ahead of him." The father sits in the kitchen, on an uncomfortable chair. "What are you thinking about, Pa?" "Nothing." "Is something wrong, Pop?" "Nothing, son, nothing at all." Coming home late one night, the son "can see the deeper darkness of his [father's] hunched shape. He is sitting in the same chair, his elbows on his knees, his cold pipe in his teeth, his unblinking eyes staring straight ahead." There is nothing to be said, neither quarrel nor reconciliation. "What do you think about, Pop?" "Nothing," answers the father, "nothing special."[22]

If we transpose this story backward in time, its only jarring note is the father's taciturn gentleness. All the rest—the impasse between the generations, the father's revery of incommunicable remembrance, the son's ache to know him—is as true of our first Hebraic immigrants as of the pogrom-fleeing Jews. Sometimes, in fact, the sons of the first Puritans asked their fathers openly for revelation of their mystery, and in a few cases a record of their dialogue survives, as when William Stoughton addressed an elderly member of his own congregation:

> You have by this time parted with the most and the choicest of your Contemporaries . . . And your eyes behold this day, that another Generation is risen up, and begin to stand thick upon the Stage, and that, even of them, there is one, to whose lot it falls to speak to you in the Name of the Lord this day. Now what is the sum of your desires, and would be the chief and top of your joyes, as to those you must shortly leave behind you? . . . O . . . shew forth and declare all the works of God unto your Children.[23]

The bad news for Stoughton, who doubtless assumed that rhetorical questions are to be answered only by those who ask them, was that a few survivors of the first generation stood up and answered on their own behalf. "We do highly prize the peace of the Churches," Charles Chauncy declared, but, "although differences be sad, yet the truth that comes to light by them, may recompence the sadness." The thrust of Chauncy's retort to the Synod of 1662 (at which the Half-Way Covenant was endorsed) was that "we must not look to Consequences in [opposing the loosened terms for church admission], but [to] the goodness of our Cause."[24]

Yet this was still an elusive language, an almost tantalizing code for what was being compromised. Searching for a way to understand and to retrieve what New England was losing, Samuel Danforth tried to invoke the original terms of Puritan self-definition. New Englanders, he said, using a phrase by which he hoped to restore the old distinction between acquiescence and commitment, must stop their drift toward becoming "spectators rather than auditors." What he and Chauncy were haltingly saying, and what one feels as the half-articulate anxiety throughout the literature of lamentation, is that the religious leadership has slipped into obsessive pragmatism—at the cost of squandering the spirit with which they had been entrusted. John Davenport, one of the founders who lived past the Restoration, put it more bluntly:

> I shall conclude [he declared in his election sermon of 1669, with such innovations as the Half-Way Covenant chiefly in mind] with a brief reminding you of the first beginning of this Colony . . . which I have the better advantage, and more special engagement to do; being one of them by whom the Patent, which you enjoy was procured . . . Churches [then] were gathered in a Congregational way, and walked therein, according to the Rules of the Gospel . . . Now therefore take heed and beware, that the Lord may not have just cause to complain of us . . . Lest you lose by God's punishing Justice what you received from his free Mercy.[25]

At the heart of the culture that Davenport was both criticizing and representing was a collapse into pragmatic focus on ends; the primary value had become to preserve institutions at all cost—institutions that were, as all Protestants were obliged to know, but "the lengthened shadows" of the men who had devised them. It was inevitable that this form of traditionalism would decline into a kind of fetishism for some, while for others the idea that "the design of our first Planters . . . consist[ed] in some little Rites, Modes, or Circumstances of Church Discipline" could be dismissed as petty formalism. Thus while Davenport and Chauncy aligned themselves against the Half-Way Covenant, others among the surviving founders, notably John Allin and Richard Mather, supported it. Increase Mather wavered; when he gave up his initial opposition he found it necessary to legitimize his new position by publishing *First Principles* (1675), an anthology of statements by the founders that could be read as endorsing the principle of latitude in baptism. Yet such discord was finally less important than the fundamental agreement on *fear* as the chief emotion of religious efficacy—a decision articulated perfectly by Urian Oakes when he declared that "serious consideration of *the latter end of a mans sinful wayes* will have a converting influence upon his affections and conversation."[26] "The latter end" becomes the incantation of Oakes's (and many other) jeremiads—a periodic refrain meant to jolt his audience into fright at their prospects for punishment. In the hands of such a minister the sermon becomes a serial of contrasting visions of plenty (if we will reform) and deprivation (if we persist in our backsliding ways). The effect of this pattern of offering and withholding is to focus the responsive mind exclusively on benefit and cost as the measures of loyalty to God. The cost of disloyalty is not shame or sorrow, but ruin: "The way of Persecution . . . ruined Pharaoh . . . the way of Rebellion . . . ruined Korah and his company . . . Contempt and ill usage of the Lords Messengers . . . ruined the State of *Israel* and *Judah*."[27]

There was, of course, some dissent among the second-generation ministers from this homiletic strategy of restricting religious discourse to the alternatives of external punishment and reward. William Adams, minister of Dedham, echoed some of the sermon titles of the founders with his *The Necessity of the Pouring out of the Spirit* (1679): "Soul-Peace, Peace with God," was Adams's evocation of New Englanders' undiminished longing, "and the testimony of that peace in their Consciences . . . an holy serenity and calmness of soul, the peace of God which passeth all understanding." Yet on the whole this language of grace as an aesthetic experience was becoming archaic. By their numerous expressions of dread, which far outweigh promises of deliverance in the literature of the second generation, and by savaging New Englanders for disregarding the God and the godly parents who had brought them across the ocean, the Jeremiahs were more and more inducing a fear of consequence rather than evoking a sense of debilitating absence. They elevated discipline to first place in their canon of value—a concession that marked the triumph of the very tendency that the fathers had resisted and from which they had sought release. The theme of ends, once it became established, grew ever and ever more dominant. Benjamin Colman, speaking to his urbane congregation at Brattle Street, reminded them that "the folly of Irreligion is, That it has no Foresight: 'tis blind, and intent only on present Gains and Pleasures, having no sense of the Soul's Duration nor the Body's Frailty." Religion had come to mean, almost exclusively, fear. "Irreligion" meant the forgetting of death.[28]

"Oh where," cried Urian Oakes, "is that *Sense* of the *evil* of *sin?*" With that question Oakes was acknowledging what Hawthorne was later to dramatize—that the tactic of preaching hell as a weapon against complacency was simply not working any more. For Oakes to charge New Englanders with having permitted the disappearance of Satan was simultaneously to demand some ongoing demonstration that they could still feel the ubiquity of God. It was a demand that went unanswered—or when it did elicit some response, it was likely to be an hysterical one: "Last night," reported Sewall in 1686, "had a very unusual Dream; *viz.* That our Saviour in the dayes of his Flesh when upon Earth, came to Boston and abode here sometime, and moreover that He Lodged in that time at Father Hull's." The dreamlife of Sewall was no match, however, for the waking life of Cotton Mather:

> I was once emptying the *Cistern of Nature*, and making *Water* at the Wall. At the same Time, there came a Dog, who did so too, before me. Thought I; "What mean, and vile Things are the Children of Men, in this mortal State! How much do our *natural Necessities* abase us, and place us in some regard, on the same Level with the very Dogs!
>
> My Thought proceeded, "Yett I will be a more noble Creature; and at the very Time, when my *natural Necessities* debase me into the Condition of the *Beast,* my *Spirit* shall (I say, *at that very Time!*) rise and soar, and fly up, towards the Employment of the Angel.[29]

By the end of the century the language of New England's spiritual leaders was becoming a self-burlesque—careening between routine moralism and a piety of grotesque proportions. They were no longer preaching conversion; they were threatening malefactors, and then shouting an incessant and frantic "Eureka."

This cry of "we have found Him" was audible most notoriously at Salem, where Oakes's question was answered, in effect, by the discovery that "the devil [was] making one attempt more upon us." As anyone who has read through the witchcraft literature can attest, the poignancy of the Salem debacle lay in the breakdown of accommodation between the diverging halves of New England's culture. "The reasonable part of the world," predicted the urbane Thomas Brattle (probably thinking of Mather's conviction that Armageddon was at last at hand), "will laugh." Before the laughter, however, came bitter discord: "What is the black man whispering to you?" demanded the court interrogator of one of the accused "witches" in 1692. "There was none whispered to me," was Susannah Martin's reply—a retort that, in all the baldness of the official transcript, spoke volumes: In order to keep alive a sense of the colony's historical continuity as a providential enterprise, the Mathers and their allies were celebrating a kind of Black Mass, their rediscovery of Satan. When they called together some town notables in the next year to witness their examination of a bewitched girl, a droll and canny merchant named Robert Calef reported (in a book that ridiculed Cotton Mather's very title, *Wonders of the Invisible World*) that "the father [Increase, sat] on a Stool, and the Son [Cotton] upon the Bedside by her . . . Then she was in a fit . . . and he [Cotton] rubb'd her Breast, etc. . . . and put his hand upon her Breast and Belly, *viz.* on the Cloaths over her, and felt a Living thing, as he said, which moved the Father also to feel, and some others."[30] Cotton Mather, who never recovered full dignity, had become the subject of pornographic satire.

This recourse to presenting evil as a "living thing" palpable by touch had miserably failed. As sin became literalized, it became laughable. By the end of the founders' century we begin to recognize in New England the moral poles that have framed American culture ever since: the skepticism and mockery of the sophisticate on the one hand; the hue and cry of the crusader on the other. Thomas Brattle ridiculed "the Salem gentlemen" for believing without experimental proof that noxious effluvia could flow through touch out of the victim back to the witch; and even as Brattle wrote, Cotton Mather was deepening his conviction (which he would refine in *The Angel of Bethesda,* completed in 1724) that the physical afflictions so evident at Salem were the interventions of Satan. To Oakes's question—"O where is that *source* of *evil* of *sin*?"—Puritanism could no longer give a collective answer: either evil was to be conceived as a monstrous thing outside the respectable self, or it could not be conceived at all. One thinks of Hans Castorp, Thomas Mann's invalid pilgrim, for whom his ancestors' practice of saying grace has shriveled into a nervous habit of hand-clasping before meals. Just so, these Puritans had only the residual forms left. "There hath been *a vital decay, a decay upon the very Vitals* of Religion."[31] The marrow of their faith— the idea of sin as alienation from God—was depleted. Satan had become the property of the reactionaries, and the modern world had been born.

And the sublime comes down
To the spirit itself,

The spirit and space,
The empty spirit
In vacant space,
What wine does one drink?
What bread does one eat?

Wallace Stevens, "The American Sublime," 1936

8 *The Puritan Legacy*

One reason it is possible to sense the depletion of what Perry Miller called "Augustinian piety" as a felt sorrow in our culture is that the real Puritanism did not entirely perish. For one thing, it got into the books. By this I mean that classic American literature (which, as we are now frequently reminded, has been exalted and delimited by such New England–oriented scholars as Miller and Matthiessen) is characteristically committed to the restoration of what the Puritans had lost: a powerful, but privative, sense of sin. Our literature can be largely understood as a minority dissent (and this implies no studious, Hawthornean sense of history on the part of all who wrote it) from what Puritanism became, and from the antebellum middle-class culture that had been seeded by its weakened forms. Classic American literature bespeaks, in other words, a continuity with the defeated tradition within Puritanism that I have identified with Cotton and Hutchinson and their first-generation followers—or, if we wish to question the substantive unity of this phase of our literature, we may prefer to say that it perpetuates the essential debate in which the "antinomians" were losers. It perpetuates it, for instance, in the contrast between Emerson ("sin, seen from the thought, is . . . shade, absence of light, no essence") and Thoreau ("all sensuality is one, though it takes many forms . . . when the reptile is attacked at one mouth of his burrow, he shows himself at another").[1] The Emersonian, or antinomian, critique of rationalized Puritanism is everywhere in our literature, though it has naturally been especially acute within the New England tradition itself. Harriet Beecher Stowe, for instance, attacked the preparationist style with a lacerating wit that could only have derived from intimacy with what she was decrying. Here she has her Southern gentleman, whom she pointedly calls "Augustine," deliver a lecture on the virtues of disorder to his New England cousin, who has just rushed out in horror from his slave-run kitchen:

My dear Vermont, you natives up by the North Pole set an extravagant value on time! What on earth is the use of time to a fellow who has twice as much of it as he knows what to do with? As to order and system, where there is nothing to be done but to lounge on the sofa and read, an hour sooner or later in breakfast or dinner isn't of much account. Now, there's Dinah gets you a capital dinner,—soup, ragout, roast fowl, dessert, ice-creams and all,—and she creates it all out of chaos and old night down there, in that kitchen. I think it really sublime, the way she manages. But, Heaven bless us! if we are to go down there, and view all the smoking and squatting about, and hurryscurryation of the preparatory process, we should never eat more! My good cousin, absolve yourself from that! . . . Don't I know that the rolling-pin is under her bed, and the nutmeg-grater in her pocket with her tobacco,— that there are sixty-five different sugar-bowls, one in every hole in the house,—that she washes dishes with a dinner-napkin one day, and with a fragment of an old petticoat the next? But the upshot is, she gets up glorious dinners, makes superb coffee; and you must judge her as warriors and statesmen are judged, by *her success*.

With its wickedly clever juxtaposition of the menial with the grand, this is nothing less than an evangelical critique of the rational Protestant heritage. It is, moreover, an informed attack, launched from within. It is Richard Sibbes's objection against "a set measure of bruising ourselves," John Cotton's dissent that "there are no steps unto [the] Altar" of salvation, Jonathan Edwards's insistence that the authenticity of religious experience can never be judged by the rigor of its method—in which there is "vast variety"—but only by its result.[2] Stowe was neither alone nor original in amplifying the dissenting voices that had preceded her, but her tirade against the attenuated preparationist orthodoxy does mark one of the first conscious resorts by the New England mind to an alien culture in order to achieve liberation from what had become of its own.

There is another mode of dissent imbedded in *Uncle Tom's Cabin* that is richly predictive of later analogues—Henry Adams, T. S. Eliot, even such cranky Yankees as Jack Kerouac, who wishes he was a "Negro, feeling that the best the white world had offered was not enough ecstasy . . ." Broadly speaking, this is the Catholic strain—a much underestimated current in American literary expression, and another form of dissent from the culture of preparationist self-discipline. Stowe gives us a New England senator who, in his support of the Fugitive Slave Act, is clearly a version of Daniel Webster: "Bold as a lion," she says of him, he has never opened himself to "the magic of the real presence of distress." This is a retort not merely to the granite Webster but to the entire Protestant lineage (including the Beechers and the Stowes) that had spawned him. It is, as is *Uncle Tom's Cabin* as a whole, a gesture of respect toward the moral efficacy of Catholic emotion—toward the Virgin and even, if only in a fleeting hint, toward the miracle of transubstantiation, "the real presence." Hawthorne, like Henry Adams after him, shared Stowe's suspicion that the Catholic emotion was critically scarce in American life, though he put forward his judgment only tentatively in his most sustained study of the Puritans, *The Scarlet Letter:* "Had there been a Papist among the crowd of Puritans, he might have seen in this beautiful woman, so picturesque in her attire and mien, and with the infant at her bosom, an object to remind him of the image of Divine Maternity . . . that sacred image of sinless motherhood, whose infant was to redeem the world."³ The force of such imagery was its reassertion of a vision of innocent humanity—in the maternal form that is the focus of Catholic devotion, and that was present in the antinomian strain of Puritanism all along.

Here is Nina Leeds in Eugene O'Neill's *Strange Interlude* (1928), lamenting the loss of just such an alternative faith:

> The mistake began when God was created in a male image. Of course, women would see Him that way, but men should have been gentlemen enough, remembering their mothers, to make God a woman! . . . We should have imagined life as created in the birth-pain of God the Mother. Then we would understand why we, Her children, have inherited pain, for we would know that our life's rhythm beats from Her great heart, torn with the agony of love and birth. And we would feel that death meant reunion with Her, a passing back into Her substance, blood of her blood again, peace of Her peace!

Hawthorne had announced the same theme much earlier in *The Marble Faun* (1860): "A Christian girl," says Hilda, "—even a daughter of the Puritans—may surely pay honor to the idea of divine Womanhood, without giving up the faith of her forefathers." But probably the most familiar expression of this recoil from what Roger Williams had called "cold societies" is Emerson's even fiercer contempt for "corpse-cold Unitarianism." Emerson's repudiation of Unitarian rationalism can only be understood as part of his lifelong commitment to the "law of laws"—here expressed in celebration of the universe as a beating, breathing (conspiring) entity that charms even as it commands:

> All things proceed out of the same spirit, and all things conspire with it. Whilst a man seeks good ends, he is strong by the whole strength of nature. In so far as he roves from these ends, he bereaves himself of power, or auxiliaries; his being shrinks out of all remote channels, he becomes less and less, a mote, a point, until absolute badness is absolute death.
>
> The perception of this law of laws awakens in the mind a sentiment which we call the religious sentiment, and which makes our highest happiness. Wonderful is its power to charm and to command. It is a mountain air. It is the embalmer of the world. It is myrrh and storax, and chlorine and rosemary. It makes the sky and the hills sublime, and the silent song of the stars is it.[4]

For Emerson, the definition of declension was the transition that his Puritan forebears had endured. Religion itself was nothing other than the always endangered conviction that evil is a privation.

This conviction was the great casualty of the early history of the New England mind. To regain it has ever since been a trial, but it has also been the searing aspiration that has produced the masterpieces of American literary art. We recognize it in the fact that our literature, when it seeks to evoke terror, focuses not on fearful monsters (as Cotton Mather tried to do) but on moments of abandonment —on the castaway Pip whose "ringed horizon . . . expand[s] around him" as he bobs alone in the sea; on Poe's living entombments; on the hiss that Scott Fitzgerald means us to hear as "the trees . . . pandered in whispers" at the close of *The Great Gatsby*. This anxiety that the voice of God may be nothing more than a trick of the wind, that the peopled landscape may be suddenly swept clean, has always been the basis of American horror. "Thou shalt stand stripped of all friends, all comfort, all creatures," the Puritan minister had said in his effort to stir his congregants into a more vivid awareness of God—whom we have come to call simply "presence." Whatever the name, the threat of *deus absconditus* has lingered in our literature—far more frightfully than Satan's threatened intrusion—ever since.[5]

We recognize the same conviction in the fact that figures of fatal pride —Cowperwoods, Ambersons, Ververs, Gatsbys, even Ahab in his calculating moods—walk through our fiction toward the catastrophe of self-reliant solitude. Our books are littered with casualties of such presumption: "When striving stops," says Augie March as he barely saves himself from his own Yankee ambition, "the truth comes as a gift—bounty, harmony, love."[6] Such an entrance into peace—a revelation in Augie's frenetic Chicago—is the objective toward which the American bildungsroman most often moves: away from the grip of social convention, not toward domesticity, but, with Natty and Huck, out toward the incorruptible "territories."

The American literary aspiration has, in other words, always been to renovate not merely persons but a backsliding people, and not by stirring them to some form of enmity (which is what our politics tends to do), but by returning them to contact with what Emerson called "maternal Reason." Classic American literature makes the call back from artifice to what it celebrates as the authentic self, which it takes to be a created, not an evolved, entity with an existence entirely independent of history. This belief in an essential self— "that Something a man is . . . divine in his own right, and a woman in hers, sole and untouchable by any canons of authority, or any rule derived from precedent"—is the inevitable recourse of a culture that has continually renewed itself through the *topos* of immigration, the experience of coming out of history into a place where time begins again, where the accretions of Old World culture can be burned away, and the unrestrained self can freely emerge in all its strident divinity:

> Houses and rooms are full of perfumes, the shelves are crowded with
>   perfumes,
> I breathe the fragrance myself and know it and like it,
> The distillation would intoxicate me also, but I shall not let it.
> The atmosphere is not a perfume, it has not taste of the distillation, it
>   is odorless,
> It is for my mouth forever, I am in love with it,
> I will go to the bank by the wood and become undisguised and naked,
> I am mad for it to be in contact with me.

Nearly twenty years after writing these lines, Whitman was still able to dispense with the dutiful caveat even as he uttered it: "For after the rest is said . . . it remains to bring forward and modify everything else with the idea of that Something a man is . . ." This is an idea that all modern historicisms—whether vigorously Marxist or resolutely liberal—find dangerously innocent. Hawthorne represented it as the idea of sculpture, to which, he noticed, Americans are peculiarly drawn: "a sort of fossilizing process," by which "feverish men [are turned] into cool, quiet marble." It is an ideal, however ill-founded, that has never been absent from Americans' dialogue with themselves. When Whitman heard from Emerson that *Leaves of Grass* must have had "a long foreground," he was, we may surmise, less than flattered by the postulates of age and influence; when fifty years later Gertrude Stein intoned that America had become the oldest country in the world, she was being knowingly cruel.[7]

Whitman's celebration of nakedness as the aboriginal—and retrievable—condition of the democratic self is a fusion of history and destiny that has been unavailable, at least to the same degree, for other postcolonial cultures. Most Americans have not had to cope, for example, with any equivalent of the "convict stain" that has "dominated all argument about Australian selfhood" for two hundred years.[8] Nor have we been required—though some historians are now pressing us to do so—to regard ourselves, as Octavio Paz says of Mexico, as "the child of a double [Aztec and Spanish] violence." American culture was, moreover, the product of a Protestant advance guard in flight from impending conflict between feudal and bourgeois orders, while the Spanish inheritance of Latin Americans derived instead from a Catholic, still-feudal civilization committed to mercantilist economic exploitation of native labor and resources. Such a beginning laid the groundwork for an entirely different process of identity-formation: Meso-American Indians, though decimated, were not exterminated, "because their labor [was needed] for the cultivation of the vast haciendas and the exploitation of the mines," and because Catholic universalism created a culture where "there were classes, castes, and slaves; but . . . no pariahs."[9] The resulting amalgamation of conquerors and conquered encouraged nothing equivalent to the distinctively American sense of immigrant heroism, nor did it revert to a religion of exclusion. Even with respect to Canada, whose historical development has run much closer to our own, the legacy of imperial conflict between France and England inhibited the formation of a unitary national myth. Its absence helps to account for the differences between American immigrant writing (in which the New World allure is always in conflict with Old World identity) and such fictions as those of the Canadian Jewish writer Mordecai Richler in which the *goyische* world, though as close as the next Montreal neighborhood, is an alien menace to be avoided or overcome—not to be joined in holy union.

Thus the American claim to "awful . . . endless endurance"—an immunity to what Lionel Trilling called "the conditioned"—has been as distinctive as it has been persistent, and furnishes at least one angle of understanding from which we may establish a place for the Puritan (and thus the first immigrant) element in American life and letters. For "after the rest is said," after the caveats and discriminations have been made, and the increasingly fractured nature of the social ground of American literary expression has been duly acknowledged, there yet remains a genuinely common inheritance at work in even the most diverse American books. One might enumerate instances of what Matthiessen called our "renaissance"—*The Deerslayer* (1841), *Walden* (1854), *Song of Myself* (1855)—or the products of a single decade a century later—*The Catcher in the Rye* (1951), *Invisible Man* (1951), *To Kill a Mockingbird* (1960). Each of these books is imbedded in a place and moment of particular regional flavor; all revisit the same "American Adam" in his career of perpetual metempsychosis. Yet especially the mid-twentieth-century versions are written out of fatigue with the historically real. Geographies of "a world elsewhere," or pastoral fantasies, or portraits of an "imperial self," or expressions of a millenarian dream, they adumbrate their authors' subsequent bile or silence. Death never comes for the Adam of these books—not for Natty or Henry or Walt; not for Holden or the nameless black wanderer or Atticus—but neither does a life in time and culture. There have rarely been sequels to these imaginings in the minds of their inventors ("no second acts," said Scott Fitzgerald, "in American lives"); but they have always been succeeded by new incarnations from some other optative poet whose imaginative reach is not yet cropped by experience or not yet exhausted by the act of giving form to the formless object of desire. Occasionally the yearning has focused backward in time on some aspect of pre-Reformation Catholicism—in the resort by Henry Adams, for example, from the accelerating chaos of industrial civilization to the putative unity of medieval Christendom; or in the quest for a poetics of salvation from time:

> If all time is eternally present
> All time is unredeemable
> What might have been is an abstraction
> Remaining a perpetual possibility
> Only in a world of speculation
> . . . . .
> We shall not cease from exploration
> And in the end of all our exploring
> Will be to arrive where we started
> And know the place for the first time.[10]

This perpetual American act of emigration out of history, this expression of desire for divine abrogation of the limits that time and culture impose on human lives, has had no end, but it did have a discernible beginning—in New England. Some of our shrewdest and most historically informed writers have, to be sure, represented it as sheerest folly. Such is the burden, for example, of Mme. Merle's response to Isabel Archer in *The Portrait of a Lady*:

> When you have lived as long as I, you will see that every human being
> has his shell, and that you must take the shell into account. By the shell
> I mean the whole envelope of circumstances. There is no such thing as
> an isolated man or woman; we are each of us made up of a cluster of
> appurtenances. What do you call one's self? Where does it begin? Where
> does it end? It overflows into everything that belongs to us—and then
> it flows back again.

The cruelty of this speech resides not in the condescension of age to youth, but in the irrefutable prophecy that youth will, as it grows old, lose the illusion that it has the power to generate itself. (Think of James's mockery of Roderick Hudson, who, in his Massachusetts twang, calls himself an "aboriginal.") One knows, upon reading this, why James regarded Whitman as a poet of "great pretensions," and one may even know why James appointed himself to write from the reverse vantage point—from the position of an exile from the New World to the Old.[11]

In their own self-banishment the Puritans would, of course, have abhorred Whitman's romantic erotics with a disdain at least equal to that of Hawthorne and James. But with all their indignation at the enthusiasts of their own time, and with their assent to the doctrine of depravity, the fact remains that they were the first Americans to enact the paradigm that underlies all romantic projects. Their typology collapsed time into what one of them called the "remaining Now";

their antinomianism (never entirely suppressed) collapsed space into an ecstatic unity wherein self and God became interfused. With as much mixed bitterness and exhilaration as Whitman was later to muster, they turned away from all forms of mediacy —historical, institutional, even scriptural—and dared to assert the direct apprehension by the believer of the divine.

This turning away, James's rebukes notwithstanding, has constituted the essential thrust of American imaginative expression ever since. Whitman's own metaphysic, which is so often accused of deficiency in its representation of evil, is much better understood as a rejection of the Manichean belief in equal warring principles in favor of the conviction that evil is a traversable gap between man and God. Dissenting from the Manichean view, which he found dominant in his fallen culture, Whitman speaks the language of sacred prurience. This lost language of our first immigrants has been the chief object of restorationist desire in American letters. When recovered by a poet of Whitman's power, it has the sureness of prophecy.

2

Yet prophecy is elegy transformed. That is why the most striking recapitulations of this experience and emotion are to be found in the literature of subsequent immigrations. When we hear in the fiction of the Jewish emigration of the early twentieth century the maternal voice calling home her renegade sons, we are hearing once again the contrapuntal theme of Edward Johnson's *History*—the chastisement of the apostate who has broken the bonds of time and blood. When we read of suburban amnesia and Old World parents afraid of shaming their assimilating children, we are hearing again the second-generation New Englanders as they condemn themselves for burying their fathers at "tearless funerals." There is an inevitable allusion in all American literature to immigration in this large sense— immigration not merely as a physical event but as a paradigm for human experience: adulthood as the assimilated state, the solvent of memory, that leaves childhood behind. The paradigm happens to be especially clear in our Hebraic literatures of exodus—the Puritan of the seventeenth century, and the Jewish of the twentieth—but it is equally and obviously present in all our immigrant writers, whose preferred form is always elegy, and whose lament is always for the vanished moment when the self was held in suspension between the Old World identity it has just discarded and the New World potentiality of which it dreams.[12]

There is one telling exception to this generalization, which, in its very difference, confirms the unity of memory and desire in the culture from which it stands apart. That exception is the literature of Afro-Americans, whose distinctiveness in this respect (think of Richard Wright's bitterness in *Black Boy* when he recalls his toadying father, from whom all self-respect has been drained) is an aesthetic measure of the violence done to their pre-enslavement memory—to their sense of natal identity. Having endured the one American immigration that was fully involuntary, they were left with no sense of parental dignity, much less heroism. They are the one American people about whom the following genealogical paradigm (aptly applied again by Hawthorne to his New England forebears) makes no sense at all:

> The early settlers were able to keep within the narrowest limits of their rigid principles, because they had adopted them in mature life, and from their own deep conviction, and were strengthened in them by that species of enthusiasm, which is as sober and enduring as reason itself. But if their immediate successors followed the same line of conduct, they were confined to it, in a great degree, by habits forced on them, and by the severe rule under which they were educated, and, in short, more by restraint than by the free exercise of the imagination and understanding.[13]

And so the literature of Afro-Americans has been—until the last thirty years or so, when a sense of their cultural continuity has begun to be painfully rebuilt—the one American literature that is not fundamentally elegiac. There are hints of elegy in certain recurrent conventions of Afro-American autobiography: in, for instance, William Wells Brown's account of being scoured for his journey "up" from the slave quarters to the plantation house, or in Malcolm X's retrospective shame at the memory of soaking his hair in a bath of lye as he tried to burn the kinks out. Such blanching of the self is the subject of many Afro-American novels that take as their theme the price of unholy conversion, acquiescence in a falsely claimed identity—what the Puritans called formal hypocrisy. But only very recently, in the work of authors who have witnessed the emergence of a black middle class and the simultaneous recovery of a living sense of Afro-American history, has it become possible for the black writer to address with full voice the theme of a younger generation's infidelity to its elders.[14]

The exuberance of American literature, the force that counteracts such elegiac undercurrents, has been its loyalty to the brave conviction that conversion—the life divinely interrupted and transfigured—is possible and wholly to be embraced. There have, of course, been dissident voices other than those of Hawthorne and James—Melville's (in his Plotinus Plinlimmon mood), or Dickinson's in her manifold resistance to transfiguration ("I should have been too saved . . . "), or Poe's in his portrayals of transcendental madness. But a remarkable array of American writers have found ways to overcome such objections and have given implicit assent to the conclusive Puritan dictum that "Ministers must not preach for fear of the law . . . [nor] for fashion sake . . . [nor] for ostentation sake," but always and only to "deliver a man from hell."[15] If we translate "God" as "presence," we may just as well translate "hell" as "history." We may, in other words, read our literature as the historically inflected product of the homiletic impulse. A simpler way to put this is to say that all American literature is essentially romantic.

It is of course necessary to recognize that the subordinate theme that underlies the Puritan experience—the resistless degradation of the conversionist idea—has also been enduring. Consider, for example, what Weber deemed the most Puritan and most representative of our books, *The Autobiography of Benjamin Franklin*. Even in this amazingly ebullient tract by our "everlasting Wanamaker" there is an unmistakable counterpoint within the celebration of the unconditioned self. Franklin's text is, among other things, a classic conversion narrative and a story of emigration—an account of a young man's refusal to accept his inherited identity. But the pathos of his book, its moments of chilling honesty, come from its barely articulate acknowledgment that in his newly discovered world (Philadelphia) the idea of conversion has retained only its destructive force with regard to the oppressive past—the Boston world of candlemaking at his father's whim. Franklin feels, to use one scholar's phrase for the desire that informs the Puritan morphology of conversion, "an absolute necessity to be another man." But he finds no divine substitute for the petty authority of family obligation that he has thrown off. He finds not even a stability in reason: "So convenient a thing it is to be a *reasonable creature,* since it enables one to find or make a reason for everything one has a mind to do." There is a literally unutterable sense of isolation in Franklin's universe of individual calculation—a sense of loss for which he barely has a language. And so he falls back on the language of "order": "In truth, I found myself incorrigible with respect to Order; and now I am grown old, and my memory bad, I feel very sensibly the want of it." This is his one whisper of the feeling of privation—what Saul Bellow calls, in defining the term, "a general love or craving [which] before it is explicit or before it sees its object, manifests itself as boredom or some other kind of suffering."[16] Every reader of the *Autobiography* (including Jay Gatz) marvels at the chart Franklin keeps to measure his progress toward the perfection of self-control. But every reader also feels a terrible vacuity in Franklin's scheme. For Franklin, and for the culture of which he was so acutely representative, the first stages of the Puritan conversion narrative—humiliation and preparation—have swollen into the totality of experience. Implantation, exaltation, and glorification have fallen out of the world.

Such has been the recurrent fate of the immigrant imagination in America—a brief and purposeful intensity followed by fragmentation and flatness—a pattern that is especially clear in the experience of groups that have undertaken the journey to America with a sense of corporate identity as a community of believers. This is most obvious if one looks at migrations by people of close cultural proximity to the Puritan founders. Examples are legion. If, for instance, one scans the communities that were formed in provincial Pennsylvania by the German pietist migrations of the early eighteenth century (which Franklin looked upon with fraternal dismay), the paradigm is vividly apparent. The Moravians under Zinzendorf developed upon arrival in the New World such vital and elaborate rituals of communal affirmation—including the exchange of personal testimonies of belief—that they came to constitute obstacles to a culture of work. But the "Brethren" who emigrated from the Rhineland in the 1720s to this "well-blessed land [where] there are neither guilds nor burdens from the authorities," found themselves internally divided almost immediately by the presence of a charismatic mystic. Their particular ecstatic, Johann Conrad Beissel, called himself "Superintendent" of the

Ephrata Commune (where family names were replaced by new names signifying the spiritual bonds of the communicants) and, claiming that Christ was hermaphroditic, demanded passionate worship of what he called "the heavenly God-femalety." It seems that he worshiped human "femalety" as well, and not with perfect celibacy: "My ascending self-will was crucified with Christ, so that now consequently his firey male property is made sinking down, which sinking is the female property, from which font mercy flows out for the salvation of the whole world." God was ontologically a woman—but in the process of teaching this doctrine, Beissel achieved a reputation for "being a seducer and destroyer of wedlock," for "dragg[ing] the gifts of the Spirit into the Flesh" at the Love Feasts over which he presided.[17] The ghost of John of Leyden, with his sexual Fanaticism, was reanimated yet again, just as it had been (to some observers) by Anne Hutchinson at Boston a hundred years before.

Other less closely allied candidates for comparison do not, to be sure, always furnish such neat or instructively distorted parallels with immigrant Puritanism; one may think of the remarkably unchanging Amish, or of certain Hasidic groups who have retained coherence in the face of secular pressures in the urban crucible. But the recurrence of the central themes of divisive change and problematic self-reference remain striking in less likely cases: here is Joan Didion commenting on the post-Castro Cuban exodus to Miami—a piece of reportage written, one assumes, without the benefit of a recent reading of Miller's *Errand into the Wilderness:* "Living in Florida was still at the deepest level construed by Cubans as a temporary condition, an accepted political option shaped by the continuing dream, if no longer the immediate expectation, of a vindicatory return. *El exilio* was for Cubans a ritual, a respected tradition."[18] Such transhistorical continuities, sometimes bizarre in the precision of their recurrence, give us more than chronological justification to grant the Puritans a continued claim to their archetypal position in our immigrant culture. Within their immigrant community the presence of an antinomian tendency and a lingering homeland allegiance distinguish them relatively little from others who have since lived through the same contradictions.

Yet they stand disproportionately thick upon the stage of our history not merely because they were first, but because they determinedly wrote themselves onto it. In their obsessive self-chronicling, which grew in intensity with their sense of dissolution as a community, they guaranteed for themselves a unique afterlife in American culture: "Whether *New England* may live anywhere else or no," Cotton Mather proclaimed, "it must *Live* in our *History*."[19] Their unwilling adumbration (by historians such as Bradford and Johnson as well as Mather) of the modern suspicion that irrational change is the only constant in human affairs arose only when their hopes for imminent social fulfillment had been destroyed.

There was indeed a moment—very brief, and very early—when it seemed that that hope might be realized (John Cotton once fixed upon the year 1655, which he did not live to see), but by the end of the first decade the keynote of New England's literature had already become its acknowledgment that the end of time was not hastening, but receding. The community was suspended in a limbo of its own making—a discovery that the Puritan founders could never quite acknowledge. We may recognize in that muted theme the first expression of what Marcus Cunliffe has called "an almost inherent American tendency to believe that one has been cut off decisively from the past as if by a physical barrier . . . [a feeling that] has . . . revealed itself in regrets and neuroses as well as in pride and exuberance."[20] This remains the somber, if secondary, melody in our most ecstatic writings—from Thomas Shepard's commentaries on his ocean crossing to the many immigrant memoirs of the twentieth century. It is the paradox to which the Puritans were the first to give expression—the conundrum that in America the yearning for rebirth involves a felt loss of identity.

The project of restoring the loss (which persists in religious forms that many intellectuals in a secular age cannot fathom) became, by the second third of the nineteenth century, the central project of American literary culture even as it moved away from explicitly theistic formulations. The rationalization of Puritanism had left this restorationist impulse dormant but not extinct—especially not in New England, which became the site of what we think of, following Matthiessen, as our national literary rebirth. "Good is positive," said Emerson (whose father occupied the pulpit of John Cotton's church) before the encrusted worthies of the Harvard Divinity School in 1838. "Evil is merely privative, not absolute: it is like cold, which is the privation of heat." One measure of New England's fatigue at that literary/historical moment was the degree to which its religious leaders could be shocked by this invocation of their original faith. It had first begun to stir again in the periodic revivals of the eighteenth century, when it divided local communities between New Lights and Old, shrank the distances between hitherto separated regions as itinerant preachers crisscrossed the country, and helped to assimilate many newly immigrant Protestants into what Melville was to call "the evangelical land." Its intellectual content was given highly explicit formulation by the chief spokesman for evangelicalism, Jonathan Edwards, who wrote, in what seems to have been a mood of trust that the old consensus was being restored, that "Divines are generally agreed, that sin radically and fundamentally consists in what is negative, or privative, having its root and foundation in a privation or want of holiness." History was to show that Edwards overestimated his countrymen's agreement on this point, but he had invoked the terms of what was, and remains, the essential familial debate.[21]

"There were," as Alan Heimert has magisterially shown, " . . . only *two* parties on the American religious scene in the period after the Great Awakening."[22] The present book has been in large part an account of the prehistory of those parties, but they have had a continuing history as well—for the apprehension of which one means has been to study what is traditionally called literary history. The usual subject for literary historians—the emergence of a mature American culture of letters out of a childhood obsession with homiletics—can be better understood as the work of gingerly secular writers who were seeking not to disclaim but to recover the imperiled conversionist intention. In its early stages this recovery proceeded uncertainly by way of forms derived from English models and therefore ungainly for American purposes. Thus fiction in the new United States was at first sentimental because it hesitated at the prospect of reorganized relations between classes and sexes in a postrevolutionary world. Verse was at first satiric because it surveyed the foibles of an unformed culture aping the old world from which it had broken away. Drama was farcical because it found comic energy in the fault-lines that divided the emerging nation—dandies from bumpkins, Old Lights from New.

None of these developing genres, however, fully articulated the radical aspirations of the new nation, because they were put to use by writers who brought to them an almost exclusively negative energy. Various inhibitions blocked the development of mature indigenous forms within the American literary mind, inhibitions that can be reasonably summed up as a fear of "promiscuous equality."[23] The first half of the conversionist paradigm (seventeenth-century Calvinists had called it preparation; eighteenth-century Federalists were cautiously willing to call it independence) could be at least partially satisfied by such a truncated literature. But, hostile to its own emerging democratic culture (as the preparationists had been hostile to the specter of free grace), it failed to assist the national rebirth into a new identity.

Eventually there came a resurgence of the fervent impulse of "promiscuous equality"—in politics (Jefferson and Jackson), literature (the Renaissance), and religion (revivalism, transcendentalism, reform)—that, following Miller, I have called Augustinian. To make such a statement may seem to betray the naive opinion that human action can be explained as somehow preceded by, or even generated by, some kind of periodicity in the life of abstract ideas. This is not my claim. I have tried in this book to make at least a beginning toward understanding how certain deeply and widely held beliefs were affiliated with the social conditions and political conflicts through which Puritanism arose. And though my primary interest has been to suggest a process of change in ideas and feelings, I willingly press the point that this change can be understood only in conjunction with the large material fact that stands at our beginning as a nation: the migration from one continent to another.

It bears saying in this connection that to follow the gradations at any time in Americans' collective thinking about the nature of evil is not to elevate falsely the mental experience of an intellectual elite. To confront in some way those moments in life which threaten to fall outside the limits of understanding is not a necessary capability restricted by class, or by gender, or by any other material category of human experience. It is a psychic obligation common to all humanity. And for those who have just completed a journey out of one culture into another (whether physical, political, or imaginative), the form of this response tends to be the hope, or at least the tolerance of the hope, that evil is incompleteness—an expectancy waiting "promiscuously" to be fulfilled. In contemporary culture we call this expectation, using the language of Progressive optimism, "each individual's potential." For the historian the challenge is to make sense of the ways that Americans, all of whom have some personal or ancestral memory of such an immigration, have dealt with the loss or mitigation of that expectancy over centuries of cultural change.[24]

This book has been chiefly concerned with only the first chapter in that unwritten narrative—a chapter that is worth dwelling on, I believe, not only because of its intrinsic interest, but because it furnishes the basic terms through which the problem of evil continues to be understood in our culture. It is well to acknowledge such recent cautions as Lawrence Buell's remark that "Puritan legacy-ism might be nothing more than an artifact of the researcher's wishful hope to break through to a unified theory of American culture." Such challenges are a deserved rebuke for the study of early America, as was R. W. B. Lewis's earlier warning that "there may be no such thing as 'American experience'; it is probably better not to insist that there is. But there has been experience in America, and the account of it has had its own specific form. That form has been clearest and most rewarding when it has been most dialectical."[25] The search for breakthrough to a unified theory of the form by which experience in America can be best represented is not likely to be given up any time soon, and there is a certain health in its continuance. I have tried in this book to identify its dialectical motion in terms that seem to me faithful to a generation of religious immigrants who were among the first to live it.

Perhaps most important for the continuing effort to come to terms with our cultural inheritance is the need to recognize that the messianic element is at work in all Western nationalisms, and furnishes no basis for a theory of American exceptionalism. We share it, but we surely have no special claim to it. It is time to exonerate the Puritans from this latest in the long list of national sins that have been laid at their feet. "Any local goddess," as Mircea Eliade has said, "tends to become *the* Great Goddess; any village anywhere *is* the 'Center of the World,' and any wizard whatever pretends, at the height of his ritual, to be the Universal Sovereign."[26] History has given us no reason to judge the tribal certainties of Americans as any more virulent than those of other peoples. There are even some grounds for believing the opposite. The extraordinary tenacity, however, with which Americans have clung to the belief that their lives can be radically renewed is a more notable cultural distinction. To give an account of this belief in American lives is to acknowledge not only its persistence as an idea but also the inevitable rebuff it suffers through experience. It is at work in the highly refined vision of a John Cotton and in the pandering promises of a Billy Sunday; in the ordeal of every immigrant and the vexed inheritance of his children. In all these forms and more—arisen and in abeyance—it has been the credo of our culture.

Epilogue: Lincoln and Everett at Gettysburg

In November of 1863 President Lincoln and former Massachusetts Governor Edward Everett went to Gettysburg to dedicate the national cemetery where thousands of Union dead had been buried four months earlier. There Lincoln, who had been perfunctorily invited by the committee of governors that had organized the event, delivered what would become the most famous speech in American history—a message of three minutes' duration that has achieved nearly scriptural status in the national imagination. Everett, for whose convenience the ceremonies had been postponed by a month, delivered a two-hour oration that, by virtue of the inescapable comparison, has become (somewhat unfairly) a symbolic instance of vapid political bombast. Both men—one a member of a restless emigrant family that had been migrating south and west for two centuries and had moved three times in his own youth, the other the scion of a distinguished and eminently stable New England clan—were descended from New England Puritans.[1] Neither made any significant reference that day to any person, doctrine, or event in their ancestral New England history, but the two performances expressed what may be called their inherited alternatives of Augustinian and Manichean politics.

Everett began with an invocation of Athenian burial traditions and likened the events at Gettysburg of the previous July to the Battle of Marathon in the fifth century B.C. "It depended upon the events of that day," he said, in a text that Lincoln had read before composing his own remarks, "whether Greece should live, a glory and a light to all coming time, or should expire like the meteor of a moment." Everett further developed his theme of the battle as critical to the survival of the nation—a battle "on whose issue it depended whether this august republican Union . . . cemented with the blood of some of the purest patriots that ever died, should perish or endure." This was not the only phrase which Lincoln would note for future use. Paying homage to the "sisters of charity" who take the field after the armies have withdrawn, Everett has them "bind up the wounds" of the fallen soldiers, and his repeated acknowledgment of providence as the essential actor on those terrible days in July may also have been in Lincoln's mind when he added "under God" in revising the last sentence of his own address.

But the differences between the two orations are far more striking than the convergences and echoes. Among them is the fact that Everett placed the Gettysburg struggle in a historical continuum reaching back over twenty centuries, while Lincoln spoke of history as if it had begun less than a century before: "Four score and seven years ago our fathers brought forth upon this continent a new nation, conceived in liberty, and dedicated to the proposition that all men are created equal." This extraordinary sentence delivers many meanings, all of which are linked and interdependent. It extinguishes, by its use of a language derived from Genesis, all history preceding the nation's birth. It uses the pronoun "our" in a much more capacious way than does Everett—for whom "our" means primarily the military aggregate fielded by the Northern states: "[General] Ewell, on our extreme right . . . had been weakened by the withdrawal of the troops sent over to support our left." While Everett's metaphors are deployed in serviceable variations—the Union "cemented by blood," the fields "moistened by blood"—Lincoln's opening sentence establishes a paradoxical relation between the terms of its central metaphor of conception and birth. "Our fathers brought forth on this continent," as if the founding fathers were simultaneously childbearers and inseminators of the maternal continent.[2]

But most important among the many differences of rhetorical technique are those between Everett's and Lincoln's representations of the enemy. For Everett, the enemy is an "invader," always singular— "*he* was repulsed with immense loss"—always unitary, never allowed to emerge into the too-vivid human reality of many dying men. Compared implicitly to the minions of Satan and of Robespierre, and carefully distinguished from the righteous rebels of 1640 and 1776, this enemy is a fiendish conspirator with designs upon the nation's capital. Everett takes pains to expose the enemy's fallacious arguments, the "wretched sophistries" upon which the Confederate based his claim to constitutional legitimacy—chiefly the idea that federal power is an agency of the sovereign states. Everett goes on to trace the "monstrous conspiracy" back beyond the outbreak of war, into the 1840s and 1850s. The presence of many military men in the audience (Everett's oration, with its decorative phrases looped around simple sentences, is an oral performance for the moment much more than a text for published preservation) seems to have led him to emphasize the details of battle, and to insist—with the potential "peace candidacy" of George McClellan in mind—on the need to prosecute the war to its conclusion.

In Lincoln's address there is no "I," a pronoun to which Everett has frequent recourse. And no enemy is ever mentioned. These absences prevent Lincoln's speech from falling into the oppositional structure—erected upon a Manichean premise—that is the essence of Everett's vision, and for more of which the audience surely remained expectant. Lincoln builds his homily instead around the word "dedicate," which he uses in varying form four times, and which builds a greater and greater sense of bound humility and transcendent possibility. The verbs with which he frames the main body of his message—"endure" and "perish"—are intransitive. They depend on no resistant object for their meaning. And the force of the whole is not to inspire or maintain enmity, but to foster a new measure of positive devotion to the principle invoked by the opening invocation of Genesis—the equality principle of the Declaration, which Lincoln elsewhere called "the sheet anchor" of the Republic. This is a universalist vision, and one that posits no Satan. The only evil it understands—with a singleness of purpose that is both appalling and sublime—is the evil of incompleteness.

Lincoln and Everett were on the same side of what was, some say, the military imposition of rule by industrial capitalist culture upon the last holdouts against modernity. But, however allied they may have been, between Lincoln's vision and Everett's there is a world of difference—for the possession of which Americans have contended long before and ever since.

Notes

Introduction

1. Raymond Williams, *Marxism and Literature* (Oxford: Oxford University Press, 1977), p. 128.
2. Miller's first developed statement of this position was " 'Preparation for Salvation' in Seventeenth-Century New England," *Journal of the History of Ideas* 4, no. 3 (1943): 253–286, which he expanded and refined as chapter four of *The New England Mind: From Colony to Province* (Cambridge, Mass.: Harvard University Press, 1953). For the revisionist argument that " 'preparation for salvation' comprises a Christian's growth in grace following conversion," see William K. B. Stoever, *"A Faire and Easie Way to Heaven": Covenant Theology and Antinomianism in Early Massachusetts* (Middletown: Wesleyan University Press, 1978), esp. pp. 12, 196; and Charles E. Hambrick-Stowe, *The Practice of Piety: Puritan Devotional Discipline in Seventeenth-Century New England* (Chapel Hill: University of North Carolina Press, 1982), pp. 21–22, 197–241. Quoted phrases are from John Norton, *The Orthodox Evangelist* (London, 1654), n.p., 53.
3. Norton, *Orthodox Evangelist*, pp. 160–161; Richard D. Pierce, ed., "Records of the First Church in Boston, 1630–1868," *Publications of the Colonial Society of Massachusetts* 39 (1961): 38.
4. Steven Marcus, *The Other Victorians: A Study of Sexuality and Pornography in Mid-Nineteenth-Century England* (New York: Basic Books, 1974) p. 30; C. S. Lewis, *A Preface to Paradise Lost* (Oxford: Oxford University

Press, 1970), ch. 9; Jerome McGann, *The Romantic Ideology* (Chicago: University of Chicago Press, 1983), p. 11. With the welcome resurgence of historicism in literary study, the idea of "timeless, cultureless, universal human essence"—the phrase is Stephen Greenblatt's, in *Renaissance Self-Fashioning* (Chicago: University of Chicago Press, 1980), p. 4 —seems to be becoming heresy. Of my own lingering respect for the essentialist idea (which Greenblatt himself is too subtle a reader entirely to banish) I would simply say that while there may no longer be, as Jürgen Habermas puts it in *Communication and the Evolution of Society* (Boston: Beacon Press, 1979), p. 140, any "need to assume a *species-subject*" in historical analysis, it seems to me that all critical writing— indeed all utterance—involves an act of faith that there is some common ground to be found between even the most disparate human consciousnesses. It is notable, I think, that the influential anthropologist Clifford Geertz, though he is readily quoted to the effect that "there is no such thing as a human nature independent of culture" (Greenblatt, p. 3) has also devoted his most famous essay ("Notes on the Balinese Cockfight") to the "thick description" of what he calls, invoking Northrop Frye as his model, "a paradigmatic human event"—"Notes on the Balinese Cockfight," in *The Interpretation of Cultures* (New York: Basic Books, 1973), p. 450. The present book is committed to the idea of culture as process, but also to the continuing possibility of comprehensible narration of paradigmatic human events.

5. Richard Hofstadter, *The Progressive Historians* (Chicago: University of Chicago Press, 1968), pp. 451–452.

6. A number of significant books have lately appeared, inspired by the groundbreaking work of the English historian E. P. Thompson, that are devoted to the recovery of a working-class "subculture" in American life: David Montgomery, *The Fall of the House of Labor: The Workplace, the State, and American Labor Activism, 1865–1925* (New York: Cambridge University Press, 1987); Sean Wilentz, *Chants Democratic: New York City and the Rise of the American Working Class, 1788–1850* (New York: Oxford University Press, 1984). Michael Denning, in *Mechanic Accents: Dime Novels and American Working Class Culture* (New York: Verso, 1987), employs a more literary method of representing the experience of working-class life.

7. Sacvan Bercovitch, *The American Jeremiad* (Madison: University of Wisconsin Press, 1978), p. 158; Myra Jehlen, *American Incarnation: The Individual, the Nation, and the Continent* (Cambridge, Mass.: Harvard University Press, 1986), p. 8; Alan Trachtenberg, *The Incorporation of America: Culture and Society in the Gilded Age* (New York: Hill and Wang, 1982), p. 144.

8. Louis Hartz, *The Liberal Tradition in America* (New York: Harcourt, Brace, Jovanovich, 1955), p. 58; Emerson, "Circles," in Stephen E.

Whicher, ed., *Selections from Ralph Waldo Emerson* (Boston: Houghton Mifflin, 1957), p. 173; Myra Jehlen, "Archimedes and the Paradox of Feminist Criticism," in *Feminist Theory: A Critique of Ideology*, ed. Nannerl O. Keohane, Michelle Z. Rosaldo, and Barbara C. Gelpi (Chicago: University of Chicago Press, 1982), pp. 189–190.

9. J. Hillis Miller, "Presidential Address, 1986," *PMLA* 102, no. 3 (1987): 281. The angriest study of recent years is Ann Kibbey, *The Interpretation of Material Shapes in Puritanism: A Study of Rhetoric, Prejudice, and Violence* (Cambridge: Cambridge University Press, 1986): "Despite their appearance of otherworldly concerns in preaching the soul's salvation, ministers such as John Cotton subordinated belief in the deity to another end: communicating the absolute rightness of their own social ideals," which included "extreme act[s] of prejudice" and "mass killing" (pp. 6, 1).

10. Henry Vane, *The Retired Mans Meditations*, 2 vols. (London, 1655), II, 415; Willa Cather, *O Pioneers!* (1913; Boston: Houghton Mifflin, n.d.), p. 3; "The Examination of Mrs. Anne Hutchinson at the Court of Newtown (1637)," in David D. Hall, ed., *The Antinomian Controversy, 1636–1638: A Documentary History* (Middletown: Wesleyan University Press, 1968), p. 338; Bradstreet, "To My Dear Children," in Jeannine Hensley, ed., *The Works of Anne Bradstreet* (Cambridge, Mass.: Harvard University Press, 1967), p. 241; Thomas Dudley, *Letter to the Countess of Lincoln* (1631), in Edmund S. Morgan, ed., *The Founding of Massachusetts* (Indianapolis: Bobbs-Merrill, 1964), p. 165; Barbary Cutter and Jane Holmes, in *The Confessions of Diverse Propounded*, ed. George Selement and Bruce C. Woolley, *Publications of the Colonial Society of Massachusetts* 58 (1981): 90, 68, Abraham Cahan, *Yekl: A Tale of the New York Ghetto* (1896; rpt. New York: Dover Press, 1970), p. 66.

11. Perry Miller, *Errand into the Wilderness* (Cambridge: Harvard University Press, 1956), p. 9. For the argument distinguishing between Puritan eschatology in England and New England, see Sacvan Bercovitch, *The Puritan Origins of the American Self* (New Haven: Yale University Press, 1975), p. 82, and his "The Image of America: From Hermeneutics to Symbolism," in Michael T. Gilmore, ed., *Early American Literature: A Collection of Critical Essays* (Englewood Cliffs: Prentice-Hall, 1980), p. 162; "All [English Puritans] knew the difference between federal progress and sacred teleology," and "no English patriot could confuse his country *per se* with the Heavenly City, or his duties as Englishman with his prospects for eternity," but in America "the case was otherwise" because there "the saint prepared for salvation within a corporate historic undertaking destined to usher in the millennium." This distinction has been challenged by Michael McGiffert, "God's Controversy with Jacobean England," *American Historical Review* 88 (1983): esp. 1168.

12. Bernard Bailyn, *Voyagers to the West: A Passage in the Peopling of America*

on the Eve of the Revolution (New York: Knopf, 1986), p. 378. Norman Pettit, in a recent essay entitled "The English in New England: Their Reluctance to Become American," in *The Transit of Civilization from Europe to America: Essays in Honor of Hans Galinsky* (Tübingen: Gunter Narr Verlag, 1986), pp. 45–52, has remarked that the Puritans' "reluctance to become American . . . [has] until now [not] been given sufficient thought."

13. Charlotte Erickson, *Invisible Immigrants: The Adaptation of English and Scottish Immigrants in Nineteenth-Century America* (Coral Gables, Fla.: University of Miami Press), pp. 23–25; W. I. Thomas, *The Unadjusted Girl: With Cases and Standpoint for Behavior Analysis* (1923), quoted in Carla Cappetti, "Deviant Girls and Dissatisfied Women: A Sociologist's Tale," forthcoming in *The Invention of Ethnicity in the United States,* ed. Werner Sollors (New York: Oxford University Press), 1988.

14. Bailyn, *Voyagers,* p. 412; see Daniel Patrick Moynihan, "What Wretched Refuse?," *New York Magazine,* 12 May 1986, p. 59.

15. Peter Heylyn, quoted in Carl Bridenbaugh, *Vexed and Troubled Englishmen, 1630 to 1642* (New York: Oxford University Press, 1967), p. 452; Darrett Rutman, *Winthrop's Boston: A Portrait of a Puritan Town, 1630–1649* (New York: Norton, 1965), p. 147; David D. Hall, "Toward a History of Popular Religion in Early New England," *William and Mary Quarterly* 41 (1984): 50; Samuel Stone, quoted in Cotton Mather, *Magnalia Christi Americana* (1702; Hartford, 1853), 2 vols., I, 437. Harry Stout, *The New England Soul: Preaching and Religious Culture in Colonial New England* (New York: Oxford University Press, 1986), is deeply read in the regular (sabbath and lecture-day) sermons of later New England, which remain mostly unpublished and therefore outside the purview of most intellectual historians, who have concentrated on the published occasional sermons, that is, those delivered on fast and election days. Stout corrects the recent overemphasis on apocalyptic themes, and calls into question some aspects of Miller's declension thesis, though it should be acknowledged that Miller did qualify his own distinction between the phases of New England Puritanism: "What has happened [in later Puritanism] is a concentration of emotion upon the destiny of a group . . . while other modes of discourse, even though kept up in ordinary Sabbath sermons, persist only as mementos of a vanished past" (*Colony to Province,* p. 33). For the first generation Stout finds a close alignment between the two sorts of sermons. Further materials are likely to emerge that will deepen our sense of "lay piety." A number of conversion relations in the possession of the American Antiquarian Society, formerly assumed to be from Richard Mather's Dorchester congregation, are being edited for publication by Mary Rhinelander of Boston University, who attributes them to Thomas Shepard's Newtown church.

16. Patricia Caldwell, *The Puritan Conversion Narrative: The Beginnings of*

American Expression (New York: Cambridge University Press, 1983), p. 125; Samuel Rogers, quoted in Kenneth W. Shipps, "The Puritan Emigration to New England: A New Source on Motivation," *New England Historical and Genealogical Register* 135 (1981): 89; Winthrop, *General Considerations* (1629) in Alden T. Vaughan, ed., *The Puritan Tradition in America, 1620–1730* (New York: Harper and Row, 1972), p. 26; Stoddard, *The Danger of Speedy Degeneracy* (Boston, 1705), pp. 23–24.

17. Winthrop, quoted in Norman C. P. Tyack, *Migration from East Anglia to New England before 1660*, Ph.D. diss., University of London, 1951, p. 102. William Hunt, *The Puritan Moment: The Coming of Revolution in an English County* (Cambridge, Mass.: Harvard University Press, 1983), p. 25; Fuller, *The Holy State and the Profane State* (London, 1642), 2 vols., II, 357.

18. Christopher Blackwood, *A Treatise Concerning Repentance* (London, 1653), p. 19 (Blackwood was among those New Englanders who returned to England in the 1640s); Hutchinson, quoted in Winthrop, *A Short Story of the rise, reign, and ruine of the Antionomians, Familists, and Libertines* (1644), in Hall, ed., *Antinomian Controversy*, p. 246; Cotton, *A Practical Commentary or an Exposition upon the First Epistle Generall of John* (London, 1656), p. 256.

19. David D. Hall, *The Faithful Shepherd: A History of the New England Ministry in the Seventeenth Century* (Chapel Hill: University of North Carolina Press, 1972), p. 90; Cotton, quoted in ibid., p. 250; Dudley, *Letter to Countess of Lincoln*, in Morgan, p. 161; Shepard, *Works*, ed. John Albro (Boston, 1853), 3 vols., II, 170, 26; Cotton, *God's Promise to His Plantations*, Old South Leaflets, no. 3 p. 14; Cotton, *The Powring out of the Seven Vials* (preached in New England, c. 1641; LONDON, 1645), p. 150.

20. Henry Adams, *The Education of Henry Adams* (1907; Boston: Houghton Mifflin, 1973), p. 7; Christopher Blackwood, *Four Treatises* (London, 1653), p. 75; Bradstreet, "To My Dear Children," in Hensley, p. 243; William Coddington, *A Demonstration of True Love unto You the Rulers of the Colony of the Massachusets in New-England* (London, 1674), p. 12; Milton, *Areopagitica* (1644); Johnson, *Wonder-Working Providence of Sion's Saviour in New England* (1654), ed. J. Franklin Jameson (New York, 1910), p. 34. Kai Erikson, *Wayward Puritans: A Study in the Sociology of Deviance* (New York: John Wiley, 1966), is a psychologically sensitive account along Durkheimean lines of the Puritans' growing need to define and expel "deviants" from their midst.

21. Emerson, *Nature*, in Whicher, p. 33; Norton, *Orthodox Evangelist*, SigA2ᵛ.

22. *The Open Cage: An Anzia Yezierska Collection*, ed. Alice Kessler-Harris (New York: Persea Books, 1979), pp. 90, 147; Shepard, Jr., *Eye-Salve, or a Watch-Word from our Lord Jesus Christ unto His Churches in New England* (Cambridge, Mass., 1673), p. 44.

23. Folger, "A Looking Glass for the Times" (1676), *Rhode Island Historical Tracts* 16 (1883): 17; Roth, *The Great American Novel* (New York: Bantam Books, 1974), p. 101.

24. Cotton, *God's Promise*, p. 6; Frederick Jackson Turner, "The Significance of the Frontier in American History," in George R. Taylor, ed., *The Turner Thesis* (Lexington, Mass.: D. C. Heath, 1972), p. 8. Among the several studies of New England communities founded by first-generation migrants, those of Kenneth Lockridge on Dedham, *A New England Town: The First Hundred Years* (New York: Norton, 1970), and Philip Greven on Andover, *Four Generations: Population, Land and Family in Colonial Andover, Massachusetts* (Ithaca: Cornell University Press, 1970) constitute, as Bruce Tucker has pointed out in "Early American Intellectual History after Perry Miller," *Canadian Review of American Studies* 13, no. 2 (1982): 145–157, sociological confirmations of Miller's declension paradigm; they tell a story of slow fragmentation over several generations as population pressures broke through the original conception of a patriarchal community devoted to subsistence farming under religious control. For a summary review, see James A. Henretta, "The Morphology of New England Society in the Colonial Period," *Journal of Interdisciplinary History* (1971–72): 379–398. More recently, social historians such as Stephen Innes, in *Labor in a New Land: Economy and Society in Seventeenth-Century Springfield* (Princeton: Princeton University Press, 1983), have contested the notion of originally cooperative Christian communities sliding into modernity, and have documented the dominance of "developmentalism, diversification, acquisitiveness, individualism, contentiousness, and stratification," from the very start (p. 171). See also John F. Martin, *Entrepreneurship and the Founding of New England Towns: The Seventeenth Century*, Ph.D. diss., Harvard University, 1985. Darrett Rutman's *Winthrop's Boston* stands between these poles, and thus accords most closely with my own view that a sense of defeat took hold within the period of the founders' control, and was undiluted by the mitigating explanation of generational decline. It happened within the founders' lifetime, and therefore could be, and frequently was, experienced by a single consciousness. For the romanticization of the shtetl in Jewish-American culture, see Sol Gittleman, *From Shtetl to Suburbia: The Family in Jewish Literary Imagination* (Boston: Beacon Press, 1978), esp. chs. 3–4.

25. Michael Gordon, "Irish Immigrant Culture and the Labor Boycott in New York City, 1880–1886," in Richard L. Ehrlich, ed., *Immigrants in Industrial America, 1850–1920* (Charlottesville: University Press of Virginia, 1977), p. 118; Caroline Kirkland, *A New Home: Who'll Follow?* (1838; New Haven: College and University Press, 1965), p. 180; Upton Sinclair, *The Jungle* (1906; New York: New American Library, n.d.), p. 20.

26. John Murrin, "Review Essay," *History and Theory* 11 (1972): 232; David

Grayson Allen, *In English Ways: The Movement of Societies and the Transferal of English Local Law and Custom to Massachusetts Bay in the Seventeenth Century* (Chapel Hill: University of North Carolina Press, 1981); Don G. Hill, ed., *Church Records in the town of Dedham, Massachusetts, 1638–1845* (Dedham, 1888), quoted in Caldwell, *Puritan Conversion Narrative,* pp. 111–112; Cotton, quoted in John Norton, *Abel being dead yet speaketh; or the life and death of that deservedly famous man of God, Mr. John Cotton* (London, 1658), pp. 29–30; Cotton, *The Churches Resurrection* (London, 1642), p. 20; Jerre Mangione, *An Ethnic at Large* (New York: G. P. Putnam's, 1978), p. 182.

27. Max Weber, *The Sociology of Religion,* trans. Ephraim Fischoff (Boston: Beacon Press, 1964), p. 139; John Hick, *Evil and the God of Love* (San Francisco: Harper and Row, 1978), p. 3; Thomas Hooker, *The Soules Exaltation* (London, 1638), p. 246.

28. Norman Grabo, "The Veiled Vision: The Role of Aesthetics in Early American Intellectual History," in Sacvan Bercovitch, ed., *The American Puritan Imagination: Essays in Revaluation* (New York: Cambridge University Press, 1974), p. 22; R. W. B. Lewis, *The American Adam: Innocence, Tragedy, and Tradition in the Nineteenth Century* (Chicago: University of Chicago Press, 1955), p. 2. Perry Miller understood, with his usual penetration, that "the jeremiad," by which he meant later American Puritanism, "could make sense out of existence as long as adversity was to be overcome, but in the moment of victory it was confused" (*Colony to Province,* p. 33). My only emendation is to claim this dilemma as a general feature of Puritanism rather than as a "technical problem inherent in the [jeremiad] convention."

29. Paul Ricoeur, *The Symbolism of Evil* (Boston: Beacon Press, 1967), pp. 26–27.

30. Peter Laslett, *The World We Have Lost: England before the Industrial Age* (New York: Charles Scribner's Sons, 1971), p. 22; Greenblatt, *Renaissance Self-Fashioning,* passim; Irvonwy Morgan, *Prince Charles's Puritan Chaplain* (London: Allen and Unwin, 1957), p. 41; Katherine Chidley, *The Justification of the Independant Churches of Christ* (London, 1641), p. 27.

31. Mary Douglas, *Natural Symbols: Explorations in Cosmology* (New York: Pantheon, 1982), pp. 102–104.

32. Ibid., p. 102.

33. Augustine, *Confessions,* trans. Edward Puscy (London: Collier Books, 1961), p. 108.

34. John Norton, *A Discussion of that Great Point in Divinity, the Suffering of Christ* (London, 1653), pp. 2, 7; for the controversy over Pyncheon, see Philip F. Gura, *A Glimpse of Sion's Glory: Puritan Radicalism in New England, 1620–1660* (Middletown: Wesleyan University Press, 1984), pp. 311–312.

35. Norton, *Suffering of Christ,* p. 5; Shepard, *Works,* II, 30.

36. Cotton, *Practical Commentary*, p. 300; Norton, *Suffering of Christ*, p. 7.
37. Freud, *Civilization and Its Discontents* (1930), trans. James Strachey (New York: Norton, 1962), p. 61; Hall, "Popular Religion," p. 51; G. M. Young: *Victorian England: Portrait of an Age* (1936); London: Oxford University Press, 1974), p. vi; Alan Simpson, *Puritanism in Old and New England* (Chicago: University of Chicago Press, 1955).

1. The Prophecies of Richard Hooker

1. Patrick Collinson, *The Elizabethan Puritan Movement* (Berkeley: University of California Press, 1967), pp. 112, 405, 407, 411, 431.
2. Richard Hooker, *On the Laws of Ecclesiastical Polity* (London: J. M. Dent, 1969), 2 vols., I, Preface, vi, 1; vii, 1.
3. Collinson, *Elizabethan Puritan Movement*, p. 404.
4. John Dod and Robert Cleaver, *Two Sermons on the Third of the Lamentations of Jeremie* (London, 1608), p. 25.
5. Patrick Collinson, "A Comment: Concerning the Name Puritan," *Journal of Ecclesiastical History* 31, no. 4 (1980): 485; Christopher Hill, *Puritanism and Revolution* (New York: Schocken, 1964), p. 327; Michael Walzer, *The Revolution of the Saints* (New York: Atheneum, 1973), p. viii.
6. Hooker, *Laws*, I, Preface, iv, 4.
7. Ibid., I, Preface, iii, 9.
8. Collinson, "A Comment," 487; Norton, *Orthodox Evangelist*, n.p.; Hooker, *Laws*, quoted in Harold Laski, *The Rise of European Liberalism* (London: Unwin, 1962), p. 47.
9. Nathaniel Ward, *The Simple Cobler of Aggawam in America* (1647), ed. Paul M. Zall (Lincoln: University of Nebraska Press, 1969), p. 12; William James, "The Dilemma of Determinism," in *The Will to Believe and Other Essays in Popular Philosophy* (1897); New York: Dover, 1956), p. 177.
10. Hooker, *Laws*, I, Preface, iii, 7; John Preston, *The New Covenant* (London, 1629), pp. 34–35; Norman Fiering, *Moral Philosophy at Seventeenth-Century Harvard* (Chapel Hill: University of North Carolina Press, 1981), p. 61.
11. Fiering, *Moral Philosophy*, p. 78.
12. Thomas Hooker, *The Soules Vocation or Effectual Calling* (London, 1637), p. 254; Hooker, *The Soules Possession of Christ* (London, 1638), p. 167; David D. Hall, "On Common Ground: The Coherence of American Puritan Studies," *William and Mary Quarterly* 44, no. 2 (1987): 212.
13. Hooker, *Laws*, I, bk. IV, i. 3.
14. Horton Davies, *Worship and Theology in England: From Andrewes to Baxter and Fox, 1603–1690* (Princeton: Princeton University Press, 1975), p. 4.

15. Hooker, *Laws,* II, bk. V, xxi, 2.
16. Peter Smart, quoted in Davies, *Worship and Theology,* p. 188.
17. Hooker, *Laws,* II, bk. V, xxi, 4.
18. Shepard, *Works,* I, 69; William Perkins, *Works,* 3 vols., (London, 1608–1609), I, 670; William Bradshaw, *English Puritanisme Containeing the Maine Opinions of the rigidest sort of those that are called Puritanes in the Realme of England* (London, 1605), p. 14; A. G. Dickens, *The English Reformation* (New York: Schocken, 1978), p. 246; J. P. Kenyon, *The Stuart Constitution: Documents and Commentary* (Cambridge: Cambridge University Press, 1966), p. 128.
19. Richard Bernard, *The Isle of Man* (London, 1627), p. 8; Bernard, *The Faithful Shepheard* (London, 1621), pp. 135–136; John Brinsely, *The Preacher's Charge and People's Duty* (London, 1631), p. 4.
20. Davies, *Worship and Theology,* pp. 12, 68–69.
21. Cotton, *Practical Commentary,*, p. 363.
22. John Prideaux, *The Doctrine of the Sabbath* (London, 1634), pp. 39, 32; Winton U. Solberg, *Redeem the Time: The Puritan Sabbath in Early America* (Cambridge, Mass.: Harvard University Press, 1977), p. 19; Thomas Shepard, *Theses Sabbaticae* (1644), in *Works,* III, 17, 26.
23. Hooker, *Laws,* I, Preface, iii, 13, 15; Hambrick-Stowe, *Practice of Piety,* p. 47; Cotton, in Roger Williams, *Complete Writings* (New York: Narraganset Club, 1963), ed. Perry Miller, 7 vols., II, 189; Gorton, Letter to Nathaniel Morton, in *Tracts and Other Papers Relating Principally to the Origin, Settlement, and Progress of the Colonies in North America,* ed. Peter Force (Washington, D.C., 1847), 4 vols., IV, no. 7, p. 6.
24. Nathaniel Homes, *The New World, or the New Reformed Church* (London, 1641), p. 23; Cotton, *Practical Commentary,* p. 232; Collinson, *Elizabethan Puritan Movement,* p. 88; Hooker, *Laws,* I, bk. 1, xvi, 6.

2. Errand out of the Wilderness

1. Virginia DeJohn Anderson, "Migrants and Motives: Religion and the Settlement of New England, 1630–1640," *New England Quarterly* 58 (1985): 348; Allen, *In English Ways,* pp. 164, 20. The estimate of the size of the emigrant ministry, which includes priests once ordained in the Church of England, university-educated Puritan lecturers, and lay preachers later appointed to New England congregations, is from Richard Waterhouse, "Reluctant Emigrants: The English Background of the First Generation of the New England Puritan Clergy," *Historical Magazine of the Protestant Episcopal Church* 44 (1975): 474.
2. T. H. Breen and Stephen Foster, "Moving to the New World: The Character of Early Massachusetts Immigration," in Breen, *Puritans and Adventurers: Change and Persistence in Early America* (New York: Oxford University Press, 1980), p. 51; The Rev. Francis Higginson to His Friends

at Leicester, July 1629, in Everett Emerson, ed., *Letters from New England* (Amherst: University of Massachusetts Press, 1976), p. 26; Anderson, "Migrants and Motives," 372–373; David Cressy, *Coming Over: Migration and Communication between England and New England in the Seventeenth Century* (Cambridge: Cambridge University Press, 1987), pp. 107–129.

3. "Migrants and Motives," p. 379; Higginson quoted, p. 375; Breen and Foster, "Moving to the New World," p. 53.

4. Cotton, *Practical Commentary,* p. 197; Hutchinson, quoted in Winthrop, *A Short Story of the Rise, reign, and ruine,* in Hall, ed., *Antinomian Controversy,* p. 272; Roger Clap, *Memoirs,* in Alexander Young, ed., *Chronicles of the First Planters of the Colony of Massachusetts Bay* (Boston, 1846), p. 346.

5. Laud, quoted in Tyack, *Migration from East Anglia, p.* 249; Paul Seaver, *The Puritan Lectureships* (Stanford: Stanford University Press, 1970), p. 255; William Haller, *Tracts on Liberty in the Puritan Revolution, 1638–1647* (New York: Columbia University Press, 1934), 3 vols., I, 10; Shepard, quoted in Michael McGiffert, ed., *God's Plot: The Paradoxes of Puritan Piety, Being the Autobiography and Journal of Thomas Shepard* (Amherst: University of Massachusetts Press, 1972), p. 49n.

6. Shepard, *Works,* I, 268; George R. Potter and Evelyn M. Simpson, eds., *The Sermons of John Donne* (Berkeley: University of California Press, 1953–1962), 10 vols., VIII, 255; III, 364–365; Edwards, *The Great Christian Doctrine of Original Sin Defended* (1758; New Haven: Yale University Press, 1970), p. 129; Thomas Hooker, *The Soul's Vocation or Effectual Calling to Christ* (London 1638), p. 520.

7. Robert Cawdray, *A Treasurie or Storehouse of Similes* (London, 1609), pp. 695–696; George Gifford, *Foure Sermons upon the seven chiefe vertues or principall effectes of faith* (London, 1582), sig B2ᵛ; Philip Stubbes, *The Anatomie of Abuses* (London, 1584), pp. 90, 106.

8. John Downame, *Christian Warfare* (London, 1609), p. 73; Richard Bernard, *Faithful Shepheard,* p. 12; Wrightson, *English Society, 1580–1680* (New Brunswick: Rutgers University Press, 1982), pp. 23, 30; Higginson, *New Englands Plantation, Or, A Short and True Description of the Commodities and Discommodities of that Countrey* (1629), in Emerson, ed., *Letters to New England,* p. 36.

9. Shepard, *Works,* II, p. 89; Stoughton, in Miller, *The American Puritans* (New York: Doubleday, 1956), p. 114.

10. John Dane, "Narrative," *New England Historical and Genealogical Register* 8 (1854): 154.

11. Hambrick-Stowe, *Practice of Piety,* p. 5; Shepard, *Works,* II, 103; Emory Elliott, *Power and the Pulpit in Puritan New England* (Princeton: Princeton University Press, 1975); Augustine Jones, *The Life and Work of*

Thomas Dudley (Boston: Houghton Mifflin, 1899), p. 16; Dudley, quoted in Cotton Mather, *Magnalia Christi Americana* (1702), ed. K. B. Murdock and E. W. Miller (Cambridge, Mass.: Harvard University Press, 1977), p. 232.

12. Hawthorne, *The Scarlet Letter* (1850; Boston: Houghton Mifflin, 1960), pp. 104–105; Richard Bushman, *From Puritan to Yankee: Character and Social Order in Connecticut, 1690–1765* (Cambridge, Mass.: Harvard University Press, 1967).

13. Perkins, *Works*, I, 628.

14. See Phyllis M. Jones and Nicholas R. Jones, eds., *Salvation in New England* (Austin: University of Texas Press, 1977), pp. 61–62. Hooker's emphasis on controlling the will makes illuminating comparison with Preston's tendency to call for its stimulation and release.

15. Henry [John] Archer, *The Personall Reigne of Christ upon Earth* (London, 1642), p. 4.

16. Perkins, *Works*, I, 627; Stoever, "A Faire and Easie Way to Heaven," p. 123; Cotton, *Practical Commentary*, p. 249; Norman Pettit, *The Heart Prepared: Grace and Conversion in Puritan Spiritual Life* (New Haven: Yale University Press, 1966), p. vii; Ames, *The Marrow of Theology*, trans. John Eusden (Durham, N.C.: Labyrinth Press, 1983), p. 161; Emily Dickinson, "He fumbles at your soul," poem #315.

17. Perkins, *Works*, I, 672; III, 699.

18. Perkins, *Works*, III, 654; Morgan, *Visible Saints: The History of a Puritan Idea* (Ithaca, N.Y.: Cornell University Press, 1963), esp. pp. 68–71, remains the most lucid account of the spirit of preparationism.

19. Hooker, *The Soules Preparation for Christ* (London, 1632), pp. 136–137.

20. Ibid., p. 138.

21. Perkins, *Works*, I, 3; E. R. Dodds, *The Greeks and the Irrational* (Berkeley: University of California Press, 1951), ch. 2.

22. Cotton, *The Way of Life* (London, 1641), p. 270.

23. Hunt, *Puritan Moment*, pp. 24, 69; Wrightson, *English Society*, p. 84; Lawrence Stone, *The Family, Sex, and Marriage in England, 1500–1800* (New York: Harper, 1979), p. 386; *The New Cambridge Modern History*, ed. J. R. Cooper (Cambridge: Cambridge University Press, 1971), 4 vols., IV, 76–77.

24. *The Winthrop Papers*, ed. S. E. Morison et al. (Boston: Massachusetts Historical Society, 1927–1944), 5 vols., IV, 129; Whately, *A bride-bush, or, a direction for Married Persons* (London, 1623), pp. 2-5; Cotton, *God's Promise*, p. 8; Bayly, *The Practise of Pietie* (London, 1616), p. 236.

25. Cotton, *The Way of Life*, p. 301; *Practical Commentary*, p. 32; *The Diary of Michael Wigglesworth, 1653–1657*, ed. Edmund S. Morgan (New York: Harper and Row, 1965), p. 5; Samuel Clarke, *A Generall Martyrologie* (London, 1677).

26. John Ward Dean, *A Brief Memoir of the Reverend Giles Firmin* (Boston, 1866), p. 16; Bradford, *Of Plymouth Plantation,* ed. S. E. Morison (New York: Knopf, 1952), p. 143.

27. Shipps, "The Puritan Emigration to New England," p. 88; Shepard, *Defense of the Answer,* in Perry Miller and Thomas H. Johnson, eds., *The Puritans* (New York: Harper and Row, 1963), 2 vols., I, 119; Gorges, quoted in Bridenbaugh, *Vexed and Troubled Englishmen,* p. 407; Shipps, p. 88.

28. Shepard, *Works,* II, 350; Preston, *New Covenant,* p. 434; Hill, "The Political Sermons of John Preston," in *Puritanism and Revolution,* pp. 239–274; Preston, *The Breast-Plate of Faith and Love* (London, 1634), pp. 278–279.

29. Donne, quoted in Raymond Southall, *Literature and the Rise of Capitalism* (London: Lawrence and Wishart, 1973), p. 90; Sibbes, *The Bruised Reede and Smoaking Flax* (London, 1630), p. 71; Rogers, *A Christian Concertation with Mr. Prin, Mr. Baxter, Mr. Harrington, For the true Cause of the Commonwealth* (London, 1659), pp. 89–90.

30. Taylor, *Church Records,* ed. Thomas and Virginia Davis (Boston: G. K. Hall, 1981), p. 333.

31. Preston, *Breast-Plate,* p. 221; Aristotle, *Metaphysics,* XII, ch. 2; Cartwright, quoted in Perez Zagorin, *The Court and the Country* (New York: Atheneum, 1970), p. 164.

32. Edwards, *Dissertation on the End for Which God Created the World,* in *Jonathan Edwards: Representative Selections,* ed. Clarence H. Faust and Thomas H. Johnson (New York: Hill and Wang, 1962), pp. 346-347.

33. Wrightson, *English Society,* p. 41; Bridenbaugh, *Vexed and Troubled Englishmen,* p. 395; Cressy, *Coming Over,* p. 69; Mede, *The Apostasy of the Latter Times* (London, 1642), p. 39; Ward, quoted in David Lovejoy, *Religious Enthusiasm in the New World* (Cambridge, Mass.: Harvard University Press, 1985), p. 9.

34. Hill, *Puritanism and Revolution,* pp. 220–221; Cotton, *Practical Commentary,* p. 233.

35. Nicholas Tyacke, "Popular Puritan Mentality in Late Elizabethan England," in Peter Clark, Alan G. R. Smith, and Nicholas Tyacke, eds., *The English Commonwealth, 1547–1640: Essays in Politics and Society Presented to Joel Hurstfield* (Leicester: Leicester University Press, 1979), p. 89; Winthrop, quoted in Darrett Rutman, *John Winthrop's Decision for America, 1629* (Philadelphia: Lippincott, 1975), p. 15; Preston, *New Covenant,* p. 350; Hill, *The World Turned Upside Down* (New York: Viking, 1972), p. 43; Wrightson, *English Society,* p. 35.

36. Laski, *Rise of European Liberalism,* p. 11; Alan Macfarlane, *The Family Life of Ralph Josselyn* (New York: Norton, 1970), p. 55; John White, *The Troubles of Jerusalems Restauration* (London, 1642), p. 13; Dodd, *Life in Elizabethan England* (New York: G. P. Putnam's, 1961), p. 25.

37. Since Miller's exposition of the covenant theology as a Puritan inno-
    vation, a number of scholars have qualified his model of legalist obli-
    gation between God and the faithful. A pioneering essay is Everett
    Emerson, "Calvin and Covenant Theology," *Church History* 25, no. 2
    (1956): 136–144; see also Michael McGiffert, "Grace and Works: The
    Rise and Division of Covenant Divinity in Elizabethan Puritanism,"
    Harvard Theological Review 75 (1982): 463–502; R. T. Kendall, "The
    Puritan Modification of Calvin's Theology," in W. Stanford Reid, ed.,
    John Calvin: His Influence in the Western World (Grand Rapids: Zonder-
    van, 1982), pp. 199–216; Dewey D. Wallace, Jr., *Puritans and Predes-
    tination: Grace in English Protestant Theology, 1525–1695* (Chapel Hill:
    University of North Carolina Press, 1982), esp. pp. 197–198; and the
    very provocative Charles L. Cohen, *God's Caress: The Psychology of Pu-
    ritan Religious Experience* (New York: Oxford University Press, 1986),
    which distinguishes (esp. ch. 2) between covenant (as conditional bar-
    gain) and testament (as conferral of the gift of grace). On the psycho-
    logical effects of the covenant of works, which demands that men meet
    a standard that they are unable to meet, Cohen says, "When the receiver
    strongly desires to respond because the sender is an influential person
    in one's life, and when the option to not reply does not exist, double-
    bind theory predicts a rising level of anxiety on the part of the respond-
    ent" (p. 62). My own sense of the psychological state of the emigrant
    Puritans suggests that this is and was a good prediction.
38. Bradford, *Of Plymouth Plantation*, p. 24; Winthrop, *Letter* of 1629, p.
    122; Rutman, *Winthrop's Decision*, p. 14.
39. Winthrop, "Particular considerations in the case of J.W.," in Emerson,
    ed., *Letters from New England*, p. 41; letter to his son Henry, in Rutman,
    Winthrop's Decision, p. 77.
40. George Garrett, *Death of the Fox* (New York: Doubleday, 1971), p. 19;
    Bownde, quoted in Collinson, *Elizabethan Puritan Movement*, p. 372;
    Bownde, *Medicines for the Plague* (London, 1604), pp. 6–7, 27; J. H.
    Adamson and H. F. Folland, *The Life of Sir Henry Vane* (Boston: Gambit,
    1973), p. 18; Wrightson, *English Society*, pp. 53–54, 19; *The Political
    Works of King James I*, ed. Charles H. McIlwain (Cambridge, Mass, 1918),
    p. 3.
41. Mary Lee Settle, *Prisons* (New York: Ballantine, 1981), p. 23; *Political
    Works of King James I*, p. 216.
42. Morgan, *Prince Charles's Puritan Chaplain*, pp. 22–23.
43. Mark Spurrell, *The Puritan Town of Boston* (Boston: Richard Kay, 1972),
    p. 4; Jones, *Life of Dudley*, p. 34; Stephen Foster, *Notes from the Caroline
    Underground* (Hamden, Conn.: Archon, 1978), p. 20.
44. Ormerod, *The Picture of a Puritaine* (London, 1605), SigA3ᵛ; Morgan,
    Prince Charles's Puritan Chaplain, p. 83; Bradshaw, quoted in Larzer
    Ziff, *Puritanism in America* (New York: Viking, 1973), p. 25.

45. Hunt, *Puritan Moment*, p. 127; Jonson, *The Alchemist* (1610), III. ii. 74–77; "A Puritan . . . heart," quoted in Collinson, "A Comment," 487.

46. Perkins, *Works*, I, 449; Ward, quoted in Samuel Whiting, *The Life of John Cotton*, in Young, *Chronicles of the First Planters*, p. 127; Morgan, *Visible Saints*, p. 19.

47. Miller, *Orthodoxy in Massachusetts, 1630–1650* (1933; New York: Harper, 1970), p. 84; Perkins, *Works*, II, 104–105; E. Brooks Holifield, *The Covenant Sealed* (New Haven: Yale University Press, 1974), p. 155.

48. Shepard, *The Clear Sunshine of the Gospel Breaking Forth upon the Indians in New England*, in Massachusetts Historical Society, *Collections* 34 (1834): 63; Hunt, *Puritan Moment*, p. 113.

49. *King Lear*, IV. ii; Cotton, *God's Promise*, p. 8; Hill, *Society and Puritanism* (New York: Schocken, 1967), p. 487; Cushman, *Reasons and Considerations*, in Dwight B. Heath, ed., *A Journal of the Pilgrims at Plymouth* (New York: Corinth, 1963), p. 94; L. C. Knights, *Drama and Society in the Age of Jonson* (London: Chatto and Windus, 1937), p. 180.

50. Stubbes, *Anatomie of Abuses*, p. 70; Fuller, *Holy State*, p. 113; L. B. Wright, *Middle-Class Culture in Elizabethan England* (Ithaca: Cornell University Press, 1958), p. 24; Hooker, *Soul's Vocation*, p. 173; Rutman, *Winthrop's Decision*, p. 20.

51. *Winthrop Papers*, I, 288.

52. Breen, *Puritans and Adventurers*, pp. 49–50; Bridenbaugh, *Vexed and Troubled Englishmen*, p. 463; Selement and Woolley, eds., *Divers Confessions*, p. 66.

53. Harris, *Davids Comfort at Ziklag* (London, 1628), pp. 16, 12; Hooker, *The Application of Redemption: the Ninth and Tenth Books* (London, 1656), X, 125.

54. Perkins, *Works*, III, 466.

55. Cotton, *Way of Life*, p. 480.

56. Josiah Royce, "The Problem of Job," in Perry Miller, ed., *American Thought from the Civil War to World War I* (New York: Rinehart, 1954), p. 20; Adams, in Morgan, ed., *Founding of Massachusetts*, p. 63.

57. Bulkeley, *The Gospel Covenant* (London, 1651), p. 431; Johnson, *Wonder-Working Providence*, p. 29; Oakes, *New England Pleaded With* (Cambridge, Mass., 1673), p. 21; for critiques of theories of the "errand" as highly purposeful, see Andrew Delbanco, "The Puritan Errand Re-Viewed," *Journal of American Studies* 18, no. 3 (1984): 343–360; and Theodore Dwight Bozeman, "The Puritans' 'Errand into the Wilderness' Reconsidered," *New England Quarterly* 59 (1986): 231–251.

58. Among modern commentators, Darrett Rutman and Alan Heimert have stressed the retrospective mood of Winthrop's sermon; see Rutman, *American Puritanism: Faith and Practice* (Philadelphia: Lippincott, 1970), p. 69, and Alan Heimert and Andrew Delbanco, eds., *The Puritans in America: A Narrative Anthology* (Cambridge, Mass.: Harvard University

Press, 1985), pp. 81–82; Winthrop, *A Model of Christian Charity* (Old South Leaflets, no. 207), p. 20.

59. Winthrop, *Model*, pp. 13–14.
60. Ibid., pp. 11, 15–17.
61. Hambrick-Stowe, *Practice of Piety*, p. 65.
62. Perkins, *Works*, III, 466; Hunt, *Puritan Moment*, pp. 32, 27; on the initial dominance of the gentry, see Bernard Bailyn, *The New England Merchants in the Seventeenth Century* (Cambridge, Mass.: Harvard University Press, 1955).
63. *The Massachusetts Body of Liberties* (1641), in Edmund S. Morgan, ed., *Puritan Political Ideas: 1558–1794* (Indianapolis: Bobbs-Merrill, 1965), p. 181; W. H. Wheeler, *A History of the Fens of South Lincolnshire* (Boston, 1894).
64. G. L. Walker, *Thomas Hooker* (New York, 1871), p. 5; *Winthrop Papers*, IV, 102; Gordon Wood, *The Rising Glory of America, 1760–1820* (New York: George Braziller, 1971), p. 5; Bradford, *Of Plymouth Plantation*, p. 23.
65. Winthrop, *The History of New England from 1630–1649 (Journal)*, ed. James Savage (Boston, 1825), 2 vols., I, 152; John Wilson, "Certeyne Questions . . . Tending to Declare How Farre C-covenant Binds the Members to Cohabite togeather and so to continue," American Antiquarian Society, *Mather Family Papers*, mss., box 13, folder 8 (I am grateful to Virginia Anderson for calling to my attention the existence of this document); Rutman, *Winthrop's Boston*, pp. 75–97; Martin, *Entrepreneurship*, passim; Edmund S. Morgan, *The Puritan Dilemma: The Story of John Winthrop* (Boston: Little, Brown, 1958), p. 87; Tyack, *Migration from East Anglia*, pp. 145–151.
66. Dane, "Narrative," 154.
67. *Notebook of Thomas Lechford*, American Antiquarian Society, *Transactions* 7 (1885): 217, 345.
68. Anthony Tuckney, *Forty Sermons upon Several Occasions* (London, pub. 1676, w. c.1640), p. 378.
69. Ibid., p. 377; see Fiering, *Moral Philosophy at Harvard*, p. 85, for the Neoplatonic tradition of "intellectual love"; Eliot, "The Metaphysical Poets," *Selected Essays* (New York: Harcourt, Brace, 1932), p. 247.
70. Fiering, *Moral Philosophy at Harvard*, p. 119; Hooker, *The Soules Possession of Christ*, p. 145; Hooker, in G. H. Williams, et al., *Thomas Hooker: Writings in England and Holland* (Cambridge, Mass.: Harvard University Press, 1975), pp. 118–119; Hooker, *Soules Preparation*, p. 192; Walzer, *Revolution of the Saints*, p. 142; Sibbes, *Works*, ed. Alexander Grosart (Edinburgh, 1862–64), 7 vols., I, 420; II, 332.
71. Francis Higginson, quoted in Bridenbaugh, *Vexed and Troubled Englishmen*, p. 464; Howe, *World of our Fathers* (New York: Bantam, 1980), p. 167.

3. City on a Hill

1. Crashaw, *A Sermon Preached in London before the right honorable the Lord Lawarre* (London, 1610), SigC^v; Bolton, *Some Generall Directions for a Comfortable Walking with God* (London, 1638), p. 58; John Knewstub, *A Sermon Preached at Paules Cross* (London, 1576), sig S2^r.

2. Crashaw, SigA^r; Hooker, *The Soules Humiliation* (London, 1638), p. 145; Perkins, *Works,* I, 666.

3. Noah Biggs, *Chymiatrophilos* (1651), quoted in Allen G. Debus, ed., *Medicine in Seventeenth-Century England* (Berkeley: University of California Press, 1974), p. 38; Crashaw, sigA2^r, sigC2^r–sigC2^v.

4. Crashaw, sigD2^r; Winthrop, *Model of Christian Charity,* p. 18; Cotton, *Christ the Fountaine of Life* (London, 1651), p. 200; Hooker, *Soul's Vocation,* p. 287.

5. Higginson, in Emerson, ed., *Letters,* p. 34; John Seelye, *Prophetic Waters: The River in Early American Life and Literature* (New York: Oxford University Press, 1977), p. 150; Jackson C. Boswell, "Check List of Americana," *Early American Literature* 9, no. 2 (1974): 5–8.

6. Spenser, *The Faerie Queene,* bk. II, l. 18; Smith, *The Generall Historie of Virginia, New-England, and the Summer Isles* (London, 1624), pp. 210, 212; Morton, *New English Canaan* (London, 1637), p. 179; Higginson, in Emerson, ed., *Letters,* p. 33; Graves, in ibid., p. 39.

7. Clap, in Young, *First Planters,* p. 351; Welde, quoted in Bridenbaugh, *Vexed and Troubled Englishmen,* p. 449; Nathaniel Shurtleff, ed., *Records of the Governor and Company of Massachusetts Bay* (Boston, 1857), 6 vols., I, 128; Wood, *New Englands Prospect* (1634), ed. Alden T. Vaughan (Amherst: University of Massachusetts Press, 1977), pp. 36–37.

8. Higginson, in Emerson, ed., *Letters,* pp. 16, 20.

9. Charlestown Records, quoted in Emerson, ed., *Letters,* p. 63; Winthrop to his wife, in ibid., p. 54; Pond, in ibid., pp. 64–65; Winthrop, *Journal,* I, 45.

10. Dudley, *Letter to the Countess of Lincoln,* in Morgan, ed., *Founding of Massachusetts,* p. 165; Morton, *New English Canaan,* p. 110.

11. Higginson, in Emerson, ed., *Letters,* p. 29; Dudley, in Morgan, ed., *Founding of Massachusetts,* p. 165; Bulkeley, *Gospel-Covenant,* pp. 209; see Cressy, *Coming Over,* p. 109.

12. Boyd Berry, *Process of Speech: Puritan Religious Writing and Paradise Lost* (Baltimore: Johns Hopkins University Press, 1976), p. 141; Paul Christianson, *Reformers and Babylon: English Apocalyptic Visions from the Reformation to the Eve of the Civil War* (Toronto: University of Toronto Press, 1978), pp. 9, 14.

13. Bercovitch, *Puritan Origins,* p. 36; Henoch Clapham, quoted in Christopher Hill, *Antichrist in Seventeenth-Century England* (London: Oxford University Press, 1971), p. 52; Bernard Capp, "The Political Dimension

of Apocalyptic Thought," in *The Apocalypse in English Renaissance Thought and Literature,* ed. C. A. Patrides and Joseph Wittreich (Ithaca: Cornell University Press, 1984), p. 98.

14. McGiffert, "God's Controversy," p. 1174; Berry, *Process of Speech.* p. 141.

15. Shepard, *Works,* II, 24; Maclear, "New England and the Fifth Monarchy: The Quest for the Millennium in Early American Puritanism," *William and Mary Quarterly* 32 (1975): 225; cf. Stout, *New England Soul,* p. 8: "Throughout the colonial period, ministers rarely preached specifically on millennial promises pointing to the end of time . . ."

16. White, *The Troubles of Jerusalems Restauration: or the Churches Reformation* (London, 1645), pp. 6, 31.

17. Stephen Marshall, *A Sermon Preached before the Honourable House of Commons, Nov. 17, 1640* (London, 1641), p. 19; Harris, *Davids Comfort at Ziklag,* p. 16; Hooker, in Williams et al., eds., *Thomas Hooker: Writings in England and Holland,* p. 246.

18. Winthrop, *Reasons to be Considered for . . . the Intended Plantation* (1629), in Massachusetts Historical Society, *Proceedings* 8 (1864–65): 424; Cushman, *Reasons and Considerations,* in Heath, ed., *A Journal,* pp. 89–90.

19. Cushman, p. 92.

20. Coddington, *Demonstration of True Love,* p. 13; Cotton, *God's Promise,* pp. 7–8.

21. Jesper Rosenmeier, "Veritas: The Sealing of the Promise," *Harvard Library Bulletin* 16 (1968): 34; Cotton, *God's Promise,* p. 7; G. H. Williams, "Called by Thy Name, Leave Us Not: The Case of Mrs. Joan Drake, A Formative Episode in the Pastoral Career of Thomas Hooker in England," *Harvard Library Bulletin* 16, no. 3 (1968): 290; Karen Ordahl Kupperman, "Errand to the Indies: Puritan Colonization from Providence Island through the Western Design," *William and Mary Quarterly* 45 (1988): p. 70–99; Larzer Ziff, ed., *John Cotton on the Churches of New England* (Cambridge, Mass.: Harvard University Press, 1968), p. 11; Winthrop, *Journal,* II, 129; Cressy, *Coming Over,* pp. 89, 26.

22. John White, *The Planter's Plea* (1629), in Massachusetts Historical Society, *Proceedings* 62 (1928–29): 396; Edward Johnson, *Wonder-Working Providence of Sion's Saviour in New England* (1652), ed. J. F. Jameson (New York: Charles Scribner's, 1910), pp. 39, 31.

23. John White, *The Troubles of Jerusalems Restauration: or the Churches Reformation* (London, 1645), p. 31; Hooker, *The Application of Redemption: The Ninth and Tenth Books* (London, 1656), p. 5.

24. Shepard and John Allin, *A Defense of the Answer made unto the nine questions* (1648), in Miller and Johnson, eds., *The Puritans,* I, 119; Preston, *The Breast-Plate of Faith,* pp. 234, 237.

25. Winthrop, *Journal,* II, 31 (italics added); Calamy, *Gods Free Mercy to*

England, Preached as a Pretious, and Powerfull motive to Humiliation . . . Feb. 23, 1641 (London, 1642), p. 4.

26. Bradford, *Of Plymouth Plantation*, pp. 61–62; Alan Heimert, in *The Puritans in America*, p. 52; *Mourt's Relation*, ed. Dwight B. Heath (New York: D. C. Heath, 1963), p. 41.

27. Mather, *Early Piety* (Boston, 1689), pp. 1–2; Hooke, *The Priviledge of the Saints on Earth Beyond Those in Heaven* (London, 1673), p. 141; Cotton, *A Briefe Exposition with Practicall Observations upon the Whole Book of Ecclesiastes* (London, 1657), p. 125.

28. Winthrop, Letter of 1629, in *Winthrop Papers*, II, 121.

29. Ibid., pp. 123–124.

30. Charles Andrews, *The Colonial Period of American History* (1934, rpt. New Haven: Yale University Press, 1964), 4 vols., I, 60; Cushman, in Bradford, *Of Plymouth Plantation*, p. 356; William Strachey, *A True Repertory of the Wreck and Redemption of Sir Thomas Gates, Knight* (1610), ed. L. B. Wright (Charlottesville: University Press of Virginia, 1964), pp. 4, 13, 10; David Shields, "Exploratory Narratives and the Development of the New England Passage Journal," *Essex Institute Historical Collections* 120, no. 1 (1984): 38–57.

31. Charles Edward Banks, *Planters of the Commonwealth* (Boston: Houghton Mifflin, 1930), p. 5; Morison, *Builders of the Bay Colony* (1930; rpt. Boston: Houghton Mifflin, 1958), p. 77; Michael Wigglesworth, "God's Controversy with New England" (1662), in Heimert and Delbanco, eds., *The Puritans in America*, p. 231.

32. Ryece to Winthrop, in *Winthrop Papers*, II, 105; David D. Hall, ed., Cotton's Letter to Skelton, *William and Mary Quarterly* 22 (1965): 484; Williams, *Mr. Cotton's Letter {To Williams} Lately Printed, Examined and Answered* (1644), in Williams, *Complete Writings* I, 393. See Richard Slotkin, *Regeneration through Violence: The Mythology of the American Frontier, 1600–1860* (Middletown: Wesleyan University Press, 1973), pp. 18, 108.

33. Williams, *Complete Writings*, II, 52–53.

34. *A Letter of Many Ministers in Old England, requesting the Judgement of their Reverend Brethren in New England Concerning Nine Positions, written Anno Dom. 1637* (London, 1643), sigA3ʳ, sigA4ʳ.

35. Coleman, quoted in John F. Wilson, *Pulpit in Parliament: Puritanism during the English Civil Wars, 1640–1648* (Princeton: Princeton University Press, 1969), p. 190.

36. John Bastwick, *A Just Defence* (London, 1645), p. 39.

37. Chidley, *Justification of Independant Churches*, p. 34.

38. Marshall, *Meroz Cursed, or, A Sermon Preached to the Honourable House of Commons, Feb. 23, 1641* (London, 1641), pp. 22, 5–6.

39. Whitefield, *The Light appearing more and more towards the perfect Day* (1651), in Massachusetts Historical Society, *Collections* 34 (1834): 103–

104; Hutchinson, *History of the Colony and Province of Massachusetts Bay* (1764), ed. Lawrence Shaw Mayo (Cambridge, Mass.: Harvard University Press, 1936), 3 vols., I, 429; Winthrop, *Journal,* II, 85; Ward, *A Sermon Preached Before the Honourable House of Commons* (London, 1647); Norton, *Sion the Out-cast Healed of Her Wounds,* in *Three Choice and Profitable Sermons* (Cambridge, Mass., 1664), pp. 11–12.

40. Gershom Bulkeley, "Preface" to *Will and Doom* (1692), Connecticut Historical Society *Collections* 3 (1895): 83, 91; Shepard, *Works,* I, 271.

41. Milton, quoted in Christopher Hill, *Milton and the English Revolution* (New York: Viking, 1979), p. 53; James, "William Dean Howells" (1886), in Edmund Wilson, ed., *The Shock of Recognition* (New York: Doubleday, Doran, 1943), p. 571.

42. Cotton, "Foreword" to John Norton, *The Answer to Mr. Apollonius* (1648), trans. Douglas Horton (Cambridge, Mass.: Harvard University Press, 1958), p. 10; Johnson, *Wonder-Working Providence,* p. 60; Higginson, in Emerson, ed., *Letters from New England,* p. 22.

43. Hutchinson, *History of Massachusetts Bay,* I, 428, 431.

44. Perry Miller, ed., *Roger Williams: His Contribution to the American Tradition* (New York: Atheneum, 1970), p. 200; Hill, *Change and Continuity in Seventeenth-Century England* (Cambridge: Harvard University Press, 1975), ch. 1; Hakluyt, *A Discourse Concerning Western Planting* (1584), Maine Historical Society, *Collections,* 2d ser., 2 (1877): 9; Cotton, *God's Promise,* p. 14; Shepard, *The Clear Sunshine of the Gospel Breaking Forth upon the Indians,* pp. 28–29.

45. *New England's First Fruits* (1643), in Morison, *The Founding of Harvard College* (Cambridge, Mass.: Harvard University Press, 1935), p. 440; Underhill, quoted in Robert M. Utley and Wilcomb E. Washburn, *Indian Wars* (Boston: Houghton Mifflin, 1977), p. 43; Alden Vaughan, "Pequots and Puritans: The Causes of the War of 1637," *William and Mary Quarterly* 21, no. 1 (1964); 256–269.

46. Francis Jennings, *The Invasion of America: Indians, Colonialism, and the Cant of Conquest* (New York: Norton, 1976), pp. 186–201.

47. Shepard, *Works,* II, 378; Axtell, *The European and the Indian: Essays in the Ethnohistory of Colonial North America* (New York: Oxford University Press, 1981), p. 170; Williams, *A Key into the Language of America* (1643), ed. John J. Teunissen and Evelyn J. Hinz (Detroit: Wayne State University Press, 1973), p. 88.

48. Bercovitch, *American Jeremiad,* p. 75; Marmaduke Matthews, *The Messiah Magnified by the mouthes of Babes in America* (London, 1659), sigA3ᵛ–sigA4ʳ; Increase Mather, *Ichabod . . . A Discourse, Shewing What Cause There Is to Fear That the Glory of the Lord, Is Departing from New England* (Boston, 1702), pp. 71-72, 64, 80.

49. White, *Planter's Plea,* in Morgan, ed., *Founding of Massachusetts,* p. 154.

50. Richard W. Cogley, "John Eliot and the Origins of the American In-

dians," *Early American Literature* 21, no. 3 (1986–87): 212; Shepard, *Clear Sunshine*, p. 64; "Appendix to the . . . Letters" of John Eliot, by "J.D." [possibly Davenport], in Massachusetts Historical Society, *Collections*, 34 (1934): 94, 93; Cogley, p. 218. James Holstun, in *A Rational Millennium: Puritan Utopias in England and New England* (New York: Oxford University Press, 1987), p. 110, observes that "The New World becomes the appointed site for the millennial encounter of clockwise and counterclockwise Israelites: the Indian descendants of Shem and Eber . . . [becoming] more and more degenerate . . . and the Puritan Israelites bearing westward the Hebrew scriptures."

51. Morison, *Harvard College in the Seventeenth Century* (Cambridge, Mass.: Harvard University Press, 1936), 2 vols., I, 341; Gookin, quoted in ibid., pp. 343–44; Richard H. Popkin, "Jewish Messianism and Christian Millenarianism," in Perez Zagorin, ed., *Culture and Politics from Puritanism to the Enlightenment* (Berkeley: University of California Press, 1980), p. 73; Peter Toon, "The Question of Jewish Immigration," in Toon, ed., *Puritans, The Millennium and the Future of Israel: Puritan Eschatology 1600 to 1660* (London: James Clarke, 1970), pp. 115–125.

52. Mather, *Ichabod*, pp. 65, 80; *A Dissertation Concerning the Future Conversion of the Jewish Nation* (Boston, 1709), sigE2ᵛ.

53. Ziff, *Puritanism in America*, p. 90; Mason, *A Brief History of the Pequot War* (w. 1637; pub. Boston, 1736), p. 21.

54. Archer, *The Personall Reigne of Christ* (London, 1642), p. 22; Thomas Cobbett, *A Brief Answer to a certain Slanderous Pamphlet called Ill News from N England; or A Narrative of New-Englands Persecution* (London, 1653), p. 8, sigA4ᵛ; Johnson, *Wonder-Working Providence*, pp. 134, 136; Coddington, in Hall, ed., *Antinomian Controversy*, p. 345.

55. Knox, "A Comfortable Epistell Sente to the Afflicted Church of Chryst" (1554), and "Letter to Mistress Bowes" (1553), in *Works*, ed. David Laing (Edinburgh, 1864), 6 vols., III, 240, 337.

56. Shepard, *Works*, II, 399, 170.

57. Mather, *Magnalia*, ed. Murdock and Miller, pp. 150, 151, 92; Shepard, *Works*, II, 26.

58. John Dod and Robert Cleaver, *Two Sermons on the Third of the Lamentations of Jeremie* (London, 1608), p. 17; Hooker, *Laws of Ecclesiastical Polity* (1593), I, bk. 1, 16, 6; Cotton, *Practical Commentary*, p. 405; Dudley, in Morgan, ed., *Founding of Massachusetts*, p. 161.

59. Winthrop, *Journal*, I, 140; Shurtleff, ed., *Records of the Governor and Company*, I, 157; Caldwell, *Puritan Conversion Narrative*, p. 122.

60. Middlekauff, *The Mathers: Three Generations of Puritan Intellectuals* (New York: Oxford University Press, 1970), ch. 6; Winthrop, Jr., quoted in Rutman, *Winthrop's Boston*, p. 40; Increase Mather, *Dissertation Concerning the Jewish Nation*, sigE2ᵛ.

61. Cotton, "Foreword" to Norton, *The Answer to Mr. Apollonius*, p. 10; Olson, *Call Me Ishmael* (San Francisco: City Lights Books, 1947), p. 14;

Increase Mather, *The Mystery of Israel's Salvation* (Boston, 1669), pp. 163–164.

4. The Antinomian Dissent

1. Jonathan Edwards, *Some Thoughts Concerning the Present Revival of Religion* (1742), in C. C. Goen, ed., *The Works of Jonathan Edwards*, vol. 4, *The Great Awakening* (New Haven: Yale University Press, 1972), p. 313; Winthrop, in Hall, ed., *Antinomian Controversy*, p. 343; Bulkeley, quoted in Rutman, *Winthrop's Boston*, p. 121; Winthrop, *Journal*, I, 217–218.

2. Mark Spurrell, *Boston Parish Church*, (Boston, England: St. Botolph's Church, n.d.), n.p.; John F. Bailey, ed., *Transcription of Minutes of the Corporation of Boston* (Boston, England: History of Boston Project, 1980), 3 vols., I, 189; William Stukeley, quoted in Spurrell.

3. Thomas Allen, "Preface" to Cotton, *An Exposition upon the Thirteenth Chapter of the Revelation* (London, 1655), sigA6ᵛ–sigA7ʳ; Cotton, *Practical Commentary*, pp. 47, 76, 31. Ann Kibbey (*Interpretation of Material Shapes*, p. 159) regards the story of Cotton's stylistic change at Cambridge as unsubstantiated legend. If this is so, it was a legend that Cotton did nothing to discourage.

4. Bailey, ed., *Corporation Minutes*, II, 647; Cotton, *Practical Commentary*, p. 149.

5. Cotton, *Practical Commentary*, pp. 5, 167, 233, 132. Several scholars have proposed chronologies of Cotton's sermons, which were often published years after delivery, and in some cases (e.g., the New England sermons on the new covenant) in significantly different versions. The most informed datings are those by Jesper Rosenmeier, "The Image of Christ: The Typology of John Cotton," Ph.D. diss., Harvard University, 1966, p. 227; Larzer Ziff, *The Career of John Cotton: Puritanism and the American Experience* (Princeton: Princeton University Press, 1962), pp. 261–268; and Everett Emerson, *John Cotton* (New York: Twayne, 1965), pp. 163–165. My own sense of Cotton's stylistic and intellectual development persuades me that the *Practical Commentary upon John* is earlier than the *Way of Life* and *Christ the Fountaine* (see Kibbey, *Interpretation of Material Shapes*, p. 153), and that the sermons on Ecclesiastes were delivered, or at least revised, in New England (Ziff places them before the migration). An authoritative study that could resolve such discrepancies is needed; the forthcoming edition of Cotton's letters being prepared by Sargent Bush will also be a major contribution.

6. Cotton, *Practical Commentary*, p. 77; *Way of Life*, p. 11; Miller, "From Edwards to Emerson," in *Errand into the Wilderness*, pp. 184–203.

7. Cotton, *Way of Life*, p. 79; Ziff, ed., *John Cotton on the Churches of New England*, p. 198.

8. William Perkins, *The Art of Prophesying*, in *Works*, I, 668; Cotton, *Way*

of Life, p. 76; Hooker, *Danger of Desertion*, p. 246; Marshall, *Sermon to House of Commons, Nov. 17, 1640*, pp. 19–20; Cotton, *Way of Life*, pp. 79, 74.

9. Cotton, *Way of Life*, p. 128; Coolidge, *The Pauline Renaissance: Puritanism and the Bible* (Oxford: Oxford University Press, 1970), pp. 52, 49; Cotton, *Gods Mercie Mixed with His Justice* (London, 1641), p. 3.

10. Cotton, *A Treatise of the Covenant of Grace* (London, 1671), p. 154; Cotton, *Practical Commentary*, p. 169; Richard Hooker, *Laws*, 2, bk. V, xxi, 2; Coolidge, *Pauline Renaissance*, p. 17; Mather, *Magnalia*, ed. Murdock and Miller, p. 93.

11. Cotton, *The Powring out of the Seven Vials*, p. 151; *Treatise of the Covenant of Grace*, p. 155; *Gods Mercie*, p. 4.

12. Sibbes, *Two Sermons upon the First Words of Christs Last Sermon* (London, 1636), p. 18; Cotton, *A Brief Exposition with Practicall Observations upon the whole Book of Canticles* (London, 1655), p. 47; *Way of Life*, pp. 385, 79, 78.

13. Cotton, *Way of Life*, pp. 270, 385; *Christ the Fountaine*, pp. 15–16.

14. Cotton, *Christ the Fountaine*, pp. 98, 110–111, 113–115, 119–120, 123.

15. Ibid., p. 137; Ulrich Zwingli, "On the Lord's Supper," in G. W. Bromiley, ed., *Zwingli and Bullinger* (Philadelphia: Westminster Press, 1953), p. 234; Holifield, *The Covenant Sealed*, p. 61; John Dod, *A Briefe Dialogue Concerning Preparation, for the Worthie Receiving of the Lords Supper* (London, 1610), p. 14; Holifield, p. 28; James Noyes, *The Temple Measured: or, A brief Survey of the Temple Mystical, which is the Instituted Church of Christ* (London, 1647), pp. 50–51.

16. Cotton, *Christ the Fountaine*, pp. 137–138.

17. Cotton, *Practical Commentary*, p. 8; *A Brief Exposition upon Ecclesiastes*, p. 24; *Christ the Fountaine*, p. 119.

18. Hudson, in *Aspinwall Notarial Records, 1644–1651* (Boston: Municipal Printing Office, 1903), p. 113; Winthrop to his wife, in Morgan, ed., *Founding of Massachusetts*, p. 186; Johnson, *Wonder-Working Providence*, p. 51; Cotton, *Gods Promise*, p. 14; Cotton, *A Brief Exposition of Canticles* (London, 1642), pp. 31–32; Hooker, *The Christians Two Chiefe Lessons* (London, 1640), p. 92.

19. Ames, *Conscience with the Power and Cases Thereof*, in Heimert and Delbanco, eds., *The Puritans in America*, pp. 60–61; Cotton, *Christ the Fountaine*, p. 129; Mather, *Magnalia*, ed. Murdock and Miller, p. 151.

20. Mather, *Magnalia*, ed. Murdock and Miller, pp. 137, 133, 92; Rutman, *Winthrop's Boston*, p. 27; Dudley, in Young, *Chronicles of the First Planters*, p. 313.

21. Morgan, *The Puritan Dilemma*, p. 91; Rutman, *Winthrop's Boston*, pp. 142, 139.

22. Rutman, *Winthrop's Boston*, pp. 43–44; Cotton in Winthrop, *Journal*, I, 152.

23. Winthrop, Journal, I, 295; Emery Battis, *Saints and Sectaries: Anne Hutchinson and the Antinomian Controversy in the Massachusetts Bay Colony* (Chapel Hill: University of North Carolina Press, 1962); Shepard, *New Englands Lamentations for Old Englands Errors* (London, 1645), p. 2; Lechford, *Plain Dealing*, p. 42.

24. Perry Miller, with characteristic brevity and bluster, made the argument thirty-five years ago that the antinomian dissent "amounted to one thing: a denial of preparation" (*From Colony to Province*, p. 59). Although this view has met with increasing skepticism in recent scholarship (see Stoever, "A Faire and Easie Way," pp. 192–199), I find that the literary evidence (chs. 4 and 5) and the nature of the migration out of Massachusetts Bay (ch. 6) confirm Miller's basic interpretative instinct.

25. Battis, *Saints and Sectaries*, p. 33.

26. Hall, ed., *Antinomian Controversy*, pp. 330, 337; Winthrop, *Journal*, I, 209; Hall, *Antinomian Controversy*, pp. 336–337.

27. Cotton, *A Treatise of the Covenant of Grace*, p. 178.

28. Shepard, *New England's Lamentation*, p. 4; Harry S. Stout, "Word and Order in Colonial New England," in *The Bible in America: Essays in Cultural History*, ed. Nathan O. Hatch and Mark A. Noll (New York: Oxford University Press, 1982), p. 23; Hooker, *Danger of Desertion*, in *Writings in England and Holland*, p. 244; Emerson, in Whicher, *Selections from Emerson*, p. 107; Hooker, *The Soules Preparation*, p. 30.

29. Bradstreet, *Meditations Divine and Moral*, no. 40, in Hensley, p. 279.

30. Edwards, *Images or Shadows of Divine Things*, ed. Perry Miller (New Haven: Yale University Press, 1948), p. 63.

31. Hall, ed., *Antinomian Controversy*, p. 312, Erikson, *Wayward Puritans*, ch. 3; James, *Essays on Literature: American Writers, English Writers*, ed. Leon Edel and Mark Wilson (New York: Library of America, 1984), p. 379.

32. Laurel Thatcher Ulrich, *Good Wives: Image and Reality in the Lives of Women in Northern New England, 1650-1750* (New York: Oxford University Press, 1982), p. 3; Battis, *Saints and Sectaries*, p. 61; J. F. Maclear, "Anne Hutchinson and the Mortalist Heresy," *New England Quarterly* 54 (1981): 77; John Knox, "A Faithfull Admonition to the Professors of God's Truth in England" (1554), *Works*, III, 269; Johnson, *Wonder-Working Providence*, p. 127.

33. Richard Sibbes, *The Bruised Reed and Smoking Flax* (London, 1630), p. 35; Bradshaw, *English Puritanisme*, p. 20; Chidley, *Justification*, p. 31.

34. Davenport, *The Saints Anchor-Hold, in all Storms and Tempests* (London, 1682), pp. 195–197; Gorton, *Letter to Morton*, p. 10.

35. Shepard, *Works*, II, 22, 26, 42, 94–95. It is true, as Michael Colacurcio says in " 'The Woman's Own Choice': Sex, Metaphor, and the Puritan 'Sources' of *The Scarlet Letter*," in *New Essays on The Scarlet Letter*, ed. Colacurcio (Cambridge: Cambridge University Press, 1985), p. 117, that "of the first generation, only Cotton fully explicated the sacred love

poetry of Canticles," but Shepard's explication of Matthew 25 rises to the same erotic intensity.

36. Shepard, *God's Plot: The Paradoxes of Puritan Piety, Being the Autobiography & Journal of Thomas Shepard,* ed. Michael McGiffert (Amherst: University of Massachusetts Press, 1972), p. 46; Edmund S. Morgan, *The Puritan Family: Religion and Domestic Relations in Seventeenth-Century New England* (New York: Harper and Row, 1966), p. 163; Shepard, *Works,* II, 45–46.

37. *A Letter of Many Ministers in Old England, requesting the Judgement of their Reverend Brethren in New England Concerning Nine Positions, written Anno Dom. 1637* (London, 1643), sigA3ʳ; Winthrop, *Short Story,* in Hall, ed., *Antinomian Controversy,* p. 206.

38. Cotton, *The Way of Congregational Churches Cleared* (1648), in Ziff, ed., *John Cotton on the Churches of New England,* p. 240; Miller, *From Colony to Province,* p. 57; Shepard, *God's Plot,* pp. 42, 65; Shepard, Works, II, 205, 133–134.

39. Shepard, *Works,* II, 377, 104; Hooker, *The Soules Preparation* (London, 1632), pp. 60–61; Gorton, in Force, ed., *Tracts,* IV, no. 7, p. 10.

40. Shepard, *Works,* II, 86, 83.

41. Winthrop, in Hall, ed., *Antinomian Controversy,* p. 203; Shepard, *Works,* II, 88; Clap, in Young, ed., *Chronicles,* p. 355.

42. Cotton, *A Treatise of the Covenant of Grace,* pp. 177-178.

43. Berryman, *Homage to Mistress Bradstreet* (New York: Noonday, 1968), p. 14; Bradstreet, "To My Dear Children," in Hensley, p. 241, 243; Shepard, *Works,* II, 244; Ormerod, *A Discovery of Puritan-Papisme,* p. 12; Hall, ed., *Antinomian Controversy,* pp. 322, 367; Berryman, p. 26.

44. Winthrop, *Journal,* I, 262; Hall, *Antinomian Controversy,* p. 214; Battis, *Saints and Sectaries,* p. 248n.

45. Shepard, *New England's Lamentations,* p. 4; Thomas Cobbett, *A Brief Answer to . . . Ill News from N England,* p. 3; Johnson, *Wonder-Working Providence,* p. 187; Shepard, Jr., *Eye-Salve,* in Heimert and Delbanco, eds., *The Puritans in America,* p. 254.

46. Hall, ed., *Antinomian Controversy,* p. 379; Winthrop, *Journal,* I, 253, 213; see also Hall, p. 415; Williams, *Complete Writings,* II, 80–82.

47. Cotton, *Brief Exposition of Ecclesiastes,* p. 12. For evidence that these sermons were delivered in the New World, probably in the late 1640s, see pp. 1, 193: "the hands of our fellow-labourers faint in *England.*" See also Whiting, *The Life of Cotton,* in Young, *Chronicles,* p. 424. Gorton, in Force, ed., *Tracts,* IV, no. 7., p. 3; Berryman, pp. 18–19.

5. The Founders Divide

1. Winthrop, in Hall, ed., *Antinomian Controversy*, p. 231; Winthrop, *Journal*, I, 220; Hooker, *The Soules Humiliation*, p. 62; Winthrop, *Journal*, I, 214, 236.
2. Winthrop, *Journal*, I, 237; 253.
3. Johnson, *Wonder-Working Providence*, p. 127.
4. Hall, ed., *Antinomian Controversy*, pp. 383, 205–206; Gorton, "Letter to Nathaniel Morton," Force, *Tracts*, IV, no. 7, p. 6; Richard D. Pierce, ed., *The Records of the First Church in Boston, 1630–1868*, in Colonial Society of Massachusetts, *Collections* 39 (1961): 25, 56; Ben Barker-Benfield, "Anne Hutchinson and the Puritan Attitude toward Women," *Feminist Studies* 1 (1972); 75; Caldwell, *Puritan Conversion Narrative*, pp. 12, 26.
5. Cotton, in Hall, ed., *Antinomian Controversy*, p. 370.
6. Bradstreet, "To My Dear Children," in Hensley, p. 241; Hooker, *Christians Two Chiefe Lessons*, p. 58; Hooker, *Soules Preparation*, p. 187; Hooker, *The Soules Implantation*, p. 36; G. H. Williams, "The Case of Joan Drake," 291.
7. Mather, *Magnalia* (1853 ed.), I, 262; Cotton, *Way of Life*, p. 346; *Practical Commentary*, pp. 40-41.
8. Cotton, *Brief Exposition of Canticles* (1642), pp. 97–98, 128; Sibbes, *Bruised Reed*, p. 73; Cotton, *A Brief Exposition with Practical Observations upon the Whole Book of Canticles* (London, 1655), p. 47; Cotton, *The Powring out of the Seven Vials*, p. 145. There are moments, mostly early in his career, when Cotton lapses into invective—though even then the form tends to be interrogative: "If sin were not an excrement, why should we purge it out?" (*Practical Commentary*, p. 231.) See, for an interesting study along broadly Freudian lines, David Leverenz, *The Language of Puritan Feeling: An Exploration in Literature, Psychology, and Social History* (New Brunswick: Rutgers University Press, 1980).
9. Bradstreet, "To My Dear Children," and "Prologue" to *The Tenth Muse*, in Hensley, pp. 243, 16; Wheelwright, in Hall, ed., *Antinomian Controversy*, p. 169.
10. Hall, ed., *Antinomian Controversy*, pp. 328, 246.
11. Isabel Calder, ed., *The Letters of John Davenport* (New Haven: Yale University Press, 1934), p. 67; Winthrop, Journal, I, 236; Hall, ed., *Antinomian Controversy*, 359.
12. Maclear, "Anne Hutchinson and the Mortalist Heresy," pp. 80–81; Cotton, *Way of Life*, p. 236.
13. Maclear, "Mortalist Heresy," p. 82; Hall, ed., *Antinomian Controversy*, pp. 360, 362, 358, 204.
14. Mather, *Magnalia* (1853 ed.), I, 325; Winthrop, *Journal*, I, 241.
15. Miller, *From Colony to Province*, p. 199; Davenport, *A Just Complaint*

(London, 1634), p. 2; Coolidge, *Pauline Renaissance,* p. 64; Lilian Handlin, "Dissent in a Small Community," *New England Quarterly* 58 (1985): 193–220; Davenport, *The Knowledge of Christ Indispensably Required* (London, 1653), p. 87; Davenport, *Saints Anchor-Hold,* p. 132; Davenport, *Knowledge of Christ,* p. 8; *Saints Anchor-Hold,* p. 170.

16. Davenport, *Saints Anchor-Hold,* pp. 51, 24, 150.

17. Ibid., p. 175; Emerson, "Experience," in Whicher, *Selections from Emerson,* p. 270; William Twisse, *A Treatise of Mr. Cottons Clearing Certaine Doubts Concerning Predestination, Together with an Examination Thereof* (London, 1646), p. 50; Davenport, *Knowledge of Christ,* p. 64.

18. Williams, *Complete Writings,* II, 80–82.

19. Cotton, *The Churches Resurrection* (London, 1642), p. 21; Shepard, in McGiffert, ed., *God's Plot,* pp. 38, 61, 89–90.

20. Ziff, *Puritanism in America,* p. 16; Hooker, *The Application of Redemption, The Ninth Book* (London, 1656), p. 3; Hooker, *The Danger of Desertion,* in Williams, ed., *Writings in England and Holland,* p. 246; Thomas Parker, *Visions and Prophecies of Daniel Expounded* (London, 1646), for example, vacillates between 1650 and 1860 as the year in which the millennium will begin (p. 64); Shepard, *Works,* III, 173. A key text that has been cited as a representative instance of the Puritans' "myth-making imagination" that construed America as the New Jerusalem (Bercovitch, *Puritan Origins,* p. 105; *American Jeremiad,* p. 113n) is Joshua Scottow's *Narrative of the Planting of . . . Massachusetts Bay* (1694). Bercovitch argues that Scottow quotes a famous poem on the westward movement of religion "in a way that precisely inverted its meaning." The poem in question is George Herbert's "The Church Militant," which includes the lines, "Religion Stands on Tiptoe in our Land, / Ready to pass to the American Strand"—lines of obvious encouragement to the American colonists, specifically to their sense of their place in redemptive history. Scottow, according to Bercovitch, quotes these lines early in his book, and, by omitting some later verses that predict Satan's tenacious hounding of the westward migrants, distorts Herbert's cautionary meaning by turning it into a ringing endorsement of the westward enterprise. Scottow's act of "misreading" has therefore become something of an epitome of the consuming power over the Puritans' imagination of their millenarian conviction. The fact is, however, that Scottow omits Herbert's darker lines not at all to deny their import for New England, but to save them for the climax of his book, where, sixty pages later, he reintroduces them with a phrase of self-reference: "As Holy *Herbert* in his Pious Poem foretold of us. 'As Gold and Grace never yet did agree, / Religion alway Siding with Poverty. / That as the Church shall thither Westward flie, / So Sin shall Trace and Dog her instantly.' " (Scottow has again left out some lines, but this time he gets the spirit right.) It is also worth noting that one of Scottow's

leading contemporaries, Increase Mather, was not content to use Herbert's poem merely as a gloss in his text on New England's declension, but displayed it, including all the ominous lines about sin, as the epigraph opposite the title page of *Ichabod, or The Glory is Departed* (1702). Herbert's prophecy, in Bercovitch's words, that "Massachusetts Bay [would] be no more than another imperfect human undertaking" was not much denied in New England by misquotation or otherwise; it was widely acknowledged.

21. Shepard, *Works*, I, 71; Shepard and Allin, *A Defense of the Answer* (1648), in Miller and Johnson, eds., *The Puritans*, I, 119; Shepard, *Works*, II, 19, 144; I, 64, 269.

22. Shepard, *Works*, II, 124; Hall, ed., *Antinomian Controversy*, p. 354; Shepard, *Works*, II, 120; Lord Saye and Seale, quoted in Gura, *Glimpse of Sions Glory*, p. 79; Hooker, *Soules Vocation*, pp. 499–500; Shepard, *Works*, II, 230, 305.

23. Shepard, *Works*, II, 394, 346, 307.

24. Shepard, in McGiffert, ed., *God's Plot*, p. 113; Shepard, *Works*, III, 82, 88.

25. Shepard, *Works*, III, 256, 30.

26. Williams, *Key into the Language of America*, p. 83; Williams, *Complete Writings*, III, 72; Miller, *Roger Williams*, p. 55; *Key into the Language*, pp. 134, 140.

27. Williams, *Key into the Language*, 170, 128.

28. Ibid., 90-91, 130.

29. Williams, *Complete Writings*, VI, 356.

30. Ibid., II, 260.

31. Ibid., II, 262, 259; I, 360; Cotton's reply, in ibid., II, 145. In "Typology in New England: The Williams-Cotton Controversy Reassessed," *American Quarterly* 19 (1967): 166–191, an important article that adumbrates his larger argument for millenarian expectation in the Great Migration, Sacvan Bercovitch contends that Cotton, drawing on a typological tradition descending from Eusebius (in opposition to Williams's Augustinian separation of history from the prophecies of revelation), maintained "a literal parallel between the biblical chosen people and the children of Israel in New England" (173). This essay significantly amplifies Miller's somewhat muted discussions of typology in Puritan thought; see Miller's Introduction (1948) to Edwards, *Images or Shadows of Divine Things*. See Ann Kibbey's comment, *Interpretation of Material Shapes*, p. 183n23.

32. Cotton, in Williams, *Complete Writings*, III, 56; ibid., II, 73, 262; III, 63–64.

33. Ibid., I, 362; Winthrop, *Journal*, I, 307; Williams, *Complete Writings*, III, 165.

34. Williams, *Complete Writings*, II, 158, 223–224.

35. Thomas Hutchinson, *History of the Colony and Province of Massachusetts Bay*, I, 129; Miller and Johnson, "Bibliographies," in *The Puritans*, I, xcix; Tyler, *A History of American Literature, 1607–1765* (New York: Collier, 1962), p. 189; Winfried Herget, "Preaching and Publication—Chronology and the Style of Thomas Hooker's Sermons," *Harvard Theological Review* 65 (1972): 237–238.

36. Hooker, *Application of Redemption*, bk. III, 205; Hooker, *Soules Implantation* (1637), pp. 28, 39, 41, 61; Hooker, *The Unbeleevers Preparing for Christ* (London, 1638), II, 6; Hooker, *The Soules Implantation into the Naturall Olive* (London, 1640), p. 50; Norton, *Orthodox Evangelist*, p. 161.

37. Hooker, *Application of Redemption*, bk. VII, 345; Hooker, *Soules Preparation*, p. 230.

38. Hooker, *Unbeleevers Preparing for Christ*, I, 201; Sibbes, *Bruised Reed*, pp. 79, 44; Hooker, *Application of Redemption*, bk. X, 153; Hooker, *A Christians Two Chiefe Lessons*, p. 32; *Application of Redemption*, bk. IV, 268.

39. Sibbes, *Bruised Reed*, p. 124.

40. Hooker, *Soules Vocation*, pp. 205, 34, 206–207.

41. Poe, "The Poetic Principle," in W. H. Auden, ed., *Poe: Selected Prose and Poetry* (New York: Rinehart, 1950), p. 415; Hooker, *Soules Vocation*, pp. 225–226, 145, 220; Hooker, *Soules Exaltation*, p. 270.

42. Hooker, *Soules Exaltation*, pp. 129–130.

43. Ibid., p. 79; Hooker, *Soules Vocation*, p. 668; Hooker, *Soules Exaltation*, pp. 310–311.

44. Hooker, *Unbeleevers Preparing*, II. 49; Hooker, *Application of Redemption*, bk. VIII, 368-369; *Unbeleevers*, II, 51; *Application*, bk. VIII, 365.

45. *Unbeleevers Preparing*, II, 52; *Application of Redemption*, bk. VIII, 369. See Sargent Bush, *The Writings of Thomas Hooker: Spiritual Adventure in Two Worlds* (Madison: University of Wisconsin Press, 1980), p. 153.

46. Albert J. Von Frank, *The Sacred Game: Provincialism and Frontier Consciousness in American Literature, 1630–1860* (New York: Cambridge University Press, 1985), pp. 24-25; Hooker, *Application of Redemption*, bk. III, 173; bk. X, 23, 25; Hooker, *Unbeleevers Preparing*, I, 106; Sibbes, *Bruised Reed*, p. 4; Hooker, *Soules Preparation*, p. 138.

47. Hooker, *Soules Vocation*, pp. 63, 411.

48. Winthrop, *Journal*, I, 184; Shepard, *Works*, II, 212–218.

49. Winthrop, *Journal*, I, 121; Cotton, quoted in Rutman, *Winthrop's Boston*, p. 145n20; Noyes, *Temple Measured*, p. 6.

50. Morgan, *Visible Saints*, esp. ch. 3.

51. Stearns and Brawner, "New England Church 'Relations' and Continuity in Early Congregational History," *Proceedings of the American Antiquarian Society* 75 (1965): 28; Caldwell, *Puritan Conversion Narrative*, p. 108; Lechford, *Plaine Dealing*, p. 23; Morgan, *Visible Saints*, p. 35. See also

Coolidge, *Pauline Renaissance,* pp. 65–66, and John O. King III, *The Iron of Melancholy: Structures of Spiritual Conversion in America from the Puritan Conscience to Victorian Neurosis* (Middletown: Wesleyan University Press, 1983), p. 44.

52. Hooker, *A Survey of the Summe of Church-Discipline* (London, 1648), pt. I, 90; Mather, *Magnalia* (1853 ed.), I, 349; *Winthrop Papers,* III, 390.

53. Hooker, *Soules Vocation,* p. 550; Hubbard, *A General History of New England, from the Discovery to 1680, Collection of the Massachusetts Historical Society,* 2d ser., 5 and 6 (1815): 173; Hooker, *Soules Vocation,* p. 309; Samuel Ward, quoted in Giles Firmin, *The Real Christian* (London, 1670), p. 19; Hooker, *Application of Redemption,* p. 37; *Soules Ingrafting,* pp. 17–18; *Unbeleevers Preparing,* I, 50; *Soules Implantation,* p. 65.

54. Hooker, *Application of Redemption,* bk. X, 151, 148, 150; Hooker, *A Comment Upon Christs Last Prayer* (London, 1659), p. 202; Davenport, *Saints Anchor-Hold,* p. 42.

55. Hooker, *Application of Redemption,* bk. X, 240; Hooker, *The Soules Possession* (London, 1638), pp. 43–44, 91, 96; *Soules Preparation,* p. 79; *Application of Redemption,* bk. X, 249, 265, 224, 220. Sargent Bush, in *Writings of Thomas Hooker,* p. 270, has remarked that although "we do not find in Hooker's surviving works any discussion of sanctification on the same scale as his treatment of earlier stages . . . this may be due more to historical accident than his own intention." My own feeling is that Hooker lingered with the earlier stages because that is where his imagination held him.

56. Barbara Kiefer Lewalski, *Donne's Anniversaries and the Poetry of Praise* (Princeton: Princeton University Press, 1973), pp. 86, 92–93; Samuel Hieron, *An Helpe unto Devotion* (London, 1614), sigA12ᵛ.

57. Davenport, *Saints Anchor-Hold,* p. 164; Hooker, *Soules Vocation,* pp. 553–554; *Application of Redemption,* bk. X, 683, 114.

58. Hooker, *Soules Vocation,* p. 317; *Soules Preparation,* p. 163.

6. Going Home

1. Charles Beard, *An Economic Interpretation of the Constitution* (1913; rpt. New York: Free Press, 1941), p. 18; James, *Pragmatism* (1907; rpt. New York: Meridien, 1955), pp. 157, 158.

2. The pioneering article is William L. Sachse, "The Migration of New Englanders to England, 1640–1660," *American Historical Review* 53 (1948): 251–278. See also Sachse, "Harvard Men in England, 1642–1714," *Publications of the Colonial Society of Massachusetts* 35 (1942–1946): 119–144; Hall, *Faithful Shepherd,* pp. 171–175; Harry Stout, "University Men in New England, 1620–1660: A Demographic Analysis," *Journal of Interdisciplinary History* 4 (1974): 375–400; and Stout, "The Morphology of Re-Migration: New England University Men and Their Re-

turn to England, 1640–1660," *Journal of American Studies* 10 (1975): 151–172. Handlin, *Race and Nationality in American Life* (New York: Anchor Books, 1957), p. 203. On later remigrants, see Lars-Göran Tedebrand, "Remigration from America to Sweden," in *From Sweden to America,* ed. Harold Runblom and Hans Norman (Minneapolis: University of Minnesota Press, 1976), pp. 201–227; J. D. Gould, "European Inter-Continental Emigration: The Road Home: Return Migration from the U.S.A.," *Journal of European Economic History* 9 (1980): 41–112.

3. Mather, *Magnalia* (London, 1702), I, 23; Levin, *Cotton Mather: The Young Life of the Lord's Remembrancer* (Cambridge, Mass.: Harvard University Press, 1978), pp. 143, 183; Kenneth Silverman, *The Life and Times of Cotton Mather* (New York: Harper and Row, 1984), p. 4; Cressy, *Coming Over,* p. 51.

4. Lord Saye and Sele, quoted in Winthrop, *Journal,* I, 333; Andrews, *Colonial Period,* I, 497; Clap, in Young, *Chronicles,* pp. 354–355.

5. Winthrop, *Journal,* I, 309, 310; II, 243; *The Illustrated Pepys,* ed. Robert Latham (Berkeley: University of California Press, 1983), p. 138; J. L. Sibley, *Biographical Sketches of Graduates of Harvard University,* 17 vols. (Cambridge, Mass.: Harvard University Press, 1873), I, 46.

6. *New England's First Fruits,* in Morison, *Founding of Harvard College,* pp. 441-442, 445, 446; John Pond, in Emerson, ed., *Letters from New England,* pp. 65–66; Frederick Johnson Simmons, *A Narrative Outline for a Biography of Emanuel Downinge* (Montclair, N.J.: privately printed, 1958), p. 78; Shepard, *Works,* II, 66.

7. Stout, "University Men in New England," 381; John Pond, in Emerson, ed., *Letters from New England,* p. 66.

8. David Grayson Allen, *"Vacuum Domiciliam:* The Social and Cultural Landscape of Seventeenth-Century New England," in *New England Begins,* ed. Jonathan L. Fairbanks and Robert F. Trent, 3 vols. (Boston: Museum of Fine Arts, 1983), I, 3; Theophilus Eaton to John Winthrop, Jr., in Massachusetts Historical Society, *Collections* 47 (1865): 469–470; Bernard Christian Steiner, *A History of the Town of Guilford, Connecticut* (Baltimore, 1897), pp. 60, 69, 67.

9. "A Copie of the Liberties of the Massachusets Colonie," in Edmund S. Morgan, *Puritan Political Ideas* (Indianapolis: Bobbs-Merrill, 1965), p. 179; Winthrop, *Journal,* II, 240; Maverick, "A Briefe Discription of New England," Massachusetts Historical Society, *Proceedings,* 2d ser., 1 (1884–85): 237; Symonds, quoted in Hall, *Faithful Shepherd,* pp. 172–173.

10. Cecelia Tichi, *New World, New Earth: Environmental Reform in American Literature from the Puritans through Whitman* (New Haven: Yale University Press, 1979), pp. 46–47.

11. Johnson, *Wonder-Working Providence,* p. 24.

12. Ibid., pp. 53, 261–262.

13. Johnson, *Wonder-Working Providence,* p. 87; William Aspinwall, *A Brief Description of the Fifth Monarchy, or Kingdome, that Shortly is to come into the World* (London, 1653), p. 1; Mather, *Magnalia* (1853 ed.), I, 237; Increase Mather, *A Brief Relation of the State of New England, from the Beginning of that Plantation to this Present Year,* 1689 (London, 1689), p. 5.

14. Johnson, *Wonder-Working Providence,* pp. 210–211.

15. Ibid., pp. 260, 251.

16. Ibid., p. 251.

17. Cotton, Foreword to John Norton, *The Answer to Mr. Apollonius* (1648), in Heimert and Delbanco, eds., *Puritans in America,* p. 111; Winthrop, *Journal,* II, 76; Sargent Bush, "Thomas Hooker and the Westminster Assembly," *William and Mary Quarterly* 29 (1972): 298, 300; the comment on Cotton is quoted in Geoffrey Nuttall, "John Cotton's *Keyes of the Kingdom,*" *Congregational Historical Society Transactions* 14 (1944): 305. The present chapter, in an earlier version published in the *New England Quarterly* (Sept. 1986), has been criticized by Francis J. Bremer, "Communications: The English Context of New England's Seventeenth-Century History," *New England Quarterly* 40 (1987): esp. 330–332, for failing to tell the story of how "orthodox colonists took inspiration from and supported the gradual rise to influence of men such as Thomas Goodwin, Philip Nye, and John Owen who advocated a New England-style church polity for England." I remain unpersuaded of the depth or breadth of that "inspiration."

18. Cotton, *Powring out of the Seven Vials,* p. 155; Bradford, *Of Plymouth Plantation,* pp. 78, 236; for the debate over Plymouth's influence on ecclesiastic form in Massachusetts Bay, see Perry Miller, *Orthodoxy in Massachusetts* (1933; rpt. New York: Harper and Row, 1970), esp. xxvii; Morgan, *Visible Saints,* ch. 3; and Larzer Ziff, "The Salem Puritans in the 'Free Aire of a New World,'" *Huntington Library Quarterly* (1957): 373–384.

19. Bradford, *Of Plymouth Plantation,* pp. 79, 81, 186, 63.

20. Ibid., p. 236; Johnson, *Wonder-Working Providence,* p. 160.

21. Lynn Ceci, "Fish Fertilizer: A Native North American Practice?" *Science* 188 (4 April 1975): 26–30, suggests that Squanto's celebrated demonstration to the Pilgrims of the value of fish fertilizer, which earned him their gratitude and respect, was actually a technique he learned while in England or from English settlers in various New World plantations, most likely Newfoundland. Ceci adduces no evidence to suggest that the Pilgrims were aware of the provenance of Squanto's lesson.

22. Hooke, *New Englands Teares for Old Englands Feares* (1640), in Samuel Hopkins Emery, *The Ministry of Taunton* (Boston, 1853), 2 vols., I, 86; *New England's Sence of Old England and Irelands Sorrowe,* in Emery, I, 125; Johnson, *Wonder-Working Providence,* p. 25.

23. Hooke, *New Englands Teares,* in Emery, I, 90; Hooke, *The Priviledge of the Saints on Earth Beyond Those in Heaven* (London, 1673), p. 151.

24. R. E. Moody, ed., *The Saltonstall Papers,* 2 vols., (Boston: Massachusetts Historical Society, 1972), I, 148; Dudley, in Morgan, *Founding of New England,* p. 171; Hooke, *Priviledge of the Saints,* p. 155.

25. Ward, *The Simple Cobler of Aggawam* (1646), ed. P. M. Zall (Lincoln: University of Nebraska Press, 1969), pp. 10, 28, 27.

26. Winthrop, *Journal,* I, 170; Clarendon, *History of the Rebellion* (Oxford, 1843), I, 75; Francis Higginson, in Emerson, ed., *Letters from New England,* p. 25; Maverick, "A Brief Description," 240.

27. Bradford, *Of Plymouth Plantation,* pp. 205, 217.

28. Charles Francis Adams, *Three Episodes of Massachusetts History* (Cambridge, 1892), 2 vols., I, 259.

29. Cotton, *Treatise of the Covenant of Grace,* p. 178; Underhill, quoted in Jeremy Belknap, *History of New Hampshire* (w. 1784), 3 vols. (Dover, N.H., 1831), I, 23; Winthrop, *Journal,* I, 219.

30. Winthrop, *Journal,* I, 224; *Defense of an Order of Court,* in Thomas Hutchinson, *A Collection of Original Papers Relative to the History of the Colony of Massachusetts Bay* (Boston, 1769), p. 69; Vane, *A Brief Answer to a certaine declaration, made of the intent and equitye of the order of court,* in Hutchinson, *Collection,* p. 72.

31. Winthrop, *A Model,* p. 9; Vane, in Hutchinson, *Collection,* pp. 75–76.

32. Hutchinson, *History of Massachusetts Bay,* I, 56; Gorton, *Simplicities Defence against Seven-headed Policy* (1646), in Force, ed., *Tracts,* 4, no. 6: 18–19; Winthrop, *Journal,* II, 57.

33. Aspinwall, *Brief Description of the Fifth Monarchy,* pp. 9, 12; Richard Frothingham, *The History of Charlestown* (Boston, 1845), p. 121; Matthews, quoted in Frothingham, p. 123.

34. William Medley [Thomas Venner], *A Standard Set Up* (London, 1657), p. 21; Frothingham, *Charlestown,* p. 126. The forthcoming study of the reverse migration by Susan B. Hardman, who has worked extensively with manuscript as well as printed sources, should yield some answers.

35. Shepard, *Works,* II, 179, 164.

36. See Fiering, p. 83, quoting the Thomistic basis (which, in turn, rests on Augustine) for the Puritan theory of the affections: "The passions 'are evil if our love is evil, good if our love is good . . . All these emotions are right in those whose love is rightly placed.' " Shepard, *Works,* I, 269; II, 377; Hooker, *Soules Vocation,* p. 411; Hooker, *Application of Redemption: The Ninth and Tenth Books,* p. 11.

37. Shepard, *Works,* II, 66; Cotton, *God's Promise,* p. 8.

38. Vane, *The Retired Mans Meditations,* II, 415; Robert G. Pope, Introduction to *The Notebook of the Reverend John Fiske, 1644–1675,* Colonial Society of Massachusetts, *Collections* (1974): xxviii; Winthrop, *Journal,* I, 295; Thomas Larkham, *A Discourse Concerning Tithes* (London, 1656), p. 4.

39. Noyes, *Temple Measured*, p. 10; Norton, *Great Point of Divinity*, sigA5ʳ.

40. Shepard to Winthrop (1642), in *Winthrop Papers*, IV, 345; Charles J. Hoadly, ed., *Records of the Colony and Plantation of New Haven, 1638–1649* (Hartford, 1857), pp. 65–73; David T. Konig, *Law and Society in Puritan Massachusetts: Essex County, 1629-1692* (Chapel Hill: University of North Carolina Press, 1979), pp. 27, 28, 30.

41. Pope, Introduction to Fiske, *Notebook*, xxvii; Shepard, *Works*, II, 152.

42. Keayne, *Last Will and Testament* (1657), ed. Bernard Bailyn, Colonial Society of Massachusetts, *Transactions* 42 (1952–1956): 296; Winthrop, *Journal*, I, 316–317.

43. Maclear, "New England and the Fifth Monarchy," 230; Tillam, "Upon the first sight of New England," in Harrison T. Meserole, ed., *Seventeenth-Century American Poetry* (New York: Norton, 1968), pp. 397–398.

44. Tillam, *The Banners of Love Displaied* (London, 1654), pp. 27, 29. Tillam's affinity with Hutchinson has been noticed by Gura, *Glimpse of Sion's Glory*, p. 137.

45. Tillam, *The Temple of Lively Stones* (London, 1660), p. 316; Hooker, *Application of Redemption: The Ninth Book*, p. 11; Cotton, *A Brief Exposition of the Whole Book of Canticles* (1642), p. 261; Shepard, *Works*, II, 88.

46. Hooke, Letter to Winthrop, in Massachusetts Historical Society, *Proceedings* 31 (1825): 184; Aspinwall, *Brief Description of the Fifth Monarchy*, p. 1; Tillam, *Temple of Lively Stones*, p. 218; Knollys, *The Life and Death of that Old Disciple of Jesus Christ and Eminent Minister of the Gospel, Mr. Hanserd Knollys* (London, 1812), pp. 16–18, 162–163.

47. Firmin, *The Real Christian*, sigB4ʳ, sigG1ᵛ, sigG3ʳ; Stoddard writes in *The Safety of Appearing at the Day of Judgment* (Boston, 1729), p. 162, that "when a sinner thinks that he is seeking after the work of Humiliation, he is opposing it." Franklin, *Autobiography* (New York: Holt, Rinehart, 1959), p. 88.

48. Richard Mather, *A Farewell-Exhortation to the Church and People of Dorchester* (Cambridge, Mass., 1657), p. 3; Firmin, *Real Christian*, pp. 10, 3, 8; Hooker, *Soules Preparation*, p. 57.

49. Blackwood, *A Treatise Concerning Repentance* (London, 1653), p. 5.

50. Winthrop, *Journal*, II, 31.

51. Blackwood, *Treatise Concerning Repentance*, p. 19; Emerson, "Divinity School Address," in Whicher, *Selections from Emerson*, p. 107; Hambrick-Stowe, *Practice of Piety*, p. 6.

52. Norton, *Abel Being Dead Yet Speaketh* (1658), in Heimert and Delbanco, eds., *Puritans in America*, p. 217.

7. Fathers and Children

1. "New England's First Fruits" (1642), in Morison, *Founding of Harvard College*, p. 466; Miller, *Errand into the Wilderness*, p. 15.

2. Jennings, *Invasion of America*, p. vii.
3. Miller, *Errand*, pp. 11, 14; "The Plight of the Lone Wolf," *American Scholar* 25, no. 4 (1956): 445–451; David Levin, "Perry Miller at Harvard," *Southern Review* 19, no. 4 (1983): 802, 804; Fiedler, *Love and Death in the American Novel* (London: Paladin, 1970), p. 222.
4. "The scene . . . New Jerusalem" is quoted by Bercovitch in *American Jeremiad*, p. 9, from Jesper Rosenmeier, "Veritas: The Sealing of the Promise," 33; Bercovitch, "The Rites of Assent: Rhetoric, Ritual, and the Ideology of American Consensus," in Sam B. Girgus, ed., *The American Self: Myth, Ideology, and Popular Culture* (Albuquerque: University of New Mexico Press, 1981), p. 8. In general, as the present chapter makes clear, I feel very little deficiency in Miller's much-assaulted theory of "declension." Despite the many qualifications that have been wrought upon it—see, in addition to Bercovitch, Emory Elliot, *Power and the Pulpit in Puritan New England* (1975), and Robert G. Pope, *The Half-Way Covenant: Church Membership in Puritan New England* (Princeton: Princeton University Press, 1969)—it remains an accurate guide to the Puritans' sense of their own experience and a powerful paradigm for understanding all subsequent immigrations. There is nevertheless a problem with the idea of declension as a way of accounting for cultural continuity. The problem is simply that the concept of declension can have no afterlife in post-Puritan America—except as an infinitely extended process that may be said to afflict any culture with even as rudimentary a sense of the past as our own. (For a cogent critique of the idea of declension as it informs American historiography generally, see Thomas Bender, *Community and Social Change in America* [Baltimore: Johns Hopkins University Press, 1982], esp. ch. 3.) In part to compensate for this perceived deficiency, a new orthodoxy concerning the place of Puritanism in the development of American culture has arisen in recent years, and has been little challenged. This now-familiar version of "Puritan legacy-ism"—the idea that Puritanism injected a millenarian strain into the American bloodstream—obviates the problem of continuity because it is all about continuity. It offers a new explanation for the old problem of why America has had no "left," by showing how the persistent rhetoric of the jeremiad constricts what we call dissent into a form of self-flattery that renders every national failure a corrective judgment from a favoring God. Unlike the old version of consensus history (of which it is a variant) it is rooted in cultural self-hatred. Its value as an account of the Puritan experience is real though limited, but it has much less explanatory power with respect to those moments when consensus has broken down, or with respect to the region whose cultural genealogy is significantly different: "Nothing about the history of the South," as C. Vann Woodward has written in *The Burden of Southern History* (New York: Vintage, 1960), p. 171, "was conducive

to the theory that the South was the darling of divine providence." There is a challenge in that remark to all theories of American culture as a unified entity.

5. Backus, *History of the Baptists in New England* (1777) presents Roger Williams and Anne Hutchinson as martyred witnesses and Thomas Hooker as a vengeful prosecutor; Oliver, *The Origin and Progress of the American Rebellion,* ed. Douglass Adair and John A. Schutz (Stanford: Stanford University Press, 1967), p. 12; Webster, *Works* (Boston, 1903), 18 vols., I, 186; Lanier, *Tiger-Lilies* (1867; rpt. Chapel Hill: University of North Carolina Press, 1969), p. 3. See Warren Susman, "Uses of the Puritan Past," in Susman, *Culture as History* (New York: Pantheon, 1984), pp. 39–49.

6. Hawthorne, *Scarlet Letter,* p. 252.

7. Ibid., pp. 256–257.

8. Ibid., p. 249.

9. Ibid., p. 192; V. L. Parrington, *Main Currents in American Thought,* vol. 2, *The Romantic Revolution* (New York: Harcourt, Brace, 1927), p. 438; *Scarlet Letter,* pp. 157, 236, 229, 231. Michael Colacurcio, in "The Woman's Own Choice," enlarges on his own groundbreaking essay "The Footsteps of Anne Hutchinson," *English Literary History* 39 (1972): 459–494, in establishing the historical specificity of Hawthorne's romance as a study in tensions within Puritan culture.

10. Davies, *Worship and Theology, 1603–1690,* pp. 26–27; Davies, *Worship and Theology in England, 1534–1603* (Princeton: Princeton University Press, 197), p. 21.

11. Morgan, "The Revolutionary Era as an Age of Politics," in *The Role of Ideology in the American Revolution,* ed. John R. Howe, Jr. (New York: Rinehart, 1970), p. 11. Cf. Louis Hartz's comment, in *The Liberal Tradition in America,* p. 65n, that "in a real sense physical flight is the American substitute for social revolution."

12. See Gura, *Glimpse of Sion's Glory;* Winthrop, *Journal,* I, 316.

13. Lawrence, *Studies in Classic American Literature* (1923); New York: Viking, 1972), p. 5.

14. Lewis P. Simpson, *The Dispossessed Garden: Pastoral and History in Southern Literature* (Baton Rouge: Louisiana State University Press, 1983), p. 2.

15. For a treatment of this theme as a prelude to the Civil War, see George Forgie, *Patricide in the House Divided: A Psychological Interpretation of Lincoln and His Age* (New York: Norton, 1979), which sees Lincoln's generation as variously oppressed by the feeling of living in "a postheroic age"; Sewall, *Phaenomena quaedam Apocalyptica* (Boston, 1927), p. 1. See also Stephen Fender, *Plotting the Golden West: American Literature and the Rhetoric of the California Trail* (New York: Cambridge University Press, 1981), p. 62, which describes the emigrants to Cali-

fornia as "being told endlessly of their forebears' achievements, and wishing to vindicate themselves by at least a token migration of their own."

16. Morgan, ed., *Diary of Michael Wigglesworth*, p. 60; Middlekauff, *The Mathers*, ch. 6; Ziff, *Puritanism in America*, p. 165; Increase Mather, *A Discourse Concerning the Danger of Apostasy* (Boston, 1679), pp. 87, 89; Torrey, Preface to William Adams, *The Necessity of the Pouring Out of the Spirit from on High upon a Sinning Apostatizing People* (Boston, 1679), sigA3ᵛ; Edward Randolph, "Report on Massachusetts" (1676), in Alden T. Vaughan, ed., *Puritan Tradition*, p. 315; Thomas Shepard, Jr., *Eye-Salve*, p. 10.

17. Increase Mather, *Pray for the Rising Generation* (Boston, 1678), p. 14; Mather, *Ichabod*, p. 69.

18. Cotton Mather, *Diary* ("Reserved Memorials"), ed. Worthington C. Ford (New York: Frederick Ungar, 1912), 2 vols., II, 207, 279.

19. The Result of the Synod of 1679, in Williston Walker, ed., *Creeds and Platforms of Congregationalism* (New York, 1893), pp. 427–431; Adams, *Necessity of the Spirit*, p. 30; Joshua Scottow, *A Narrative of the Planting of the Massachusetts Colony* (Boston, 1694), p. 38; Hall, *Faithful Shepherd*, p. 227.

20. Emerson, "Divinity School Address," in Whicher, *Selections from Emerson*, p. 106; Jonathan Mitchell, *Nehemiah on the Wall in Troublesome Times* (Cambridge, 1671), p. 26; Shepard, *Works*, II, 269; William Hubbard, *The Happiness of a People* (Boston, 1676), p. 9; Joshua Moodey, *Souldiery Spiritualized or the Christian Souldier Orderly, and Strenuously Engaged in the Spiritual Warre* (Cambridge, 1674), p. 23; John Cotton, *The Keys of the Kingdom of Heaven* (1644), in Ziff, ed., *Cotton on the Churches*, p. 161; Urian Oakes, *New England Pleaded With* (Cambridge, 1673), pp. 47–48. See Hall, *Faithful Shepherd*, p. 273: "Order [became] an end in itself, not (as it had once been for the founders of New England) a quality conjoined with the freedom of the kingdom."

21. Hubbard, *Happiness of a People*, pp. 29–31; *A Narrative of the Troubles with the Indians* (Boston, 1677), pp. 78–79; John Higginson, *The Cause of God and His People in New-England* (Cambridge, 1663), p. 11.

22. Howe, *World of Our Fathers*, p. 262.

23. William Stoughton, *New-Englands True Interest* (Cambridge, 1670), pp. 22–23; David Leverenz, *The Language of Puritan Feeling*, pp. 268, 333n21, notes that following their migration, second-generation Puritan and Jewish sons paid a peculiarly high "psychological price for breaking away" from the fathers.

24. Charles Chauncy, *Anti-Synodalia Americana* (Boston, 1662), pp. 3, 2.

25. Samuel Danforth, *Errand into the Wilderness* (1670), in A. W. Plumstead, ed., *The Wall and the Garden* (Minneapolis: University of Minnesota Press, 1968), p. 58; Davenport, *A Sermon Preach'd at the Election of the*

Governour, at Boston in New-England, May 19th 1669 (Boston, 1670), p. 15.

26. Emerson, "Self-Reliance," in Whicher, *Selections,* p. 154; Benjamin Colman et al., *The Gospel Order Revived* (New York, 1700), n.p.; Richard Mather and Jonathan Mitchell, *A Defence of the Answer and Arguments of the Synod Met in Boston in the Year 1662* (Cambridge, 1664); and John Allin, *Two Sermons* (Cambridge, 1672); Increase Mather, *First Principles of New England* (Cambridge, 1675); Oakes, *New England Pleaded With,* p. 11. See the penetrating article by E. Brooks Holifield, "On Toleration in Massachusetts," *Church History* 38 (1969): 188–200, which suggests that "traditionalists" who continued to oppose the Half-Way Covenant into the 1670s were more inclined than its "more liberal" supporters to favor toleration of the Baptists—because the Baptists' commitment to reserving the seals for those professing a gracious experience was in better accord with the spirit of the founders.

27. Oakes, *New England Pleaded With,* pp. 59–60.

28. Adams, *Necessity of the Pouring,* p. 5; Miller writes of "the subtle shift in fast-day proclamations from sensible judgments to the ravages of sin" (*From Colony to Province,* p. 76); see, for a similar argument, David Minter, "The Puritan Jeremiad as a Literary Form," in Bercovitch, ed., *The American Puritan Imagination,* p. 50; Benjamin Colman, *Practical Discourses upon the Parable of the Ten Virgins* (Boston, 1707), p. 96.

29. Oakes, *New England Pleaded With,* p. 28; Sewall, *Diary,* ed. M. H. Thomas (New York: Farrar, Straus, Giroux, 1973), 2 vols., I, 91; Cotton Mather, *Diary,* I, 327.

30. Cotton Mather, *Wonders of the Invisible World,* in Heimert and Delbanco, eds., *Puritans in America,* p. 240; Thomas Brattle, *A Full and Candid Account of the Delusion called Witchcraft (1692), Collections of the Massachusetts Historical Society,* 1st ser., 5 (1798): 64; William E. Woodward, ed., *Records of Salem Witchcraft* (Roxbury, Mass., 1864) 2 vols., I, 200; Robert Calef, *More Wonders of the Invisible World,* in George L. Burr, ed., *Narratives of the Witchcraft Cases* (New York: Scribner's, 1914), pp. 325–326.

31. Brattle, *Full and Candid Account,* p. 63; Samuel Torrey, *A Plea for the Life of Dying Religion* (Boston, 1683), p. 11.

8. The Puritan Legacy

1. Emerson, "Experience," in Whicher, *Selections,* p. 270; Thoreau, *Walden* (New York: Modern Library, 1950), "Higher Laws," p. 198.

2. Stowe, *Uncle Tom's Cabin* (1852); Cambridge, Mass.: Harvard University Press, 1962), p. 218; Sibbes, *Bruised Reed,* p. 35; Cotton, *A Treatise of the Covenant of Grace,* p. 36; Edwards, *Narrative of Surprising Conversions* (1735), in *Representative Selections,* ed. Faust and Johnson, p. 80.

3. Kerouac, *On the Road* (New York: Viking, 1975), p. 180; Stowe, *Uncle Tom's Cabin*, p. 93; Hawthorne, *Scarlet Letter*, pp. 57–58.

4. O'Neill, *Strange Interlude*, Act II; Hawthorne, *The Marble Faun, or the Romance of Monte Beni* (Boston: Houghton Mifflin, 1888), p. 71; Emerson, "Divinity School Address," in Whicher, *Selections*, p. 103.

5. Melville, *Moby-Dick* (1851; New York: Norton, 1967), p. 347; Fitzgerald, *The Great Gatsby* (1925; New York: Scribner's, 1953), p. 182; Shepard, *Works*, I, 37.

6. Saul Bellow, *The Adventures of Augie March* (1954; New York: Avon, 1977), p. 574.

7. Emerson, *Journals and Miscellaneous Notebooks*, 17 vols., ed. Alfred R. Ferguson, Jr. (Cambridge, Mass.: Harvard University Press, 1953), IV, 348; Whitman, *Democratic Vistas* (1870) and *Song of Myself* (1855), in James E. Miller, Jr., ed., *Whitman, Complete Poetry and Selected Prose* (Boston: Houghton Mifflin, 1959), pp. 464, 25; Hawthorne, *Marble Faun*, pp. 31, 145; Emerson, Letter to Whitman, July 21, 1855, in Whicher, *Selections*, p. 362; Stein, *The Autobiography of Alice B. Toklas* (1933), in *Selected Writings of Gertrude Stein*, ed. Carl van Vechten (New York: Vintage, 1972), p. 73.

8. Robert Hughes, *The Fatal Shore* (New York: Knopf, 1987), p. xi.

9. Octavio Paz, *The Labyrinth of Solitude: Life and Thought in Mexico*, trans. Lysander Kemp (New York: Grove Press, 1961), pp. 100–103.

10. Hawthorne, *Marble Faun*, p. 144; Trilling, *The Opposing Self* (New York: Viking, 1959), pp. 90–91; Richard Poirier, *A World Elsewhere: The Place of Style in American Literature* (New York: Oxford University Press, 1966); Quentin Anderson, *The Imperial Self: An Essay in American Literary and Cultural History* (New York: Knopf, 1971); Leo Marx, *The Machine in the Garden: Technology and the Pastoral Ideal in America* (New York: Oxford University Press, 1965); Bercovitch, *American Jeremiad;* T. S. Eliot, "Little Gidding."

11. Henry James, *The Portrait of a Lady* (1881; New York: New American Library, 1963), p. 186; James, review of *Drum-Taps*, in *Essays on Literature: American Writers, English Writers*, ed. Leon Edel and Mark Wilson (New York: Library of America, 1984), p. 630.

12. Werner Sollors, in *Beyond Ethnicity: Consent and Descent in American Culture* (New York: Oxford University Press, 1986), advances a formidable argument for the theme of Americanization as the obsessive concern of American writing from the typological imagination of the Puritans to the ethnic self-consciousness of the present day, or, as he puts it, "from Cotton Mather to *Young Frankenstein*" (p. 7). His readings, however, are more heavily weighted toward the "consent" side of his paradigm than the texts seem to me to warrant. See ch. 7 for an interesting discussion of what Sollors deems the critical deficiencies of the category "generation" for explaining cultural change.

13. Wright, *Black Boy* (1945; New York: Harper and Row, 1966), p. 43:

"From the white landowners above him there had not been handed to him a chance to learn the meaning of loyalty, of sentiment, of tradition"; Hawthorne, "Dr. Bullivant," quoted in Michael J. Colacurcio, *The Province of Piety: Moral History in Hawthorne's Early Tales* (Cambridge, Mass.: Harvard University Press, 1984), p. 69.

14. William Wells Brown, *The Black Man, his Antecedents, his Genius, and his Achievements* (1865; Miami: Mnemosyne, 1969), p. 12; *The Autobiography of Malcolm X* (New York: Grove Press, 1964), pp. 54–55. See, for an instance of the new black fiction, David Bradley, *The Chaneysville Incident* (New York: Avon, 1982), esp. pp. 67–68. Eugene Genovese, *Roll, Jordan, Roll: The World the Slaves Made* (New York: Vintage, 1976), and Herbert Gutman, *The Black Family in Slavery and Freedom* (New York: Vintage, 1977), are among the extraordinary works of historical scholarship that have helped in the last two decades to foster a new sense of the complexity—indeed, the recoverability—of the Afro-American past.

15. William Perkins, *The Calling of the Ministerie*, in *Works*, III, 438.

16. Lawrence, *Studies*, p. 10; Howard M. Feinstein, "The Prepared Heart: A Comparative Study of Puritan Theology and Psychoanalysis," *American Quarterly* 22 (1970): 168; Franklin, *Autobiography*, pp. 32, 85; Bellow, *Augie March*, p. 216.

17. Gillian Lindt Gollin, *Moravians in Two Worlds: A Study of Changing Communities* (New York: Columbia University Press, 1967), p. 20; Donald F. Durnbaugh, ed., *The Brethren in Colonial America* (Elgin, Ill.: Brethren Press, 1967), pp. 34, 77; Peter C. Erb, ed., *Johann Conrad Beissel and the Ephrata Commune* (Lewiston, N.Y.: Edwin Mellen Press, 1985), pp. 16.

18. Joan Didion, "Miami," *New York Review of Books*, 28 May 1987, p. 46.

19. Mather, *Magnalia*, ed. Murdock and Miller, p. 94.

20. Cotton, *An Exposition upon the Thirteenth Chapter of the Revelation*, p. 93. For discussion of Cotton's waning millenarianism, see Rosenmeier, "The Image of Christ," p. 100; and Jeffrey A. Hammond, "The Bride in Redemptive Time: John Cotton and the Canticles Controversy," *New England Quarterly* 56 (1983): 78–102; Marcus Cunliffe, "American Watersheds," *American Quarterly* 13 (1961): 489.

21. Emerson, "Divinity School Address," in Whicher, *Selections*, p. 103; Jonathan Edwards, *A Treatise Concerning Religious Affections* (1746; New Haven: Yale University Press, 1959), p. 118.

22. Alan Heimert, *Religion and the American Mind: From the Great Awakening to the Revolution* (Cambridge, Mass.: Harvard University Press, 1966), p. 3.

23. Benjamin Welles, "Political Methodism," in *The Federalist Literary Mind*, ed. Lewis P. Simpson (Baton Rouge: Louisiana State University Press, 1962), p. 55.

24. See Katherine Newman, *Falling from Grace: The Experience of Downward*

Mobility in the American Middle Class (New York: Free Press, 1988).

25. Lawrence Buell, "The New England Renaissance and American Literary Ethnocentrism," *Prospects* 10 (1985): 410. See also William Spengemann, "The Literature of British America," *Early American Literature* 18 (1983): 316. Lewis, *American Adam*, p. 8.

26. Mircea Eliade, *Myths, Rites, and Symbols,* quoted in Robert Weisbuch, *Atlantic Double-Cross: American Literature and British Influence in the Age of Emerson* (Chicago: University of Chicago Press, 1986), pp. 59–60. Recent extensions of the millenarian argument as a way of accounting for America's current behavior in the world include Loren Baritz, *Backfire: A History of How American Culture Led Us into Vietnam and Made Us Fight the Way We Did* (New York: William Morrow, 1984), pp. 26–27; John Hellmann, *American Myth and the Legacy of Vietnam* (New York: Columbia University Press, 1986), esp. pp. 20–23; and A. G. Mojtabai, *Blessèd Assurance: At Home with the Bomb in Amarillo, Texas* (Boston: Houghton Mifflin, 1986), esp. ch. 11.

Epilogue

1. Lincoln himself spoke only of a "vague [family] tradition, that my great-grand father went from Pennsylvania to Virginia; and that he was a quaker," but the Lincolns who migrated to Hingham, Massachusetts, in the seventeenth century were apparently his direct ancestors: see Roy P. Basler, ed., *The Collected Works of Abraham Lincoln* (New Brunswick: Rutgers University Press, 1953), 9 vols., I, 456; James Savage, *A Genealogical Dictionary of the first Settlers of New England* (Boston, 1860–1862), 4 vols., III, 91–95; C. E. Banks, *Planters,* pp. 193–194; and *New England Historical and Genealogical Register,* 15 (1861): 25–27.

2. Lincoln knew the Bible well and revered it as "the best gift God has given to man." It seems likely that he was drawn, just as Cotton and others among the Puritan founders were before him, to the image of "nursing fathers" in *Numbers* and *Isaiah.*

Index